THE DOCTRINE OF THE JAINAS

LALA SUNDARLAL JAIN RESEARCH SERIES

General Editor

PROF. SATYA RANJAN BANERJEE

Editorial Board

PANDIT DALSUK BHAI MALVANIA
DR. PADMANABH S. JAINI
PROF. W.B. BOLLEE
PROF. DAYANAND BHARGAVA
PROF. KLAUS BRUHN

VOLUME XV

Walther Schubring

The Doctrine of the Jainas

Described after the Old Sources

Translated from the revised German edition by

WOLFGANG BEURLEN

With the three indices enlarged and added by
Willem Bollée and Jayandra Soni

MOTILAL BANARSIDASS PUBLISHERS
PRIVATE LIMITED • DELHI

First Edition: 1962
Reprint: Delhi, 1978, 1995
Second Revised Edition: Delhi, 2000

ISBN: 81-208-0933-5

Also available at:

MOTILAL BANARSIDASS

236 Sri Ranga, 9th Main III Block, Jayanagar, Bangalore 560 011
41 U.A. Bungalow Road, Jawahar Nagar, Delhi 110 007
8 Mahalaxmi Chamber, Warden Road, Mumbai 400 026
120 Royapettah High Road, Mylapore, Chennai 600 004
Sanas Plaza, 1302 Baji Rao Road, Pune 411 002
8 Camac Street, Calcutta 700 017
Ashok Rajpath, Patna 800 004
Chowk, Varanasi 221 001

Printed in India
BY JAINENDRA PRAKASH JAIN AT SHRI JAINENDRA PRESS,
A-45 NARAINA, PHASE-I, NEW DELHI 110 028
AND PUBLISHED BY NARENDRA PRAKASH JAIN FOR
MOTILAL BANARSIDASS PUBLISHERS PRIVATE LIMITED,
BUNGALOW ROAD, DELHI 110 007

PREFACE TO THE SECOND REVISED EDITION

As the stocks of the *Doctrine of the Jainas* reprinted in 1978 are drawing to a close the publisher allowed me to prepare a new edition. The title-page of the first edition of the English version indicates that it was "translated from the revised German edition." This is ambiguous as the German original published in 1935 has never been reprinted, but for reasons not given in the Preface of the English edition, Schubring (1881-1969) condensed the first chapter containing the historical survey of Jain scholarship. Because the *Doctrine* is a standard work, it would seem desirable, however, to have this survey in its original form at a time when the old sources are hard to find. Moreover, many readers were not quite satisfied with the English of the German translation.

A new translation was therefore considered in which also some evident errors would be eliminated. Schubring's personal copy of the *Doctrine* is in the possession of Professor Adelheid Mette, who kindly informed me that Schubring had noted the confusion of Devakī and Rohiṇī on p. 32 (§ 17), but may not have notified the publisher; at any rate the mistake remained in the reprint of 1978. Further, it is unclear why e.g., in § 47 Malayagiri, the author of the *vṛtti* on the Rāyapaseṇaijja, was replaced by Abhayadeva in the English version, for Schubring possessed the *pothi* print (Bombay, 1925) himself. Updates would be certainly desirable in the bibliographical data of the canonical texts or by way of adding the titles of Schubring's own and others' works after 1962. Moreover, mentioning the results of new studies, as e.g., at the beginning of § 14 with a note on Norman's new etymology and original meaning of *patteya-buddha*, would have been appropriate.

Therefore the collaboration of Dr. Jayandra Soni was requested, and readily obtained. The latter found that the condensation mainly concerned the first chapter. In Schubring's Preface the omission of the survey is excused by the impossibility of updating it now (though it would seem valuable even as it is, i.e., up to about 1933). To make up for it, at least as far as the Śvetāmbara canonical scriptures are concerned, the reader is referred to Royce Wiles' *The "Śvetāmbara Canon" A descriptive listing of text editions, commentaries, studies and indexes*", in preparation in Canberra which we hope to have soon at our disposal.

As for the indices of this standard work on Jainism, we cannot imagine that Schubring would have willingly left them out as they are the key to it. Deference to the author's final version made us eventually give up our original plan to make a fresh translation and to add some notes as indicated above, which, moreover, would have made the book unavailable for yet a longer time. Nonetheless we decided to add the indices of which Dr. Soni checked the English catchwords and prepared a neat uniform computer script of my scribbled conversion of the page numbers of the German original into paragraphs. Besides, the Subject Index was considerably enlarged, It is hoped that in this way Schubring's *magnum opus* has been made better accessible, all the more because it seems improbable that the German original will ever be reprinted, much less revised in view of "the conditions of the present epoch", to quote from Schubring's Preface.

In Schubring's copy Professor Mette found a slip of paper with a handwritten citation from W. Norman Brown's *Story of Kālaka. Texts, History, Legends, and Miniature Paintings of the Śvetāmbara Jain Hagiographical Work The Kālakācāryakathā* (Washington, 1933), p. iv pasted inside the cover and apparently intended by the author as a motto for his book. It runs: "It is perhaps permissible to record here my appreciation not merely of the courtesy and scholarship of Jain monks and laymen but also of their lofty ideals and noble lives. They are of the greatness that is India. There is a spirit of helpfulness, tolerance, and sacrifice coupled with their intelligence and religious devotion that makes them as one of the world's choice communities."

Bamberg, September 1999 W. Bollée

PREFACE

When in 1934 the original edition of this book, "Die Lehre der Jainas, nach den alten Quellen dargestellt" (Grundriss der indo-arischen Philologie und Altertumskunde Vol. III No. 7), had been published, there were voices from India regretting that the book had not been written in English and demanding for a translation. Of the various projects regarding such a version none has been effected until the matter was taken up by the reputed publishers whose names appear on the title-page of this English book The present writer is highly indebted to the able translator, Herr Wolfgang Beurlen, with whom to collaborate was a pleasure at all stages of the difficult task.

In harmony with the character of the "Grundriss" certain limits had to be respected. Often outlines and references had to suffice, though, especially in the first chapters, the description thus came near to a sketch. The author consciously neglected the treatment of other religious and philosophical systems and historical facts of Old as well as of Mediaeval and New India in order not only to avoid an excessive extent of the book, but also, eventually, to give the old sources, i. e. the Śvetāmbara Canon, their due, but not neglecting Digambara writers. It need not be said that it was impossible to render all details themselves or even to register all references to the same. Hence the reader must be warned against taking this book for a bibliography or an encyclopedia. The names of the Jain authors and Jain works can but serve to indicate the untiring zeal of scholars and the grand liberality of donators in favour of their noble religion. That the bibliographical survey of the first edition has been altogether dropped seems to be excusable, since the conditions of the present epoch did not allow of bringing forward a survey of all that in the mean time had been printed and published on the field of Jainism in India.

On the other hand our Jain friends might come to obtain an idea of what much has been accomplished by Western scholars—including many Germans—during a period of about one hundred and fifty years, burning the midnight-oil with a view to make the world acquainted with one of the finest products of the Indian mind.

It may be hoped that the results will be, in general, applauded by Jain circles and that errors and shortcomings, inevitable as they are in such vast a field, will be kindly excused.

मैं अल्पज्ञ बहुत दोषी हूँ । यह ग्रन्थ है महान ॥
मिथ्यालाप दुष्कृत्य करूँ । सुधार जो विद्वान ॥

(अमोलख ऋषि)

CONTENTS

Preface to the second revised edition v
Preface vii
Abbreviations xi

I. A short History of Jain Research 1
Origins 1 From Weber to Pischel 3 Jain Editions 6 Later Western Research 7 Jain Activity 11 · Historical Position of Jainism 13

II. An historical Sketch of Jainism 18
Heroic Legend 18 Pāsa 28 Mahāvīra 31 Gosāla 35 Goyama and Suhamma 44 Early Jain Church 45 Jina - Statues 49 Schism 50 Early Literature 57 Digambaras 61 Śvetāmbaras 63 Sthānakvāsī 65 Other Sects 67

III. The Canon 73
Puvvas 74 Sections 78 Commentaries 82 Angas 85 Uvangas 96 Paiṇṇas 107 Cheyasuttas 109 Nandī and Aṇuogadārā 114 Mūlasuttas 115 Angabāhiras 121

IV. Cosmology 126
Fundamental Facts 126 Units 129 Atom 132 Bodies 137 Physiology 139 Soul 152 Cognition 156 *naya* 159 *nikkheva* 163 *siyā* 164 *kevala*-Cognition 169 Spiritual Function 170 Karman 172 Binding 173 Realization 178 Kinds of Karman 180 Ejection 183 Life 185 Kinds concluded 187 Reincarnation 188

V. Cosmography 204
The World, its Shape 204 Beings 206 Lower World 210 Centre World, Jambuddīva 216 Periods 225 Oceans and Ṛing-Continents 227 Gods and Stars 231 Upper World 237 Its Gods 240 Īsīpabbhārā 246

VI. Renunciation 247

General 247 Community 248 Ranks 253 Outfit 256 Daily Life 260 Study 266 Begging Tour 270 Asceticism 274 Confession and Atonement 278 Lay Folk 284 Death 288

VII. Victory 291

Similes 291 Human Character 292 Influence (*aṇhaya*) and Stoppage (*saṃvara*) 296 Lay Vows 297 Monastic Vows 300 Control 304 Ethics 305 Reflections 307 Resistance 308 Right Conduct 310 Asceticism 311 Meditation 313 Miracles and Magic 316 Conditions of Karman 319 *guṇaṭṭhāṇa* and *seḍhi* 320 Annihilation 324 Kevalin 327 Siddha 328

Glossary 331

Index of Proper Names 367

Subject Index 377

Additions 386

ABBREVIATIONS

Bh.	Bhavnagar.	Bo.	Bombay.
C.	Calcutta.	Lpz.	Leipzig.
T.	Tattvārthādhigamasūtra.		

Sanskrit Commentaries to Prakrit Texts :

Ācār. Śīlānka Ācāraṭīkā. As to Āyār. I and II, note that I means the AUTHOR'S edition of 1910, II JACOBI'S edition of 1882, pp. 49-137.

Āvaśy. Malayagiri, Āvaśyakaṭīkā

Prajn. Malayagiri, Prajnapanāṭīkā

Sthān. Abhayadeva, Sthānāngavṛtti

Vy. Abhayadeva, Vyākhyāprajnaptivṛtti

Periodicals

ABHORI Annals of the Bhandarkar Oriental Research Institute, Poona

ĀGRM Ātmānanda-Grantha-Ratna-Mālā. Bhavnagar

Āg. S. Āgamodaya Samiti. Mhesana, Surat, Bombay

AO Acta Orientalia. Oslo

ĀSG Āgamodaya-Samiti-Granthoddhāra, Bombay

BSOS Bulletin of the School of Oriental Studies. London

CII Corpus Inscriptionum Indicarum

DLJP Devcand-Lālbhāī-Jaina-Pustakoddhāra. Bombay

ERE Encyclopedia of Religion and Ethics. London

GGA Göttingische Gelehrte Angeihen. Göttingen

IA Indian Antiquary. Bombay

IHQ Indian Historical Quarterly. Calcutta

JAs Journal Asiatique. Paris

JASB Journal of the Asiatic Society of Bengal. Calcutta

JBORS Journal of the Bihar and Orissa Research Society. Patna.

JUB	Journal of the University of Bombay. Bombay
MKJMM	Śrīman-Mukti-Kamala-Jaina-Mohana-Mālā. Baroda
NIA	New Indian Antiquary. Bombay
OC	International Congress of Orientalists. Various Places
OLZ	Orientalistische Literatur-Zeitung. Leipzig, Berlin
QJMS	Quarterly Journal of the Mythic Society. Bangalore
SAWW	Sitzungsberichte der Phil.-Hist. Clesse der Kaiserlichen Akademie der Wissenschaften. Wien
SBE	Sacred Books of the East. Oxford
SBJ	Sacred Books of the Jainas. Arrah, Lucknow
SIFII	Studi italiani di filologia indo-iranica. Roma
SJS	Singhi Jain Series, Bombay.
SPAW	Sitzungsberichte der Kōniglich Preussischen Akademie der Wissenschaften. Berlin
WZKM	Wiener Zeitschrift für die Kunde der Morgenlendes Wien
YJGM	Yaśovijaya Jaina (or : Jaina-Yaśovijaya) -Grantha-Mālā. Benares
ZDMC	Zeitschrift der Deutschen Morgenländischen Gesellschaft. Leipzig, Wiesbaden.

I

A SHORT HISTORY OF JAIN RESEARCH

§ 1. It was in the year 1807 that in the Asiatic Researches (Calcutta and London), Vol. IX, there appeared three reports published under the title "Account of the Jains" and collected by Major (later Lieutenant Colonel) Colin MACKENZIE supplemented by an abstract from his diary of 1797 and from that of Dr. F. BUCHANAN[1], the latter containing some notes of a Jain gentleman. These publications were immediately followed by H. Th. COLEBROOKE'S "Observations on the Sect of Jains"[2]. They were based upon those researches as well as on Colebrooke's own, and it was in them that, apart from bare descriptive recording, some scholarly spirit first made itself felt by a critical standpoint taken and by facts being combined. Jain research thus dates from somewhat more than 150 years ago.

In H. H. WILSON's "Sketch of the Religious Sects of the Hindus" we find some stray notes about the Jains, but no details are given, though, on the other hand, the author dwells upon Vol. I of the Transactions of the Royal Asiatic Society (1827) which contained an essay by DELAMAINE and one more by BUCHANAN (=F. Buchanan HAMILTON), both with the title "On the Srawacs or Jains" and followed by a few remarks of the latter and of W. FRANCKLIN about some Jain temples, by COLEBROOKE'S account of two inscriptions, and by WILSON's own review of COLEBROOKE's study "Sect

1. BUCHANAN published "A Journey from Madras through the countries of Mysore, Canara and Malabar" (Lo. 1807, 2nd ed. Madras 1870, comp. GUÉRINOT JAs. 1909, p. 55). In this work the Jains are often mentioned. BUCHANAN's Journal kept during the Survey of the Districts of Patna and Gaya in 1811-12", ed. by V.H. JACKSON, Patna 1925, contains a description of his visit to the place where Mahāvīra died. Comp. JACOBI SPAW 1930, p. 561.

2. Printed in Colebrooke's Miscellaneous Essays, 2nd, ed. (1872) vol. II, 191-224.

of Jina" in his "Essays on the Philosophy of the Hindus"[1]. In the same year, 1827, FRANCKLIN'S "Researches on the Tenets of the Jeynes and Boodhists" were published, the first book that had the Jains in its title. Its descriptive portions are readable even now, whereas this cannot be said of its mythological and speculative deductions.

We abstain from cataloguing here which was printed after 1827, since this can be found in GUÉRINOT's Bibliography (s.b.). We must confine ourselves to mention that "Sketch" of WILSON, because it represents the most important treatment of the subject at that time. He gives a report on the numerable Jain manuscripts both privately owned by him and by the Calcutta Sanskrit College. His "Descriptive Catalogue of the Mackenzie Collection"[2] dealt with 44 South Indian Jain manuscripts that had come to the East India Company in London. But even the earliest essays were partly based upon texts as was COLEBROOKE'S first one in that it concerned Hemacandra's Abhidhānacintāmaṇi and the Kalpasūtra of the Jain Canon. Still he made use of both in a selective manner only and was far from editing or translating them completely, and twenty years had to pass until the first Jain text was published. Again it was Hemacandra's work that was edited by BÖHTLINGK and RIEU with a German translation in 1847 (St. Petersburg), whereas the Kalpasûtra, along with the Navatattvaprakarana, appeared in 1848 in STEVENSON's English rendering[3]. That this was a rather imperfect performance[4] is easily explained by

1. We should not like to pass over in silence the earliest references to the Jains. Comp. WINDISCH in his Geschichte der indo-arischen Philologie etc., p. 29 ; ZACHARIAE WZKM 24, 337-344 (reprinted in his Kleine Schriften, p. 41-47) and Festschrift Winternitz p. 174-185 ; RANDLE JRAS 1933, p. 147. The Greek glossator Hesychios (5th century A.D.) mentions '*gennoi*' as naked philosophers, a word in which M. SCHMIDT in his 2nd ed. (1867) of Hes. p. 342 surmises the Jains, comp. GRAY and SCHUYLER, Am. J. of Philol. 22 (1901), p. 197. LASSEN, Ind. Altertumskunde 4 (1861) and LÜDERS KZ 38, p. 433 are not against SCHMIDT's suggestion, whereas STEIN in Megasthenes and Kautilya, p. 293 f. maintains a cautious attitude.

2. The Mackenzie Collection. A descriptive Catalogue...By...H.H. WILSON. C. 1828, 2nd ed. Madras 1882.

3. The Kalpa-Sūtra and Nava Tatva. Two works illustrative of the Jain religion and philosophy. Transl. from the Magadhi by J. STEVENSON. Lo. 1848.

4. Comp. JACOBI, The Kalpasūtra of Bhadrabāhu, p. 27ff.

the fact that STEVENSON was the first European scholar to be confronted with the canonical Prakrit[1]. The Abhidhāna-cintāmaṇi in 1858 was followed[2] by WEBER'S edition of Dhaneśvara's Śatruṃjayamāhātmya[3] with a detailed. preface. So,then, the textual basis was rather narrow for LASSEN's sketch of Jainism[4] in his "Indische Altertumskunde" 4, 755-787 (1861).[5]

§ 2. The mentioned edition had been WEBER's first attempt in Jain research, but years later it was actually his great study "Über ein Fragment der Bhagavatī etc." that was epoch-making. It appeared in two parts in the Abhandlungen der Königlichen Akademie der Wissenschaften zu Berlin 1865-66 and in a separate edition (1866-67), that is to say again twenty years after the first Jain text (s.a.). Obsolete as it is now, yet it marks in our field the beginning of a philological and creative epoch. As to it, the reader may be referred to WINDISCH's precise description rendered in the Grundriss (Encyclopedia of Indo-Aryan Research). But the fundaments laid down by WEBER in self-sacrificing zeal cannot be passed over here: his treatise "Über die heiligen Schriften der Jaina" in Indische Studien Vol. 16 and 17 (1883-85) based upon the Jain manuscripts acquired by the Royal Library of Berlin 1873-78, and his "Verzeichnis" of the same (1888-92), the latter[6] represented by two monumental volumes, being a most accurate description which even extends to literature and history. A work of that scope going beyond the usual limits of a catalogue was not out of place at that stage. The Jain manuscripts purchased in

1. PISCHEL, Grammatik der Prakrit-Sprachen in § 17 deals with the history of research in the Ardha-Māgadhī.

2. PAVIE's French analysis of the Padmāvatīcaritra in JAs 5, T. 7 may also be mentioned.

3. Albrecht WEBER, Über das Catrumjaya Māhātmyam. Ein Beitrag zur Geschichte der Jaina. Leipzig 1858.

[4.] The w d Jainism is an English rendering and etymologically not correct. In German works of LEUMANN, WINTERNITZ, the AUTHOR and others the student will read "Jinismus" and "Jinistisch" derived from Jina, as are, in all languages, "Buddhism etc." from Buddha. "Bauddhism" etc. has never and nowhere been said.

5. Translation by REHATSEK JA 2, 193-200; 258-265.

6. "A good deal of my visual faculty has been buried therein", Verz. II, 3. p. XVIII.

later years have been catalogued by the AUTHOR not earlier than in 1944[1].

Some time about those eighties the first prints of canonical texts (1880 ff.) came to Europe adding to foster Jain research work over there. Their inaugurator was Rāy DHANPATI SIMHA Bāhādur at Azimganj or Murshidabad in Bengal. Those huge volumes served their purpose until they were replaced by more handy ones some thirty years after (s.b.).

The manuscripts described by WEBER had come to Berlin thanks to an agreement between BÜHLER and the Department of Public Instruction at Bombay which had commissioned him and other scholars in their service with the careful examination of private collections and the purchase of manuscripts at government costs. He was allowed to acquire manuscripts even for foreign libraries, provided they were doubles. The examined and purchased manuscripts were catalogued and listed in the valuable reports of R.S. and S.R. BHANDARKAR, BÜHLER, KIELHORN, PETERSON, and others. The manuscripts acquired by the Government have been deposited in the Deccan College, now Bhandarkar Oriental Research Institute in Poona. The Jain works among them have been minutely described by H.R. KAPADIA in Vol. XVII of the Descriptive Catalogue of the Institute (1935-48). An appendix is devoted to graphic peculiarities (comp. JUB Vol. 5 and 6)[2].

BÜHLER, through his Reports, has not only become a patron of Jain philology indirectly, but thanks to a number of original works and essays has been a direct promotor in our field, as, in the course of years, WEBER, too, had been, and, moreover, they both have inspired younger scholars. JACOBI'S critical edition of the "Kalpasūtra of Bhadrabāhu" (AKM 7, 1 1879) clearly shows traces of BÜHLER'S spirit, while LEUMANN'S

1. Die Jaina-Handschriften der Preussischen Staatsbibliothek. Neuerwerbungen seit 1891. Leipzig 1944. (1127 mss. on 647 pages.)

2. WEBER already dealt with this topic (Verz. II 3, p. XII ff.). LEUMANN discussed the influence of the shape of the leaves upon the text (ZDMG 46, 583f.). Miniatures in manuscripts were treated by HÜTTEMANN, Baessler-Archiv 4, 2; BROWN, Jaina Gazette 28, p. 77-83 (reviewed by Hirananda SASTRI ibid. 113 f.); BROWN, Kālaka (§ 24) with a bibliography. The Bibliography of Indian Archaeology may also be consulted.

"Aupapātika Sūtra" (AKM 8, 2; 1883)—originally a thesis of Leipzig—is influenced by WEBER and the Berlin Collection. It may be mentioned here that WEBER successfully co-operated with LEUMANN in his great essay referred to above. The editions of both JACOBI and LEUMANN are masterpieces of philology, and it was only a predilection for the old Prakrit grammarians that led PISCHEL in his famous "Grammatik der Prakrit-Sprachen" (§ 19, footnote 3) to call HOERNLE's "Uvāsagadasāo" (1890) the only "critical" one[1].

§ 3. JACOBI's introduction to the Kalpasūtra has come to be fundamental for all further research. This research has been described up to the twenties of this century by WINDISCH and need not be repeated here[2]. Its starting point was, due to JACOBI[3], the definite removal of any doubt whether the Jains or the Buddhists were of earlier origin[4], a doubt resulting from some inward and outward similarities between those two world-denying religions. Jain creed had sprung into existence long before Gautama Buddha's time, Vardhamāna Mahāvīra was not its founder, but a reformer of what Pārśva had taught, whom tradition credibly maintains to have lived 250 years before him. It may be added here from a later deduction of JACOBI's that Mahāvīra's Nirvāna was in 477 B.C. As we know from Pali sources, he was a contemporary of Gautama and is likely to have survived him by seven years[5].

Pali texts, moreover, give numerous details about thinkers and their schools in the Buddha's time. F.O. SCHRADER, a pupil of Leumann, made them the subject of his thesis in 1902[6].

1. A reflex of Pischel's remark can be seen in Antagaḍadasāo ed. BARNETT, p. X, comp. LEUMANN JRAS 1907, p. 1080. As to the Uvās., see LEUMANN's review WZKM 3, 328-350.

2. For Jain studies in Italy mostly going back to JACOBI see the indological bibliography up to 1911 in Rivista degli Studi Orientali 5, 219-271.

3. See his introduction to the Kalpasūtra and to SBE 22 and 45.

4. COLEBROOKE found it necessary to investigate the precedence of the Veda and of Brahmanism before the said religions (Observations etc., Misc. Essays II 196 ff.). FRANCKLIN had no doubt that the original religion of India was that of the "Boodh" and the "Jeyne" (Researches p. 137).

5. SPAW 1930, p. 557ff. (§19). Counter-arguments brought forward by KEITH Bull. School Or. Studies 6, p. 859-866.

6. Über den Stand der indischen Philosophie zur Zeit Mahāvīras and Buddhas. Strassburg 1902.

The most important of those philosophers was Gośāla Maskariputra, the head of the Ājīvika sect, whose interesting career has been repeatedly treated by HOERNLE[1]. That Aśoka knew the Jains under the name of *nigaṇṭha* (Topra edict 7, 26) was BÜHLER's statement[2]. Their early history in so far as it is reflected by Hemacandra in his Pariśiṣṭaparvan (the Sthavirāvalī) and in legends pertaining to it, is due to JACOBI no less than is the right interpretation of what is called the schism that led to the separation of the Śvetāmbara and Digambara communities. They did not, as old time would have it, separate by an act of violence but gradually, until, eventually, both partners became aware of their differences.

§ 4. It might have been expected that continued Jain research in Europe should have led to the origin of a Jaina Text Society as a counterpart to the well-known Pali Text Society. PISCHEL expressed his hope in this direction[3], but things took a different course. The edition of canonical texts—which, of course, was the most important—did not go on methodically, but as circumstances would have it. We are glad to say that the Jains themselves came to help, if, to be true, in their own style. The Āgamodaya-Samiti, founded at Mhesana in 1915, has published most works of the Śvetāmbara Siddhānta and many more non-canonical texts. These handy prints mark a great progress as compared with the monstrous volumes mentioned above. The classical commentary in Sanskrit has been added. It is wanting in the Jain Sūtra Battīsī which was a rather primitive undertaking (Haidarabad 1920), though Ṛṣi (i.e. Sādhu) Āmolak[4] had contributed a Hindi paraphrase.

1. Uvās. II app.; Encyclop. of Religion and Ethics 1, p. 259ff. Later publications see § 18.—A full account of Schools and Sects in Jaina Literature by Amulyachandra SEN, C. 1931.

2. ZDMG 46, p. 91; Ep. Ind. 2, 274. Acc. to the former place the discovery is due to LASSEN.

3. SPAW 1903, f 11. PISCHEL lived half a century too early to see the foundation of the Prakrit Text Society on a large scale in 1953. For the first Volume see § 56.

4. The same as Amolakh Ṛṣijī, the author of Mukti Sopān (Haidarābād 1915), born in S. 1933, as is evident from the preface.

The most recent print[1] is without any commentary whatever. Its name, taken from Ardhamāgadhī, is Suttāgame. Both the Battīsī and the Suttāgame are Sthānakvāsī prints and, for that reason, they contain no more than 32 Āgamas out of the traditional 45.

§ 5. The old texts, in many cases, have been handed down to us in a very curious shape which makes them rather unintelligible for the unprepared reader. The copyists of olden time being confronted with innumerable repetitions have recoursed, as can be easily understood, to abbreviations which, however, violated the context. Up to this day, the printed books pass over them as through thick and thin. The reader, indeed, is prepared to forbear as traditional and respectable peculiarities of Jain style a certain monotony of question and answer, dry lists, and long complexes (though not altogether void of euphony) of what has turned out to be metrical passages[2]. But he is longing for a less clumsy wording. This might be easily achieved by a rational method of dissolving those abbreviations and by providing the necessary references, a method which would result in a readable text where the valuable trend of thought now often concealed would eventually appear in a lucid form. It goes without saying that critical examination and comparison of traditions will remain indispensable. Let it be admitted that the want of controllable oldest manuscripts is often a stumbling stone in the way towards that ideal of a critical edition. Hundreds of Jain works are still preserved in partly subterranean bhaṇḍārs where they were deposited centuries ago, and those precious libraries remained inaccessible since the conservatism of the owners could not overcome their disinclination towards their treasures being published. When BÜHLER was allowed to have a glance into the *baṛā bhaṇḍār* of Jaisalmer, he was misled as to the mass of what was preserved there. It was not earlier than a few years ago that a scholarly examination of bhaṇḍār manuscripts became feasible, and our thanks and res-

1. Shri Sutragama Prakashak Samiti, Gurgaon Cantt., E. P.

2. The Veḍha metre, discovered by JACOBI Ind. Stud. 17, p. 389ff.; later treatments by the AUTHOR, Worte p. 3f.; ALSDORF in Asiatica (Festschrift Weller), p. 16

pects are due to Munirāj PUṆYAVIJAYA for his working towards that noble aim[1].

§ 6. The 'classical' Sanskrit commentary to the Śvetambara canon represents the climax of a vast scholastic literature. Its predecessors in Prakrit, the Nijjuttis and Cuṇṇis, were, for a long time, neglected by scholars. We might even say that, in a certain sense, this is still true to-day, for the publications of Cuṇṇis issued in the course of the last decades do not contain even the slightest illustrative or critical addition, though the merits of Muni JINAVIJAYA Acharya in laying them before the reader are undisputable. It was nearly half a century earlier (1892) that LEUMANN, on the ground of his own subtle investigations based not upon prints but upon manuscripts, has shown (ZDMG 46, p. 586) the importance of those voluminous products for not only Jain dogmatics but for the history of literature in general. Unfortunately the author did not pursue those researches he had characterized as "indispensible for the exploration of the Jain literature of several centuries", pointing out that the Kathās in the old commentaries often appear in non-Jinistic works. Still we possess his "Āvaśyaka-Erzählungen" (AKM lo, 2; 1897) which after the most subtle examination of the best manuscripts give the pure text of those old moral illustrations. It is a point of regret that no more than but four forms of that work should have been printed and that a continuation, though promised, should never have seen the light of the day. It was younger recensions of Jain stories that were translated and explored as to their motives and their importance for comparative history of literature by HERTEL and others. In his essay "On the Literature of the Shvetambaras of Gujarat" (1922) we find the following remarkable passage : "During the middle-ages down to our own days the Jains and especially the Śvetāmbaras of Gujarat, were the principal story-tellers of India. Their literature contains, in huge masses, the materials which the students of folklore, who wish to do true scientific work, should thoroughly study in preference to all the other Indian narrative

1. See ALSDORF in Festschrift Schubring, p. 59f.

literature." But HERTEL did not leave any doubt that in his opinion not even the preliminary condition, i.e. of critical texts and precise translations was fulfilled. As to his intrinsic studies of the Kathānakas for which he succeeded to produce parallels even from non-Indian sources, the reader is referred to WINTERNITZ' History of Indian Literature Vol. 2.

Jain Sanskrit in the Stories, according to HERTEL, is a common people's language with its usual carelessness and some borrowings from Prakrit or from the author's provincial tongue; it must not be measured by the standard of classical Bhāratī. This definition serves to weaken a severe judgment pronounced by BÜHLER (loc. cit. p. 14). At other places in scholarly literature, too, peculiarities of Jain Sanskrit have been noted down. BLOOMFIELD in the second of four systematical collections[1] has pointed out, (1) the influence of Prakrit and an early stage of New Indian (Gujarati and Marathi) already mentioned, (2) in some cases hyper-sanskritization of words apparently Prakritic, (3) borrowings from dictionaries and grammars, (4) use of words of un-known origin. Apart from Amitagati's Dharmaparīkṣā (ed. MIRONOW) this judgment was based upon Śvetāmbara works. A description of the origin and progress of linguistic studies in the Prakrits (Ardhamāgadhī, Jaina-Māhārāṣṭrī, Jaina Śaurasenī) and Apabhraṃśas in Jain literature is beyond the scope of this book.

When stopping further publication of the "Āvaśyaka-Erzählungen" LEUMANN had consoled the reader with his "Übersicht über die Āvaśyaka-Literature" to come out "in the very next time." Materials from manuscripts and manuscripts only, a long list of which LEUMANN has given in ZDMG 45 and 46, had been collected for the purpose of laying bare the different layers of an extensive scholastic literature concerning certain indispensable (*āvaśyaka*) formulae of daily devotion. By this great work he was many decades ahead of his

1. Life and stories of the Jain Saviour Pārśvanātha (Baltimore 1919); p. 220; Some Aspects of Jaina Sanskrit (Antidōron, Festschrift Wackernagel 1923, p. 220 ff.; The Śālibhadra Carita (JAQS 1923, p. 290-316); On Diminutive Pronouns in Jaina Sanskrit (Festschrift Lanman 1929, p. 7 ff.).

time. But, unfortunately, in this case too, printing was stopped when the 14th form (in folio) had been composed. Not until 34 years later this fragment, rich in contents, but difficult to study, was published by the AUTHOR who was fortunate enough to find the proofs being preserved[1].

§ 7. All history of literature, a building, as it were, has for its ground-floor the bio-bibliographical materials. Jain research would have enjoyed the great luck of having them at its disposal, if KLATT's Onomasticon had been completed and printed. Eight volumes from his own hand in alphabetical order contain what was within his reach to collect data concerning Jain authors and works. But he fell severely ill and never recovered. The work was estimated to fill some 1,100 pages in print, but no more than 55 pages have been printed as a specimen thanks to WEBER and LEUMANN[2]. The first to become a bibliographer of Jainism was GUÉRINOT by his "Essai de bibliographie jaina" (1906). A modern standard was not reached until 1944, when VELANKAR's Jinaratnakoṣa appeared, where the Jain works have been catalogued, while a second volume containing their authors is still waiting for being published. A primitive forerunner had been the "Jaina Granthāvalī" published by the Jain Śvetāmbara Conference in 1908.

Another fundament for Jain history are the inscriptions. GUÉRINOT's "Essai" was followed in 1908 by a "Répertoire d'épigraphie jaina." Though not the work of a specialist, yet LÜDERS' "List of Brāhmī Inscriptions from the earliest time till about 400 A.D. with the exception of those of Aśoka" is valuable thanks to innumerable inscribed allusions to the Order of Jain laymen and monks. (EI 10, App. L.C. 1912.)

It seems to be a digression from our subject when we note that BÜHLER in his academical lecture "Über die indische Sekte der Jainas" (1887) was the first to call up the interest of

1. LEUMANN, Übersicht über die Āvaśyaka-Literatur, aus dem Nachlass hrsg. v. Walther SCHUBRING, Hamburg 1934. Obituary by the same, ZDMG 87, p. 69-75.

2. Specimen of a literary-biographical Onomasticon by Dr. Joh. KLATT Leipzig 1892.—His obituary by LEUMANN IA p. 23, 169.

non-scholars for Jainism, legitimated as he was to do so thanks to 17 years of official service in the then Bombay Presidency. Mrs. S. STEVENSON, trained in the Christian Mission of Gujarat, wrote her book "The Heart of Jainism" in 1915, thus challenging a strong resentment at least among the Digambaras[1]. It is curious to see that, while this authoress regretted to miss true warmth of heart in the religion she described, PERTOLD in a public lecture approved of its being excluded from it[2]. GUERINOT'S book "La religion djaina" (1926) was exposed to criticism as was the book just mentioned[3]. One year before (1925) H.v. GLASENAPP's by far more instructive and comprehensive work "Der Jainismus, eine indische Erlösungsreligion" had come into the hands of many grateful readers.

To the same author we owe his contribution to the Handbuch der Literaturwissenschaft representing Jain literature and writing according to the different literary species. WINTERNITZ' History of Indian Literature Vol. II, p. 289-356 (1920) which deals with the same subject is too well known for its merits for being praised here.

§ 8. Thus far we have registered western working for the public knowledge of Mahāvīra's religion. As to the countless pamphlets and journals through which the Jains themselves, for the purpose of propaganda, appeal to the general public, we but mention them here in passing. Of the publications useful for scholars we refer to VIJAYADHARMA Sūri's (s.b.) Jainatattvajnāna (in Festschrift Winternitz), JAINI's "Outlines of Jainism", P. C. Nahar's "Epitome of Jainism" and Ch. R. JAIN's "Jaina Law." Research further receives great help by *compilations* as are catalogues of private libraries, collections of Paṭṭāvalis and of Praśastis, biographies, etc. They

1. Jagmanderlal JAINI : A Review of the H. of J., Ambala 1925. Earlier, Mrs. STEVENSON published "Notes on modern Jainism", Oxford 1910.

2. O. PERTOLD, The Place and Importance of Jainism in the Comparative Science of Religions (Bh. without year), p. 21 : "I think this sentimental aspect is the least desirable in a modern religion, which must go parallel with the fast development of sciences".

3. Critically reviewed by Charlotte KRAUSE ZDMG 84, p. 192-202 ; comp. also FRAUWALLNER WZKM 36, p. 336 ff.

all, however, are overshadowed by the "Abhidhānarājendra", a Sanskrit encyclopedia in 7 volumes, whose Prakrit catchwords are taken from the canonical and scholastical literature of the Śvetāmbaras, a monumental work by VIJAYARĀJENDRA Sūri (1827-1907, Ratlam 1913-25). A glossary of the Canon in three languages is the Illustrated Ardha-Magadhi Dictionary of Muni RATNACANDRA in 5 volumes (Indaur 1923-32). Prakrits of all kind including that of the Jains have flown together to mix in the ocean called "Pāia-Sadda-Mahaṇṇavo, a complete Prakrit-Hindi Dictionary" (1928) by Pandit Hargovind Das SHETH. Precise data of places as well as large supplements will increase the value of that great work. Among the *periodicals* we should like to mention the Anekānt, Jain Antiquary, Jain Hitaiṣī where literature and history are being discussed by Jain authors, many of whom, of course, have contributed also to non-Jinist journals. Nearest related to the periodicals are the series (*grantha-mālā*). In many cases they represent a very remarkable file including rare and significant works provided with a scholarly introduction. It is a pity that many Granthamālās should have become known in the West only in fragments, if at all. The Śvetāmbaras can be proud of the volumes, apart from the Siddhānta, published by the Āgamodaya-Samiti, by the Devcand Lālbhāi-J.-Pustakoddhāra, the Ātmānanda-Grantharatnamālā (Bhn, 1911 ff.), the Yaśovijaya-J.-Gr., started in 1904 and apparently the oldest Jain series, and many more literary undertakings which cannot be enumerated here. Our thanks are equally due to the Digambaras. A parallel to the Siddhānta are the classical Digambara authors. They have been printed and translated in the Sacred Books of the Jains (Arrah 1917 ff.; Sanātana-J. Gr.-M. (Ben. 1917 ff.); Śrī Rāyacandra-J. Śāstra-M. (Bo. 1916 ff.) Māṇikcand-J.-Gr.-M. (Bo. 1915 ff.). The most recent series is the Jnānapīṭha-Mūrtidevī-J.-Gr.-M. (Banaras 1948 ff.), a younger counterpart to the Singhī-J.-Gr.-M. (Bo. 1933 ff.) of the Śvetāmbaras, edited by Muni JINAVIJAYA.

§ 9. These intimations are merely meant to demonstrate the respectable activity within the Jain communities as to their almost inexhaustible stock of literature, an activity radiating as far as to the field of Western research. This state of affairs can be dated from the first two decades of this century. It is true that it was HOERNLE who, as early as in 1890, could dedicate the first volume of his Uvāsagadasāo to VIJAYĀNANDA Sūri (Ānandavijaya=Ātmārāma, 1837-97) in grateful acknowledgment of various suggestions and corrections, though it is equally true that it was VIJAYADHARMA Sūri (1868-1922), never failing to help when being consulted by European scholars[1], who proved by far more effective. The renaissance just mentioned with the Śvetāmbaras at least is due to his lasting impulse.

For a long time research in Europe and America was known to the Jains to but a certain degree, that is to say, as far as their knowledge of English allowed. Books and articles in German and other Western languages frequently remained beyond their reach. Hence it follows that quite a number of data produced by them are well-known in Western literature. It is evident, therefore, that of all works of JACOBI's (1850-1937)[2] none have come to their knowledge than those written in English. But even this crop harvested on the Jain field by an all-round genial indologist was abundant enough for a Jain Conference in 1914 held on the occasion of JACOBI's second stay in India, to bestow upon him the honorary title of Jaina-darśana-divākara. We are thus justified in this historical sketch in reproducing how to him, in several publications[3], Jainism presented itself in view of its relation to other creeds and systems.

§10. On the foregoing pages it has been said already that research started from the similarity observed between

1. Western acknowledgments and recollections by WINTERNITZ, GUÉRINOT, BELLONI-FILIPPI and others; A.J. SUNAWALA, V. Dh. S., His Life and Work. With a prefatory note by F. W. THOMAS, Cambridge 1922, the SAME, Adarsha Sadhu, an ideal monk, 2nd ed. Cambridge 1934; VIJAYA INDRA Sūri, Reminiscences of V. Dh. S., Shivpuri 1924.

2. Obituary by H.v. GLASENAPP ZDMG 92, p. 1-14; the AUTHOR, Jain Gazette 1937.

3. On the Metaphysics and Ethics of the Jainas (Transact. 3rd Congr. for the History of Religion 2, p. 59-66; Die Entwicklung der Gottesidee bei den Indern (1923) p. 21 ff.; Gött. Gelehrte Anz. 1919, p. 16 ff,; Encyclop. f. Rel. and Ethics 7, p. 465 ff,; SPAW 1929, p. 322 ff.; a summary in Forschungen und Fortschritte 6, p. 36.

Mahāvīra's and the Buddha's, teaching, those two coeval features which both result in a monk's life, touching each other in many respects and agreeing in considering Right Knowledge to be the means of how to get rid of the endless chain of rebirth. There is, however, a difference (among others) between them in that the Buddha does not share the high opinion of ascetic practices which, in Mahāvīra's belief, are essential for reaching the ultimate goal. Further differences will be found in metaphysics. But here the partner of the comparison[1] is not so much Buddhism as is the Sāṃkhya. In the Sāṃkya the development of the world starts from matter that is imperishable and infinite as to quality going on in a determined sequel defined by means of Brahman terms. The Jains, being far from the Brahman way of thinking, do not acknowledge such a sequel, since, in their eyes, the world is eternal, though they agree with the Sāṃkhya in considering matter as being capable of developing in whatever direction. Moreover, logic compels them, as does the Sāṃkhya, to consider as important the' transition (*pariṇāma*) from the one status to the next. And third, both are in harmony as to the original conception of the soul. "The Jainas call *jīva* all souls, the Sāṃkhya those that exist in the concrete world. Thus it seems that "soul" has been abstracted from "living being", that is to say, from a popular view." The same idea appears in the conception that the soul is as large as the body, a conception which is apparent with the Jains, while it is at least inferable from the original Sāṃkhya and Yoga. Both Jainism and Sāṃkhya pretend a plurality of bodies. It seems that this conception replaced the primitive idea of a plurality of souls at a time when the doctrine of the One Ātman could not be neglected any longer. This applies to the doctrine of Karman and of reincarnation following from the former and which, by the by, is a primitive idea as well. Both Karman and reincarnation are the fundaments of the Sāṃkhya system as well as of that of the Jains. The very fact that both these systems, as they now stand, are so very

1. Comp. W. BOHN, Die Religion des Jaina und ihr Verhältnis zum Buddhismus, Zeitschr. f. Buddhismus'3, p. 113-140; LEUMANN, Buddha und Mahāvīra, ibd. 4 (separate offprint, Munich 1921).

unlike to each other contributes to their common features being extremely significant, and this explains itself by their having embodied elements of common-sense view (Volksglauben). The time when this happened can be calculated thanks to non-Jinist testimonials of spiritual development as well as to chronology. Both agree in going back as far as the 8th century B.C.

The Jain system, moreover, exhibits archaic traits not found in other systems. Among them we have the theory of the elementary particles (earth, water, fire, wind) possessing souls, and the names of *dharma* and *adharma* for the media of motion and stop. The former can be rubricated as animism, whereas in the latter there appears the conception of "invisible fluids which by contact cause sin and merit"[1], a conception coming near to primitive sorcery. In later chapters of this book we are going to point out some more characteristics of such primitive or popular thinking ("Volksglaube"). It is very well imaginable that, apart from this basis, Mahāvīra made use of the conceptions of other systems[2], though his is not dependent on other systems we know of[3]. On the other hand it is probable that the Jains influenced the Yoga as taught by Patanjali, but in subordinate items only. There is no relation to the Vaiśeṣika system assumed by JACOBI, though it shares its atomistic character with that of the Jains. Since the similarity between both of them cannot possibly be ignored, the Jains maintained that a heretic[4] named Chaluya Rohagutta was the inventor of the Vaiśeṣika system. For scholars[5] take the word Chaluya as an illusion to the six (*cha*) categories in the "owl" (*uluya*)-philosophy, i.e. the teaching of the Kāṇādas or "crow-eaters", i.e. "owls." The doctrine imputed to Rohagutta is that he under-

1. JACOBI at frequent places.

2. "Mahāvīra probably borrowed much more from other sects than we shall ever be able to prove", JACOBI SBE 45, p. XXXII.

3. A conjecture that Umāsvāti in T. 7, 5 ff. was influenced by the Yoga-sūtra was not maintained by JACOBI SPWA 1930, p. 607. Some contact between both of them is stated by him ad T. 2, 52 and 9, 46.

4. This was the 6th heresy of the 7 known in tradition (§ 17).

5. JACOBI (following WEBER) Kalpasūtra p. 119, SBE 45, XXXV ff., ad T, 9. Most important LEUMANN, Ind. Stud. 17, p. 121 ff.

took to add a third category (*rāsī*) called *nojīva*, to the natural and traditional ones, viz. *jīva* and *ajīva*. It seems impossible to prove that the Vaiśeṣika took its origin from that rather funny doctrine. Rohagutta was defeated dialectically by 144 items the detailed list of which, being based on the Vaiśeṣika, turns out to be a secondary addition.

§11. It is in this connexion that, last not least, we wish to refer to a subject common to both Jainism and Hinduism, without being entitled to pretend that the latter influenced the former. The belief in the force of magic syllables has its roots in the primitive stage of mankind. In Brahman literature it appears ever since the remotest times of antiquity. No wonder, then, that in later centuries we find it even in Jainism where a great many of Stotras resound with those incantations which even an illiterate might master[1]. But the Jains, moreover, have found a way for educated people to bring forward their praise and desire in writing. A *vijjā* or magic formula appears in the peculiar manner of each consonant having the virāma and being followed by the respective vowel akṣara (e.g. *t*+*u* instead of *tu*). In the Canon the Mahānisīha is the only representative[2] and thus goes conform with the Angacūliyā, Āyāravihi, Vihimaggappavā and other texts of a decidedly later date. On principle the Stotras are directed to an Arhat, though other persons, among whom there are certain Hindu goddesses, receive veneration all the same. But an Arhat is far beyond the reach of human affairs. Being in the state of pure cognition exclusively and without both sentiment and will, he cannot bestow grace and favour unto those who appeal to him. Hindu influence seems to have been at work in placing at his side two adjutants, one male (*yakṣa*) and one female (*yakṣī*, *yakṣiṇī*), the former presumably being not more than the shadow of the latter[3]. and it is these two that take care of a devout supplicant. That,

1. Comp. Ch. KRAUSE, Ancient Jaina Hymns, Ujjain 1952 ; the AUTHOR in Festschrift Nobel 1959.

2. The AUTHOR, Mahanis. p. 73 and 74ff. Studien (§) p. 66, 88, 106.

3. The AUTHOR, see footnote 1.

on a large scale, Hindu mythology was adopted by the Jains and brought in accord with their own principles is a fact known too well that it should be treated here in detail. The remarkable process of making out of a Bodhisattva a Roman Catholic Saint[1] finds its not less remarkable counterpart in the Jain ability of transforming epic heroes and other individuals into venerable persons of their own creed. The difference is that the said process in the West, thanks to translating a wandering subject into many languages, was unconscious, while the Jains with conscious energy satisfied their pious requirements at home.

1. E. KUHN, Barlaam and Josaphat, comp. WINTERNITZ, History 2, p. 416 f.

II
AN HISTORICAL SKETCH OF JAINISM

§12. Any historical sketch of the Jain religion has to deal not only with the objective results of research but also with the facts maintained by this religion. We shall consider the latter first. They are based on the assumption of the world having neither beginning nor end, i.e. being everlasting. Incessantly, though only within a small part of the universe, the wheel of time revolves with its spokes (*samā*), the gradations ranging from the paradisical to the catastrophical period (§ 120) and back to the former, ceaselessly passing through the point denoting the present. The descending half-circle, and it is this where we find ourselves, is called *osappiṇī*, the ascending *ussappiṇī*. Either produces a number of prophets of salvation (*titthagara*) as Mahāvīra is, and just as his teaching (*tittha*) is destined to last not longer than 21,000 years (Viy. 792a, comp. also § 120), so the teachings of all his precursors were doomed to degenerate and so will be those of all that come after him. But from every degeneration a new prophet will save the teaching, if only but after an immeasurably long intermediate period (*antara*). Since all this occurs periodically, the Jains can afford to be quite easy in stating the inevitable impendency of degeneration.[1]

§13. Next to the spiritual supermen, to whom we shall return in due course, we have the temporal heroes. It is in them, in their social standing as well as in their personal names and those connected with them, that we first and most distinctly behold the influence of non-Jain conceptions and, mainly, of such pertaining to the Kṛṣṇa mythology. There are grand sovereigns or world-emperors (*cakkavaṭṭi*) who are the immediate counterparts of the common-Indian *cakravartin*. In the *baladeva* and *vāsudeva*, comprised as *dasāra-maṇḍala* by Samav. 152b, the two homonymous heroic figures have been generalized

1. Comp. AUTHOR, OLZ 1926, col. 910 ff.

into types, and Samav. 153a is consequent in calling these half-brothers *duve rāmakesavā* by then adding their names. The *kulagara*, finally, reflect the Brahman *manu* and the law-constituting ancestral fathers. During every half-circle covered by the ever revolving time-wheel[1] there arise 24 prophets, 12 grand sovereigns, 9 *baladeva* and as many *vasudeva*, and either 7, 10 or 15 legislators. It is these latter only that are traced back (Samav. 150 b) over the present half-course to the one immediately preceding, whereas for the one to succeed all different classes are noted (comp. also Ṭhāṇ. 455b, 457b ff.). And, what is more, from the uniformity regarding the cosmographic structure (§ 119) it follows that the appearance of all these men in our southernmost continent of Bharaha has its counterpart in the northernmost of Eravaya. So that, then, we hear (Ṭhāṇ. 76a ; Samav. 72b, 153b) of the corresponding men also in this continent, if only by their names, and, indeed, they make their appearance even in the nearest continents (§ 122), as Ṭhāṇ. 123b, if only by way of indication, shows (see also below). In this respect the continent of Mahāvideha is but rarely mentioned (Viy. 791a and, accordingly, Ṭhāṇ. 201a).

For discussing the individual classes we have to start from the fact that every half-course contains 6 periods (§ 120) within which the condition of the world either deteriorates—as is the case in the *osappiṇī*—or improves—as in the *ussappiṇī*. In the third of these periods, illustrated by the wheel-spoke of 'good-bad" (*susama-dūsamā*), that is to say in its last third, the legislators and founders of civilisation (*kulagara*) made their appearance, 15 in number acc. to Jambudd. 132b, and 7 acc. to Ṭhāṇ. 398a ; Samav. 150b ; Āv. 148. Their names are : Sumai, Paḍissui, Sīmaṃkara, Sīmaṃdhara, Khemaṃkara, Khemaṃdhara (thus far in Jambudd. only), Vimalavāhaṇa, Cakkhumaṃ, Jasamaṃ, Abhicanda, Candābha (in Jambudd. only), Paseṇaī, Marudeva, Nābhi, Usabha (in Jambudd. only). The last of these names is due only to unnecessarily adding the 1st Titthagara. Without it we have 14 names after the example

1. *ega-samae ega-juge* Ṭhāṇ. 76a ; Nāyādh. 223a.

of the 14 Manu[1], though the 7 first names are for the most part rather poorly invented, and most certainly the second row of 7 is the original one. Now the kulagaras introduced punishments (*daṇḍa-nīi*) which, however, consisted in not more than in admonition, warning and reprimand (*hakkāra, ma-kkāra, dhikkāra*). Every new kind[2] came to be of common usage with the 6th and 11th kulagara (Āv. 165 f. : 1.3.5.).

The following period "bad-good" (*dūsama-susamā*) contains all *Baladeva* and *Vāsudeva* (Jambudd. 164b) or *dasāra* (Than. 76a ; 123a f. ; Samav. 72b). The former, dressed in dark, is characterised by the palmtree, the latter, dressed in yellow, by the Garuḍa in the banner ; other attributes of the *baladeva* are the ploughshare, the club and the arrow, whereas of the *vāsudeva* they are the shell, the discus, the club, the spear, and the sword, so that the description (Samav. 152b f.)[3] closely follows the epic pattern. They both are masters of half the Bharaha. We come to know (also Ṭhāṇ. 447a) their names in their pre-existence, their fathers and mothers, their teachers, the towns where they first came to wish for a certain form of existence (*niyāṇa-bhūmi*), the cause for this wish (*n.-kāraṇa*), and their 9 opponents, *padisattu*, later called *prativāsudeva*. Since these informations are for the most part given in the way of popular verses we may well suggest the general knowledge of certain legends marked with regard to content. In the Canon, however, the individual *baladeva* and *vāsudeva* scarcely appear at all (Samav. 63a). It is only *Kaṇha Vāsudeva* who in Antag. 5[4] plays an actual part, and in the Jain version of the epic Draupadī legend in the Nāya

1. This is the number in the Dig., comp. v. GLASENAPP, Festgabe für Jacobi p. 337.

2. Ṭhāṇ. 398a renders the *daṇḍa-nīi* as seven-fold : the above mentioned plus *paribhāsa, maṇḍala-bandha, cāraga, chavi-ccheya*. Acc. to Āv. 166f. the last 4 constitute the *daṇḍa-nīi* coming in with Bharaha.—To the common *nīti* it has to be added that its means are *sāma, bheya* and *daṇḍa* (Ṭhāṇ. 151a). These three *attha-joṇi* are lacking *dāṇa*.

3. In Veḍhas interspersed with prose.

4. Comp. KENNEDY JRAS 1908, 505-521.

16 of the 6th Anga[1]. Here in Kavila (Kapila) we come to know a *vāsudeva* contemporary with Kaṇha, though pertaining to a different continent (see above).

As to the world emperors we are informed in a similar way by Samav. 152a, though in Jambudd. 3 we have a detailed description concerning the career of the 1st *cakkavaṭṭī* Bharaha. This career consists in the obtaining of 14 imperial crown-treasures. In the armoury hall of his palace at Viṇīyā the wheel (1) settles first and then shows him the way to the succeeding ventures[2]. Bh. proclaims his sovereignty at three points of the sea-shore, at the Sindhu and at a cave in the Veyaḍḍha mountains. At the two latter places he gains a magic fleece (*camma-rayaṇa*) (2) and the rod (3) and by the former serving him as a ship he crosses the stream. The people of the Avāḍa-Çilāya are assisted by the Nāgakumāra causing a tempest to rage over the headquarters for seven days which Bh., however, is able to resist by means of his magic umbrella (4) and the crown-jewel (5), and the Av.-C. surrender. Further acquisitions made in this district are : the prototype of all measures of capacity (*kāgiṇī*)[3] (6), a spouse (7), and a sword (8). On the Gangā Bh. receives 9 objects of priceless value (nihi, Ṭhāṇ. 448b ; Jambudd. 256b). Then there follows the ceremonial entry into Viṇīyā. The imperial crown-treasures equally include the general (*seṇāvai*), the chamberlain (*gāhāvai*), the architect (*vaḍḍhai*), the domestic chaplain (*purohiya*), horse and elephant (9 to 14). After a long reign he performs the act of purging called *apuvva-karaṇa* (§ 183), obtains the Kevala-cognition (§ 81) and enters the Nirvāna on the Aṭṭhāvaya mountain. This career is typical of all grand-sovereigns, for Ṭhāṇ. 298a says that they all gain the 14 crown-jewels. They are all considered to be animate (§ 101) as we know from Indian dramatic plays a.o. Apart from being distin-

1. Comp. LEUMANN, VIH OC III, 2, p. 541 ff. In addition there is the "Legend of Dvāravatī's fall and Krishna's death" provided by Devendra in the comm. on Utt. (JACOBI ZDMG 42, 493-529 ; CHARPENTIER ibd. 66, 675-678).

2. The AUTHOR also GGA 1932, p. 293f. ALSDORF ZDMG 92, 472 f.

3. For a description see Ṭhāṇ. 434a ; Jambudd. 225a.

guished by their names (Samav. 152b) the 12 *cakkavaṭṭī* are also distinguished by their bodily size[1], but this they share with the *baladeva* and *vāsudeva* on the one hand and with the *titthagara* on the other. Their period, too, is the *dūsama-susamā* with the exception of Bharaha who already lived in the *susama-dūsamā* as did the 1st Titthagara. But there are still other relations existing between the two species. The 5th to the 7th grand-sovereigns came to be the 16th to the 18th *titthagara*, and of the latter the first was actually an emperor (Samav. 42b), even though he is not listed as such a one.

In the following we give the Śvet.-names of the series[2] in Bharata as have been discussed above. The *kulagara* temporally precede the *cakkavaṭṭī*, Bharaha is the son of Usabha. The 5 first members of the series 2 to 4 lie between cakk. 2 and 3, the 6th and 8th fall in the time of cakk. 7 and 9, the 7th and 9th lie between cakk. 8 and 9, and between 11 and 12 resp.[3].

1. *cakkavaṭṭī* : Bharaha, Sagara, Meghavaṃ, Sanaṃkumāra, Santi[4], Kunthu[4], Ara[4], Subhūma, Mahāpauma Hariseṇa, Jayaṇāma or -seṇa, Bambhadatta.—2. *baladeva* : Ayala, Vijaya, Bhadda, Suppabha, Sudaṃsaṇa, Āṇanda, Nandaṇa, Pauma (=Rāma Dāśarathi), Rāma (=Balarāma).—3. *vāsudeva* : Tiviṭṭha (-ṭṭhū), Duviṭṭha, Sayaṃbhū, Purisuttama, Purisasīha, Purisapuṇḍarīya, Datta, Nārāyaṇa, Kaṇha.—4. *paḍisattu* : Assaggīva, Tāraga, Meraga, Mahukedhava, Nisuṃbha, Bali,

1. The size most certainly also determined the measures of the three giant figures representing Bharaha's younger brother Bāhubali. Acc. to the legend Bh. himself raised a statue to him with B. measuring 325 dhaṇu. He is often called Kāmadeva among other names, and acc. to M. GOVIND PAL IHQ 4, 270-286, the Kanarese name of Gommaṭa, by the mediation of the Konkaṇī, stems from the synonymous word Manmatha. The most ancient, largest and most famous of the three statues (57 ft. high) was raised about 980 A.D. by Cāmuṇḍa Rāya—Gommaṭa Rāya near Sravana Belgola in Mysore, a second, dated Śaka 1353, near Karkala, and a third, dated 1525 by Saka, near Yenur (Venur), both places in South-Kanara. Comp. PAL ibd. ; VENKATASUBBIAH IHQ 6, 290-309 ; early reports by MACKENZIE IA 2, 129-133; BURNELL ibd. 353-357.

2. For the deviations of the Dig. see v. GLASENAPP, Festgabe f. Jacobi, p. 337f.

3. Comp. the tables AV 242a and v. GLASENAPP, Jainismus, p. 261.

4. *titth.* 16—18 (s.b.). JACOBI (SBE 45, 86) thinks it possible that this name developed from Kakutstha, but this derivation asks for a number of hypothetical links.

Pahāraga, Rāvaṇa, Jarāsaṃdha. By adding the spiritual series of the 24 *titthagara* to these temporal series 2 to 5 later authors come to count 63 men "of mark" (Śvet. : *śalākā-puruṣa*, Dig, : *lakṣaṇa-p.*) leaving the mentioned identities out of consideration. 27 out of these 63 are related to the Kṛṣṇa legend. This has been led back by JACOBI to the spreading of the teaching towards the west[1]. But we have seen already that Kaṇha had been playing a part at all times, and also Ariṭṭhaṇemi, a brother-in-law of Kṛṣṇa, is included in the system since the time we know it.

§14. In now turning to the spiritual heroes we have to distinguish between such who *find* and such who *preach* salvation, and as to the former we may denote them as the *patteya-buddha*. Viy. 895a places them next to the latter though fails to give any particulars for doing so, nor do we find any in the two only remaining and, by the way, later passages of Samav. 123a and Nandī 203a. The appertaining persons first appear in the narrative tradition of the Āvassaya[2]. The *preachers of salvation* (*titthagara, arahaṃ, jiṇa*; Viy. 583a and Ṭhāṇ. 302a : *devādhideva*) of the current *osappiṇī* are called : 1. Usabha, 2. Ajiya, 3. Saṃbhava, 4. Abhiṇandaṇa, 5. Sumai, 6. Paumappabha, 7. Supāsa, 8. Candappabha, 9. Suvihi Pupphadanta, 10. Sīyala, 11. Sejjaṃsa, 12. Vāsupujja, 13. Vimala, 14. Aṇanta, 15. Dhamma, 16. Santi, 17. Kunthu, 18. Ara, 19. Malli, 20. Muṇisuvvaya, 21. Nami, 22. Ariṭṭhaṇemi, 23. Pāsa, 24. Vaddhamāṇa or Mahāvīra. For Paumappabha and Candappabha Viy. 792a has Suppabha and Sasi ; in an isolated inscription (§ 25) Ara is called Nāndyāvarta ; Ariṭṭhaṇemi is frequently shortened into Nemi. The entire series is closely dealt with by Samav. 150a and Āv. 230 ff. though this is being done in comprising gāhās only. They record the names of each in their pre-existence, those of their parents, of their first alms-givers, pupils both male and female, and other items. What else we find in the Samav. and in the Ṭhāṇ. as well

1. Reports of the VIIth OC (Vienna 1889), p. 75-77 ; IA 16, 163f.

2. The part they play with the later commentators Devendra and Bhāvavijaya has been dealt with by CHARPENTIER in the light of the Jātaka and epic texts (Paccekabuddhageschichten. Uppsala 1908 ; JAS. 1911, 201-255).

rests in correspondence to the purpose of these works, on figures which, faithful to the system, are mostly very large. Thus we learn, though but incompletely and frequently without any recognizable principle, at what age a Titthagara devoted himself to monastic life, how many groups of disciples and group-leaders he had, how many among his followers owned a certain amount of spiritual knowledge and were endowed with certain kinds of cognition, how old he came to be, how tall he was, etc. Jinac. 184-203 in dealing with those from 2 up to 21 confines himself to giving the distances of the one from the other, from Mahāvīra or from the present of that time. A number of them is attributed certain colours of the body (Ṭhāṇ. 98b)[1], and, what is more, in pairs : 6 and 12 are *pauma-gora* red, 8 and 9 *canda-gora*, white, 19 and 23 *piyangu-sāma* dark, and 20 and 22 *nīl'-uppala*, blue. The remaining are golden. For a smaller part these colours are due to the names of their bearers, and this, too, goes back to legends. Such is equally the case with reports stating, for instance (Samav. 42b), that 23 preachers of salvation (2-24) were minor princes (*maṇḍali-rāya*) prior to their monastic life, or, as Ṭhāṇ. 351b gives it, that five (12. 19. 22-24) were *kumāra* when becoming monks. By the earliest plastic image of a Titthagara handed down to us (§ 25, comp. also § 24) it is proved that their representation showing merely their typical features was given personal traits by adding a symbol. The Canon does not refer to such symbols. For the most part they consist in animals (for 1-4 : bull, elephant, horse, monkey : for 23 and 24 : snake and lion), but also in the red and blue lotus (6 and 21), in patterns (7, 10, 15, 18), in the water-jug (19) and in the shell (22)[2]. A direct reference to the name of the Titthagara is made merely by the bull of the Ṛṣabha ; Mahāvīra's lion may be connected with the words : *sīh'ubbhava*[3]-

1. For minor deviations with the Digambaras see JAINI, Outlines of Jainism.

2. For a specification see v. GLASENAPP, Jainismus p. 491.

3. So instead of *sīhabbhava* (the AUTHOR ZDMG 104, p. 262). Comp. the *siṃhāvalokita* and other lion-like behaviour of the new-born Bodhisattva in Lalitavistara VII.

bhūeṇaṃ appāṇeṇaṃ kucchiṃsi gabbhaṃ vakkante Āyār. II p. 121, line 22 (to supply *gabbhaṃ*).

No more than the Canon refers to the symbols does it refer to the two deities of male and female sex associated with every Titthagara. They are called *yakṣa* and *yakṣiṇī* or *yakṣī* or *sāsaṇa-(śruta) devatā.* The latter may well have inaugurated the conception in so far as it was the commandment of Jina that first took on human shape, i.e. female shape in correspondence with basic Indian conceptions. Moreover, there was the demand for granting powers establishing for laymen since the preachers of salvation were beyond reach of their supplications[1]. Their names, again, disclose obvious suggestions of the Brahman sphere of ideas[2]. For these as well as for other persons and objects pertaining to the later cult comp. v. GLASENAPP, Jainismus p. 362ff., 492[3].

§15. At the beginning of her pregnancy the mother of a Titthagara has experienced 14 visions by dreaming as has such of a *cakkavaṭṭi*, whereas the mother of a *vāsudeva* has visioned 7, such of a *baladeva* 4, and such of a *maṇḍaliya* 1 out of those 14. The germ for these figures is in the 14 dreams of Mahāvīra's mother (Jiṇac. § 32 ff.)[4]. Acc. to Viy. 709a we have (to refer to this here) 42 normal and 30 major dreams (*mahā-suviṇa*) of the kind of dreams in pregnancy mentioned above. Ten dreams were visioned by Mv. when still a *chaumattha* (§ 81, also Ṭhāṇ. 499a). 14 dreams immediately lead to true cognition and in most cases to salvation within the same existence. The dream belongs to the 8 possible omens (*nimitta*, Ṭhāṇ. 427a) and is considered rather incongruently[5]

1. About the importance of the yakṣī cult in South India see DESAI Jainism in South India, 1957.

2. For the picture-teaching of the Dig. comp. BURGESS IA 32, 459-464; XIII. OC, 74; in The Indian Sect of the Jainas (§ 4); J. L. JAINI IA 33, 330-332. For the Śvet. see Helen M. JOHNSON, IA 56, 23-28.

3. A movement against the Śruta-d. see § 33.

4. A representation in colours was reviewed by HÜTTEMANN, Baessler-Archiv IV, H. 2. The Dig. know of 16 dreams.

5. *nimitta* as well as *uppāya* a. o. pertain to the region of the pāva-suya-pasanga (Ṭhāṇ, 45/a).

as a special kind of visionary power (Ṭhāṇ. 430b) together with *sammad-daṃsaṇa* etc. up to *kevala-d.* (§ 82) to which Sthān. 430b remarks that, properly speaking, the *svapna-darśana* pertains to the *acakṣur-d.* (§82). It comes in during the state of semi-trance (*sutta-jāgara*) and it is either true (*ahātacca*), of temporal extension (*payāṇa*), goes back to some day-event (*cintā-suviṇa*) or not (*tavvivarīya*), or, finally, it is vague (*avvatta-daṃsaṇa*). The dream of a *saṃvuḍa*, i.e. of one who exercises *saṃvara* (§169), is necessarily true, however, while this is not positive with the *saṃvuḍa* and the *saṃvuḍāsaṃvuda*. All this is taught by Viy. 16, 6 (709a ff.) perhaps in identity with the Suminabhavaṇa referred to by Vav. 10, 28, or with the Mahāsuminabhāvaṇā quoted at other places.

The schematic structure of the life as lived by a preacher of salvation equally becomes clear by Jambudd.5 describing the ceremonies conferred by the gods on every new-born Titthagara. The *disākumarī* perform the preparations. Sakka and his gods, the latter being summoned by Hari Negamesi (§ 17), betake themselves to the birth-place. After the mother has been sunk into deep sleep a copy of the child is being created along with 5 Sakka who themselves take the Titthagara to the sacred place in the Paṇḍaga grove of the Mandara. Here it is Accuya who, with the assistance of the other gods, performs the act of consecration by anointing and adorning. Īsāṇa creates 5 of his like who wash the Titthagara, Sakka 4 white bulls whose horns join above in the shape of water streams so that a vast flood pours down upon the head of the consecrated. 5 other Sakka then take him back to his mother's side removing the copy. By order of Sakka and Vesamaṇa the Jambhaga gods finally bring in all sorts of treasures, and in the end they all return to their abodes.

The end of the Titthagara career is discussed by Jambudd. 156b, though the text fails to mention any fixed locality. Acc. to the legends it is invariably the mountain of Sammeta or Pārasnāth, a name referring to Pārśva (Pāsa). It was only Usabha who found the Nirvāṇa on the Kailāsa, Vāsupujja in

Campā, Ariṭṭhaṇemi on Girnār, and Mahāvīra (s.b.) in Pāvā. The cremation of the corpse is performed by all godly princes under Sakka's leadership. As we read in Viy. 502b the relics enjoy adoration in the heavenly sphere. This description holds good in any case even though the author here but refers to *Usabha* whose biography which for the most part coincides closely with Jinac. 204-228 is related in the preceding passages. Ranging first in the sequence and, for that reason, frequently called Ādinātha in later times Usabha (Ṛṣabha) enjoys the advantage of a more detailed representation which in Āv.2 is explicitly proclaimed to be universally accepted; anything the like does not occur until the end of the sequence (s. b.). Ṛṣabha who, acc. to Viṣṇu-Purāṇa 2, 1 was a world emperor to become a naked ascetic and to die the fasting-death[1] is sure to have come to the Jains most opportunely as ranging first in their sequence.[2] The extended description of the late Bḥāgavata-P. (5, 6, 8-11) is connected with a vengeful allusion to Jainism flourishing in "Konka, Venka and Kuṭaka" thanks to Ṛ.'s travels in those regions. As is mentioned ibd. 5, 15, 1, but not in Viṣṇu-P., the same has happened with *Sumati*, Bharata's son. The person of *Malli* is (Ṭhāṇ. 400b) identical with that of the king's daughter referred to by Nāya. 8. There she is called by the name of Malli *arahā* and incidentally so from the moment (Nāyādh. 148a) when, on account of her report in front of her six suitors, she comes to remember earlier adventures. Her naming as Arhat always remains masculine, and the gods hail her (Nāyādh. 151a none else than Mahāvīra, Jinac. 111) as *Bhagavaṃ loga-nāha*. Nor does the latter figurative representation distinguish her in any way from the others. All this is a matter of course since sexual qualities are not inherent in a Siddha any longer. The Digambaras do not know of Malli having been a girl (comp. § 30).

1. The first allusion made to the above mentioned passage was by WILSON (Works, Vol. 7, 104). Comp. also JACOBI IA 9, 163.

2. No trace in the Yajurveda of "the Tīrthankaras Ṛṣabha, Ajitanātha and Ariṣṭanemi", as Radhakrishnan (Indian Philosophy I, 28f.) will have it.

§ 16. JACOBI expressed the idea[1] that among the Titthagara such men were admitted who were dear to those communities that had attached themselves to Mahāvīra. This would have its counterpart on a larger scale in the structure of the Hindu pantheon. Provided that Mahāvīra's community really gained in strength by the incorporation of whole bodies of sects, we must, however, bear in mind that the Titthagara are separated from each other by "astronomical figures", whereas those persons must have lived more or less distinctly in the memory of the contemporaries. As is the case with so many characters of the Brahman legends we can neither prove nor can we definitely dispute the assertion that the preachers of salvation relie on individual persons. The lowest rungs of the Titthagara ladder leading from primeval times up to the present are more or less clearly visible in the light of history.[2] Yet we would be more correct in saying that the ladder reaching from an historically attested experience on dogmatic grounds far up into the past is still hit by this light at a point not far from its foot. The question to be asked is how far up this is the case. We meet *Ariṭṭhaṇemi* in Nāya 5; Antag. 1-5; Vaṇhid.; Utt. 22. He is placed within the Kṛṣṇa circle as the brother-in-law of Kaṃsa; the scene is Dvāravatī (Bāravaī). In spite of his being more frequently referred to than his precursors, yet Ariṭṭhaṇemi—he lived to the age of a thousand years—is by no means historically more tangible than they are. The only thing to be advanced might be that in the year of Mahāvīra's Nirvāṇa he had been dead for 84,000 years (Jinac. 182f.), because it should be remembered that the figure of 84 or either of its plurals frequently appear with the Jains and elsewhere where they only fail to give precise details for something founded on fact. Acc. to Jinac. 184 Ariṭṭhaṇemi's precursor, Nami, died half a million years back, and as is the case with all other figures in the lives of the Jinas, so these intervals, too, increase into the gigantic by retrogradation. *Pāsa*, however, acc. to Jinac. 168 f. died 250

1. SBE 45. XXXII.

2. By discussing this problem Chimanlal J. SHAH starts his book on Jainism in North India 800 B.C.—526 A.D. Lo. 1932. Review by the AUTHOR in OLZ 1934, col. 126-128.

years before Mv. (1230 minus 980) at an age of one hundred years. Ever since STEVENSON came to point out this moderation in quoting figures[1] these two dates have served as an argument for Pāsa's being an historic person, though what else we are told of him in Jiṇac. 149f. is merely a copy of Mahāvīra's biography with the exception that Pāsa is said to have been born in Benares and to have died on the Sammeya mountain in Bihar. Nor do we learn anything of importance[2] from Pāsa's rôle Nāyādh. II 1 and Pupph. 1, 3. But he is attested as a historic personality by other passages in rendering his teaching and reporting on his followers. Mahāvīra's parents are said to have belonged to Pāsa's lay-followers (*Pāsâvaccijjā samaṇôvasagā*, Āyār. II, 15, 16), and in his lifetime—as is confirmed by the Sāmaññaphala-Sutta of the Dīgha-Nikāya)[3]—there have been teachers (*P. ijā therā bhagavanto*, Viy. 134b, 247b) and monks (*aṇagāra*, Viy. 99a, 439a) in accordance with Pāsa's intentions. The word *avaccijja* (also Therāv. 2) indicates the spiritual filiation[4]. Pāsa was obviously of a winsome nature, for he bears the constant title of *puris' ādāṇiya* which seems to be the oldest precursor of the modern occasional titles of Lokamānya, Deśabandhu, Mahātman, etc. *ādāṇiya* means as much as *ādejja* which in the Karman theory stands for "suggestive"[5]. Both sects were on absolutely friendly terms, and for this we are given some valuable proof by the conversation of two of their leading representatives Rāyap.[6] and Utt. 23[7]. We are assured (Viy. 247b, 454a) that already Pāsa had conceived both the shape and the eternity of the world (§ 103) in a way as taught by Mahāvīra, though (in the second passage) the latter insists that he came to discover it independently. Yet

1. Kalpa Sūtra S. XII. Comp. JACOBI IA 9, 162f. COLEBROOKE (Misc. Ess. II, 212) does not make any use of this argument when calling P. "perhaps the real founder of the sect".

2. What Isibhās. 31 is given as his utterances has no individual character.

3. Comp. JACOBI, SBE 45, XX.

4. Since dhamm'antevāsī is one of the 10 terms for "son" (Ṭhāṇ. 516a).

5. *puruṣāṇām madhya ādānīya ādeya* Vy. 248b.

6. Comp. LEUMANN, VI. OC III,[2] (Leiden 1883), p. 509-524.

7. Comp. JACOBI, SBE 45 XXII.

we are not able to draw any immediate inferences on Pāsa's system from this conception of his since the idea of a lower, an intermediate, and an upper world is in itself not singular. Mahāvīra's laymen are instructed (Viy. 138a) by Pāsa teachers that self-discipline (*saṃjama*) leads to the suppression of the "influence" (*aṇaṇhaya*, § 168) and asceticism (*tava*) to purification (*vodāṇa*, also 140b), and to this Mahāvīra agrees. And yet, perhaps, he himself went beyond it, provided it was he who placed those two pairs into the causal association known, acc. to Ṭhāṇ. 156b, as: *savaṇa, nāṇa, vinnāṇa, paccakkhāṇa, saṃjama, a., t., v., akiriyā, nivvāṇa, siddhi-gai-gamaṇa-pajjavasāṇa*. But it cannot be disputed that in practical ethics we see a development beyond Pāsa's ideas where the four-fold morality, the *cāujjāma dhamma*, is replaced by the *panca-mahavvaiya sapaḍikkamaṇa dh.* Pāsa's postulation (Rāyap. 118a; Thāṇ. 201 a) was: not to damage anything living, not to commit anything untrue, and neither to take what has not ben given (*adinn'ādāṇāo veramaṇa*) nor to give away (*bahiddhādāṇāo v.*). The last word by Sthān. 202 a is taken as *bahirdhādāna* and commented as "accepting (*ādāna*) from outside", i.e. the accepting of things not belonging to the monk's standard outfit. This prohibition is said to include the "possession" of a female individual. Thus, as Abhayadeva adds, Pāsa's *fourth* commandment would correspond with Mahāvīra's both fourth and fifth (sexual abstention and non-possession (§ 171). The former of these two LEUMANN sees expressed in *bahiddhā-dāṇa* (sic), "a decent term for copulation[1] (the delivery of sperm)". Thus it is Pāsa's *third* vow that corresponds with both the third and fifth of Mahāvīra's including prohibition of any appropriation other than by gift as well as by acquisition. At any rate, it is a merit of Mahāvīra's that he did away with a certain vagueness in the terms of his predecessor and made his fifth commandment applicable for both sexes. Utt. 23, 26f. and probably also 87 indicate that this act of extension was at the same time a process of revival, and this, to be sure, is the case, since it was in the nature of the two founders. Moreover, this is indicated by the above-mentioned view according to which

1. Buddha und Mahāvīra p. 33.

the teaching experiences a decline until a new preacher of salvation comes to make his appearance. And it was also the difference existing between the teachings of Pāsa and Mahāvīra that had to be perpetuated within this view. This was done in a way (Viy. 791 b; Ṭhāṇ. 201a) that all Titthagara prior to Pāsa are considered preachers of the *cāujjāma dhamma* with the exception of Usabha[1], and in the timeless continent of Mahāvideha (§ 113) it is even all 24. Likewise there is a difference being construed (Ṭhāṇ. 296a) in that the same preachers of salvation including Pāsa had no difficult career as teachers whereas Usabha and Mahāvīra had (*purima-pacchimāṇaṃ jiṇāṇaṃ duggamaṃ bhavai, taṃ-jahā: duāikkhaṃ duvibhajjaṃ dupassaṃ dutitikkhaṃ duraṇucaraṃ*). It is possible, to be true, that the system handed down to us was complete already with Pāsa, though it fails to be probable, and certainly it cannot be proved. What is said by Āyār. II 15, 16 about the religious life and death of Mahāvīra's parents is out of the question with regard to Pāsa's teaching, particularly since it includes the confession (*āloettā. . . paḍikkamittā*). For it was by this confession that Mahāvīra's rules differed from those of Pāsa, or else one would not have spoken of the *panca-mahavvaiya sapaḍikkamaṇa dhamma* in contrast with his *cāujjama dh.* Mahāvīra appears as much too original a thinker than that he should have but repeated what had been in existence since long without adding something of his own.[2] Otherwise the system would show junctures. But this is not the case.

§17. For our knowledge concerning Mahāvīra's life and personality we have as ancient coherent sources[3] the Uvahāṇasuya Āyār. I 9, then Āyār. II 15 (the Bhāvaṇā) and basing upon it Jiṇac. 1-148, finally Āv. 458ff. A number of detailed traits is rendered by Viy.[4] The birthplace of Mahāvīra was the

1. This proportion of 2 to 22 also applies to the future.

2. The way how he came to gain his ideas is expressed by the word Ṭhāṇ. 173a. acc. to which for him the *dhamma* was *suadhijjiya, sujjhāiya, sutavassiya.*

3. Present day monographies are : Manak Chand JAINI, Life of Mahavira (Allahabad 1908) and Bimala Churn LAW, Mv. his Life and teaching, Lo. 1932).

4. Comp. The AUTHOR's Worte Mv. 's p. 18ff.

northern borough of Vaiśālī, the Besāṛh of our days, called Kuṇḍapura (Āyār.) or Kuṇḍagrāma (Jiṇac.), the Basukuṇḍ of to-day[1]. It was here where the nobleman (*khattiya*) Nāya lived whose name is rendered in Pali by Ñātika and in Sanskrit texts rightly by Jnātṛ. The father belonging to this clan—and consequently also his children—were Kāśyapa acc. to the Gotra, while the mother was a Vāsiṣṭhī. Their names are Siddhattha and Tisalā with two more being added to each, the latter being but sporadically referred to and probably so as to serve merely the uniformity with the three names of the son to be mentioned presently. Tradition gave great importance to Mahāvīra's Kshatriya and not Brahman descent, and with the Śvetāmbaras at least it did so to the degree that it adopted the legend of Baladeva's embryonal transplantation from Rohiṇī into Devakī[2] and represented Mahāvīra as being the physical son of the Brahman couple of Usabhadatta and Devāṇandā in the Brahman borough of Kuṇḍapura. Acc. to Viy. 456a, however, Devāṇandā is acknowledged by Mahāvīra as being his true mother. In Viy. 218a he refers to the rôle of transplanter played by Hari Negamesi[3], but he does so without any relation to himself.

The name of Mahāvīra is an attribute inspired by profound reverence and traced back to the gods. The curtailed form is Vīra. *samaṇa*, as he is said to have called himself, is as far from being a proper name as is, for instance, "the Son of Man." His civil name is Vaddhamāṇa, "the prospering one", which in the texts, however, is interpreted as "the promoter". The verb *vaddhai* does not occur,[4] but only *vaddhai* leading up to the by far less frequent form of Vaḍḍhamāṇa (Āyār. II, 15, 12; Samav. 151a). As a member of the clan of the Nāya Mahāvīra is called *Nāya* (*putta*) (Viy. 323b), as a Kāśyapa *Kāsava* (a. o. Utt. 2;

1. Comp. JACOBI, SPAW 1930, p. 564f. See before HOERNLE, Uvās. II, p. 3ff. and Proceedings As. Soc. Beng. 1898, 40; JACOBI, SBE 22, XI. F.

2. Comp. JACOBI SBE 22, XXXI; ERE 7, 466b 6.

3. About him see WINTERNITZ IRAS 1895, 149ff.

4. Only *vaḍḍhāvei* "to congratulate", comp. PISCHEL, Gr. § 291. F. An historical mon. of Vaiśālī was compiled by VIJAYENDRA sūri (Bo. 1958; Guj.).

Dasav. 4), after the town of Vaiśālī, in whose sphere of influence he was born[1], by the name *Vesāliya* (Sū. I 2, 3 end; Utt. 6 end)[2], and *Videha-dinna* after his native country (Āyār. II 15, 17; Jiṇac. 11 0). He is addressed as *bhante*.

Vaddhamāṇa married Jasoyā, a Kauṇḍinyī[3], with whom he had a daughter bearing the name of Aṇojjā or Piyadaṃsaṇā. She later became the mother of a girl. Her husband is not referred to in the two biographies, but we know[4], if not from Viy. 461a ff. so from the Āvassaya tradition, that his name was Jamāli. His name was suppressed since it was with his son-in-law (who is said to have been also his nephew from the side of sister) that Mahāvīra went through the trying experience of disobedience and heresy which came to be the "first heresy"[5] in the history of the Jain church. Since his grand daughter is called a Kauśikī, the *khattiya-kumāra* Jamāli must have been a Kauśika as well.

§18. Vaddhamāṇa having kept his promise not to leave his parents as long as they lived[6] and having obtained the consent probably to be given by his elder brother Nandivaddhaṇa, left his native country at the age of thirty after having arranged the distribution of his property and his heritage in the course of one year. It speaks for his inclination towards asceticism that he did so at the beginning of the cold season. Thirteen months later, i.e. in winter again, he decided to rid himself of his clothes as well[7]. This was to be the first great step out of Pāsaism which,

1. JACOBI, SBE 22 X f.

2. In this connexion it may be assumed that he was spoken of as *Vesāliya sāvaya* as was the *niyaṇṭha* Pingalaga of Śrāvastī (Viy. 112b, in the comm. a fantastic explanation).

3. This doubtlessly underlies the *Koḍinna* of the texts. Comp. also Ajjava Koḍinna Samarāicc. with Ārjava Kauṇḍinya Samarādityasaṃkṣepa 1, 65.

4. For the following see LEUMANN Ind. Stud. 17, 97 ff.

5. Out of 7 referred to by Ṭhāṇ. 410a and the Āvassaya tradition, comp. LEUMANN's essay, Ind. Stud. 17, 91-135. These 7 heresies (*pavayaṇa-niṇhava*) are more interesting in other respects (§ 38) that as to the history of dogmatics. For Jamāli's heresy see Viy. 461a ff. For the 8th *niṇhava* of the Boḍiya Sivabhūi see § 26.

6. This interpretation of *samatta-painna* implies that they were not willing to let him go. Gautama the Śākya paid less respect to his father's wish to keep him at home. Another interpretation of *s.-p.* would be that he now was in a position of keeping his vow (?) to become a homeless monk.

7. As SHAH, Jainism in Northern India, p. 25, supposes he did so in a state of trance.

as is demonstrated by Utt. 23, 19, knew of clothed adherents only. The ballad Āyār. I, 9, describing his early ascetic life and the austerity of his conduct further tells us of the *samaṇa bhagavaṃ* devoting himself to meditation behind a wall of man's height surrounding him on all sides (*porisi tiriya-bhitti*). This caused a great sensation, while, on the other hand, by his solitary and disobliging bearing he annoyed the people who did not fail to vent their anger on him. Festivities, though he took part in them, were indifferent to him. For more than two years he neither drank nor used cool water, and it was during this period that his ideas grew to maturity: it may be mentioned here that he came to cognize the animatedness of all physical substances, plants and animals, the up and down in the forms of existence, the Karman as being its cause, its influx by sensual perception and activity, and the woman as its mediator. The monastic basic laws equally took shape in that time. Perhaps we are correct in interpreting Āyār. I 9,1,22 by saying that after those two years and two months Mahāvīra resolved to take up that vagrant life which was to last for more than twelve years[1]. Travelling towards the east he came as far as Lāḍha in West Bengal (Lāḍh, Rāḍh, Ṛāṛh) containing Vajjabhūmi and Subbhabhūmi, the land of the Suhmas. This period was characterized by utmost privations caused by inhospitable and and verminous quarters and many hardships owing to climate, stinging plants and insects, and wicked inhabitants who set dogs at him and ill-treated him. Mahāvīra himself made his life ascetic by the choice of his food, by fasting and by standing back behind animals and humans in need of help, while nothing is being said of self-castigations in bodily positions as incorporated into the system. The Uvahāṇa-suya closes by rendering that description. The two other texts have merely vague generalities ending up those twelve years by Mahāvīra's entering into omnicognition. In the Bhāvaṇā "both the possession and the acquisition of cognitions . . . thread the preceding biographical

1. Āyār. II, 15, 25; Jiṇac. 120. *pa-telasa* Āyār. I 9, 2, 4 means the same as is clearly stated by the Cuṇṇi.

sketch (p. 121 f., 130 f. of the edition)"[1]. Here from the dogmatic view it is traced that even when still an embryo Mahāvīra was in possession of the first three kinds of cognition (*tinnāṇô-vagaya*)[2] and the way how at the beginning of his monastic career the fourth (*maṇapajjava-nāṇa*) made its appearance[3]. By the fifth kind, the *kevala-vara-nāṇa-daṃsaṇa*, coming in he started teaching. But, to be true, by all this we are not given the description of an intellectual development in our sense.

In the sources hitherto considered there is not a single word being said concerning the rôle that is acted by Gosāla Maṃkhaliputta in Mahāvīra's life. He was the head of the Ājīvikas[4] and in this position, acc. to Pali reports, he was the successor to Kissa Saṃkicca and Nanda Vaccha. Thus it follows that the sect must have existed for some time yet. Viy. 15 gives a report regarding Mahāvīra's relations to Gosāla[5]. According to them Gosāla came to be Mahāvīra's pupil in the latter's second year as a monk and remained to be so for six years. Then their relations came to a rupture, however, and Gosāla went his own ways. It was not until 16 years later that both met again though for a violent contest only. Gosāla died nearly immediately after, i.e. 16 years before his antagonist. This report of Viy. has long since been judged as biassed and hateful. Critics went to the length of making Mahāvīra a disciple or adherent of Gosāla to whom they say he was indebted for the biological system proclaimed by himself to be his own. For these and further questions the reader is referred to BASHAM who has exhaustively treated the matter offered by literature and inscriptions, including materials from the South[6]. Gosala is said to have introduced

1. The AUTHOR, Worte p. 11.

2. But the words immediately following: *caissāmi tti jāṇai, cue mi tti j.* up to *pannatte* clearly have nothing to do with *mai-*, *suya-* and *ohināṇa*. The same Jiṇac. 29 and 30.

3. The Jiṇac, does not refer to them, but it speaks (112) of the *āhohiya* for which comp. § 81.

4. Comp. HOERNLE ERE 1, 259 ff.

5. Detailed summary by HOERNLE, Uvas. II ? pp. See also LEUMANN WZKM 3, 328-339.

6. History and Religion of the Ājīvikas. Lo. 1951 (rev. by the AUTHOR ZDMG 104, p. 256-263).

a division of humans into six different colours which has its parallel in the Jain *leśyā* theory[1]. This theory appears to be strange in Mahāvīra's system (§ 97), but here, again, it is not certain that it were borrowed from Gosāla's teaching, and it may well be possible that here as well as there the idea reflects primitive conceptions. On the other hand JACOBI has made it to appear probable[2] that some practices of ascetic nutrition as exercised by Jains originate from the Ājīvikas, and if Mahāvīra, as we have seen, put up with clothing thirteen months after having entered into monastic life, then it follows that this fell in the very second year which is reported to have brought about his relation to Gosāla. When, on a summer's night, the cognition of omniscience flashed upon him, Mahāvīra was on the field of the farmer Sāmāga near the town of Jambhiyagāma on the northern bank of the Ujjuvāliyā. Not far off that place there stood a Sāl tree which accordingly entered into the hagiology as Mahāvīra's *ceiya-rukkha*, thus reminding us of the Buddhists, and which served as an example for that of all preceding Titthagaras (Samav. 152a). This experience naturally did not put an end to his vagrant life, but with his fame increasing the vicissitudes he had to suffer from the side of humans ceased and changed into respect and reverence. As before (Jinac. 119) Mahāvīra continued to be on the way for two thirds of the year putting up in villages for one night and in towns for up to five; for four months he remained stationary owing to the rainy season. Jinac. 122 gives as unverifiable list of the places where he did so, i.e. in the course of the time up to fourteen times. We here but mention as such also known elsewhere those of Campā, Vesālī, Rāyagiha, Nālandā, and Sāvatthī. None of these places is situated on the sea, though in the similes attributed to Mahāvīra (Nāya 8. 11) the sea plays an important part, to say nothing of the Jainist world view (§110. 121). Places related to Mahāvīra's activity as a teacher are frequently referred to by the Canon, and those mentioned in the Viy. are to a certain degree trustworthy thanks to its special position (§ 45). Rāyagiha, of all places the most frequently mentioned

1. LEUMANN, loc. cit. 330 f.
2. SBE 45, XXX f.

both in the Viy. and the Jiṇac.[1], was the capital of Prince Seṇiya, the Bimbisāra of the Buddhists. Mahāvīra was a relative of his by Cellaṇā, the daughter of his uncle Ceḍaga, Prince of Vesālī[2], and Seniya's successor, Kūṇiya (called Ajātasattu in Pali texts)[3], was also his protector. To the list of the cities mentioned above the Viy. adds further the name of Kosambī[4]. The various other places referred to in either text cannot, however, be mentioned here. Mahāvīra did not stay at these places themselves, nor even during the interval of the long rainy season but—as is shown in Jiṇac. 122 by the word *nīsāe* attached to the indication of place—following the examples of other preachers he dwelt at a nearby *ceiya* regularly mentioned by its name, while nothing is being reported concerning its outward appearance[5]. As is described in the Uvav. at great length in poetical language, the princes, their noble attendants and the crowd used to leave the town in order to listen to his preachings, and *samosaraṇa* is the word designating not only Mahāvīra's going out to preach and the pouring out of those eager to listen, but also his setting up the fundamental teachings and both the place where the Kevalin teaches prepared by other religious-philosophical sects (Sūy. I 12) and later (Āv. 5) also by celestials, and the audience assembled around it.

§19. Acc. to the Pali texts Mahāvīra was a contemporary of Gautama Buddha, but although for decades they both wandered about one and the same area by no means very extensive preaching and teaching, there is no word being said as to their having met. Buddha is said to have survived Mahāvīra. This

1. A monography on Rāyagiha in ancient Literature was published by B. C. LAW (Delhi 1938).

2. Comp. the summary SBE 22, XV.

3. For his militant policy comp. JACOBI SPAW 1930, 557 ff. (review by the AUTHOR OLZ 1932, 143 ff.) and the original reports in Niray. and Viy.

4. At one time the believers in Vesālī were cared for by Jayantī who belonged to the laity (*Vesāliya-sāvayāṇaṃ arihantāṇaṃ puvva-sejjāyarī*). She was the sister of Sayāṇīya, Prince of Kosambī, who consequently took Migāvaī, another daughter of Ceḍaga, for his wife from Vesālī. Her son was Udāyaṇa (Viy. 556b).

5. Differently with the Buddhists, comp. B. C. LAW, Studia indo-iranica p. 42 ff.

information, however, is due to the Buddhists confusing the city of Pāvā, where Mahāvīra died, with the Pāvā, where Buddha stayed shortly before his end, thus concluding that he survived Mahāvīra[1]. The latter's Pāvā is referred to as *majjhima*. This may indicate that for once (perhaps owing to illness) he dwelt in the city proper, and he may well have done so since his quarters were in the residence of a high official in Prince Hatthipāla's service. At any rate he died there in his 72nd year, forty-two years after he had become a monk. Acc. to modern belief Pāvā is the village of Pāvapurī in the district of Patna[2]. Thus Mahāvīra's life passed within a narrow frame of space. All his days he, the aristocrat, had enjoyed the sympathy and the support of the nobles of the country. We have already mentioned his princely relations[3], and in Viy. 792b we read that the notables and the noble families of his time adhered to him and his teaching which they helped to spread. Now the collegial princes (*gaṇarāyāṇo*) of the Mallaki and Licchavi families gave a lamp-ceremony in commemoration of him. Mahāvīrā's death or, rather, in terms of spiritual language, his entry into Nirvāṇa represents to the Jains the point from where their chronology starts. The Śvetāmbaras (§ 26) place it 470 years before the beginning of the Vikrama era (57-56 B.C.), the Digambaras (§ 26) 605 years before the Śaka era (78 A.D.), the latter being also erroneously taken for the Vikrama era[4]. By critically dealing with these statements which both lead back to 527-526 B. C., JACOBI[5] (1879) calculated the year of 467 B.C., and CHARPENTIER[6] tried to support this date by a new line of argument. In 1891

1. CHARPENTIER in the essay to be presently mentioned; JACOBI SPAW 1930, 557ff. where ref. are made to: Journal of Francis BUCHANAN etc. see §1 f.—Comp. also Puran Chand NAHAR, Pāvāpurī and its Temple Prashasti (1698) IHQ 1, 116-119.

2. Imp. Gaz. of I. 20, 81.

3. Without himself having shut his eyes to the abusive reigning of major and minor princes (Thāṇ. 125b).—The author of the Angacūliyā considers Mahāvīra's teaching aristocratic to a degree that he refers to the transition of the *dhamma* to the Vaiśyas (*cattāri vaṇṇāṇa majjhe vaissa-hatthe dhammo bhavissai*) as a bad omen.

4. For passages comp. the writings presently mentioned and Satis Chandra VIDYABHUSHANA, Logic, p. 11; PĀTHAK IA 12, 21f.

5. Kalpasūtra p. 8.

6. IA 43 (1914), 115 ff.

JACOBI[1] himself decided in favour of 477 or 476 basing his deductions SPAW 1930, 557 ff. on the year 477.

§20. As to Mahāvīra's success as a teacher Jiṇac. 134 provides us with monumental figures which we can leave as they are. The only point worth mentioning is that women are by far in the majority. The nuns were headed by Ajja-Candaṇā also referred to by Viy. 458b where it tells us of Mahāvīra introducing his mother Devāṇandā to her. The monk very rightly mentioned as the first was Indabhūi, better known by his Gotra name as Goyama, though sporadically we hear of a "second" and a "third" Gautama, Aggibhūi and Vāubhūi[2]. Since, acc. to Viy. 153 a, they all appear simultaneously it is likely that Therāv. 1 by denoting all three as oldest, second and youngest monk of Mahāvīra was lead by a desire for classification. As one putting questions to his master Goyama as compared with a number of other persons is by far the most important, and as such he appears even where, as is the case in the Viy., there is no longer any real dialogue thinkable or probable, but where question and answer have come to congeal into mere forms of style[3]. In Viy. 755a, however, Goyama appears as a living person where we are told of his having wiped the floor with an antagonist and of his being commended for his ready wit by Mahāvīra who, acc. to Viy. 646b, also informs him that they both had been friends already for a number of existences. These two passages are probably the only ones in the Canon reflecting something like the note of a personal feeling on Mahāvīra's side. For as well as always he remains impersonal, and even where he rejects contradicting—often rather foolish—teachings of other preachers (*annautthiya*), he does so by speaking in naked antithesis. It was probably in his nature to be non-committal and stern[4]. Though it were wrong to judge Mahāvīra merely by how he appears to us in the dialogues of the Canon. He would never

1. Pariśiṣṭaparvan p. 6: corr. 2nd ed. (1932) p. XX f.
2. Comp. the 3 Kassapas (Uruvelā-, Nadī- and Gayā—K.) with 500, 300, and 200 followers, Mahāvagga 1, 15.
3. The AUTHOR, Worte Mv.'s p. 10.
4. Comp. the attractive confrontations by LEUMANN, Buddha un Mahāvīras, p. 28 and Maitreya-samiti p. 1-3.

have been able to succeed without giving his words a touch of originality and power, and his oratorical gift is certain to have excelled the high measure customary in India by far. He is said to have spoken Ardhamāgadhī[1], that is to say Old AMg., an idiom prior to the language of our texts[2]. Traces of the diction characteristic of him can clearly be demonstrated.[3] In this connexion we have to mention the similes. We have a large quantity of them in the Ṭhāṇ., esp. in Ṭhāṇa 4, and we shall refer to them later in § 116. In them Mahāvīra renders proof of his extensive practical experience and of both his profound knowledge of the world and of human nature, and had they been handed down to us in an oratorical form, the Canon of the Jains would certainly not be inferior to that of the Buddhists aesthetically[4].

§21. Even individual traits borrowed from nature have been incorporated into the total conception by Mahāvīra, the systematizer, as is shown by many passages of the Viy. Thus his explanation for a hot spring he must have visited near Rāyagiha (§ 94), his theory of the wind (§ 110), and the life-community of fire and wind (§ 105). The fact that the movement of a flying object slows down (Viy. 176 b; Jīv. 374b) was probably concluded by Mahāvīra from the effect of gravitation. Nor should we omit the wind *kavvaḍaya* (Viy. 499b) arising between the heart and the liver and causing within a galoping horse the sound of *khu khu*. Above all, however, the most versatile thinker we know of in ancient India had a liking for figures and arithmetic, that characterizes his speeches most extraordinarily, In most cases we are not able to prove which considerations are his own and which are of others, but he calls himself the author of a theory of the 7 possible lines (*evaṃ khalu, Goyama, mae satta seḍhīo pannattāo*, Viy. 954b). Acc. to Viy. 866b such a line is either

1. Uvav. § 56. Each listener heard him in his own language, comp. the Acts of the Apostles 2, 7 ff. This applies to all *buddha* or *arahaṃ* (Samav. 60 b).

2. The discovery was due to LÜDERS (1911). In the Jain Canon he showed up traces of Old AMg. in 1913, comp. Philologica Indica, p. 280 f.

3. The AUTHOR, Worte Mv.'s p. 21 ff.

4. Comp. LEUMANN WZKM 3, 331 f.

straight (*ujjuy'-āyaya*), has 1 break (*egao-vaṃka*), 2 breaks (*duhao*-v.), forms an open rectangle on one side (*egao-khaha*), forms a rectangular Z (*duhao-kh.*)[1], is circular (*cakkavāla*) or semicircular (*addha-c.*). As a general principle there is neither a beginning nor an end to a line, whereas either is the case within the world since the world is finite. In the infinite non-world (§ 103) this applies to the tangential straight lines that touches a border plane[2] of the world. A line leading from the non-world and meeting with the world border has no beginning, a line leading from the latter into the non-world is without an end, and a line leading all around the world in one way or other has neither beginning nor end (Viy. 866a with comm.). As to geometrical forms (*saṃṭhāṇa*)[3]—to add them in this connexion—Viy. 860a refers to orbicular (*vaṭṭa*), triangular, rectangular, elongated ones (*āyaya*), and to the ring (*parimaṇḍala*)[4], and in them the atoms are arranged either two-or three-dimensionally (in *payara* or *ghaṇa*), in the elongated form also one-dimensionally (in *seḍhī*). In referring to them the minimum and maximum numbers of the atoms and space units are being discussed, and this leads us up to the calculative reflections. In them a certain family likeness seems to become apparent, and where it goes together with a special liking for applying it we are probably confronted with an original idea of Mahāvīra's. The frequency of their occurrence alone is not decisive, or else it would be he, too, who had come to find the root of 10 and to apply it in the sense of the figure of π[5]. But this certainly asked for a wider knowledge of mathematics than Mahāvīra had, if we are

1. Since these determination are intended to describe the movements of atoms, aggregates, and souls we should rather speak of "path" instead of "line". But the following principal reflection, especially since it comprises the non-world, makes it necessary to use the latter word.

2. *kṣullaka-pratara* (Vy. 867a).

3. Opposite to these ideal forms a 6th forms is called "faulty" (*aṇit-thaṃtha*). (Than. 389 a).

4. Another sequence contains the first three of the above mentioned between the long and the short one (*dīha and rahassa*) on the one hand and between the wide (*pihula*) and the circular one on the other hand (Ṭhāṇ. 389a).

5 LEUMANN, Aup. p. 165. For a proof among many others see Jambudd. 15a. In discussing the figure of π with the Hindus JPAsB N. S. p. 22 (1926) 25-42, Bibh. DATTA does not mention the Jains.

allowed to judge by the favourite ideas he presumably cherished. Nor is the astronomy of the Jains, as, above all, it is offered to us by the Sūrapannatti, a creation of his own, but it rather reflects the thinking of generations. This becomes equally clear by the usage of "we" instead of "I" and by the absence of polemics[1]. As to the aspect of the world, however, it bears Mahāvīra's stamping by his doubling the widths of geographical units, a geometrical line with the quotient 2 (§ 122). This, perhaps, accounts for the contention that there are two suns and moons over Jambuddīva, which then leads up to the doubling of further stars (§ 128). The arithmetical line is applied in Mahāvīra's teaching to the sums. Of a sum (*jumma* or *rāsī* or *rāsi-jumma*)[2] continuously diminished by 4 there remains 4 (or 0), 3, 2 or 1, and it is called accordingly by the terms used at dice-playing *kaḍa-jumma*, *teoya*, *dāvara* or *kali-oya* (Viy. 744b)[3], and even *khuddāga* may be paced at the head of these names of *khudda-jumma* (Viy. 948b). They are called small "sums" as against the "large" ones, *mahā-j.* (Viy. 964b). They are sums expressing by their name not only the final remainder but also the number of the factors, the latter always preceding in the bipartite names of *kaḍa-jumma-kaḍajumma*, *k.-teoya*, etc.[4]. These calculations —to be found in the last passages of the Viy.—are applied in the most different connexions[5], though even Abhayadeva

1. We here give the different kinds of arithemetics as known from Ṭhāṇ. 263a, 496a: *parikamma*, the elements, and *vavahāra*, the application, are followed by *rajj ū*, geometry, and *rāsī*, addition, *kalā-savaṇṇa*, fractions, *jāvaṃ-tāvaī*, multiplication, and *vagga*, *ghaṇa*, *vagga-vagga*, involution to the square, the cube and the fourth power. Comp. also Bibhutibhushan DATTA, Origin and History of the Hindu Names for Geometry: Quellen u. Studien z. Gesch. d. Math. 1, 113-119. The SAME, The Jaina School of Mathematics; Bull. of the Calcutta Mathematical Soc. 21, 115-145; D. M. ROY, The Culture of Mathematics among the Jains of S. India in the Ninth Century: in ABHORI 8.

2. Even the totality of things characterized by either the presence or absence of soul (*jīva*) is called *rāsī* (Samav. 7b. 133a).

3. Thus *jumma* denotes the even and *oya* the odd sums (Viy. 860a; Vy. 745b).

4. Examples: 16 is *kaḍa-jumma* (i.e. the lowest possible), since it is divisible by 4 with 0 remaining. The division is done 4 times, and 4 is in itself *kaḍa-j.* Accordingly 16 is called *kaḍajumma-kaḍajumma*. 19 is *ṭeoya* (i.e. the lowest possible), since it is divisible by 4 with 3 remaining. The division is done as above. Hence 19 is called *kaḍajumma-teoya.*—6 is *dāvara*, since it is divisible by 4 with 2 remaining. The division is done once, and 1 is *kali-oya.* Hence 6 is called *kalioya-dāvara.*

5. Comp. also Thāṇ. 237 a.

fails to know what to do with the latter[1]. Other speculations related to permutations[2] are arrived at by crossing different lines of conceptions. Thus, for instance, it is being examined how many beings occupying one and the same hell exercise one of the 4 main passions, i.e. anger, pride, fraud, and greed (§ 167) (Viy. 68b), with the result that each of these four passions occurs with all beings, with all minus 1, with several ones and with a single one. Or, it is being demonstrated in which way 1-10 hell-beings (§ 109) divide among the 7 regions (Viy. 439b ff.). In order to give a characteristic example of the calculatory intelligence we here refer to the statements made on the maximum and minimum (*jahanneṇaṃ* and *ukkoseṇaṃ*) of most of the figures of the system, to the qualification of being both the first and not the first, both the last and not the last of one's like (*paḍhama* and *apaḍhama*, *carima* and *acarima*) (Viy. 731b), to which the Carama-paya Pannav. 10 goes back, to the discrimination made between the beginning and the continuation of a certain condition (a. o. *aṇantara-siddha* and *paramparas.*, Viy. 877a, also *-neraiya* Ṭhāṇ. 513b), and finally to the teaching of the relative number (T. 1, 8: *alpa-bahutva*). It answers the question of *kayarā kayarehiṃto appā vā bahugā vā tullā vā visesāhiyā vā* ? Such statements (in the Viy. first 235b) are comprised in Pannav. 3, the Bahuvattavvaya-paya. An object exists in proportionally a smallest number (*savva-tthovā*), others in either undecidedly, uncountably, or infinitely as many numbers (*saṃkhejja-guṇā*, *asaṃkhejja-guṇā*, *aṇantaguṇā*). The terms mentioned here—and to be represented in this book by the figures of x, i, ∞— are very frequent. In this connexion *aṇanta* specifically means nothing else but any other high figure. It is applied in a similarly naive way as is the idea of time, which, at least within the cosmography, means a quality among others, and which, as such a one, may be either attributed or denied to a region (§ 128).

§22. As to Indabhūi's life nothing authentical is known,

1. *etac c'aivam ājnā-prāmāṇyād avagantavyam* Vy. 745b.

2. Permutations dating from later times are dealt with by LEUMANN, Übersicht p. 41 b.

and the same applies to the two other Goyamas (s. a.). All three appear with eight more as the eleven "group-leaders" (*gaṇahara*) of Mahāvīra's, since, however, two times two of them share in leading a *gaṇa*, we have but nine "groups" (Ṭhāṇ. 451b) each comprising 300, 450 or 500 monks. For these statements as well as for the following the Therāvalī annexed to the Jiṇacariya is responsible (§ 1.2). It adds that merely Indabhūi and Suhamma (to whom we shall refer presently) survived Mahāvīra. Thus also Jiṇac. 127 says the same of Indabhūi who when his master had passed away cut the bond of attachment towards him, since for love there is no room in true monkhood. There can be scarcely any doubt that the other nine Gaṇaharas are fictitious for the purpose of dividing the followers of Mahāvīra and even the case first occurring in the 6th generation, acc. to which a *gaṇa* had two leaders, is already claimed for the origins[1]. The Maṇḍiyaputta mentioned by Viy. 181a ff. also helped to establish that fiction. Sudharman (Suhamma) was teacher of Jambū and is considered to be the originator of canonical texts as far as they are introduced passage-wise by the question of the latter for their contents. Hence they are supposed to render the wording Suhamma is said to have had from Mahāvīra personally. Acc. to Therāv. 2 it was also Indabhūi and Suhamma who, after Mahāvīra's death, came to obtain the power of omniscience and acc. to the tradition rendered in Hc. Par. 4 also Jambū[2]. Suhamma is said to have died 20 years, and Jambū 64 years after Mahāvīra; they were the last of the Kevalins, and thus the canonic text left by them is considered to be above any objection. All successive teachers up to Sthūlabhadra incl. are called *śruta-kevalin*. Jambū's grandson-pupil by the way of *Prabhava* is said to have been *Śayyambhava*[3] (*Sejjaṃbhava*), who is considered to be the author of the Dasaveyāliya.

1. The 11 Gaṇaharas are dealt with by Āv. 591-665.

2. Since *jambū* is fem., as a proper name it will be an abbreviation such as other names may be suppossed to be. Hemacandra in the Par. avoids all cases other than the nom.

3. This is considered to be the Sanskrit form, though probably it goes back to Svāyambhuva.

§23. The most easily accessible source for the remotest history of the Jain Church is Hemacandra's Pariśiṣṭaparvan laid down between samvat 1216 and 1229[1]. But Hemacandra naturally goes back to older sources comprising not only such in the Āvassaya literature and in other comments on the Canon, but also in the Vasudevahiṇḍi[2] (6th century A.D. at the latest). Here already we find the sequence of the lords spiritual being linked with that of the lords temporal. Thus it is said to have happened 60 years after Mahāvīra's death that the son of his protector named Kūṇiya or Ajātasatru, King Udāyin of Magadha, was murdered and followed by Nanda becoming the head of a new line (since 9 of this name are known) (Par. 6, 243), We do not come across any date before Nanda's fall (155 after Mv., Par. 8, 339) caused by Cāṇakya in favour of Candragupta. C.'s son, Bindusāra, as well as his grandson, Aśoka, and the latter's son, Kuṇāla, and grandson, Samprati, appear within the frame of the Par., which mixes the anecdotical and the historical in the well-known way. The history of the Jain Church goes as far as to *Vajra Svāmin* to whom Āv. 764-773 refer in all sorts of things, as it does to his successor, *Ārya Rakṣita*.

Śayyambhava, by the way of *Yaśobhadra* and next to *Sambhūtavijaya* (s.b.), is followed by *Bhadrabāhu*. Belonging to the 6th generation since Mv. or Goyama, resp., he lived in the 2nd century after them at the latest, i.e., in the 3rd century B.C. He died 170 (thus Par. 9, 113) or 162 years (thus the Dig. tradition) after Mahāvīra. In the Therāv. we have apart from the "shorter" list of names a more "comprehensive" one[3] which by starting from Bhadrabāhu lists the male and female disciples of every Gaṇahara, the *gaṇa* founded by them. their *sāhā* (*śākhā*), and (from Suhastin onward) also their *kula*. It may well be assumed that this list, on the whole, can be relied upon, since in locally confined regions it is confirmed by inscriptions, as first

1. BÜHLER, Leben Hc.'s p. 43.

2. Comp. the proof furnished by JACOBI, Sthav. (2nd. ed.) p. v ff.

3. For their relation to each other and other lists of teachers in the Nandi and the Āvassayanijjutti see JACOBI. loc. cit. S. XIII ff. One of the results is (XVIII) that only a few of the *thera* that have actually existed have survived by name.

was shown by BÜHLER[1]. These inscriptions come from the district of Mathurā, and as far as they[2] are dated they start with the 4th year of the Kaniṣka era=132-133 A.D.[3]; these oldest Śvetāmbara evidences thus outdate that literary tradition by years and, moreover, improve them[4]. It now speaks for Bh.'s importance that the more comprehensive list starts with him, for thus we are given evidence of the part he acted in spreading the religious belief (as will be mentioned below § 26). He also deserved well of preserving the doctrine. Acc. to Par. 9, 55 ff.[5] a food crisis lasting in the country for twelve years forced the monks to emigrate "to the coast" for some time, and it was due to these circumstances that the exact preservation and encouragement of the Jina teaching was interrupted. Here Bh. proves an expert of the sacred tests to a degree never reached again, for he is said to have been the last to know not only the 11 Anga but also the 12th, the Diṭṭhivāya, containing the remains of 14 so-called Puvva or Pūrva (§ 37). When now a synod collecting the endangered texts met in Pātaliputra and sent for Bh. for the Diṭṭhivāya, since he was on the way to Nepal, the attendants whom he was willing to instruct on the spot were able to comprehend but details of those 14 Pūrvas, with the only exception of Sthūlabhadra who brought with him 10 of them by memory. For Bh. as the supposed author of comments see § 43. Owing to his long, though not definite absence from the centre of the community it was not Bh. who was its formal head but his fellow-pupil with Yaśobhadra named *Sambhūtavijaya* who was followed by the above mentioned *Sthūlabhadra* as a leader, so that the latter was the pupil of either. His relations to Bh., however,

1. WZKM 1-4.

2. Their investigation is referred to by LÜDERS, List (§ 4).

3. Comp. KONOW Ep. Ind. 19, 1-15. Another calculation comes to 78 A. D.

4. SBE XXII, p. 291 under e. read *Vāraṇa*, p. 292 above read *Prītivarmika* (Pkt. *Pīivammiya*), under g.h. *Thaṇija*.—Corr. to Therāv. p. 80 above Rakkhiya, Rohagutta, Bambha and Soma ought to have been mentioned on p. 292 as l. m.

5. It goes back to a kathānaka rendered by Āv. 17, 11 after the catchwords in the Āv. cuṇṇi and by Haribhadra and translated by LEUMANN, Übers. p. 25.

were not undisturbed[1], and disturbances of this sort recurred even more intensively between Sth.'s two pupils, Mahāgiri and *Suhastin*, after the latter had taken the lead of the order. As mentioned above, Suhastin is notable in that the Therav., from him onward, lists also *kula* as parts of the *gaṇa*, and, moreover, in that he is said to have won the King Samprati, grandson of and successor to Aśoka, for Jainism (Par. 11, 55 ff.).

§24. The oldest region known to have been frequented by itinerant monks and nuns and handed down to us in Kappa 1, 51 comprises Anga-Magadha to the east, Kauśāmbī to the south, Sthūṇā to the west, and Kuṇālā to the north. The sentence succeeding 1, 52 speaks of allowing communication in regions where the teaching had been successful in gaining a footing, and it is therefore considered as a supplementary addendum which is said to go back to Samprati's times[2]. Thus Hemacandra, too, reports that Samprati devoted himself to Jain mission work among the Andhra and Dramila in South India, i.e. in the Telugu and Tamil countries, which both are said to have been subject to his command (Par. 11, 89 ff.). Since Samprati is said to have resided in Ujjayinī we might see in this city an early western colony of Jainism, and even so if Suhastin had resided there only temporarily as is reported by Par. 11, 23; 66. Acc. to the same passage, provided that we acknowledge the reports in question to contain a grain of historical truth, the Jains played a rôle even in the 1st century B. C. when their ecclesiastic Kālaka took revenge on Gardhabhilla, the prince of that place, for having seduced his sister, and called the sovereign (*sāhāṇusāhi*) of the Śaka to take over the country[3]. We

1. Comp. Par. 9, 101 ff. The inner reasons are explained by LEUMANN, Übersicht p. 26 f.

2. The AUTHOR, Kalpasūtra p. 38.

3. Comp. the Kālakācārya-kathānaka first published and reviewed in its different versions by JACOBI and LEUMANN (ZDMG 34 and 37). For a review on the Kālaka problems and for a selection of the K. texts see W.N. BROWN, The Story of K., Washington 1933 (reviewed by the AUTHOR OLZ 1934, col. 449 f. also Indian Linguistics 4, p. 165-182. We know of at least 3 K., i. e. apart from the above mentioned the teacher called Śyāma (synonymous with Kālaka) of the system laid down in the Pannavaṇā and him who antedated the *pajjosavaṇā-pancamī*.

may add that Vikrama, the successor to Gardhabhilla, is said to have been won for Jainism by Siddhasena Divākara[1]. Yet this report contains as little tangible data as do such statements of the same contents that were made with regard to other distinguished personalities and which in this connexion may be omitted as negligible. There are even doubts as to the question whether Vikrama's political importance was as great as the Jains wish it to be[2].

With Samprati we find ourselves somewhere near the turn of the 3rd to the 2nd century B.C., and somewhere near this time there lived the King Khāravela of Kalinga (Orissa) provided that, on account of his great inscription at Khandagiri (Hāthīgumphā), the years between 182 and 180 B.C. allow of dating his accession to the throne[3]. This much mutilated inscription[4], it is true, begins with a Jinist formula of veneration, but what tangible deeds in favour of the Jains scholars were inclined to interpret from it have turned out to be untenable or remained inexplicable. We may presuppose that Jain communities flourished within Kh.'s realm. They stand side by side with those that existed in Tāmraliptī (Tamluk, Midnapur Distr., Bengal), Koṭivarṣa (Bāṇgaṛh, Dinājpur Distr., Bengal) and Puṇḍravardhana (North Bengal), and which went back to a pupil of Bhadrabāhu's (Therav. 5)[5].

§25. In contrast to the unconfirmed report of Samprati and Suhastin the spreading to the west becomes evident for the 2nd century B.C. and the following owing to the finds made at the ancient town of Mathurā,[6] which are most revealing also in

1. Vikramacarita, comp. Vikrama's Adventures, ed. and trans. by EDGERTON Harvard Oriental Ser. 26.

2. Comp. EDGERTON loc-cit. O. P. I, LXII.

3. Thus KONOW AO 1, 35.

4. Last by JAYASWAL in JBORS 3 and 4; KONOW AO I, 12-42. For earlier bibliography see LÜDERS, List under No. 1345. Details by different authors in Anekānt 1.

5. *agajina* and *satikalariya coyaṭhiaga.*

D. R. BHANDARKAR, ABhORI 12, 104 f. 106 f. is not very convincing in attributing their revival to Mahāvīra's wandering in Lāḍha. A fourth colony not yet indentified was (ibd.) Dāsīkharbaṭa.

6. V. A. SMITH, The Jain Stûpa and other Antiquities of M. (Archaeolog.). Survey of India. New. Imp. Series Vol. 20). Allahabad 1901.

factual respects[1]. From the inscriptions we learn, as mentioned before in confirming the texts, of *śākhā* and *kula* as subdivisions of the *gaṇa*, though the mutual relation of the two first is not altogether clear,[2] and added to this there is the *saṃbhoga* illustrated by the literary document of Vav. 5, 19f. and 7, 1-3. It goes without saying that there were preachers (*vācaka*), but this does not necessarily involve the existence of an established ritual text[3]. The Titthagaras were distinguished from each other by their symbols (§ 14) since we know that for Ara there stands a name formed after his attribute of Nandyāvarta (*arahato Nāndiāvatasa pratimā*). The stūpa to which the erect figure of this Arhat belonged, was supposed to have been the work of the gods (or either of one of them) (*deva-nirmita*) suggesting that it had been standing since times immemorial when the inscribed monument was erected in the 49th year of the Kaniṣka era, i.e. in 177-178 A.D. It furthermore suggests that the Jains had erected stūpas since long, as also the Canon refers to them (*thūbha*)[4].

It may be noted here that also the effigies of the Jinas (*jiṇa-paḍimā*) are spoken of in the Canon Nāyādh. 210b; Rāyap. 87b, 94a, etc. In the course of its most detailed description of a godly residence[5] Rāyap. refers to 4 sitting Jina figures (Usabha, Vaddhamāṇa, Candāṇaṇa, Vāriseṇa[6]) of natural size surrounding a stūpa towards which they turn their faces, adding that a special building (*siddh' āyayaṇa*) contains 108 *j.-paḍimā*. Their cult on the part of the god equals that of to-day consisting in the attendance of the figures by uttering devotional formulae. In the large hall (*sabhā*), however, there are spherical boxes (*gola-vaṭṭa-samugga*) containing the sacred remains (*j.-sakahā*, comp. § 15) and hanging on hooks (*nāgadanta*) by means of cords (*sikkaga*). The whole description most certainly follows earthly

1. LÜDERS, List (§ 4); BÜHLER WZKM 1-5; SAWW 1897= IA 27, 49-54; HOERNLE Proceedings As. Soc. Bengal 189, p. 49-53.
2. JACOBI SBE 22, 288[1].
3. This is meant by v. GLASENAPP, Jainismus p. 42.
4. For passages comp. PISCHEL, Gr. § 208.
5. Comp. LEUMANN VI. OC III, 2, p. 489 ff.
6. The two last ones are the counterparts of the two first ones in the continent of Erāvaya (§ 119).

examples. The room enclosing the figures mentioned in Nāyādh. is called the *jiṇa-ghara*. Aṇuog. 158d; Paṇhāv. 123a do mention the *ḍeula* '*devakula*' next to the *thūbha* and profane establishments (Comp. also Jambudd. 207a)[1].

§26. The discoveries made at Mathura seem to prove by the nakedness of the sculptured figures[2] that the schism of the Order into Śvetāmbara and Digambara dates from as early as the 2nd century A.D. Mahāvīra had put up with clothing, and it was generally considered worthy to follow his example. He who in the one or the other formality took his conduct as a model for his own was in the state of *jiṇa-kappa*[3]; ordinary monks followed the *thera-kappa*[4]. The question of clothing was treated liberally, and there is reason to assume that especially those monks adhering to Pāsa's teaching kept their clothing[5]. Hence it follows that even in the early days of antiquity there was a duplicity existing which we may call the germ of the later schism of the Order into the "Naked" (*digambara, āśāmbara, dig-vāsas*) and the "Whites" (*śvetāmbara, śveta-paṭa, sitāmbara*, etc.). The Śvetāmbaras report (Āv. nijj. 418a) on the heresy committed by Boḍiya Sivabhūi in the year 609 after Mv., who wanted the *jiṇa-kappa* to be made generally acknowledged and who himself accepted it notwithstanding the warnings of his guru. Originally, however, this has nothing to do with the Digambaras[6] and was related to them only later. The year given by the Dig. is 136 Vikrama=79 A.D.[7], and it is at this time that the Śvetāmbaras

1. *Nemi-Pāse subhatta* (=subhakta)-*sālāsu vibhāga-kusale* (i.e. the royal architect).

2. BÜHLER WZKM 4, 330 f.

3. Comp. Devendra ZDMG 38, 6.

4. There is a parallel to this in that the texts of the Canon are said to be partly the words of the Jina disciple Sudharman and partly those of the *thera*, either being equally obliging for the community. The translation of *thera-kappa-ṭṭhiī* K. 6, 14 must be altered corr. to the above.

5. For this and the following comp. JACOBI ZDMG 38, 1ff. (*jina-kalpa*. p. 7); 40, 92 ff. and SBE 45, XXXI; also WEBER, Kup. p. 797 f.

6. Differently BHANDARKAR Rep. 1883-84, Notes p. III.

7. The same year is reported (Daṃs. 11ff.) by the Dig. Devasena (S.909). for the separation of the Sevaḍa Sangha, i.e. the Svetāmbara, from the Dig, owing to the heresy of Jinacandra who in teaching it slew his teacher Śānti, a pupil of Bhadrabāhu (Devasena in the Bhāvasaṃgaha, comp. Daṃs. p. 55 ff.). It is said to have taken place at Valahī where the monks had emigrated

are said to have developed from the Ārdhapālika or Ārdhaphālaka who are called "partly clothed partly unclothed" by the Dig. Ratnanandin in the Bhadrabāhucarita (4,50). This expression fails to be clear. Both reports on the origin of either[1] when viewed under the aspect of JACOBI's critical study make us see that their authors could not remember any actual dissension having taken place and hence invented one instead, in which case, as we observe, the Dig. go so far as to state a gradual alienation. This turns out to be true, and certainly so not only in regard of historical time but of regional space as well. Isolated groups of the Jain Order were eager to be most faithful in living up to the monastic ideal, and the result was that, when again coming into touch with the original community standing in the current of development, they made themselves conspicuous as renegades or, resp., considered themselves orthodox the way the Dig. are known to do.

A self-isolation of this kind found its expression in the accounts of an emigration from Bihar. In the Par. there are two passages (8, 193; 377) that refer to a twelve years, famine falling in the years of Sthūlabhadra and Susthita and forcing the latter to send away his gaṇa, though where it was directed to we are not told. Once before already we heard of an equal crisis in the times of Bhadrabāhu and, to be careful, of its possible effects (§ 23). The tradition of the Śvet. (Ther. 5) does not trace its spiritual descendants beyond his pupils, and it is but from one of them, called Godāsa, that it derives 4 *sāhās* to locate them in Tāmraliptī, Koṭivarṣa, Puṇḍravardhana and Dāsīkharbaṭa, and at least by the first and the third name it becomes clear that they point to the east and south-east. In this the tradition of the Digambaras

from Ujjayinī owing to the 12 years' famine predicted by Bhadrabāhu. Devasena thought of the Synod of Valabhī (§ 39) in which he was mistaken, the more so since Bhāv. 70 he refers to the then written śāstra. He is equally confusing where he deals with subjects lying beyond the Dig. sphere. Thus Daṃs. 20 Makkhali Gosāla is reflected as Makkaḍi-Pūraṇa, the pupil of a Gaṇin of the Pāsa-saṃgha, since he had heard something about Pūraṇa Kassapa (the same Srutaśāgara, Chappāhuḍa 5, 89: Maskari-Pūraṇa).

1. A counterpart to the former is the statement derived from an anonym. Dig. source rendered in Jineśvara's Pramālakṣaṇa with ref. to v. 404, acc. to which the Śvet. made their appearance in 609 after Mahāvīra at Valabhī (comp. Daṃs. p. 61f.).

differs. Thanks to an inscription at Śravaṇa Beḷgoḷa dedicated to the memory of an ācārya Prabhācandra and first reported by RICE[1] we know that Bh. had predicted a famine lasting for twelve years and, what is more, to occur in Ujjayinī, where upon the whole saṃgha moved to the south where it reached a flourished country. The Bhadrabāhu-Kathā (about 800) and the Bṛhat-kathākośa (931) report that toward the end of his life Bh. ordered his followers to move away to Punnāṭa (South-Mysore), whereas Ratnanandin's Bh.-carita (2nd half of the 16th cent.) says that he himself took the lead and died on the way.[2] Bh.'s death is being linked with that of the Candragupta or -gupti whom even other inscriptions delivered by RICE report to have been Bh.'s pupil. C. who had resigned the throne to follow Bh. put an end to his life by fasting as is said at the same place as Bh. did, i.e. at Śravaṇa Beḷgoḷa.[3] As to Candragupta the Śvet. report partly more partly less. Acc. to Par. 8, 433; 445 he saw in the monks his gurus and he died the *samādhi-maraṇa;* Cāṇakya, his minister, who himself was the son of a Jain layman, equally sympathized with the monks. This we know from the Āvassaya tradition[4]. The Viyāhacūliyā describes a prophesy made by Bhadrabāhu at Pāḍalipura on account of 16 dreams of the queen[5]. Among other symptoms of decline in religion and morals they mean a twelve years' *dukkāla*, the *dhamma's* changing over to the Vaiśyas,

1. RICE IA 3, 153-158; the SAME, Mysore Inscriptions transl., Bangalore 1879, p. LXXXVI-VIII, the SAME Inscr. at Sravana B. (= Epigraphia Carnatica II, 1889, p. 1; new ed. of this vol. by NARASIMHA-CHAR (1923); Epigr. Indica (ed. FLEET) 4, 27. Improvements by FLEET made as early as in IA 21, 158; also LEUMANN WZKM 7, 383.

2. For the first and third source see LEUMANN, Übersicht, p. 24 for the second comp. RICE (on the ground of an information given by PATHAK) Ep. Carn. III-IV, P 2, p. 1. RICE loc. cit. (1889) also draws upon the Rājāvalīkathe of the Devacandra (19th cent.). For a synopsis of the tradition see NARASIMHACHAR loc.cit.p.36ff. If the last named Prabhācandra who was a pupil of the Akalanka living in the 2nd half of the 8th cent., was the same as the one mentioned in the memorial inscription, then in spite of the strong opinion held by FLEET the latter must be later than the 1st of the 8th cent.

3. V. A. SMITH, Oxford History of India, p. 75; NARASIMHA-CHAR Ep. Carn. 2 (rev. ed.).

4. JACOBI, Sthav. (2nd ed.) p. IX following LEUMANN.

5. The Dig. equally have it, comp. the Rājāvalīkathe with RICE IA 3, 155.

the sermon[1] of the *jiṇa-magga* in the south, a rise of the middle classes and insurgent activities of princes—altogether gloomy prospects for the future that caused Candragupta to resign in favour of his son. As to the manner of his death nothing is being said. Hence in the times of the Viyāhacūliyā it was also the Śvet. that linked Bhadrabāhu's name with the migration to the south leading to the schism of the Order. Provided we take Candragupta's piety strictly it does not harmonize with an allusion of Vimala's Paumacariya (89, 42) disclosed by JACOBI[2] which in consequence of political troubles and religious apostasy speaks in retrospective prophesy of a decline of Jainism in the "time succeeding the Nanda." In opposition to the Dig. passages of Bhadrabāhu it was FLEET who contended[3] that it concerned a second bearer of his name who acc. to an ancient list of the Dig.[4] came to be the head of the Order in 492 after Mv., and that instead of Candragupta we have to think of Guptigupta or Arhadbali as being the pupil and later follower of "Bhadrabāhu II.". LEUMANN, however, points out[5] that in this list already existing in the 8th century, "the second Bh. is but a chronistic repetition" and that "apart from the above Dig. dating nothing of him is known that were not assigned to him from the older." The migration itself seems to be historical, nor does FLEET argue against it. For a religion in process of spreading necessarily flows from the country of its origin over into regions capable of absorption[6], no matter whether it be by some forced impulse or not.

§27. For the inscriptions of Mathura the above mentioned list of LÜDERS (1912) prevails; the bibliography of the later will

1. It is significant of the Śvet. text that it speaks of a sermon (*pannavissanti*) only and not of a flourishing status.

2. ERE 7, 473 footnote.

3. IA 21, 156-160; EI 4, 26. Reply to the first passage of RICE, Inscr. of the Mysore District (=Ep. Carn. III-IV), PI (1894), p. 5 footnote.

4. BHANDARKAR, Rep. 1883-84, 124; HOERNLE IA 20, 341-361; 21, 57-84.

5. Ubersicht p. 24. 27.

6. Acc. to a conjecture made by DESAI (Jainism in S. India p. 2 ff.) there were Jain communities in South Canara even before Bhadrabāhu's arrival, a fact that made it easier for him to choose that country.

be found together with a summary of the spiritual and temporal genealogies in GUÉRINOT's Répertoire d'épigraphie jaina (1906). Partial collections containing the text are for the Śvet. the Prācīn Jain Lekh Saṃgrah, Bh. 1.2 (the latter KJIṂ 6, 1921) compiled by JINAVIJAYA acc. to the places of discovery and the Jain Lekh Samgrah (also under the title of Jaina Inscriptions) by Puran Chand NAHAR, Bh. 1-3, the latter with the inscriptions of Jaisalmer (C. 1918-29), for the Dig. Hīrālāl JAINS Jainaśilālekhāsaṃgraha, whose 1st vol. (MDJGM 28, 1928) offers the inscriptions of Śravaṇa Beḷgoḷa already collected by RICE (Inscriptions at Sr. B., Bangalore 1889, 2nd. ed. by NARASIMHACHAR 1923). The fact that in the 12 vols. of RICE'S Epigraphia Carnatica (1886-1904) comprising the last-mentioned as vol. 2, chiefly Jain inscriptions are being rendered and evaluated, is explained by the course of history. For it is South India and predominantly Mysore that became the domain of the Digambaras. It was in these parts of the sub-continent, as is proven by the inscriptions, that for centuries they flourished and exercised their influence. Their tradition is based on the migration of Bhadrabāhu's monks to the south[1], but it is very much later that we find South Indian communites supported by inscriptions, i.e. towards the end of the 5th century by the copper plates of Halsi in Belgaum going back to a Kadamba prince[2] and of Śaka 556-634 in Aihoḷe, Kaledgi Distr. in Bijāpur.[3] The two Ganga documents of Nonamangala placed by RICE at about 370 and 425, resp., are possibly older[4]. The former would be the earliest Jaina inscription existing after Mathurā though separated from it by centuries. Among the genuine documents[5] of nearly the same age we have Udayagiri (South Gwalior) by

1. Mahāvaṃsa 10, 97-99 goes still much farther beyond this date. Acc. to this Pali work in Anuradhapura under the reign of the second predecessor of Tissa in the 4th cent. B. C. there lived also *nigaṇṭhas* apart from other heretics (*pāsaṇḍika*).

2. FLEET in IA 6 and 7; Rép. No. 96ff.

3. KIELHORN EI 6, No. 1; Rép. No. 108.

4. Ep. Carn. 10, Malur Taluq No. 73 and 72; Rép. No. 90 and 94.

5. That is after having eliminated the older or younger fabrications compiled by FLEET IA 7, 209 ff.; 18. 309 ff.

Gupta 106=425[1]; Mathurā by G. 113=423-3[2] and Kahāuṃ (in an eastern tip of the Uttar Pradesh to the north of the Ganges) by G. 141=460-1[3]; they, too, belong to the Digambaras. Though any day there may be discoveries being made bridging to a certain degree the historical gaps, yet the inscriptions will always prove the small outward effect of the Jain Order during the early centuries of our Christian era. For the Śvet. JACOBI assumes "a comparative obscurity as an exclusive sect" lasting up to the 7th century and supposes that in Haribhadra's time (8th century) they had not yet come to the south beyond the Tapti[4]. It is, moreover, worth mentioning that in the classical drama there appears no Śvet. Jaina[5].

§28. As a rule the inscriptions contain as a subject the donation of statues, building-ground, building-money or tax-returns to the Jaina community by laymen and princely patrons, in the former case of either sex and (in Mathurā) frequently at the suggestion of a specified member of the Order intimately connected with the donor. It is not so much the facts that are interesting to us as the genealogical and chronistic statements accompanying the reports. They considerably add to our knowledge concerning the history of both the dynasties and the Order. Individually as well as in their subsequent members quite a number of princely houses, a.o. the Ganga, Rāṣṭrakūṭa, Cālukya, Hoysaḷa have proved friendly to the Jains. And yet, taking into account the well-known versatility of Indian princes in religious affairs, we must be careful not to overrate the rôle acted by Jainism in political life, and it is rather bold to speak of "adeptes du jainisme" in this connexion. It may be assumed that more often than not it was for reasons of prudence that it was thought necessary to suit the Order so influential owing to its wealthy laymen, whereas true conviction may be taken for

1. FLEET CII 3, No. 61; Rêp. No. 91.
2. BÜHLER EI 2, No. 39; Rêp. No. 92.
3. FLEET CII 3, No. 15; Rêp. No. 93.
4. Samarāiccakahā p. XIII. VII. That R. G. BHANDARKAR Rêp. 1883/84, p. 125 considered the Jains "a very unimportant sect" far up in the 2nd century is explained by a different context.
5. Comp. PISCHEL, Gr. § 17 end.

granted wherever the populace was struck hard by serious ahiṃsā-commandments, in other words, wherever its displeasure was not dreaded, and where, acc. to Jain rites, death through fasting was believed to crown one's life. For these rites some pieces of evidence are given by inscriptions[1]. As in Candragupta and Cāṇakya (s.a.), so the Jains see great supporters of their religion also in Vikrama, Śālivāhana, Munja, Bhoja and others. Up to now, however, their respective reports lack authentication by monumental or non-Jainist literary documents. Recently, Toramāṇa, the prince of the Hūna who invaded India about 500), and different members of the house of Gupta have been added to the above-mentioned list[2]. For, acc. to the introductory verse of the Kuvalayamālākathā composed by Uddyotana Sūri in Śaka 700 (=778), Torarāya (as here he is called) had as a guru the ācārya Harigupta from the Guptavaṃśa, a pupil of his was the poet (*kai*) Devagupta. If these harmless reports prove true it may be said that the Jains had exercised at least a certain influence upon Toramāṇa, though this influence did not extend to his son Mihiragula or -kula after he had ascended the throne, since it was Mihiragula who by his cruelty testified to him by Brahmans and Buddhists had also been hard on the Jains. We are indebted to PATHAK for having offered proof that he is identical with Kalkin (*Kakkī*), the Indian Antichrist[3].

For the Śvet. the case of the Kumārapāla of Gujarat (*s.* 1200-1229) represents a show-piece of how a prince was won for their Order. We are informed of this case in all details since BÜHLER has rendered a masterly biographical representation of the originator of the conversion, the scholar Hema-

1. Rép. No. 152. 163. 298.

2. JINAVIJAYA Jaina-Sāhitya-Samsodhaka 3, 169 ff. N. C. MEHTA JBORS 14, 28 ff.

3. IA 47, 18 ff.; Festschr. Bhandarkar p. 216. Apart from Uttarapurāṇa 76 comp. also Mahānis. 5 IV (the AUTHOR p. 43) and Dhaneśvara. Śatrumjayamāhātmya 14, 203 f.—Previously (IA 46, 145 ff.) JAYASWAL had seen in Kalkin the Yaśodharman, the conqueror of Mihiragula. In a chronological treatise SHAMASASTRY Annual Rep. of the Mysore Archaeol. Dep. 1923 (p. 24) asks for two Toramāṇas and two Mihiragulas.

candra, by separating the historical from the legendary[1]. According to that there is no doubt that starting from *s.* 1216 Kumārapāla "tried to make Gujarat in some manner a Jain model state" and forced his subjects to go far in putting into practice the *ahiṃsā*, etc., acc. to his example. At the same time Hemacandra by his versatile scientific work established the basis for a typical Jain culture[2]. But even Kumārapāla did not leave off favouring the Śaivas with whom up to then he had been intimately connected, so that after his death they again won the upperhand. Finally there is the belief in being able to call the Emperor Akbar a Śvetāmbara Jain. He requested them to send him Hīravijaya (1526,7-1595), an Ācārya from the Tapā-Gaccha (§ 34). He, the so-called *jagad-guru* spent some years at the court of Delhi. After his departure in 1584 Śānticandra, Bhānucandra and Vijayasena were successively active in the same direction of making Akbar familiar with the Dharma. As is known Akbar was not converted (*prabodhita*), but similarly to Aśoka under Buddhist, so he under Jain influence edited some regionally and temporarily limited prohibitions in accordance with their teaching[3].

§29. The successes previously mentioned mostly go back to the outward reputaion of the Jain Order, which again goes back to the number and the importance of its adherents, whereas its publicity explains itself by the substance of the doctrine. Since about 80 A.D.[4] when a pseudo-Bhadrabāhu (§ 43) first came to put the traditional text comment into shape, the Śvet., for centuries, have tried hard for this substance, although, as was said, mostly in the pale of the community. It is true, the investigations into the details of this intellectual acomplishment started by LEUMANN remained stuck in their first stages in public (§ 4), but yet they allow us to realize the comprehensive

1. On the Life of the Jain Monk Hemacandra. (Vienna 1889, transl. by Mani Lal PATEL, Singhi Series 11). For the following comp. p. 39. 41 f 51. Rev. by LEUMANN ZDMG 43, 348-352.

2. Acc. to JACOBI, Par. (2nd ed.) p. XXIII this effort tended to the very details of versification.

3. V. A. SMITH, Festschr. Bhandarkar, p. 265-276; the SAME, Akbar, the Great Mogul, p. 47 ff.

4. LEUMANN, Übersicht p. 28b.

character of that scholasticism. The names of those that stand behind it we do not know[1], and presumably we shall never do; and it is not until we come to the ending stages in Prakrit that we have several names, see Chapter III. A wide circulation of the Śvetāmbara texts had become possible by the redaction of the Canon under the direction of Devarddhi (980 or 993 after Mahāvīra). Owing to the schism of the Order the Dig. had since long become estranged from the Canon, and there were only very few passages of some texts which partly in a shape prior to its definite fixation continued to live in their memory[2]. Hence they first appear with the so-called *prakaraṇa*, and, what is more, they represent the first authors of this kind of literature with the Jains[3]. By *prakaraṇas* we understand systematic treatises[4], i.e. treatises following a fixed plan and leading the subject instead of being led by it as is the case with works that start from something given. With its beginnings the *prakaraṇa* period reaches back as far as the period of comments. Among the Śvet. it opens with Umāsvāti, Siddhasena Divākara and Haribhadra (750 A.D.), among the Dig. with Vaṭṭakera and Kundakunda[5] who both wrote Prakrit and preceded Umāsvāti[6] who wrote his *prakaraṇa* in Sanskrit. With this we do not intend to establish a historical criterion, for in the literature of comments the change over to Sanskrit was first started by the above mentioned

1. On account of a passage in the Āvaśyaka tradition LEUMANN gives Siddhasena *khamā-samaṇa* (Divākara) as the author of the oldest interpolations in pseudo-Bhadrabāhu's Nijjuttis', the so-called *mūla-bhāṣya*. For S. Divākara and S. Gaṇin between whom we have Haribhadra comp. JACOBI, Samarāicc. p. III.

2. (The Dig. redaction of the Āvaśyaka) "is . . . the only remainder of the Canon worth mentioning among the Digambaras, of the Daśavaikālika they have retained in their memory but some Ślokas (I. 1. IV 7 f. VI 54. 56. 65 VIII 17a) !" (Footnote:) "Aparājita still quotes (on Ārādhanā 415 and 601) different passages from Ācārānga, Sūtrakṛta (II, 1, 58), Niśītha, Uttarādhy. (II 6a. 7. 12b. 34. XXIII 12b-14) and Daśavaikālika. Some of these passages run quite differently in the traditional Canon, and some of them it lacks completely", LEUMANN, Uebersicht p. 3.

3. Somewhat different JACOBI, Samarāicc. p. XII.

4. JACOBI, loc. cit. p. xi.

5. This sequence after LEUMANN, Übersicht 15b.

6. For K. comp. PETERSON, A fourth Report p. XX; JACOBI, Tattv. p. 288; LEUMANN, Uebersicht p. 3a. The Dig. call him Koṇḍakunda after his birth place. His spiritual name is Padmanandin. Comp. DESAI esp. p. 55 f. 37.

Haribhadra who was a Brahman by birth and probably also for this reason frequently proved considerably impartial in his treatises[1], and accomplished by Śīlānka (872 A.D.), and Prakrit treatises have long continued to be written. But the use of Sanskrit coming in was significant. By editing his Tattvārthādhigama in the shape of Sūtras (imitated by Haribhadra in his Dharmabindu) Umāsvāti followed Brahman models, and by doing so he led the Śvet. out of the narrow circle and made them become competitive. Umāsvāti also appears in the lists of the Dig.; but there is no doubt that he was a Śvet., since the Dig. do not acknowledge the Bhāṣya he himself wrote for his Sūtras, but use their own comments instead. They have changed the basic text[2], too, if only inconsiderably. Among the authors following Umāsvāti the above mentioned competitiveness led to arguments and disputes of remarkable dialectic refinement with both Buddhists and Brahmans[3]. On the part of the Śvet. we have to mention Siddhasena Divākara and Haribhadra as contestants to Dharmakīrti (about 650)[4], while among the Dig. we have Samantabhadra (1st half of the 8th century), Akalanka (2nd half of the 8th century), Vidyānanda (Pātrakesarin) and Prabhācandra (1st half of the 9th centurry) as opponents to Kumārila and Śāntarakṣita. Vidyānanda also stood up against Śaṃkara. After the unanimously testified decline of Buddhism in South India it was in the personality of Kumārila that "the Mīmāṃsā flourished for a short while. It was followed (thanks to the Dig.) by a Jain reaction culminating during the reign

1. LEUMANN ZDMG 46, 582; For H.'s life and works see JACOBI, Samarāicc, p. I ff. The Yogabindu (Bo. 1911) and Yogadṛṣṭisamuccaya (DLJP 12, Bo. 1912) ed. by SUALI are no Jain works.

2. For a confrontation of the two versions of the Tattv. see edition by JAINI SBJ 2. A critical discussion about them and the author of the Bhāṣya by GHATAGE JUB 4 p. 105-111.

3. Hinted at already also by U. himself, comp. compilation by H. R. KAPADIA ABhORI 14, 142-144. For polemics of Buddhists and Brahmans against the Jains see v. GLASENAPP in Festschrift Schubring p. 74-84. —SCHRADER assumes (Philos. p. 51) that these disputes had helped to bring the Syādvāda to life.

4. JACOBI Z II 5, 307.

5. JACOBI, Samarāicc. p. XIII. For chronology and system of either logician see Satis Chandra VIDYABHUSANA, History of the Mediaeval School of Indian Logic. C. 1909.

of the Rāṣṭrakūṭa Amoghavarṣa I. (815-877)"[1]. In the end, however, Hinduism triumphed. By the Canarese literature we are able to trace how Jainism loses ground to the Śaivas and the Vaiṣṇavas. That this did not happen until the 2nd half of the 12th century easily explains itself by the solid tradition flowing from Śravaṇa Beḷgoḷa. In the region where the Tamil language was spoken the change over in favour of Viṣṇuism and Śivaism was in full swing not until the end of the 10th century after both had come to rise here already some centuries earlier. Soon after the middle of the 12th century the Vīraśaiva who had increased in importance owing to the propaganda of the Basava, joined the enemies of Jainism. The contest between the different religions soon took the form of bloody persecutions[2], such as the Jains in northern India, i.e. presumably mainly Śvet., had to endure by the hands of Mohammedan conquerors in the 13th century.

The above remarks allowed of being confined to the densest possible form since the author made use of the historical chapter in v. GLASENAPP's "Jainismus" (1926) including various details and references to sources[3]. It was followed by Ch. L. SHAH, Jainism in Northern India (1929); the South was treated in DESAI's book previously mentioned (1957). His predecessors were M.S. Ramaswami AYYANGAR, South Indian Jainism, and B. Seshagiri RAO, Andhra Karnata Jainism, both combined under the title studies in South Indian Jainism (1922). S. B. DEO gives an historical account in his History of Jaina Monachism (1956) p. 57-130.

§30. After having dealt with the exterior adventures of Jainism we now turn to its inward changes. The teaching proper was scarcely affected by any of them. The so-called schisms of the early times (§ 17) concerned quite subordinate

1. The investigator of these polemics and shiftings is PATHAK, comp. IX. OC I, 186-214; JBBRAS 18, 214-238; a series of essays in ABhORI 11 and 12.—The Praśnottararatnamālā, however attributed to the A. by some avoids strict partiality.

2. Comp. R. G. BHANDARKAR in this Grundriss 3, 6, p. 48 ff., 131 ff., 140 ff.

3. For Rajputana comp. also the booklet by UMRAO SINGH TANK, Jaina Historical Studies (Delhi 1914).

points and were overome in the pale of the Order itself. The new formations which developed to remain are nearly exclusively concerned with formalities. This becomes evident already by the alienation between Śvet. and Dig. which goes back, as we know, to a more uncompromising conception of monkdom on the part of the latter. It crystallizes around the idea of the ideal monk, i.e. the Kevalin. He no longer takes any earthly food but is merely kept alive by a constant influx of material particles, a process the Śvet. would call *lom'āhāra* (§ 96). To think that he ate and digested was most certainly shocking[1], as much as in the view of Dig. it was against his dignity to decorate his temple figure, and, especially, against that of Mahāvīra to imagine him owing his origin to an operation performed by some divine gynaecology (§ 17), or to think that he was married. If, furthermore, there can be no salvation without nakedness[2] (Chapp. 3,23,), then it follows that all female persons, since they cannot go without clothes, are excluded from it (and that is why Arhat Malli—§ 15—is said to have been by no means a girl). The extreme conclusion, however, that accordingly there should be no nuns at all, is not yet drawn by Vaṭṭakera in the Mūlācāra, an early work, nor by others (§ 137). But we come across it in the Chappāhuḍa (3, 24f.), which is attributed, though wrongly, to Kundakunda[3]. The Dig. on the whole deny the *strī-mukti* up this day, but yet we find that the attitude of the Śvet., since ever more capable of adaptation, has penetrated into their thinking here and there. Among the Dig. there were so-called *saṃghas* called Kāṣṭhā, Mūla, Māthura, and Gopya or Yāpanīya. Acc. to the Śvet. Guṇaratna[4], who, it is true, lived, as late as in the 15th century (s. 1466), they are *ācāre gurdu ca deve ca* equal to the Śvet. so the *Gopya* equal them

1. With regard to digestion we have the same attitude with the Śvet. *pacchanne āhāra-nīhāre, adisse maṃsa-cakkhuṇā* (a śloka line, to read *pacchann'* Samav. 60a), and also in Chapp. 4, 37 we have to understand the word in this way.

2. For this there are 9 reasons, see Dharmasāgara in the Kuv. (§ 32) in WEBER, Kup. p. 798.

3. The AUTHOR ZDMG 107, 557 f.

4. Comp. Haribhadra, Ṣaḍdarśanasamuccaya ed. SUALI p. 111.

in using as a salutation the word of *dharma-lābha*[1] and in allowing women to find salvation and the Kevalin to live on food. The by far older Devasena, who may perhaps deserve some credit with questions concerning the Dig. (§ 26), traces (Daṃs. 29) the *Yāpanīya* back to a Śvet., i.e. the Sirikalasa at Kalyāṇa (s. 705)[2]. Among the different customs of the Kāṣṭhā-s., which is said to have been established s. 753 by Kumārasena in Nanditaṭa (Daṃs. 33 ff.), we may in this connexion mention the *dīkṣā* of female persons[3].

As regards the Mūla- and the Māthura-s., Guṇaratna refers to them merely with respect to their adherents being distinguishable by the whisks (*piccha*) of different kind used by them as hand-brooms (§ 145) which he also mentions in connexion with the aforesaid. Acc. to Devasena (Daṃs. 40ff.) the *Māthuras* branched off 200 years after the Kāṣṭhā-s., and they did so thanks to a certain Rāmasena at Mathurā who, among others, believed in Padmanandin (i.e. Kundakunda) less than in Bhūtabali and Puṣpadanta both referred to as pupils of Arhadbali in the inscriptions (s. b.). The place mentioned concerns Mathurā on the Yamunā, since it is at Dakkhiṇa-Mahurā, i.e. Madurā, where in s. 526 the *Drāvida*-s. is said to have originated (Daṃs. 24 ff.). Its founder was Vajranandin, a pupil of Pujyapāda (Devanandin). He and his like were less scrupulous about the *ahiṃsā* than the traditional teaching wanted it, and so they were liberal in questions concerning nutrition and civil activities.[4] Of the Mūla-s. we learn nothing from Devasena

1. The other three *s.* with "*dharma-vṛddhi*".

2. A second Ms. has 205. The occurence of Yāp. in Khāravela's large inscription discussed by SHAH, Jainism, p. 180 f. appears to be rather doubtful. For recent investigations see UPADHYE JUB 1, p. 224 ff. and DESAI p. 163 ff.

3. Further characteristics of this *saṃgha* under the proviso that he coincides with the Gopucchikas (comp. footnote 1 on p. 46) see Śrutasāgara on Chapp. 1.

4. For the sake of completeness we mention the prophesy rendered Dams.45f. acc. to which after 1800 years hence the monk Vīracandra of Puṣkara in the Vindhya mountains in Deccan will destroy the teaching by the Bhillaka-saṃgha.—In Nītisāra 10 Indranandin speaks of the five *jain'ābhāsa* or false Jains by whom he means the Śvet., the Drāviḍa-and Yāpanīya (IA 21, 68; Yāpulīya) —saṃghas, the Niḥpiṃchas (i.e. as shown by Gunaratna the Māthura-s.) and the Gopucchikas who may stand for the Kāṣṭhā-s. (called *camarīvālaiḥ picchika* by Guṇaratna) (but IA 21, 68 instead of Gop. : Kekīpiccha).

since this does not mean a branch but the religious centre of the Digambaras. For it was the *Mūla-saṃgha* from which by means of integration (*saṃghaṭṭana*) in earlier times Arhadbali had formed the *saṃghas* called Siṃha, Nandi, Sena[1], and Deva. This we learn from inscriptions dated 1398 and 1432 A.D.[2], from the Nītisāra[3] composed by Indranandin between 1524 and 1565, and from Paṭṭāvalis of the last centuries[4]. In the latter works those four names are explained by the special praxis of individuals, and the fact is stressed that these four saṃghas harmonized with each other, though the measures taken by Arhadbali were meant to be an act of pacification after controversies had shown up in the course of time (*kāla-svabhāvāt*). Acc. to the latter inscription the classification was made after Akalanka's death (2nd half of the 8th century). In the 12th-13th century, however, there was once more a *Mūla-saṃgha*. At least the Nandi-s. was divided into *gaṇa*, *gaccha* and *vali* (*bali*), and its adherents had as a second name of the words of *candra*, *kīrtideva*, *bhūṣaṇa*, and *nandin*[5].

§31. We now turn back to the Śvetāmbaras. If we were certain about the time when the three smaller texts going by the name of *cūliyā* were composed, we should know at what date the declines from the normal level described by them had occurred. The prophesy pointing at 1990 after Mv. rendered in the Vaggacūliyā leads to the 15th century A.D. which cannot be the date of their origin. Here we are told of the disrespect shown towards sacred texts. From the Angacūliyā we learn that partly with the superiors' knowledge and consent persons slipped in without being formally accepted. Their exposure then led to

1. IA 20, 350; Vṛṣabha.

2. First (with translation) ed. by RICE, Ep. Carn. 2, 77, 82, improved by NARASIMHACHAR, loc. cit. (rev. ed.) p. 123, 129, comp. also p. 87 f.

3. HOERNLE IA 21, 84.

4. HOERNLE IA 20, 341 ff; 21, 57 ff.

5. Ep. Carn. 2, 123. In the Paṭṭāvalī IA 20, 350; 21, 71 fails to have the word of *deva*. The Sena-s. has the words: *rāga*, *vīra*, *bhadra*, *sena*; the Siṃha-s. *siṃha*, *kumbha*, *āsrava*, *sāgara*; the Deva-s.: *deva*, *datta*, *nāga*, *tunga* (I.A 21, 69; there *langa* instead of *tunga*). For a biographical list of the Ācāryas of the Arungala-anvaya which was a subsection of the Nandi-s. since Akalanka, see HULTZSCH ZDMG 68, 695-700.

quarrels and schisms[1]. The Viyāhacūliyā, finally, by the means of 16 interpretations of dreams designs a picture typical of the time of its origin. In addition to the details already mentioned in §21 we may, in this connection, point to the loss of texts for instruction, the corruption of monastic morals, the flourishing of heresy, the disregard for the Order on the part of outsiders, the deficient training of preachers owing to the absence of *theragas*, and bickering and biting among the monks.

Since detailed reports are missing, it may be assumed that the grievances here referred to were of an importance going far beyond the regional. The custom, however, of using the cult-places as living quarters as well (*caitya-vāsa*) seems to have been observed at certain times especially in Gujarat. According to ancient prescriptions (§ 147) the monk is expected to ask for his quarters in ordinary homes (*vasati-nivāsa*). Those who acted differently may have referred to the Canon saying that sermons and instructional talks invariably took place at a *ceiya* (§ 18) which may have developed into taking one's quarters there. The argument[2] in favour of and against the *ceiy'ālaya* quoted in the Mahānisīha is not motivated therein. The early leaders of a Gaccha (§ 34) saw their task in opposing the *caitya-vāsin*, and so energetically was it refuted at Gujarat by Jineśvara in s. 1080 that for this refutation[3] he came to be given the surname of Kharatara (after which his Gaccha[4] was accordingly called), whereas the *caityavāsin* were called *kuvala*. Jinadatta (12th-13th century s.), the chronicler of this Gaccha, is, moreover, very desirous in pointing out, that Haribhadra was not a *cīvāsī*, while Śīlāṅka is spoken of with respect even though he belonged to them.[5] So, then, even Haribhadra had stood up against the abuse of sanctuaries by profane music and other worldly

1. Comp. the AUTHOR, OLZ 1926, col. 910 ff.
2. The AUTHOR, Mahānis. p. 100.
3. WEBER, List II, 1038, Also R. G. BHANDARKAR Rep. 1882-83 p. 46.
4. Comp. § 34.
5. Gaṇadharasārdhaśataka 57 and comm. on 60, comp. WEBER, Verf. II, 988 f. and GOS 37, p. 94f., ref. by JACOBI, Samarāicc. IX f., (for on p. IX read 57).

diversions, above all, however, as is equally reported by Jinadatta in his Caccarī,[1] Jinavallabha (who died in s. 1167) restored them as *vidhi-caitya-gṛha*, i.e. by turning out trespassers and by enforcing a dignified conduct for their dignified use. In his Uvaesarasāyaṇu and his Kālasvarūpakulaka,[2] Jinadatta renders a sinister report on the state of affairs prevailing among the Śvet. in the 12th century.

§32. The antagonism between dwelling places and such devoted to cultic activitiesr evives many centuries after in the name of the Sthānakvāsī. By this name such Jains are designated that practise their religious duties not in the temple but exclusively at some profane place (*sthānaka*), i.e. in the Upāśraya. Their reason for doing so is that they refuse the cult of the Jina statues, and they refuse it because only the living deserve veneration but not dead matter like the *pratimā* or *bimba* to which particularly the Canon does not refer. The latter argument is wrong, for at least Rāyap. mentions statues of Titthagaras (§ 25). The Sthānakvāsī, however, are not the originators of that conception, they merely pursue or either revive it in the beginning of the 18th century. As early as s. 1508 there appeared a sect headed by a certain Lumpāka or Lonkaśa from Ahmedabad and calling itself after him by the name of Lumpāka, Lunka, Lonka or Launka, since when professionally copying manuscripts he had discovered that they contained nothing about the cult of images. The arguments referred to are attributed to Lumpāka in Dharmasāgara's polemic work bearing the title of Kuvakkhakosiyasahassakiraṇa and composed at a time (*s*. 1629) when the Sthānakvāsī had not yet existed. They did not appear until s. 1710 in Surat under the leadership of Lava(ji), the son of Vīra, who reorganized Lonkaśa's Order. The community also passes by the name of Bāvīs (or Vīs) Tole Panth, and its members are called either Ḍhuṇḍhiyā or Ḍhuṇḍhak, the latter meaning futile "seekers" in the script[3] and the former owing its name to the fact that the sect goes back to

1. Caccarī 12 ff.
2. Both following the Caccarī in GOS 37.
3. For a different explanation comp. MILLET IA 25, 147 following IBBETSON, Outlines of Panjāb Ethnography, p. 132, § 25 f.

22 groups (*tolā*) under named leaders.[1] Notwithstanding this fundamental difference various Sthānakvāsīs still to-day call themselves Śvetāmbaras[2] though without acknowledging all of their texts, i.e. repudiating 13 out of its 45, including the Mahānisīha, for their attitude towards the *paḍimās*. Hence the Battīsī mentioned §4. An earlier branch of Lonkaśa's community dating from either s. 1531 or 1533 was represented in Rajputana and in Gujarat by the Veṣadharas who must have stood out by wearing some conspicuous costume.[3] A counterpart to the name of the Bāvīs Tolā is that of the Terāpanth, the "path of the thirteen", which appeared in Marwar in s. 1817. The Terāpanthī, within the frame of their strict orthodoxy, equally reject the cult of images since the founder of their sect, Bhīkanjī, was a Sthānakvāsī, but they equally counted themselves among the Śvetāmbaras[4].

§33 The afore mentioned publication of Dharmasāgara, known also by the title of Pravacanaparīkṣā[5], is up to now the only contemporary source for the Lumpākas and the Veṣadharas, though for its polemic character it has to be valued accordingly. While the aversion to images represents an actually far-reaching disparity of views, Dh., on the other hand, deals with a number of other sects whose principles vary but insignificantly from the standard rules. We therefore content ourselves with rendering but a few statements. The Paurṇamīyakas (s. 1159) derived

1. Comp. p. 2, 29 of the publication mentioned § 56.

2. "Seeker" (i.e. Kesari Chand BHANDARI), Notes on the Sthānakwasi or non-idolatrous Shwetambar Jains. (Indore) 1911.—STEVENSON, Heart p. 87 f.; the SAME ERE 12, 123 f.; JACOBI, Archiv f. Religionswiss. 18, 271 f.—SRI PREM CHAND, Mithya Khandan, containing origin of Jainism. Ludhiana 1914.

3. R. G. BHANDARKAR, Rep. 1883-84, p. 153.

4. For details see JACOBI loc. cit. 272; Kesree Chand KISHORY in the Census of India 1921, vol. I, p. I, App. IV; JAYACARYA, Bhram Vidhvaṃsan (C. s. 1980); KANAMALLA Svami, Kālu Bhaktāmarastotra (C. s. 1987), p. ga ff.; Terāpanthīkṛt Granth Samgrah (Bo. 1876); A short History of the Terapanthi Sect of the Jain Swetambar Community (*C.* 1933). —On the above mentioned sects partly diverging Muni Ātmārāmjī ĀNANDAVIJAYA IA 21, 63, 72 (also on other different branches).

5. BHANDARKAR, Report 1883-84, p. 144-155; WEBER, Über den Kupakshakauçikāditya des Dharmasāgara, Streitschrift eines orthodoxen Jaina, vom Jahre 1573. SPAW1882, 793-814, merely discusses the fragment of a ms. of which the most important parts are missing.

their name from the confession act on full moon-day (*pūrṇimā*) to which they attached as great an importance as to Jina figures being erected exclusively by laymen without the assistance of monks (*śrāvaka-pratiṣṭhā*). Banished from Gujarat by Kumārapāla (§ 28) they gained ground once more as Sārdha-P. after his death (s. 1236), which possibly expresses itself by their name- as "sesqui"P. unless, as some want it, Sādhu-P. is the authentical form. The Āgamikas or Tristutikas[1] (s. 1250) would not hear of any worship of the *śruta-devatā*[2] (§14), in other words, they felt it to be an adulteration of the true teaching. They as well as the Lumpākas, though they did not share the latter's aversion to images (1, 75), resembled those who had appropriated the *mata* of a certain Bīja (s. 1570) who himself was no man of spiritual rank (? *vaṇṇa-vihīṇa*). The followers of Kaṭuka (s. 1562 or 1564)[3] were equally connected with the Āgamikas though the rendering of this connexion is not altogether clear. On the other hand they were radical enough in rejecting monkdom and insisting as laymen on the right of preaching and converting. This most certainly resulted from observing the Sādhus leading a non-religious life, so that here, too, it may be assumed that their decisive reforms coincided with the preservation of true belief and good conduct.

§34. Apart from dealing with the Digambaras, Dharmasāgara in his publication finally refers to a number of branches which for the lack of essential material divergencies would scarcely be designated as *kupakṣa* by any impartial author. He himself belonged to the Tapā-Gaccha. In linguistic usage the *gaccha* follows on the *gaṇa*.[4] In the course of time there are said to have been numerous *gacchas* or Orders which is frequently

1. Rājendra Suri (s. 1883-1963) was a great promotor of theirs as is told in the biographical sketch mentioned §8. The Tristutikas are opposed to the Catuḥstutikas.

2. BHANDARKAR loc. cit. p. 153 as compared with Kuv. I, 73 probably by mistake: *kṣetra-devatā*.

3. s. 1524 after the list laid down by Kalyāṇa *s.* 1685, Kalyāṇa, who himself was a Kaṭuka, controverts for his part the Tapā to be dealt with presently. Comp. KLATT, in Festgruss an Böhtlingk (1888) p. 58 f.

4. The change of the earlier name into the later can be pursued in the Mahāṇisiha (the AUTHOR, Mahāṇis. p. 78).

expressed by the figure of 84 (§ 16)[1], but only few of them have come to gain any considerable and lasting importance. Thanks to the disposition of the Jains for chronicling we have comprehensive lists of teachers to inform us accordingly.[2] They usually go by the name of *paṭṭ'āvalī* in the sense of *paṭṭadhar'āvalī* since in this connexion *paṭṭa* means "place of honour, throne". He who occupies it bears the title of Sūri, and he personally appoints his successor. Frequently the lists (chronicles) are traced back to Sudharman, or even to Mahāvīra who, however, is not everywhere considered as *paṭṭa-dhara*.[3] The Upakeśa-Gaccha, to refer to this list first, even goes back to Pāsa which follows from an intended relation to Keśin, the disciple of Pārśva known from Uvanga 2. The fabulous *paṭṭ'āvalī* of this Gaccha probably written in the 2nd half of the 17th century,[4] proves as an exception to the rule that these chronicles are mines of reliable dates regarding the history of Jain Orders and writings.[5] Upakeśa is said to be the later Os near Jodhpur from where the commercial Jain caste of the Osvāl derive. A collection of the Śvet. lists in a Paṭṭavalīsamuccaya has been started by Muni DARŚANA-VIJAYA (Bh. 1, Cāritrasmāraka-GM. 22. Vīramgām 1933).[6] Now it is Dharmasāgara who, in a Prakrit-Gurvāvalī[7] with an individual Sanskrit comment, notes the history of the Tapā-Gaccha who, so he says, took this name but as the sixth after that

1. Comp. the lists given by Muni JINAVIJAYA in Jaina-Sāhitya-Saṃśodhaka 3, 30-34.

2. Other proofs are the *praśasti* at the end of Jain works and the *vijnapti*, annual reports in the shape of letters (partly illustrated). Comp. the exhaustive study by Muni JINAVIJAYA: Vijnapti-triveṇi (Bh. 1916), also K. P. J (AYASWAL) JA 46, 276.

3. (*tīrthakṛtāṃ*) *svayam eva tīrtha-pravacanena kasyāpi paṭṭadhara-tvābhāvāt* Dharmasāgara on verse 2 of his Gurvāvalī as against the Kharataras presently to be mentioned.

4. Transl. by HOERNLE IA 19, 233-242; complete text: JINAVIJAYA in Jaina-Sāhitya-Samsodhaka 1; Paṭṭāvalīsam. (see presently) 1, 177-194.

5. A second exception is the "apocryphal Paṭṭāvalī" rendered by KLATT in Festgruss an Böhtlingk (1888, p. 54-59).

6. For the names of 17 Paṭṭ. s. see KLATT-LEUMANN IA 23, 170.

7. KLATT, IA 11, 251-256; WEBER Verz. II, 651 f. 997-1015; for this and for chronistic predecessors and successors of Dh. see KLATT-LEUMANN IA 23, 179; compl. text and comm. Paṭṭavalīsam. 1, 41-77, followed by further Tapā-tradition.

of the *nirgrantha-* and those of Koṭika-, Candra-, Vanavāsī and Vaṭa-Gaccha, altogether names which are explained in different ways. Different from two other lists presently to be mentioned, this list by starting from Uddyotana, the 35th Sūri (till s. 994), follows its own way as that of Vaṭa- or Bṛhad-G. and leads up to the 44th Sūri, Jagaccandra, who equally gained fame as a reformer and as a triumphant disputant, but who as a stern fasting ascetic came to be given the surname of Tapā (*Tapā-biruda*) (s.1285)[1]. Still today the Tapā-G. enjoys a high reputation. This also applies to the Kharatara-G. and others, whom to attack is a special concern of Dharmasāgara's in his work. In their *paṭṭ'āvalī*[2] the Kharatara, too, appear beyond the time of Uddyotana just as the formation of the above mentioned 84 gacchas is said to go back to the same number of Uddyotana's pupils who are said to have been blessed by him individually in a ceremony before he died.[3] One of them, and hence the first Kharatara-Sūri proper, was Vardhamāna (till s. 1088)[4], by origin a *caityavāsin*, who were energetically attacked by his own pupil, Jineśvara (s. 1080), as we have seen in § 31. This report of the Kharatarasa, however, Dharmasāgara[5] declares to be false owing to historic dates,[6] and he refutes the statements it contains also elsewhere. Acc. to him it was Jinadatta (s. 1204) who came to be the first Kharatara, and it is said that his activities equally account for his further names[7]: Cāmuṇḍika, because Jinadatta dedicated a prayer to Cāmuṇḍā, and Auṣṭrika, because he fled on a camel. As to the peculiarities of the Kh. we hear of them from Jinadatta himself by an Utsūtrapadâghāṭanakulaka (30 G.), by a Sāmāyārī, and

1. Tapā seems to be the intimate form for a name beginning with *tapas* as Yaśā is said to have been for Yaśovijaya (§ 36).

2. KLATT IA 11, 245-250; WEBER, Verz. II, 1030-1056.

3. KLATT loc. cit. 248a; WEBER loc. cit. 1035. By this the Gacchas are legitimated by the Tapā.

4. This will not agree with s. 994 which date is given by the Tapās as the death year of his immediate precursor, Uddyotana. 1088 is the first year referred to in the Kharatara chronicle.

5. BHANDARKAR, Report 1883-84, p. 149.

6. This, too, is the object of an assumed dispute bearing the title of Kharātmajānām nihnava-sthāpanā-vāda-yuto mūlapuruṣa-vādaḥ.

7. DHARMASĀGARA, Gurv. in Ajitadeva Sūri (No. 41); WEBER, Kup. p. 804.

again, most comprehensively, from Dharmasāgara in his Auṣṭrikamatotsūtrodghāṭanakulaka commented by himself (18 G.)[1]. By a change of the sign the last small text implicitly teaches us to know the standpoint of the Tapās. The various points of divergence scarcely concern anything but irrelevant matters of praxis. As being of some slightly greater importance we, therefore, but mention that women may not worship the Jina (*itthī-jiṇa-pūya-nisehaṇa*), that there is no fasting beyond the *cauttha* (§ 156), that laymen will not exercise *paḍimā* (§ 163), that the Cāmuṇḍā and other local deities may be worshipped, and that the ceremony of Mahāvīra's being put into another womb is to be celebrated as his sixth *kallāṇaga*[2].

§35. Among Uddyotana's pupils we have Sarvadeva, the teacher of Padmadeva. With them as the 36th and 37th Sūri there begins the *paṭṭ'āvalī* of Ancala-Gaccha[3] who, though under Padmadeva he was still called Śankheśvara-G., was soon after named Nānaka-G. and under Āryarakṣita (No. 47) Vidhipakṣa G. by which name he is still known to-day. The name of Ancala does not occur here at all. But Dharmasāgara does deal with the Ancala-G. as such[4] where he discusses the Ancaliya (Āncalika) or Pallaviya (Pallavika), once even Stanika (?). The reciprocal notes have one thing in common: that in the *paṭṭ'āvalī* it was an *upādhyāya* Vijayacandra, in the Gurvāvalī a certain Narasiṃha, who was one-eyed, as a Sūri was given the name of Āryarakṣita. The origin of the Vidhipakṣa-G. is there said to be the year s. 1169[5], whereas here the Ancala-G. is said to date from s. 1213, So we have two completley different occurrences, and we certainly cannot charge the Āncalika of to-day with

1. All incl. the text referred to in footnote 6 in : Dharmasāgara, Iryāpathikīṣaṭtriṃśikā (Āg. Ś, 49).

2. The traditional 5 festive days in honour of all Jinas are: conception, birth, becoming a monk, the first notion of the Kevala cognition and entering into Nirvāṇa.

3. KLATT-LEUMANN IA 23, 174-178 after a Gurupaṭṭāvalī published in the Śrīmad-Vidhipakṣagacchīya śrāvaknā daivas'ādik pānce Pratikramaṇa Sūtra, Bo. 1889, 2nd print 1905.

4. Gurv. in Ajitadeva Sūri (No. 41); for the Kuv. comp. BHANDARKAR, Report 1883-84, p. 152 and WEBER, Kup. p. 805 f.

5. A list defying any closer determination and ed. by BHANDARKAR loc, cit. p. 14 gives s. 1159 for the Ancala-G.

saying that acc. to Dharmasāgara the *ancala* or *pallava*, i.e. the corner of a dress, had stood for the face cloth by way of imitating an individual case, and that later also the hand-broom and even the act of confession had been dismissed. At least the latter does not apply to the praxis of the Vidhipakṣa.

In conclusion we have to add that the Kuv. was also concerned with the Gaccha of the Pāśacandras[1] whose foundation goes back to an *upādhyāya* bearing the same name and being descended from a sidebranch of the Tapā-G. as such frequently developed being called *gaccha* as well or, as was the case already in ancient days, *śākhā* (comp. § 25). In this case it was a *Nāgapurīya*--Tapā-G. which had developed at Nāgaur (Rajputana) in *s*. 1174 and within which Pāśacandra established his *mata* in *s*. 1572. He distinguished himself as an independent writer and as a commentator of canonic texts who as such a one also calls himself Pārśvacandra.[2] Since his Bālāvabodha and Vārttika are still being acknowledged he is not likely to have departed very far from the principles of the doctrine. Nor did he ignore the scholastic comments and the Chedagrantha as he is blamed for having done by Dharmasāgara. He is said to have had different points of contact with the Lumpākas. BHANDARKAR is not fully intelligible in reporting on a system developed by Pāśacandra.[3]

§36. Since the forming of a Śvet.-Gaccha[4] of the kind described above lastly always comes as a protest against the traditional state of affairs in order to replace it by a better one, there can be no doubt that in return reformatory efforts were made within its body. This we may conclude from the discrimination still made to-day between monks of a higher and lower class.[5] The former are the Sādhus and the latter the Yatis. Contrary to the linguistic usage in mediaeval times when both

1. KLATT-LEUMANN IA 23, 181 f.
2. Comp. the Calcutta ed. of the Āyāra II 280; WEBER Verf. II, 542.
3. BHANDARKAR loc. cit. p. 155.
4. Or else of a *śākhā*, comp. the development of the Vijaya-śākhā IA 19, 234.
5. STEVENSON, Heart p. 233; v. GLASENAPP, Jainismus p. 72, 341, 352 ff.

words meant the same, the Yatis are the spiritual successors of those monks who had not participated in the reform. The point where this process starts is found with the Tapā-Gaccha. Of this Tapā-G. Yaśovijaya Gaṇin[1] of Gujarat was a member. After having been trained in Jain learning at home his Guru Nayavijaya of Benares made him become a master of logics who as such proved extremely productive. He died in *s*. 1745. Without occupying a leading position in the Order[2] he carried out his reforms on the initiative of Vijayasiṃha whom the Vijaya-śākhā calls their first Sūri, although Vijayadeva who had appointed him Sūri in s. 1682 outlived him, who died in s. 1709, by four years.[3] In the way he opposed both the Digambaras and the Ḍhuṇḍhiyas[4] so he was successful first in his own Gaccha. He who followed him came to be called a *saṃvegi* dressed in saffron, whereas he who refused him continued to dress in white, and that is why to-day we hear him being called not only a *yati* but a *gorji* as well. This differentiation obviously spread from the Tapās over to the Kharataras, for in our days here, too, we come across the white Yatis who even have a hierarchy of their own. So, then, in concluding our historical sketch we observe among the Śvetāmbaras the same capacity to which in remote antiquity they owe their origin: to cling faithfully to the values of tradition even though reformed.

1. Satis Chandra VIDYABHUSANA JASB 6 (1911), 463-69; M. D. DESAI, Shrimad Yahovijayaji (a Life of a great Jain Scholar). Bo. (after 1910); SAUBHAGYAVIJAYA in the ed. of Y.'s Nayopadeśa; forewords to editions of other writings of Y.

2. Then his name would be Vijayayaśas.

3. HOERNLE IA 19, 234.

4. For his polemics against the former see § 195; for those directed against the Dig. and the latter comp. a.o. his so-called Vīrastutirūp hundīnū stavan and his letter to Śā Devrāj, both in PK 3, 569-710.

III

THE CANON

§37. In the canonical texts[1] (Uvav. and (a.o.) Viy 134b; Ṭhāṇ. 176a) Mahāvīra's teaching is called *niggantha pāvayaṇa* (Viy. 792b : *pavayaṇa*[2]), more precisely *duvālas'anga gaṇi-piḍaga* (a.o Viy. 792b; 866b=Nandī 246b; Samav. 106b). This means "the basket of teacher(s)[3] containing 12 Angas". Samav. 73b speaking of Angas 1-3 calls one individual Anga *gaṇi-piḍaga*. The consonance with the *tipiṭaka* and the *anga* of the Buddhists (for the latter word comp. a.o. WINTERNITZ, History 2, 8) is apparent. As to *anga*, a reminiscence of the Vedāngas is equally possible. But while *vedānga* means "auxiliary members" (to the Vedas), the Jain Angas are members of a unit formed by themselves. The collection through which this unit must have been established, is due to a council at Pāṭaliputra described by the Śvetāmbaras in Par. 9, 57ff. Considering that Bhadrabāhu who belonged to the 6th generation following Mahāvīra played an important role in it (§ 23), this council must have taken place in the 2nd decade of the 4th century B. C. On the other hand it must be mentioned that, as was pointed out by JACOBI,[4] the oldest texts owing to metrical observations seem to date from times not earlier than the end of the 4th and the beginning of the 3rd century, the more so since the value of literary products is acknowledged not earlier than a good time after their being composed and then leads to their collection.

1. They have been treated exhaustively by H. R. KAPADIA in his learned book "A History of the canonical literature of the Jainas" (Bo. 1947), and it is with pleasure that the AUTHOR, while suppressing some minor criticism, refers the reader to that work for many details which could not be mentioned here.

2. In company with *pāvayaṇa* Āv. 127.

3. Śīlānka to Sūy. nijj. 136 (p. 253 b) is correct, the contrary Abhayadeva Samav. 107a; Malayagiri Nandiv. 193a.

4. SBE 22, XXXI ff.; ZDMG 38, 590-619; 74, 255.

We have seen that the Angas are not additions to something previously existing. Tradition, on the other hand, will have it differently in speaking of the so-called Puvva. They are no longer in existence. To explain the word, Abhayadeva in his comm. on Samav. 130b says that the Angas were composed by Mahāvīra's Gaṇadharas (§22) either immediately in the spirit of the preceding (*pūrva*) oral tradition or indirectly after first (*pūrva*) having established that tradition[1]. But he does not derive the Angas from the Puvvas. If this had been the case, the Puvvas would have been absorbed in the Angas. Instead we read in the survey of what the A. contain (Samav. 129a; Nandī 236b) that the 12th of them (which was lost) included the P. and other topics. Hence it follows that the two series were parallel to, not dependent on , each other.

§38. It is in harmony with the misunderstanding according to which the P. were the most ancient evidences[2] that some of them are said (Dasav. nijj. 15-17) to have been the sources for canonical texts, viz. P. 6 (Saccappavāya) for Dasav. 7 (Vakkasuddhi);7 (Āyapp.) for Dasav. 3 (Dhammapannatti= Chajjīvaṇiyā); 8 (Kammapp.) for Dasav. 5 (Piṇḍesaṇā). The remaining chapters of Dasav. are said to come form the Paccakkhāṇa-P. (9), *vatthu* 4, and from the same, *vatthu* 3, *pāhuḍa* 20, as the Āv.-nijj. will have it, the Cheyasutta Dasão,Kappa, and both Vavahāra and the Ohanijjutti. Utt. 2 (Parīsahā) is derived from P. 8, *vatthu* 20. Moreover, one of the Gāhās preceding the Pannavaṇā refers to the P. (another one to the Diṭṭhivāya, s.b.). For the present writer it is beyond doubt that it was merely a relationship in contents that has led authors to construe those origins, provided that the Puvvas did actually lie before their eyes. This supposition is necessary since at all times imagination is keen on filling up evident gaps.

In reality the name of *puvva* was due to the apologies of which the texts must have consisted. The lists mentioned count 14 P. and summarize them as *puvva-gaya*. With the

1. Comp. Āv.92 (106b) *attham bhāsai arahā, suttam ganthanti gaṇaharā niuṇam.*

2. JACOBI SBE 22, XLIV ff.; BAGCHI, J. Dept. Letters (Univ. of C.) 14, Nr. 9—.

exception of four they all have *pavāya* in their individual title which means the utterance of a contradictory view (*pravāda*). They are combined with various fundamental questions and ideas, viz. *uppāya* (1), *vīriya, atthi n'atthi, nāṇa, sacca, āya, kamma, paccakkhāṇa, vijjā* (3-10; 10; *vijjāṇuppavāya*). It follows that they were adversary objections evidently not preserved out of historical interest, but as instructions how to refute them. Similarly we read Viy. 380b that Mahāvīra's monks having refuted their opponents, proclaimed the Gaippavāya[1] who was called an *ajjhayaṇa* and hence was intended to set them right by an adverse view (in this case the right one). Whether the *pavāya* of the Diṭṭhivāya (the 12th Anga) were fiction or fact we do not know. The names of P. 2 Aggeṇīya of Aggāṇiya[2], 11 Avanjha, 13 Kiriyāvisāla, and 14 Logabindusāra for their obscurity all speak in favour of their factitive nature.

From Ṭhāṇ. 199a; Samav. 128b; Nandī 235b we learn[3] that the Diṭṭhivāya consisted of the sections *parikamma, suttāiṃ, puvva-gaya, aṇuoga*[4], and (with P. 1-4) *cūliyāo*. Here, evidently, the course of a dispute is reflected where *puvva-gaya* is the same as the well-known *pūrva-pakṣa*. The "introduction" is followed by the "sūtra" which may have been construed *ad hoc* and which then are "attacked" whereupon a close "examination" unveils the truth. The 12th Anga thus, under the title of a "discourse on (heterodox) views"[5] (which is but one of other titles showing a didactic or polemic meaning, comp. Ṭhāṇ. 491b) was an instruction to apology and quite naturally fitted closely in the doctrine laid down in Angas 1-11. In the course of time it was lost. JACOBI (SBE 22, XLV) explains this fact by saying that later generations thought the

1. Quite another *gai-ppavāya* (five-fold) Pannav. 16 (end) (Malayagiri: *gati-prapāta* or *pravāda.*)

2. Angacūliyā: *Āgrāyaṇīya-pūrva.*

3. For the Digambaras about the Puvva see Nemicandra, Gommaṭasāra Jīv. 343 ff.; 360 f.; Sakalakīrti, Tattv. 1, 106 f.; BHANDARKAR, Rep. 1883-84, S. 108 f. 395; Subhacandra, Angapannatti 219 f. 38 f.

4. Hemac. Abhidh. 2, 160 has *pūrvānuyoga* before *pūrva-gata*, the same Gommaṭas. Jīv. 360 *paḍhamaṇijoga* before *puvva.*

5. Sthān. 491b both *Dṛṣṭivāda* and *Dṛṣṭipāta*. The latter gives a good sense, too; "Collapse of refuted views."

discourses of their early predecessors not to be important any longer. It is more likely that their preservation appeared to be undesirable since the study of such disputes was apt to arouse heretical thoughts and activities. Some quotations from the Puvvas indeed have been preserved in the reports on the early schisms (§ 17) exclusively.

We have seen that our interpretation of the word *puvva-gaya* is, partly, based upon what both Samav. and Nandī say with regard to the contents of Anga 12. Though there can be no doubt that these are merely rhetorical, we must suppose that the names of the sections have been preserved just as faithfully as those of Anga 11. The minute descriptions of the subsections, on the other hand, seem to be fictitious, and all attempts of an interpretation are useless, since he who wrote down the alleged contents had the Diṭṭhivāya no longer before him.[1] No less fantastic, therefore, is the extent in *vatthu* or "subjects" attributed to the Puvva (to be seen also in Samav. 25a; 26b; 35b; 44b and in Ṭhāṇ.), to say nothing of their number of words. Their alleged size corresponds with their gradual loss, as referred to by the Śvetāmbaras and registered in the posthumous spiritual titles of *cauddasa-* (*coddasa-*), *dasa-*and even *nava-puvvi.* The last to know all 14 of them was Sthūlabhadra (§ 23). For it was he whom they were told by Bhadrabāhu upon the request of the Council of Pāṭaliputra, but he was forbidden to teach others more than ten (Par. 9, 110). After the seventh patriarch following Sthūlabhadra even these were lost. And that is why Mahāgiri and his successors up to Vajra are called *daśapūrvin.* So far the Śvetāmbaras; the Digambaras have eleven *daśapūrvadhārin* with other names. The last of them, Dharmasena, is reported to have died in 315 A.M.[2]

§39. The gradual loss of the Puvvas, which must have happened according as an apology in general or in the shape

1. The AUTHOR, Worte p. 5.—LEUMANN (VI. OC III, 2, p. 258) thought to see a close relation of a small Śaiva text with the Diṭṭhivāya, Parikamma 1. Possibly the so-called contents of the Diṭṭhiv. have been composed after the model of that kind of texts, since the real facts were no longer known, not vice versa, as LEUMANN believed.

2. Sakalakīrti, comp. BHANDARKAR loc. cit. S. 125.

taught by the Diṭṭhivāya was no longer necessary or desirable, has been copied by the Digambaras with regard to the Angas. They give the names of five patriarchs whom they say to have known 11 Angas, and of nine more who knew 10, 9, 8, 7 (?) and 1 Angas only, until eventually that too—the 1st—was lost. This report is based upon the Digambaras in very early times having become alienated from the collection of the Angas, from which it followed that they no longer acknowledged them as authoritative. Hence, for the Digambaras, the Angas of the Śvetāmbaras are younger productions, and when the latter give the number of words in them (Samav. 107 ff.; Nandi 209b ff.)[1], the former bring up other figures against them[2]. To a certain degree it is justified to look upon the Angas as being of a younger age, since they have not come down to us in their original shape. This follows from comparing their present state with tradition and subjecting it to a critical view. As the saying goes, new wine has been poured into old bags. The method was to form a unit out of parts and fragments, to supply lost portions and even works, and, in many cases, to arrange the text suitably. It is probable that all this was the result of two councils,[4] the one taking place at Mathurā, the other at Valabhī (Kathiawar), and both presided by Skandila and Nāgārjuna respectively. In the course of time the former must have gained the upper hand, for, when in one more Valabhī council Devarddhi undertook to lay down the wording of the text definitely, he gave the Nāgārjunīya pāṭhas not the first but the second place, even though he stood in the *paramparā* of their originator (s. b.), Devarddhi is reported to have got copies of the holy works multiplied with a view to provide with them as many communities as possible. Memorial verses serve to faci-

1. Up to Anga 4 the figure is doubled, Anga 5 has 84,000 words (a favourite figure), and the rest *saṃkhijja* words (see § 21).

2. Gommaṭ. Jiv. 357 ff.; Suyakkh. 9 ff.; Tattv. 1, 75 ff. ; Angap. 15 ff.; Comp. also JAINI, Outlines p. 135 ff.

3. The AUTHOR, Worte p. 11 ff.

4. We here follow KAPADIA p. 61 ff. who gives the sources. BHANDARKAR, Rep. 1883-84, p. 128; JACOBI, Kalpasūtra p. 117 and SBE 22 294 can be added.

litate the survey of the contents for the monk students. This, of course, had to be preceded by collecting the works within reach.[1] Here we have the origin of the Canon. This event took place, according to Jiṇac. § 148, in 980 or 993 A.V.

§ 40. Nandī 202a, 153b; Aṇuog, 6a; Pakkhiya-S. 61b divide the substance of the teaching into *anga-paviṭṭha* and *aṇanga-p.* or *angabāhira*. While history, as we have seen, is concerned with the Angas only, we here learn that there were more works in existence. This is no wonder since the Angas do not include any regulated prescriptions for the monks' discipline which must have been observed from early times onward. Its germ are the 6 *āvassaya* (§ 151), i.e. formulae for daily recital, the knowledge of which was, indeed, "indispensable". They were the starting point of discipline and, therefore, alone are opposed to all other *aṇanga-paviṭṭha* or *āvassaya-vairitta*. These again are divided into *kāliya* and *ukkāliya*, i.e. into those that are to be learnt within certain hours devoted to study (§ 150) and into those that are not. The *kāliya*-list is an extension of what is prescribed to the monk in Vav. 10, 20 ff. and elsewhere. In a certain way, the *ukkāliya*-list runs on parallel lines with it. In either list the titles partly are unica, since the works themselves do not exist any longer or at least did not reappear as yet, partly they belong to works incorporated into the Canon or are à la suite of it, and partly they are mere sections of both the last named kinds. Let us presuppose that the authors of the Vav. list (which attributes certain texts to certain years) must have been guided by paedagogic points of view, but we are unable to recognise them in the succession of the texts. Still this succession has furnished a basis for the grouping in the Canon. For among the Uvangas and Paiṇṇas some texts appear one after the other in the same order as they do in their quality as *ukkāliya* subjects nos. 5-8 and 11-15.[2]

This is the opportunity for introducing the canonical sections following the Angas, viz.: the Uvangas, Paiṇṇas, Cheya-

1. Comp. JACOBI, Kalpasūtra p. 114 ff.; p. 15ff.; SBE 22, XXXVIIff.
2. Ind. Stud. 17, 13 ff.

and Mūla-suttas, of which only the first name seems to be old. To judge[1] from its appearance in the introduction to Uvangas 8-12 there was a time when no more than just these Uvangas were called by this name, i.e. "secondary Angas" because of their being closely related in contents and style with Angas 8, 9 and 11[2]. Later on out of those and other texts (all of which may be found among the *aṇanga-paviṭṭha*) there was a group formed by imitation of the 12 Angas not only as to numbering but as to its inner structure as well. For just as the Anga group starts with two works mostly composed in a high poetical and prosaic style (Bambhac. and Gāhāsolasaga) and then proceeds with dogmatical ones (Ṭhāṇa and Samav.) followed by minor legendary accounts (Uvās. etc.), so does the Uvanga section[3], as can be seen in the course of this chapter. Apart from the Angas, the Uvangas are the only section of a stationary size. Most various is the number of the Paiṇṇas or "mixed text". But the different lists betray a nucleus formed by Paiṇṇas of a disciplinary character, and among these we find a group of ten which are the most frequently quoted.[4] The various classes of the Āgama seem to have been arranged according to the diminishing number of their members, for, historically, the Cheyasuttas ought to have preceded the Paiṇṇas. The latter dwell upon the monks' practice in more or less broad gāhā treatises, that is to say, in a remarkably imitative way, while among the Cheyasuttas (of which there are 5-7) we have the most ancient summaries of discipline. The name of this group appears as *cheya-ggantha* in Āv. 8,55 and certainly means the punishment of *cheya*, i.e. the shortening of either a monk's or a nun's seniority. And it is this seniority upon which the communal life of either is based. When seniority is dropped altogether this is called *mūla* and, indeed, the culprit then must start from the "root". But this is the situation of novices, too,

1. The AUTHOR, Worte p. 8 .

2. Possibly also Anga 10 which once looked different from the one we have before us to-day (§ 46).

3. The AUTHOR, Worte p. 8.—But it is a fiction held by Jambūdv. Ib and others that the Angas and Uvangas bearing the same number were related with each other.

4. Comp. v. KAMPTZ, Sterbefasten p. 5 ff.

and it is no more than logical to interpret the name of Mūlasutta in this direction on account of their clearly being selections and treatises about fundamental subjects for the instruction of young monks and nuns. From this point of view we understand why the diminuation mentioned above is interrupted and why its mechanical principle is replaced by a methodical one[1]. For in the solemn list the Mūlasuttas are preceded by two propaedeutic works, viz. Nandī and Aṇuogadārā. In both of them the theory of knowledge is treated in the style of the time. The number of the Āgamas is 45 with the Śvetāmbaras, but 13 of them are rejected by the Sthānakvāsī, their puritan offshoot mentioned before[2] (§ 32). As to the Digambaras, it was already said that the Angas are missing there on account of their gradual passing into oblivion. This applies to the other texts, too. Some of them were lodged in their lists of lost works[3]: The 5 Pariyammas of the Diṭṭhivāya are equated with 5 Pannattis, four of which we know as Uvangas, whereas the 5 Cūliyās are said to teaeh different kinds of sorceries. Among the so-called Paiṇṇayas of the Angabāhirayas current with the Digambaras we find the names of Śvetāmbara Paiṇṇa-, Cheya-, and Mūla-texts.

§41. We now proceed to give the common survey of the extant Svetambara Canon (*āgama*, *siddhanta*). *Angas*: 1. Āyāra (quoted as Bambhacerāiṃ, Cūlāo, Bhāvaṇā, Vimutti), 2. Sūyagaḍa, 3. Ṭhāṇa, 4. Samavāya, 5. Viyāhapannatti, 6. Nāyādhammakahāo (quoted as Nāya and Dhammakahāo,), 7. Uvāsagadasāo, 8. Antagaḍadasāo, 9. Aṇuttarovāiyadasāo, 10. Paṇhāvāgaraṇāiṃ, 11. Vivāgasuya. *Uvangas*: 1. Rāyapaseṇaijja,[4] 2. Uvavāiya (quoted as Samosaraṇa and Uvavāiya), 3. Jīvābhigama, 4. Pannavaṇā, 5. Sūrapannatti, 6. Jambuddīvapannatti, 7. Candapannatti, 8. Nirayāvaliyāo. 9. Kappavaḍiṃsiyāo, 10. Pupphiyāo, 11. Pupphacūlāo, 12. Vaṇhidasāo. *Paiṇṇas*. Causaraṇa, Āurapaccakkhāṇa, Bhattaparinnā, Saṃthāra, Mahāpaccakkhāṇa, Candāvijjhaya, Gaṇivijjā, Tandulaveyāliya,

1. The AUTHOR, Worte p. 1.

2. "Seeker", Notes (§ 32) p.90. The AUTHOR, Mahānis. p. 100 must be corrected.

3. Gommatas, Jiv. 360. f., 366 f.

4. The AUTHOR, Worte p. VIII to be corrected.

Devindatthaya, Vīratthaya and others. *Cheyasuttas*: Āyāradasāo (Dasā 8, "Kalpasūtra"=Jiṇacariya, Therāvalī, Pajjosavaṇā-kappa; Dasā 10=Āyāiṭṭhāṇa), Kappa, Vavahāra, Nisīha, Mahā-nisīha, Pancakappa, Jīyakappa. *Nandī*, *Aṇuogadārā*. *Mūlasutta*: Uttarajjhāyā, Āvassayanijjutti, Dasaveyāliya, Piṇḍanijjutti, Ohanijjutti. The homogeneity which, as we are led to assume, unites these titles is often merely an apparent one. Nearly all old and various later canonical works are composed of parts which frequently are rather incongruent, as may be seen from the brackets given above. Apart from such cases striking the eye there are others where parts and particles of some chapters, on the ground of higher criticism, can be connected in a new manner.

§42. Thus, when we replace the mechanical arrangement just given by a critical one, the result is as follows.[1] Apart from the āvassaya formulae the most ancient style presents itself in the Āyāra, Sūy., the Utt., the old Cheyasuttas, the Isibhā-siyāiṃ, and in portions of the Dasaveyāliya. Significant are old grammatical forms, the triṣṭubh, jagatī, vaitālīya, and aupacchandasaka metres, a primitive form of the Āryā,[2] the opening formula *suyaṃ me*, *āusaṃ*, etc., the concluding one *ti bemi*, and, of course, the subjects, especially so far as they are formed by the will of self-preservation and the fundaments of the order. A metrical investigation made by JACOBI, as was said before, resulted in surmising the origin of the most ancient texts at about the end of the 4th and the beginning of the 3rd century B.C. It hardly needs to be mentioned that the characteristics referred to are distributed differently upon the individual texts. The younger parts of the Canon show the younger grammatical forms, the common Āryā taking the place of the Śloka, and partly in them a symmetrical arrangement of subjects. This can be observed in most Paiṇṇas and in the Nijjuttis among the Mūlasuttas which are not far from the commentaries bearing the same name (§ 43). A good number of texts join in groups thus unveiling the peculiar taste of the author's times and later on

1. The AUTHOR, Worte, p. 2 ff.

2. Āyār. II 9; Sūy. I, 4 (see ALSDORF Ind. Ir. J. 2, 259 ff.); Utt. 8, comp. JACOBI ZDMG 38, 590 ff.; LEUMANN Z I I 7, 160-162.

becoming a mere habit. Considering the rôle the figure 10 plays in the titles, we speak of *dasā-texts*. In the second half of the Angas we come across clichés of stories called *vagga*, and thus we may sum up Dhammak., Antag., Aṇutt. and Uvanga 8-12 as *vagga-texts*. In Ṭhāṇ. and Samav. conceptions and concrete subjects occurring in the teaching have been arranged according to number just as has been the case with details from discipline taught in the Āyāradasāo and some other texts by the *therā bhagavanto*, so that we are entitled to speak of *category-texts*. Further, there is the veḍha metre, the locus classicus of which are Samos. and Jiṇac. They are the prototype for numberless passages in tne later Angas, the Uvangas and the Āyāradasāo, passages meant to introduce or to characterise a scene or an object. Here catchwords indicating the opening and the ending of the passage to be supplied served the purpose. Hence we find many artificial *veḍha-texts* next to the genuine ones mentioned to which we have to add Anga 10, 6 and 4 sections in Jambudd. The same distinction applies to the case of the *dialogue-texts*. On the one hand we have Viy. alone. It is true that here already question and reply are conventional, but the general impression is that of true life thanks to the variety of questioning individuals as well as to personal traits in Mahāvīra's answers. At any rate, the Viy. is the prototype for the various artificial dialogues where the appearance of antiquity was combined with methodical fitness. The latter, above all, seemed necessary for the systematical explanations in the Uvangas. Their typical name is *pannatti*.

§43. The commentaries on the canonical texts exhibit the usual preferences and defects of scholastic literature, i.e. they represent the apprehensions of their time. We cannot neglect them, though, frequently, we are not in a position to follow them. Most popular among them are, of course, the Sanskrit explanations (*ṭīkā*, *vivaraṇa*, *vṛtti*) composed, as regards the Angas and Uvangas, by the classical scholars Śīlānka or Śīlācārya, who concluded his Ācāraṭīkā in Śaka 798=872 A.D., Abhayadeva, who wrote in s. 1135 or 1139, and Malayagiri, who composed his Sanskrit Grammar between s. 1200 and 1230[1]. These great

1. KIELHORN NGW Gott. 1892, 318-327; PAṬHAK ABHI 1, 7.

works mark the end of a long development; what follows them (*dīpikā* or *avacūri*[1]) is insignificant and mostly no longer independent. The personalities mentioned are preceded by Haribhadra who, among various other scholarly works, wrote the Nandī-ànd Āvaśyakaṭīkā. As has been proved by JINAVIJAYA[2] he belongs to the middle of the 8th century. His epoch is significant by its definitely turning away from the Prakrit commentaries in favour of such in Sanskrit. The development of the former at that time had reached the stage of the *cuṇṇis*. A *cuṇṇi* is a composition in prose[3] of a kind wherein a change of language announces itself by a more or less intensive penetration of Sanskrit words and phrases into Prakrit. The object of the explanation is not confined to the canonical text, the Sutta, but also refers to the foregoing commentary, the Bhāsa or the Nijjutti. A *Bhāsa* is in metres and of a considerable length. Comprising thousands of Gāhās it far surpasses each Cuṇṇi, the name of which —Sanskrit: *cūrṇi*—dispersion[4]—is not badly chosen when compared with the block called *bhāsa*.[5] This again is the Nijjutti. for us the Nijjutti (*nirvyukti*[6]) is the earliest tangible stage in the Śvetāmbara commentaries, but itself it is the *gāhā*-skeleton for the body of prose explanations which had existed long before and were the ancestors of the material exhibited in a Cuṇṇi. The usual size of a Nijjutti, as we know it, is relatively small (a few hundred gāhās), but even there Bhāsa verses have been inserted. As long as such insertions were limited, the title of Nijjutti remained, in which case we find, in the course of time, a Nijjutti followed by a *Cuṇṇi*. But when the size of the latter had swollen

1. Often, but wrongly, *avacūrṇi*.

2. JACOBI, Samarāiccakahā p 1 ff. on account of JINAVIJAYA's results exposed in Sanskrit and published Poona 1919 under the title the Date of Haribhadra Sūri. Thus LEUMANN's calculation ZDMG 43,349 (s. 904) is obsolete now.

3. Wrongly called metrical by CHARPENTIER Utt. p. 52.

4. The word is not confined to the Svetāmbaras nor even to the Jains. We find it, though apparently in a different meaning, in the Śivajnānabodha of the Shivaites, see SCHOMERUS, Der Çaiva-Siddhānta p. 26. Here *cūrṇikā*, *vārttika*, and *udāharaṇa* are rendered as "assertion., argument, example".

5. *bhāsa* and *cuṇṇi* were confounded by JACOBI, Sthav. (2nd ed.) p. VI.

6. WEBER, Ind. Stud. 17, 57. CHARPENTIER, Utt. S. 48.

up owing to an extraordinary number of Bhāsa verses, it was they that gave the whole work its title.[1] Both Bhāsa and Cuṇṇi do not furnish much information about individual words. What they do have to say is dictated by abstracts and is very schematical to the degree that we seldom find a connection with the Sūtra.[2] Instead, their importance as to history of thought and of literature will be great, when one day all of them will be accessible and subjected to scholarly study.

The Nijjuttis are looked upon as works composed by Bhadrabāhu, but they are centuries later than the leader of the Order who bore this name in the 3rd century B.C. (§ 23. 26) as is proved a.o. by their being a domain of the common gāhā which was far from being in use at that time.[3] LEUMANN holds that the collection of Nijjuttis to be mentioned presently, came into existence about 80 A.D.[4] "It follows that 'Bhadrabāhu' is an author's name of the kind we meet with in India in great number (e.g. in law-books and many other literary products".[5] The author of Āv. 2, 5, a great scholar, sees his task in writing a Nijjutti on *Āvass.*, *Dasav.*, *Utt.*, *Āyār.*, *Sūy.*, *Dasāo*, Kappa, Vav., Sūrap., and Isibhāsiyāiṃ. Those belonging to the works in *italics* are at hand and have been printed with the exception of the Utt.-and Dasā-nijjuttis. The printed Bhāsas will be registered below. Some Cuṇṇis are—or were—independent of Bhāsas, they partly belong to canonical works, a.o.to Viy., Jiv., Pannav., partly to non-canonical ones as Pakkh. and Jīyakappa. But we must not forget that the word *cūrṇi* in Sanskrit commentaries may denote the famous Āvassayacuṇṇi.

The authors of ṭikās and vṛttis often register a different reading (*pāṭhāntara*, *vācanā'ntara* or sim.), and the same occurs in the Cuṇṇis (*paḍhijjai ya*). Such variants, partly considerable in

1. LEUMANN, Übersicht 15 b.

2. Comp. Dasav.-nijj. with Dasav. 4 (LEUMANN ZDMG 46, 587 f.).

3. CHARPENTIER Utt. p. 49 wrongly finds fault with the metrics of the Bhāsas and Nijjuttis. On the contrary, their authors have sacrificed grammar in favour of metrical correctness.

4. Übersicht, p. 28 b.

5. Ib. p. 23 b. JACOBI, Sthav. (2nd ed.) p. VI calls the author a namesake of the 6th patriarch.

size, in Āyār., Sūy. and Utt. are attributed to the Nāgajjuṇijja or Nāgārjunīya (s. a.) who sometimes are called *bhadanta* or *sakkhiṇo*[1] in a friendly or respectful manner. The explanation acc. to CHARPENTIER[2] is that the authors of those commentaries were friends to Devarddhi, the editor of the Āgama who was a *paramparā-guru* of Nāgārjuna[3]. From this it follows that this time was later than the end of the 5th century A.D. LEUMANN[4] dates the Āvassayacuṇṇi from about 600 to 650 A.D.

§44. We now proceed to render a survey of the canonical works and some more closely related to the Siddhānta. In some respect our survey has to be elastic in that not all details of the contents can be given. The general praise of the mendicant's life, for instance, could be, in many cases, omitted as being evident. On the other hand, care has been taken to enable the reader to find out subjects that should interest him, especially since it was impossible to incorporate all details into the description contained in chapters IV to VII.

The Angas

§45. Anga 1-5. 1. *Āyāra*. 2. *Suyakkhandha*: 9 (8) Bambhaceräiṃ and 4 Cūlāo. The 6th chapter once was followed by a seventh called Mahāparinnā which was lost. Both in his edition and his translation (s. b.) the AUTHOR undertook to solve many problems we find ourselves confronted with in the Bambh. by its mixing prose and verses or either by the fragments of such ones.[5] The subjects in chapters 1-6 and 8 are Ahiṃsā, the avoidance of weakness and relapsing, and, on the other hand, endurance in hardships. The last chapter (9) offers in ancient Āryās a vivid sketch of Mahāvīra's early career as an ascetic. What was begun here was continued in the 4 Cūlās. In the first we find

1. The AUTHOR, Ācār. p. VIII.
2. Utt. p. 53.
3. See ante.—PANIKKAR (Indo-Asian Culture 5, 46) attributes the predicate of *bhadanta* to the great Buddhist philosopher Nāgārjuna.
4. Übersicht p. IV b.
5. Comp. the AUTHOR, Worte p. 15 ff. The commentators do not see metrical portions amidst those in prose. It follows that Jīv. 259 a the Satthaparinnā (=Āyār. I, 1) is called *acchando-baddhā*.

detailed prescriptions for the begging for alms, wandering, speech, the way how to ask for garments and alms-bowl, and such concerning the question of residence; in the second Cūlā we have prescriptions regarding ascetic postures and study, easing nature, and indifference towards external influences including favours and nursing. These chapters have been arranged according to the diminishing number of their sections, as is done in Sūyagaḍa I. The third Cūlā is called Bhāvaṇā after the instructions for the right understanding (*bhāvaṇā*) of the 5 Great Vows which in their turn form the climax of Jain ethics and as such are rightly annexed to the above stated topics. But, as to quantity, by far the greatest space of this Cūlā is devoted to Mahāvīra's biography up to his leaving the worldly life. Since right conduct on the ground of the vows will lead to salvation, "Vimutti" is treated in the 6th Cūlā. For the Nisīha as once having formed a further part of the Āyāra see § 51.

Comm. : Nijjutti; Cuṇṇi[1] by Gandhahastin (printed); Ṭīkā by Śīlānka (concluded in Saka 798); Dīpikā by Jinahaṃsa. Ed.[2]: ĀS (along with Nijj., Ṭīkā, and Dīpikā, C. s. 1936.—The Āyāraṃga Sutta of the Çvetāmbara Jains. Ed. by Hermann JACOBI. (Pali Text Society.) Lo. 1882.[3]—Ācārāṅga-Sūtra. Erster Śrutaskandha. Text, Analyse and Glossar von Walther SCHUBRING. L. 1910. Rev.: JACOBI, Archiv. f. Religionswiss. 18. 283 ff. Nāgarī transcr. Jaina-Sāhitya-Saṃśodhaka-Gr.-M., Poona 1924.—Āg.S. (along with the Ṭīkā), Bo. 1916. —1. *suyakkh.*: Bo. 1916.—*Transl.*: (Engl.) by JACOBI SBE 22, Oxford 1884.—The Bambhac. by SCHUBRING in: Worte Mahāvīras, Göttingen 1926, p. 66 ff. Rev.: LEUMANN Z I I 7, 157-162.

1. As to the Cuṇṇis in general, see KAPADIA, History p. 190 ff. As far as they have been printed, they, with few exceptions, have not come into the hands of Western scholars. Those the AUTHOR has seen and used, unfortunately are lacking any hint as to editor, among whom, as we understand, is ĀNANDASĀGARA Sūri, place and year, to say nothing of interpretation.

2. As to prints of the complete Canon the reader is referred to § 4. These prints are mentioned neither here nor on the following pages.

3. The second suyakkhandha (p. 49ff.) seems to have been printed without any revision on the part of the editor.

2. *Sūyagaḍa*. In Sanskrit this name is reflected as Sūtrakṛtānga, sporadically even as Sūtrakṛdanga.[1] But, as a matter of fact, *sūtra* in Ardhamāgadhī appears in the form of *sutta* exclusively.[2] Possibly we have *sūcī=dṛṣṭi*, Pkt. *sūi=sūya*[3]. At any rate the name is taken from the discussions in Sūy. I 12, II 1. 5-7 of heretic systems and views. 2 *suyakkhandha*: Gāhāsolasaga and Mahajjhayaṇāṇi. The Gāhāsol. consists of 15 metrical chapters arranged in the manner mentioned in Āyāra. Quite contrary to its title (*gāhā*) the 16th chapter is in prose devoted to Mahāvīra explaining the terms of *māhaṇa, samaṇa-bhikkhu,* and *niggantha.* Old Āryās appear in I 4 as they do in Bambh. 9 and Utt. 8. In I 5 we are given an elaborate description of the hells and the tortures therein, 2 uddesa. The 7 Mahajjh., "great chapters", are indeed actually four big ones on prose, the following two are in verse, and the last is in prose again. As to contents see above. But we specially mention II 2 Kiriyaṭṭhāṇa, forms of activity; 3. Āhāraparinnā, a description of all forms of life and of their origin, as "told in olden ages" (*pur' akkhāya*); 4 Paccakkhāṇakiriyā, a discussion on guilt accumulated either consciously or unconsciously.

Comm.: Nijjutti; Cuṇṇi (printed); Ṭīkā by Śīlānka; Dipikā, by Harṣakula.—*Ed.*: ĀS 2 along with Nijj., Ṭīkā, and Dīpikā, Bo. s. 1936.—Āg. S., with Ṭīkā, Bo. 1917.—AMP 5, with Nijj., by P. L. VAIDYA, Poona 1928. Ed. with Guj. transl. by Muni MĀNEK, Surat 1922.—Some separate prints of I 6, Mahāvīrathui.—*Transl.*: (Engl.) by JACOBI SBE 45, Oxford 1895; 7 chapters by SCHUBRING in: Worte Mahāvīras, Göttingen 1926 (see above).—Detailed Studies: GHATAGE IHQ. 12, 270-281, ALSDORF (Itthīparinnā, I 4).

3. *Ṭhāṇa*. A list of dogmatic topics which can be grouped in 1-10 categories, cases or possibilities (*ṭhāṇa*). But for the cosmographical dates placed at the end of each chapter (section),

1. Comp. BARNETT, BM (1908) s.v.

2. Kappasūya in PISCHEL, Gr. § 19 etc.=Kalpasūtra is a mere fiction.

3. Samav. 109 b; *Sūyagaḍe ṇaṃ sa-samayā sūijjanti* etc.=*sūcyante* Abhay.—Gommaṭas. Jīv. 355 and Brahma Hemacandra, Śrutaskhandha 10 have Suddagaḍa.

no leading principle is recognizable. Many categories appear in other canonical texts, whereas other ones are not to be found elsewhere. Ṭhāṇa as well as Samavāya (s. b.) refer to texts that got lost, and those we still possess are, partly, listed as having other sections.

Comm. : Vṛtti by Abhayadeva.—*Ed.* (along with the Vṛtti): Ās 3, Ben. 1880.—Āg. S., 1. 2. Bo. 1918-20.

4. *Samavāya.* A supplement of, and a continuation to, Ṭhāṇa according to groups of 1 up to 10^{14} (*sāgarovama-koḍākoḍī*) objects. The last third of Samav. is an appendix and in general describes the *duvālas' anga gaṇi-piḍaga.* In one further appendix the qualities of all beings are described in query and reply. A third appendix, in common Gāhās, shows the dates of the spiritual and (temporal) heroes. There is no doubt whatever that these appendices found their place in the Samav. on account of their numberings.

Comm.: Vṛtti by Abhayadeva. —*Ed.* (along with the Vṛtti): ĀS 4, Ben. 1880.—Āg. S., Bo. 1918.

5. *Viyāhapaṁnatti.* This is the true old name frequently perverted to Vivāhap. as which PISCHEL unfortunately quotes it in his grammar. The later title of Bhagavaī is no more than an adjective occasionally attributed to Āyāra and Sūyagaḍa likewise.[1] What we have before us is a "proclamation of explanations" rendered by Mahāvīra as an answer to individual questions asked by disciples and, by far in most cases, directed to Goyama. 41 *saya* of which 1-20 seem to form the germ of the whole, and to which 25 can be added. *Saya* "one hundred" aptly means a great number of interviews taking place at different places and not interconnected by a distinct thread of thought. Their sequence is frequently merely superficial and similar to what can be stated in the Bambhacerāiṃ. Apart from the germ thus characterized, sayas 24 and 30 as such and 21-23 (subdivided into *vagga*, etc.), 26-29, 31 and 32, 33 and 34, 35-40 form groups of uniform contents. Frequent references to other works, especially so to Pannavaṇā and Jīvābhigama, by which the preceding or subsequent topics are either introduced

1. Comp. Samav. 92 a, Āyāranijjutti, 1, Sūyagaḍa-nijj. 1.

or explained. No other texts furnished a picture of Mahāvīra's character and activities as distinct as that of the Viy. in spite of the style being mostly conventional.

To analyse the whole Viy. would go beyond the frame of this book. Its motley character will become sufficiently clear in a specimen, for which we have chosen saya 2.

Udd. 1.—1 (109 a). Breathing. 2 (110 .b). A *madāi niyaṇṭha* (§ 154). 3(112 a.). The scene: Chittapalāsaya near Kayangalā. The Brahman monk Khandaga Kaccāyaṇa, a disciple of Saddabhāli, is instructed by Mahāvīra. On his part, Kh. had no reply to the questions of the layman Pingalaga of Vesālī. The subjects are: the resp. finiteness and infiniteness of the world, the soul, *siddhi* and *siddha*; unwisely and wisely dying; Kh.'s conversion, spiritual career, fasting to death and post-existences.—*Udd.* 2. (129a.). The 7 *samugghāya* (§ 89): reference to Pannav. 36.—*Udd.* 3 (130 a). The 7 regions: ref. to Jīv. 3, 1. 2.—*Udd.* 4 (131 a). The 5 senses: ref. to Pannav. 15.—*Udd.* 5. 1 (131b). Against *annautthiya*: gods and goddesses in their mutual relations; the soul has one gender exclusively. 2(133a). Embryology. 3. (133b). The embryo is product (*putta*) as well as cause. 4. (133b). Sexual intercourse is lack of self discipline (*saṃjama*). 5(134b). The scene: Pupphavaī near Tungiyā. Some Pārśva teachers (names) are teaching some laymen about the reward for self-discipline, ascetics, karma and worldliness (*sangiyā*). Mahāvīra approves of them in every respect. 6 (140b). The reward for having served a true (*tahā-rūva*) *samaṇa* or *māhaṇa* by degrees will lead to *siddhi*. 7 (142a) Against *annautthiya*: an explanation as to how a hot spring comes into existence.—*Udd.* 6 (142a). The speech: ref. to Pannav. 11.—*Udd.* 7 (142b). The regions of the gods: ref. to Pannav. 2 and Jīv.3, 4. 2.—*Udd.* 8 (144a). The *sabhā* of the god Camara.—*Udd.* 9 (146a). Samayakhetta.—*Udd.* 10 1 (147b). The Fundamental Facts.

Comm.: Vṛtti by Abhayadeva.—*Ed.* (along with the vṛtti): ĀS 5, Ben. s. 1938.—Āg. S. 1-3, Bo. 1918-21.—Both text and vṛtti transl. into Gujarātī by BECHARDĀS, saya 1-6, Ahm. ca. 1927. WEBER, see § 2.

§46. Anga 6-11. 6. *Nāyādhammakahāo.* This title is a

dvandva with the *a* lengthened at the end of the first member, comp. Anga 10. WEBER was wrong in taking the name as Jnātṛdharmakathā. Gommatasāra, Jīv. 355, speaks of Nāhassa Dhammakahā. *nāya* (*jnāta*) acc. to Ṭhāṇ. 253b and Dasav. nijj. 51-85 is a story serving as an example, while *dhamma-kahā* means a sermon or lecture. Of the 2 *suyakkhandha* the first contains the *nāyāiṃ*, whereas the second is said to be the *dhamma-kahāo*. But, actually, there is no more than 1 *kathā* multiplied over 200 times, with various places and names. This feature, frequent in the Siddhanta, must be taken as an attempt to attain completeness where materials were not at hand. In the case of Nāy. the great number of repetitions may reflect an intention of giving the second suy. a similar size as had the first. Prose along with Veḍhas in most of the *nāya*. In the following lines no reader will expect more than the skeleton.

1. *suyakkhandha*. 1. Ukkhitta. Intending to become a monk Prince Meha in his resolution is strengthened by Mahāvīra telling him how, in a previous existence, he himself, being a strong elephant, *patiently* protected a hare seeking refuge below his own lifted foot. 2. Saṃghaḍaga. Dhamma, a merchant, being thrown into jail and chained together with the murderer of his little son, *kindly* shares his meal with him. 3. Aṇḍa. Sāgaradatta impatiently breaks an egg hatched by a peacock, while Jinadatta *patiently* waits until it is hatched out. 4. Kumma. One turtle is killed by a jackal because it exposed itself to the danger, another one, being *cautious*, remained unhurt in its shell, since it waited until the beast had gone. 5. Selaga. King Selaga, converted to monkhood by Suya, a disciple of Ariṭṭhaṇemi, had grown weak owing to the hardships, but was *strengthened* by the encouragement given him by Panthaga, his former minister. 6. Tumba. A gourd cased with eight layers of clay will sink to the bottom when thrown into water, but will rise to the surface when the clay has dissolved. Just so the soul when *released* from its Karman burden will rush up from Saṃsāra to the place of the Siddhas. 7. Rohiṇī, Rohiṇī, in contrast to her four careless sisters, *shrewdly* sows and cultivates 5 corns of rice (cp. Matthews chap. 25; Luke 19). 8. Princess Mallī, by means of drast'c simile contrasting beautiful

features and ugly intestines, *sets right* six suitors who thereupon take the vows (§ 15). 9. Māyandi. M's. son, Jiṇapāliya, *firmly* resists the temptations of the cruel goddess of Rayaṇadīva, while Jiṇarakkhiya, his brother, yields to them and perishes miserably. 10. Candimā. The waning moon compared with the fickle monk, the waxing with the *persevering* one. 11. Dāvaddeva. Just as the *dāvaddava* trees growing on the ocean shore are strengthened by land and sea-winds (*dīviccaga* and *sāmuddaga*) so are *true* monks exposed to praise and blame. 12. Udaga. Matter is subject to change, as is demonstrated to King Jiyasatta by his minister Subuddhi by means of putrid water cleared to purity by seven times filtering. This method, as is explained by Subuddhi, was taught by the Jina, and thus *cleverly* the king's interest is roused for the Creed which eventually leads him to salvation. 13. Maṇḍukka. Nanda, a layman, is reborn as a frog in a pond he had made for the general amusement of his fellow citizens. *Feeling his guilt* now he goes on a pilgrimage to see Mahāvīra, but on his way he is injured by a horse and dies saying "*namo tthu ṇaṃ*", whereupon he becomes a god. 14. Teyalī. Poṭṭilā, wife of minister Teyaliputta, had innocently lost her husband's affection and became a nun to be reborn as god Poṭṭila. As such she preaches him the Teaching , as has been stipulated previously, but it is not before he has lost his high position that she is successful in making him accept it. 15. Nandiphala. Some travellers, though warned by their guides, rest in the pleasant shadow of *nandi* trees and feed on their poisonous fruits so that they perish; others *avoid* both shadow and fruits and thus remain healthy and alive. 16. Avarakankā. A monk, Dhammarui, eats poisonous alms thus *sacrificing* rather *himself* than exposing to certain death ants which, as he saw, are dying when tasting them. Nāgasirī, who had provided the alms, is stricken with poverty and illness, and, finding no husband, in her next life becomes a nun, Sukumāliyā, thereupon a courtesan in heaven, then Princess Dovaī, who in her svayaṃvara chooses the 5 Pāṇḍavas. She is raped by King Paumaṇābha of Avarakankā, but Vāsudeva Kaṇha defeats him and returns her to her five husbands. Four of them and Dovai himself then join the Order. 17. Āinna. Some wild horses (*āinna*) ignorantly fall into the trap laid out for them and get caught, while others which are *clever* remain free. 18. Suṃsumā. S., the daughter of a merchant, was raped and killed by a brigand, called Cilāya. Her father and his sons discover her body and eat of it from want of food. Dhanna, her father, later becomes a monk. 19. Puṇḍarīya. P., a layman, is a lay king, succeeds in persuading his younger brother Kaṇḍarīya to remain firm in his monkhood, though fickleness and illness have befallen him. On the next occasion, however, he is not equally successful and the two brothers change places, the one taking the other's position, but K. dies soon after.

The 2nd *suyakkhandha* has 10 *vagga*, which in pairs consist of 5. 54. 32. 4. 8 *ajjhayaṇa*. This comes up to 206 ajjh. But no more than the 1st *kahā* of the 1st *vagga* (247a) was completed. With names and places changed it serves as a cliché for the whole remaining part (250b). Having heard Pāsa's sermon, Kālī takes the vows with a certain nun, Pupphacūlā, as her superior. But she cannot bring herself to desist from tending her body as she is demanded to do, and so she goes her own way. Hence she is not granted salvation, and since her self-castigation fails to reach the full mark she is reborn as the goddess Kālī. When as such she approaches Mahāvīra respectfully, he gives Goyama an account of her past and her future.

Comm.: Vṛtti by Abhayadeva. —*Ed.* (along with the vṛtti) AS 6, C. 1877.—Āg. S., Bo. 1919.—Paul STEINTHAL, Specimen der Nāyādhammakahā. (Thesis.) Berlin 1881. The text goes on up to fol. 52a of the Āg. S.-ed. Notes and glossary have been added.—Nāyas 1, 16 and 14 were treated by LEUMANN VI OC III, 2. p. 539 ff.; all the Nāyas by W. HÜTTEMANN, Die Jnāta-Erzählungen im sechsten Anga . . . (Thesis.) Strassburg 1907.

7. *Uvāsagadasāo*. 10 *ajjhayaṇa* concerning pious laymen in Mahāvīra's time. In the title we should expect *dasā*, comp. the next Anga. 1. Āṇanda and his wife take the Minor vows. Mahāvīra speaks about the principal offences against the same. He further says that even laymen can obtain *ohi-nāṇa*. 2. A god

tries to intimidate Kāmakesa, but fails. 3. Culaṇīpiyā does not allow his meditations being disturbed though a god kills his three sons, but he drives away the ogre who threatens his mother. Yet he ought not to have interrupted his meditation. 4. 5. The same about Surādeva and Cullasayaga with the only difference that it is their health and property (resp.) that are endangered. 6. Kuṇḍakoliya defends his creed against a god who is an adherent of Gosāla. 7. Both Mahāvīra and Gosāla vie with each other in winning the Ājīviya Saddālaputta and his wife. The latter is threatened by a god as was the mother of Culaṇīpiyā. 8. Mahāsaga when fasting refuses to be seduced by his wife and prophesies her death and subsequent abode in hell. His fault was, so says Mahāvīra, that he gave her a reply at all. 9.10 are repetitions of 1 with the names of Nandiṇīpiyā and Sālihīpiyā.

Comm.: Vivaraṇa by Abhayadeva.—Ed. (all along with the Viv.): ĀS 7, C. 1977.—Āg. S., Bo. 1919.—Bo. 1895.—The Uvās. or the religious profession of an Uvāsaga. . . ed. (Vol. 2: trans.) by A. F. Rudolf HOERNLE. (Bibliotheca Indica.) C. 1888-90. Rev. by LEUMANN WZKM 3, 329-350; GRIERSON IA 16, 78-80; revised ed. by P. L. VAIDYA, Poona 1930, rev. by the AUTHOR, OLZ 1931, 1082 ff.

8. *Antagaḍadasāo*. Legends partly dating from the time of Ariṭṭhaṇemi and dealing with individuals who "put an end to existence" (though this does not apply to the first story). *dasāo* in the title rightly (comp. Anga 7) means groups of 10, as are formed by 4 chapters out of 8. The chapters are called *vagga* and contain original legends (I-VIII) and such running parallel to them, but the former have been distributed unequally among the *vagga*. As to disposition and contents the Antag. are closely related to Anga 9. In the time of Ṭhāṇa 506a, where the chapters of both Angas are enumerated, the contents were quite different.[1]

1. (I) Ariṭṭhaṇemi induces Prince Goyama to take the Great Vows. 9 parallels with other names. *2*. 8 (the colophon says: 10) parallels to 1. *3*. 7 parallels.—(II) Gaya-Sukumāla, a son of

1. See the AUTHOR, Worte, p. 6f.

Queen Devaī, renounces dignity and marriage and becomes a monk under Ar. Somila, the father of his bride, brings him to death and himself dies on the flight.—5 parallels to 1. *4*. 10 parallels to 1. *5*. (III) King Kaṇha Vāsudeva advises the inhabitants of his town Bāravaī which, as prophesied by Ar., will be destroyed, to take the vows and induces his wife, Queen Paumāvaī, to do the same. 9 parallels to Paumāvaī. *6*. (IV) Makāi enters the order and practises asceticism, parallel to Gangadatta Viy. 16, 5, 1. 1 parallel.—(V) The gardener Ajjuṇaga, obsessed by the god Moggarapāṇi and thus caused to do much evil, gets rid of him thanks to the layman Sudaṃsaṇa and becomes a member of the order.—11 parallels. (VI) Prince Aimutta (comp. Viy. 5, 4) does the same when being led to Mahāvīra by Goyama.--(VII) The renunciation of King Alakkha, parallel to Udāyaṇa Viy. 13, 6. *7*. 13 queens like Paumāvaī. *8*. (VIII) The great fasts of the nun Kālī who previously had been a queen.—9. parallels to different fasts.

Comm.: Vṛtti by Abhayadeva.—*Ed.* (along with the vṛtti): ĀS (along with Anga 9), C. 1875.—Āg. S. (along with Angas 9 and 11), Bo. 1920.—Along with transl. in Hindi, Lahore 1917.—(Along with A. 9:) ed. with introd., gloss., notes and an app. by P. L. VAIDYA, Poona 1932.— *Transl.*: (and the Aṇutt.) transl. by L. D. BARNETT, Lo. 1907. Rev. by LEUMANN, JRAS 1907, p. 1078 ff.

9. *Aṇuttarovavāiyadasāo*. Legends of persons who were reborn in the uppermost heavens. 3 vagga of which the first and the third, in correspondence with the title of the whole (comp. Anga 8), have been filled up to 10 *ajjhayaṇa*. We have but 2 original pieces. *1*. vagga. Jāli with 9 parallels. *2*. 13 further parallels. *3*. Dhanna, who was the most successful among Mahāvīra's 14,000 adherents. 9 parallels. Comp. Anga 8.

Comm.: Vṛtti by Abhayadeva.—For *Ed.* see Anga 8. The text also Bo. 1914 and in BARNETT, see Anga 8 (with transl.).

10. *Paṇhāvāgaraṇāim*. The title means "questions and explanations" (comp. Anga 6), but it is justified neither by the contents nor by the survey given Ṭhāṇ. 506a. We have a loquacious and comparatively modern treatise in prose mixed with

Veḍhas about the 5 Great Sins and their consequences on the one hand (*dāra* 1-5) and the 5 Great Renunciations on the other (*dāra* 6-10). 5 *ahamma-* or *aṇhaya-d.* (*pāṇa-vaha* etc.) and 5 *saṃvara-d.* (*ahiṃsā* etc.) the latter are followed by five times five *bhāvaṇāo*, partly differing from those given in Cūlā 5 of the Āyāra.

Comm.: Vṛtti by Abhayadeva.—*Ed.*: C. 1877 and Bo. 1919.—Amulyachandra SEN, A critical introd. to the P. (Thesis), Hamburg 1936.

11. *Vivāgasuya.* 2 *suyakkhandha.* Ṭhāṇ. 10 calls this Anga Kammavivāgadasāo, thus indicating that there were 10 chapters relating to the consequences of Karman which, generally, are expected to be evil ones. It seems that the resp. chapters correspond almost precisely with those we have before us. Later there were other 10 chapters added in order to show the reward for meritorious doings. But, nearly as poor as in Nāyādh. 2, etc., we find but one story with 9 parallels.

1. Duhavivāgā. Mahāvīra tells Goyama about the previous existence of somebody miserable and briefly prophesies his future lives. We learn that 1. Miyāputta a cripple, had once been Ekkāi, an unjust governor; 2. Ujjhiya, an evil-doer, has been Gottāsa, who had slaughtered cows; 3. Vijaya, a brigand, had once been Ninnaya, who had bought and sold eggs; 4. a certain Sagaḍa had lived as Channiya, who was a venison dealer and a cook; 5. Bahassaidatta, a purohita, had once been Mahesaradatta, a child murderer; 6. Prince Nandiseṇa (in the beginning Nandivaddhaṇa), the police-master Dujjohaṇa; 7. Umbaradatta, now suffering from a severe illness, had once been Dhammantari, a cruel surgeon; 8. Soriyadatta, a fisherman who is suffering from an incurable disease, had once been Sirī, a woman master-cook; 9. the tortured Devadattā, King Sīhaseṇa who burned his wives alive; 10. Aṃju, now dangerously ill, had once been the courtesan Puḍhavisirī. 2. Suhavivāgā. Prince Subāhu, a layman, had been hospitable towards the pious Sudatta when once he had been a certain Samūha. 2-10 are parallel to 1.

Comm.: Vṛtti by Abhayadeva.—*Ed.* (along with the

vṛtti): ĀS 11, C. 1877. Āg. S. see Anga 8.—MKJMM 10, c. 1920.—*Ed.* with introd. and notes by P. L. VAIDYA, Poona 1933, 2nd ed. 1935.—1, 1 (Miyāputta) with transl. in BANARSI DAS JAIN, Ardha-Māgadhī Reader, Lahore 1923.

The Uvangas

§ 47. Uvangas 1-3. 1. *Uvavāiya* (this, not Ova-, is the true old name). Two parts not numbered of which the second gives the name to the whole Uvanga. The first part calls itself Samosaraṇa and describes the preparations made for the approach of Mahāvīra and the sermon he is going to deliver in the presence of King Kūṇiya near the town of Campā. This extensive description in veḍha metre appearing in so-called *vaṇṇaga* has provided the modell for many canonical texts, including Angas 8 and 9 where they are indicated merely by catchwords. The second part deals with reincarnation (*uvavāya*) and salvation as the reward for certain actions and principles (the story of Ambaḍa and Daḍhapainna), describes the *kevali-samugghāya* (§ 89), the entrance into Nirvāṇa (an interpolation), the physical conditions necessary for it, and the abode of the Siddhas. All this, with a few exceptions, is told as being a reply of Mahāvīra to a question of Goyama. The Uvavāiya, accordingly, is of a very composite nature.

Comm.: Vṛtti by Abhayadeva.—*Ed.* (along with the Vṛtti): Ās 12, C. 1880.—Āg. S., Bo. 1916.—Das Aupapâtika[2]Sûtra, 1. Teil (the only one published.). Von Ernst LEUMANN. Introd. with extensive summary of contents, text and glossary. Leipzig 1883. Rev.: H. JACOBI, Literatur-Blatt f.d. oriental. Philologie, 2, 46-49.—Transl. of a number of §§ in Antagaḍa, see Anga 8.

2. *Rāyapaseṇaijja.* The Sanskrit name of Rajapraśnī seems to reflect the original title which may been that of Rāyapasiṇijja, i.e. "the questions of the king." LEUMANN contents that the name of King Paseṇai (Prasenajit) influenced the title,

1. The AUTHOR, Worte, p. 3 ff.

2. Thus tradition wrongly has it instead of *aupapādika*.

for it is he who appears in the Buddhist version of the Paesī story which in this Jain text we have before us. Paseṇaī once possibly was a figure in that story. We find him Ṭhāṇ. 280 a.

The god Sūriyābha pays homage to Mahāvīra who gives Gŏyama a description of his abode and his glory and then of his previous existence as King Paesī. Citta, his charioteer, brings him to Kesi, a disciple of Pārśva's, who in a discource persuades him to become a layman. He is poisoned by his wife, Queen Dhāriṇī, who feels neglected by him, and he will be reborn as Daḍhapainna (see Uvavāiya). The discourse mentioned concerns the existence of a soul different from the body. Kesī denies this to be so, but Paesī affirms it and, moreover, says that the soul is invisible and invariably of the size of the body it dwells in.

Comm.: Vṛtti by Abhayadeva.—*Ed.* (along with the Vṛtti): AS 13, C. 1880; Āg. S., Bo. 1925.—The Rāyap. was treated exhaustively by LEUMANN, VIth OC III, 2, p. 490 ff.

3. *Jīvābhigama.* In the introduction and at the end the work calls itself *Jīvājīvābhigama*; i.e. "Classification of Animate and Inanimate Objects", though it treats no more than the first category. The originators are said to have been the *therā bhagavanto* who obediently complied with what the Lord had meant and taught. This is not in harmony with the conventional form of question and reply as mostly found in the text. It has 2 times 9 *paḍivatti* "meanings" (8a, 463a) where in a non-polemic manner it is being said how some (*ege*) classify the beings from two-up to tenfold. In the Colophon there is no reference made to *paḍivatti*. As to major and minor interpolations see below.

I. Beings in the Saṃsāra are either immovable or movable (=2). II.: female, male and neuter beings (=3). III. Hell-beings (H), animals (A), human beings (M), and gods (G). the latter in 2 *vemāṇiya-uddesa* (=4). IV. Beings with one up to five senses (=5). V. Earth-, water-, fire-, wind-beings, plants, and animals (=6). VI. H(without sexual differences) and AMG both female and male (=7). VII. HAMG in the first and the last moments of their existence as such (=8). VIII. Beings with one sense (=5) and those with two up to five senses (=4). IX. Beings with one up to five senses as in VII (=10).—The following divisons are no longer confined to the Saṃsāra, but include the Siddhas. I'. Beings in the Saṃsāra and above it having organs of sense, body, activity (*joga*), etc. etc., and such having not (=2). II'. Beings capable of believing limited (*paritta*), developed, fine, having the inner sense, capable of salvation, and movable, or either representing the opposite or being subjected to a third condition (=3). III'. Activity, sex. belief, self-control in beings (=4). IV'. HAMG plus Siddhas (=5), or the same five having and not having the 4 passions. V'. Beings having and not having the five senses or the five bodies (=6). VI'. Four elementary beings, plants, movable beings (=AHG) and Siddhas (=7), or beings having and not having the *lesa* (=6+1). VII'. Beings in possession of the five kinds of right and the three kinds of wrong cognition (=8). Beings as in VI plus the Siddhas (=8). VIII'. A^{1-4}, (A^5:) HAMG plus the Siddhas (=9). The same as in VII (=9). IX'. Beings as in VIII plus the Siddhas (=10). Beings as in VII plus the Siddhas of the two kinds (=10).

Ṭhāṇ. 126a, 205a says that, apart from the Canda-, Sūra- and Jambuddīvapannatti[1] the Dīvasāgarapannatti, too, had an independent existence. But we only know it as being an interpolation in the Jīv. where it begins right in the middle of the discussion concerning the star-gods in III (176a). It closes (373a) with the words *dīva-samuddā samattā*, and we find no sections[2] as is equally the case in Jīv. and Jambudd. (§ 48). For the relation between the latter and the Dīvas. see below. As indicated by the title, the contents—in question and reply—refer to the ring-continents and oceans. But the description opens with the Jambuddīva. A summary of the Dīvas. is the Dīvasāgarapannatti-saṃgahaṇī, 223 Gr., as we are informed by the Jainagranthāvalī p. 64, the latter counting it among the Paiṇṇa.[3]

1. For this sequence see LEUMANN, Ubersicht 21 b.

2. Only the Comm. has *iti Mandaroddesakāḥ samāptāḥ* at the end of the chapter describing the Lavaṇa ocean, 326 b.

3. The Vihimaggappavā (WEBER, Verz. II, 876) wrongly names the Paiṇṇa Dīvasāgarapannatti.

The Dīvas. are followed (373b-375b) by some small interpolations merely interconnected by the word of *poggala* applied in various meanings. After them the star-gods begin anew.

Comm.: Ṭīkā by Malayagiri, but making no difference between Jīv. and Dīvas.—Ed. (along with the Ṭīkā): ĀS, Ahmedabad 1883.—Āg. S., Bo. 1919.

§48. Uvangas 4-7. 4. *Pannavaṇā*, frequently with the addition of *bhagavaī* as found with several Angas. A systematic treatise in the common shape of question and reply, based upon the preparatory work of Ajja Sāma[1] as indicated by Gāhās 3 and 4 (out of 9 preceding the text). There we learn that Ajja Sāma was the 23rd *dhīra-purisa* in the *vāyaga-vaṃsa*, and in Gāhā 5 we are told that the text applied for teaching is qualified as *Diṭṭhivāya-nisanda*. The subject-matter is divided among 36 *payas*.

1. Lifeless as well as living things with all their subsections can be the object of "proclamation". *2*. Ṭhāṇā. The places where beings reside. *3*. Bahuvattavvaya. 27 dāra for indicating the relative number of the beings, i.e. place, kind and sex, one-sensed up to five-sensed, one-sensed only (5), activity, sex, passions, *lesā*, standpoint (10), cognition, creed, self-control, distinct spiritual function, taking in of matter (15), speech, individual body, development, fineness, power of reason (20), aptitude for salvation, fundamental facts, place as last or not last, number in the 3 worlds (25), binding and other qualities, number of *poggala* in the 3 worlds, total number of beings. *4*. Ṭhiī. Duration of life. *5*. Visesa. Conditions (*pajjava*) of living and lifeless objects. *6*. Vakkanti. Reincarnation (7 dāra). *7*. Ūsāsa. Breathing. *8*. Sannā. 10 directions of consciousness. *9*. Joṇi. 4 times 3 kinds of places of origin. *10*. Carama. Objects as being relatively last and not last and their relative numbers. *11*. Bhāsā. Speech. *12*. Sarīra. The 5 bodies as to their being inhabited either now or previously (*baddhellaga* or *mukkellaga*). *13*. Pariṇāma. 10 kinds of changes in living and lifeless substances. *14*. Kasāya. The 4 passions. *15*. Indiya. The senses, in 2 *uddesa*. In the first *udd*. a few peculiarities.[2] *16*. Paoga. 15 applications of inner sense, speech, and

1. Also Kālaka acc. to tradition, comp. § 24.
2. The AUTHOR Worte, p. 13 footnote.

body. 5 kinds of getting somewhere (*gai-ppavāya*, comp. § 38 footnote) along with their sub-sections; the first of them is the the *paoga-gai*. *17*. Lessā, 6 udd. *18*. Kāyaṭṭhiī. Remaining in the same shape of a body for more than one life. *19*. Sammatta. True, wrong and mixed insight. *20*. Antakiriyā. How to reach the end of active being. *21*. Ogāhaṇāsaṃṭhāṇa. Size and shape of the 5 bodies. *22*. Kiriyā. 2 times 5 kinds of activity. *23*. Kammapagaḍī. The 8 kinds of Kamma, in 2 udd. *24*. Kammabandha. Binding of several Kamma species when some of them are being bound. *25*. Kammaveya. Sensation of several kinds of Kamma when being bound. *26*. Veyabandha. Binding (as in *24*) when being felt. *27*. Veyaveya. (as in *25*) when being felt. *28*. Āhāra. Attraction of matter. *29*. Uvaoga. 2 kinds of spiritual function. *30*. Pāsaṇayā. 2 kinds of seeing. *31*. Sannī. The beings in possession of reason. *32*. Saṃjaya. Self-control. *33*. Ohi. Its 2 and 6 kinds. *34*. Pariyāraṇā. Embodiment and sexuality (with the gods). *35*. Veyaṇā. 3 kinds of sensation, four more, three times three more, two times two more. 36. Samugghāya. The 7 kinds of explosive annihilation.

Comm.: Ṭīkā by Malayagiri.—*Ed.* (along with the Ṭīkā): ĀS, Ben. 1884.—Āg.S., Bo. 1918-19.

5. *Sūrapannatti*. The physics of the sky, though chiefly concerned with the activity and the effects of the sun and the moon. In the opening passages we have the usual legendary introduction of Goyama's questions directed to Mahāvīra, but later on either personality disappears completely, and both question and reply are impersonal.[1] The question invariably has *tā kahaṃ te . . . āhite 'ti vadejjā* with the word of *tā* invariably introducing a sentence. This style is peculiar for the Sūrap. With the Jīv. the Sūrap. shares the usage of *ege* in all chapters with the only exception of the main portion of the 10th. These *ege* following one after the other produce their *paḍivatti*; but, finally, the true teaching is brought up against them all (*vayaṃ puṇa evaṃ vayāmo*), a method reminding us of the Kauṭalīya. The Sūrap. has 20 *pāhuḍa*, each subdivided into *pāhuḍapāhuḍa*,- and

1. *Samaṇāuso* 846 ff. is most exceptional.

in 10, 1 we have a *vatthu*, all this being equally reported of the Diṭṭhivāya. The individual *pāhuḍa* bear no names, but instead there are catchwords in the introductory ślokas. The contents were rendered by WEBER, Ind. Stud. 10, 254ff. (1868), THIBAUT JASB 40, 107 ff., comp. also his "Astronomie" in the Grundriss p. 20ff., 29.[1] It may be mentioned that these descriptions are based not so much on the text itself but on Malayagiri's commentary.

1. The narrower and wider circles (*maṇḍala*) formed by the 2 suns around Mount Meru according to the seasons. 8 p.-pāh., of which the 4th,5th,6th, and 8th have 3 up to 8 *paḍivatti*. Possibly this *pāhuḍa* is the Maṇḍalappavesa in the list of *anga-bāhira* texts (§ 40). *2.* The horizontal way of either sun through the quarters of the compass (8 *paḍ.*), their transition from one circle over to the next (2 *paḍ.*), the distance covered by one sun during 1 *muhutta* (4 *paḍ.*). *3.* The range illuminated by both sun and moon (12 *paḍ.*). *4.* The figure (*saṃṭhii*) formed by the bright light (*seyā*) of both suns and moons above the earth and upon it (12 *paḍ.* each, of which the first is accepted). *5.* The atoms of the Mandara (sic) are impervious (*paḍihaṇanti*) to the light of the sun (20 *paḍ.* exclusively due to the 20 names of the Mandara). *6.* The time in which the power of the sun's rays remains constant (25 *paḍ.* according to the resp. time measured). *7=5*, only *varayanti* instead of *paḍihananti* (20 *paḍ.*). *8.* The course of the sun in relation to day, night and other earthly time measures (*udaya-saṃṭhii*) (3 *paḍ.*). *9.* How the earth-temperature is effected by the sun (3 *paḍ.*).[2] The length of the shadow (*porisicchāyā*) depends on the hight and the light of the sun (25,2, and 96 *paḍ.*, the latter on the ground of opinions that the shadow has the length of 1, 2 up to 96 *porisī*. The truth is that in the first and the last moment of the day it measures 59 *por.* and a fraction). The shadow has 25 names according to shape

1. To be exact we will not pass over SHAMA SHASTRY QJMythic Soc. 15, 138-147; 16, 201-212 under the misleading title of "A brief Translation. . . ".

2. The introductory question is missing. Instead we find the one leading up to the next subject.

and angle. Possibly this 9th *pāhuḍa* is the Porisīmaṇḍala listed among the *anga-bāhira* texts.

In the 10th *pāhuḍa* and in most of the following it is no longer the sun but the moon and the stars that are dominant. We, therefore, venture to assume that it was here where the *Candapannatti*, the so-called 7th Uvanga, came in. All we know of it from manuscripts apart from differences in spelling is identical with the Sūrapannatti.[1] Pāh. *10* has 22 *p.-pāhuḍa*. They contain the list (*āvaliyā*) of the 28 nakṣatras (5 *paḍ.*) according to its begining and end; the duration of their conjunction (*joga*) with the moon; the portions (*bhāga*) of day or night when the conjunction starts; the moment when it starts; (5.) the narrower or wider relationship (*kula*, *uvakula*, *kulôvakula*) of the nakṣatras with the months; the days of full and new moon in their relation to the *kula*, etc.; the shape (*saṃṭhii*) of every individual nakṣatra; the number of their stars (*tār'agga*); (10). the nakṣatras as guides (*netā*)[2] of the months and as the measures of the shadow casted in them by the sun; the position of the nakṣatras to the course of the moon (*canda-magga*) and the orbit of the moon during 15 days (*c.-maṇḍala*); void of n. or not; the gods of the nakṣatras (Bambhadevayā, Viṇhu-d., etc.); the names of the 30 *muhutta*; the names of the 15 days and nights of a half-month; (15.) the 5 names recurring three times, of the 15 *tithis* and their nights; the gotras, of the n. (*Moggallāyāṇa*, *Sankhāyaṇa*, etc.); the food conducive to trade affairs under a certain n.; the frequency of a conjunction of a n. with moon and son (*canda-cāra* and *āicca-c.*) in the course of the 5 years' Yuga; the names of the 12 months; (20.) the 5 kinds of years and their sub-species; the gates of the nakṣatras (*joisassa dārā*), 7 of each opening into a cardinal direction (5 *paḍ.*); and, finally (*nakkhatta-vijaya*) the duplicity of sun, moon, and n., their junction with the 62 full moon-and new moon-days in one Yuga, the coincidence of the movements of the 2 moons, 2 suns, etc. *11*. The beginning of each of the 5 years of a Yuga. *12*. The 5 kinds of years forming the sub-species of one of the 5

1. Malayagiri's quotation from the Candap. Sthān. 415a=Sūrap. 173b.

2. Comp. JACOBI ZDMG 74, 258.

years treated in *10*, 20; the 6 seasons, the *omaratta* and 6 *airatta*, i.e. missing and surplus days; the 5 solstices in a Yuga in their relation to nakṣatra and moon, the tenfold joga. *13*. Both the waxing and the waning of the moon, full and new moon, the circles formed by her movement. *14*. The bright and dark halves of the month (*dosiṇā-pakkha* and *andhakāra-p.*). *15*. The velocity of moon, sun, planets, nakṣatras, stars, both relative and absolute. Circles formed by moon and sun both during 1 day and 1 month. *16*. *canda-lessā* and *dosiṇā*, *sūra-l.* and *āyava*, *andhakāra* and *chāyā* are homonymous pairs. *17*. For the change of existence (*cayaṇôvavāya*) of the gods embodied in moons and suns there is no fixed time (25 *paḍ.* as in *pāh. 6*), but each of these gods is bound to live his or her time as destined by his or her Karman. 18. The altitude of the stars[1] above the earth (§ 126) (25 *paḍ.*,) though this altitude does not concern the moral level of their resp. gods. Their attendance and the latter's distance from the Mandara. The innermost, outermost, topmost and lowest nakṣatra relative to the Jambuḍḍīva (Abhiī, Mūla, Sāī, Bharaṇī): The shape, the size, and the tractive power (*vimāṇa*) of the star-gods. The velocity of the stars (as in *15*), their power (*iḍḍhi*), their mutual distance, their princely life, their duration, their relative number. *19*. The number (12 *paḍ.*) of the stars above the human world, with 40 Gāhās mentioning Rāhu as the originator of the moon's waxing and waning, their normal course, their shape, the vacancy of a seat. The fixed stars beyond the human world. The remote ring-continents and -oceans, and the stars above them. *20*. Moons and suns are powerful gods (2 *paḍ.*), and so is Rāhu (2 *paḍ.*); his 15 names, his *vimāṇa*, his doings, his twin character as *dhuva-R.* and *pavva-R.* The names of *sasī* and *āicca* of moon and sun, their princely life. The 88 *mahaggaha*.

Comm.: Ṭīkā by Malayagiri.—*Ed.* (along with the Ṭīkā),: Āg. S., Bo. 1919.—J. F. KOHL, Die Sūryaprajñapti. Versuch einer Textgeschichte. Stuttgart 1937. Rev. by the AUTHOR, OLZ 1938, col. 562f.

6. *Jambuddīvapannatti.* A description of the Jambuddīva,

1. This includes both the moon and the sun.

the centre of the physical universe. In the Divasāgarap. (§ 47) we have portions describing the Jambuddīva in the same words, and KIRFEL (Z I I 3, 50ff) was right in inferring that once both texts formed a whole and that, when they were disjoined, the position of the Jambudd. were repeated in the Dīvas. for the purpose of acting as a fundament and a starting-point. The usual costume of question and reply was dropped altogether in the continuous portions; as in the Jīv. there are no sections, but the comm.has 7 *vakṣaskāra*, an expression occurring in the cosmography (§ 115) only.

I. The Jambuddīva in general, its enclosure with the gates therein. The continent of Bharaha. II. The division of time in Bharaha, the conditions of life in its different epochs *susama-susamā*, etc. (§ 120). The life of the 1st Titthagara Usabha during the *susama-dūsamā*, etc. mostly in correspondence with Jiṇac. 204-228. The solemn cremation of his corpse. III. Here a *Bharahacakkicariya* is inserted with the intention of showing how King Bharaha came to rule over the world thus giving the *Bharaha vāsa* its name.[1] IV. The remaining continents of the Jambuddīva and the "benches" separating them. V. How the gods honour a new-born future Titthagara by solemn ceremonies (§ 15). VI. A brief statistic survey of the geographical details of Jambuddīva (*Eravaya* here stands for *Erāv.*), continued at the end of the work,and here followed by VII,an astronomical section. In its contents (though not in its style) it frequently corresponds with the Sūrap., especially so with Sūrap. 18, 19. and parts of 10. New subjects dealt with are: visibility, presence and temperature of the suns (458b=Viy. 392a), circles of the nakṣatras (474a), sun and moon with ref. to Viy. 5, 1 and 10 (480a), the *karaṇa*, the beginnings of the year, the half-year, the months, etc., the mutual distance of the stars (531 b). The statistic survey now proceeds in giving dates regarding the Titthagaras, the Emperors etc. and their state-jewels in Jambuddīva, as well as the latter's dimensions, eternity, duration, contents, and names. Ending up in the legendary frame with which I. had been opened.

1. Comp. the AUTHOR, GGA 1931, p. 293-298.

Comm.: Ṭīkā by Śānticandra.—*Ed.* (along with the Ṭīkā): DLJP 52. 54. Bo. 1920.

7. *Candapannatti*. This work is contained in all lists of the Siddhānta and in the older ones (e.g. Ṭhāṇ. 126a) it marches at the head of the three *pannatti*, comp. LEUMANN, Übersicht p. 26 b ff. But we have reason to assume that it is embodied in the Sūrapannatti, s. a.

§49. Uvanga 8-12 form 1 *suyakkhandha* called after the first of its 5 *vagga*. There are relations of these texts to Angas 6 and 8, comp. the AUTHOR, Worte p. 7 ff. where it is being suggested that it was they that first had been called Uvangas.

Comm.: Vivaraṇa by Candra Sūri (Srīcandra).—*Ed.* (along with the Vivaraṇa): ĀS 19-23, Ben. 1885,—Āg. Ś., Bo. 1922. Ed. Dānavijaya, Ahm. 1922. With Introd., Gloss., Notes and Appendices by P. L. VAIDYA Poona 1932.

8. *Nirayāvaliyāo*. 10 *ajjhayaṇa*. 1. Kālī, a wife of King Seṇiya residing at Rāyagiha, is informed by Mahāvīra that her son Kāla who with his stepbrother Kūṇiya went to war, will fall in the battle and be reborn in one of the hells. Asked by Goyama, Mahāvīra tells him how this war came to pass. Cellaṇā, Seṇiya's first wife, had felt a *dohaḍa* to eat flesh of her husband, a *dohaḍa* which apparently was satisfied by a trick of her stepbrother Abhaya. She now fears evil consequences for the dynasty from the part of her child and wishes to remove it, but she does not succeed in doing so. Indeed Kūṇiya, scarcely having grown up, puts his father into prison. Cellaṇā, however, makes him understand that when she had exposed him it had been Seṇiya who had saved him, whereupon Kūṇiya hurries to release his father. Tragically enough, Seṇiya, in the wrong belief that his son comes to execute him, commits suicide. Now Kūṇiya, as a king, resides at Campā. Soon after he comes to quarrel with Vehalla, his genuine brother, about some precious objects in Vehalla's possession. V. seeks refuge with his grandfather Ceḍaga, king of Vesālī, who refuses to surrender him to his pursuer, and Kūṇiya in company with his ten stepbrothers, including Kāla, starts war.—*2-10*. The same story with reference to Kāla's nine brothers Sukāla. etc.

Separate edition: Nirayāvaliyāsuttam, een upāñga der Jaina's. Met inleid., aanteek., en glossaar. Van Dr. S. WARREN. Amsterdam 1879. Rev. by JACOBI ZDMG 34, 178 ff.

9. *Kappavaḍiṃsiyāo*. 10 *ajjhayaṇa*. *1*. Pauma, son of Kāla (s. a.) and Paumāvaī, becomes a monk (as did Mahabbala, Viy. 11, 11, 1) against his parents' resistance. He is reborn in the Sohamma kappa (hence the title) and will attain mokṣa later. —*2-10* have the same story with reference to the sons of Kāla's nine brothers, Sukāla, etc.

10. *Pupphiyāo*. 10 *ajjhayaṇa*. The title derives from story *3*. *1*. The god Canda goes to pay homage to Mahāvīra (as does Sūriyābha, comp. Rāyap.) who when being asked by Goyama gives an account of his pre-existence as a certain Angai of Sāvatthī. He is converted by Pāsa and dies from fasting, is reborn as a god and will find salvation in the near future. *2* and *5-10* are parallels, but in the latter group the converters are the *therā bhagavanto*. As to their frame, *3* and *4* also are parallels, but the corresponding pre-existences are dealt with in greater detail. *3*. The Brahman Somila of Vāṇārasī consults Pāsa (reference to Somila's questions directed to Mahāvīra Viy. 758a) but does not become converted. He plants trees and decorates the groves with flowers (hence the title of the whole), honours Brahman ascetics and practises asceticism himself. He is finally convinced by a god that the Brahman method is wrong since, after all, he has consulted Pāsa. Somila thereupon allows himself to be converted. *4*. Subhaddā, a sterile housewife, on consulting some nuns becomes a lay woman and then a nun herself. As such a one she makes it her hobby to nurse children and to adorn them for their festivities. Though reprimanded for doing so she does not listen and returns home, though still remaining a nun. In her present existence she is a goddess Bahuputtiyā, and in her next life she will be[1] Somā, the daughter of a Brahman. In the course of 16 years Somā will give birth to 32 children, then she will become a lay woman and a nun; after that she will be reborn to live among gods, and finally she will attain salvation.

1. The text has the past tense.

11. *Pupphacūlāo.* 10 *ajjhayaṇa.* 1. The goddess Sirī going on a pilgrimage in order to pay homage to Mahāvīra had been Bhūyā converted by Pāsa in her pre-existence. One day she is reprimanded by her lady superior for having thoroughly washed her body, but yet she repeats doing so. That lady is called *Pupphacūlāo ajjāo* (comp. Nāy. II 1). The duration of Bhūyā's existence and her *mokṣa* are consonant with *2—10* except the name of the goddess.

12. *Vaṇhidasāo.* Not "ten" *ajjhayaṇa,* but 12. *1.* Prince Nisaḍha, son of King Baladeva and his wife Revaī of Bāravaī, was converted to laymanship by Ariṭṭhaṇemi. When being asked by Varadatta, one of A.'s disciples for the reason of N.'s bodily perfection, Ariṭṭhaṇemi gives an account of N.'s pre-existence as Prince Vīrangaya who was converted by a master called *Siddhantā nāmaṃ āyariyā.* N. later becomes a member of the order; after his death he will be reborn as a god, and, finally, he will gain salvation. *2-12* are of the same tenor, but the princes are called differently. They all belong to the same dynasty of the (Andhaka-) Vṛṣṇi (comp. Nandī 418f.), whence the title of the text.

The Paiṇṇas

§50. The number of the Paiṇṇas varies, but, as mentioned in § 40, we find a central group or core. It consists of 10 of them. Since these have no standard order we are justified to deal with them in an order suitable to their contents. There will be added a few works that surround the centre group in a wider circle.

Editions: Dasapayannā mūla sūtra. Ben. 1886, containing: Tand., Dev., Gaṇiv., Caus., Saṃth., Āurapacc., Bhattap., Mahāpacc., Cand., Maraṇavibhatti.—Payannā samgrah. Bhāg 1. Ahm. s. 1962, containing: Bhattap., Caus., Mahāpacc., Āurapacc., Ārādhaṇāprakaraṇa by Somasūri, Ātmabhāvanā (Guj.) by Buddhisāgara, Paramānandapacīsī (25 Skt.-śl.).—Śrī Caus., Āurapacc., Bhaktaparijnā, Saṃthāraga. Cār payannāno samgrah. Bh. s. 1966.—Catuḥśaraṇ'ādi-Maraṇasamādhyantaṃ prakīrṇaka-daśakam. (Āg. S.) Bo. s. 1983, containing: Caus., Āurapacc., Mahāpacc., Bhattap., Tand., Saṃth.,

Gacchāyāra, Gaṇiv., Dev., Maraṇasamāhi.—Caus. and Āurap. along with other texts, Ahm. s. 1957.—Vividh Payannāvacūri, Jām. 1912.

Five out of the ten disciplinary Paiṇṇas mentioned above have been dealt with by VON KAMPTZ.[1] They are partly interrelated with each other and their context has suffered from misconceptions. Here we restrict ourselves to but a few remarks regarding the essential contents.

Causaraṇa. "The Recourse to the Four", i.e. to the Arhats, the Siddhas, the Sādhus, and the Dharma. 63 G. Comm.: Bhuvanatunga Sūri. Avacūri on the Caus. and the subsequent texts by Guṇaratna.

Bhattaparinnā. The ritual for the "Renunciation of Food". 172 G.

Saṃthāra. "The Death Bed". Preparations, ritual, legends. 123 G. Comm.: Bhuvanatunga.

Āurapaccakkhāṇa. "The Renunciation of the Sick" as to all that is evil, his preparation for death. 70 G. along with a formula of confession containing a list of 63 objects.

Mahāpaccakkhāṇa. "The Greater Renunciation" 141 G. instead of 70. Here we add the *Maraṇasamāhi* or *Maraṇavibhatti*, 660 G., with three more in the ed. quoted above. In them the anonymous author appears to confess having used "the Maraṇavisohi, the Samlehaṇāsuya, the Bhattap., the Āurapacc., the Mahāpacc., and the Ārāhaṇāpaiṇṇa". The first as well as the second of these texts belong to the *anga-bāhira.*

Candavejjhaya. "Hitting the Mark" (*candraka-vedhyaka*= *vedhya-candraka*, Cand. 127 ff.; Āurapacc. 54; Saṃth. 122 *candaga-vijjha*). On monastic discipline, the virtues (*guṇa*) of a teacher and of a pupil in education (*niggaha*) through discipline, knowledge, practice, and in dying. 171 G., the first of which, since it refers to the Tand., most certainly is out of place here.

Gaṇivijjā. "A Gaṇin's Knowledge" as to the dates either propitious or not for anything planned in monastic life. 9 *dāra*: natural days, tithis, nakṣatras, karaṇas, days of the planets,

1. Über die vom Sterbefasten handelnden älteren Paiṇṇa des Jaina-Kanons. (Thesis.) Hamburg 1929.

muhūrtas, bird-omina, constellations, more omina. 82 v., śl. and G. at equal parts.

Tandulaveyāliya, so called after a calculation (*vicāra*) as to how many grains of rice (*tandula*) a normal individual would consume in the course of 100 (years) times 360 (days) times 30 (hours) times: 3773 (breaths). (They would fill 22 1/2 *vaha.*). A jumble of prose, G. and śl. of varying origin. Embryology, the human stages of life, the duration of life in remote times (including a description as to the bodies of Arhats, Cakravartins, etc.) and nowadays when the maximum age comes upto not more than 100 years (s. a.). Measures of capacity and of time. The parts of the body, the quantity of fluids contained by a human being, the body as an impure mass. A contemptuous description of the mothers, mostly laid down in comparisons and etymologics.

Ed. s.a. The text along with Vijayavimala's Vṛtti and the Caus. DLJP 59, Bo. 1922.—The text with transl. in Guj. by HĪRĀLĀL Haṃsraj. Jāmnagar without year.

Devindatthaya. A layman commencing to praise (*thaya*) Vardhamāna (Mahāvīra) is interrupted by his wife the moment he mentions the *devinda*, the woman asking him to explain the meaning of the word to her. By way of personal information he systematically treats the 20+16+12 Bhavaṇavāsī, Vāṇamantara, Joisiya, and Vemāṇīya kings as to their seats, duration of their lives and faculties, moreover reporting on the Vemāṇiyas also as to their size, sexuality, etc. 302 G.

Vīratthaya. A stotra of Mahāvīra whose various names are listed in 43 G.

As to the *Titthogālī* and the *Ārāhaṇāpaḍāgā* which occasionally appear among the Paiṇṇas the AUTHOR has come to know them through manuscripts as abstracts of the entire teaching (1233 G. and 930 G.).

The Cheyasuttas

§51. *Āyāradasāo*, abbreviated to Dasão, Skt. Daśāśrutaskandha. 10 *dasā* (Thāṇ. 506a): *1*. 20 precipitancies of temper (*asamāhi-ṭṭhāṇa*). *2*. 21 offences against the vows (*sabala*). *3*. 33 cases of disrespect (*āsāyaṇā*) on the part of the pupil. *4*. 8

requisite qualities of a Gaṇa-leader (*gaṇi-saṃpayā*) and two times four modes as how to gain self-control on the part of a younger. *5*. Transcendent cognition is gained by right conduct (*citta-samāhi*), 10 cases. *6*. 11 stages of laymanship (*uvāsaya-paḍimā*). *7*. 12 stages of monkhood (*bhikkhu-p.*). These 7 *dasā* are ascribed to the *therā bhagavanto* and together with Utt.16 and Dasav.9, 4 they constitute the remains of a code of discipline arranged in the fashion of both Angas 3 and 4.[1] It is only in *6* that we are surprised to come across an exposition of the *kiriyā-* and *akiriyā-vāī* which is quite out of place here. Prose with the exception of 17 śl. appended to *5*. The remaining *dasā* differ completely from the previous ones as well as among themselves.

8. This *dasā* ends up in the Pajjosavaṇākappa (the Sāmāyārī) offering prescriptions for monastic life during the rainy season (§146). In joint connexion with the two texts preceding this code of duties (presently going to be mentioned) this *d.* forms the so-called Kalpasūtra. The first part is the Jiṇacariya, a lengthy account of Mahāvīra's birth and life rendered in many Veḍhas owing to which the text has come to serve as a model as does the Samosaraṇa (§ 47). At the very end a date, see § 39. Then there follow the biographies of the preceding 23 Jinas, but in a much shorter and stereotype way. The second part is the Therāvalī, a list of the immediate disciples of Mahāvīra's and of the patriarchs following them, of affiliations and schools. In many cases the names appear in Gāhās, and we equally find them in the concluding part. At the end of this chronology we have Devarddhi (§ 39) from which we infer that those lists were started in his time or else soon after. Thus in the Kalpa-sūtra there are rather disparate portions probably due to the fact that it was intended to prove that both teaching and custom went back to very remote days.[2] From tradition[3] we understand that the K. was recited before a King Dhruvasena in order to comfort him for the loss of his son. *9*. 39 *moha-ṭṭhāṇa* to show that illusion (*moha*) results in evil deeds. 39 śl. which in a legendary

1. The AUTHOR, Worte p. 9. ff.
2. The AUTHOR, Worte p. 12. ff.
3. JACOBI's ed. p. 114 ff.; SBE 22, 270.

introduction are attributed to Mahāvīra. *10.* Āyāiṭṭhāṇa. The splendid show presented by King Seṇiya and his Queen Cellaṇā and their retinue arouse a *niyāṇa* in the hearts of monks and nuns. Mahāvīra defeats it by means of 9 analogous examples given as to such ambitions for the future life (*āyāi*) which will have detrimental consequences. Only he who abstains from all desires is certain to reach the end of existence.

Comm. on the Dasāo: Nijjutti, Cuṇṇi (printed), Ṭīkā by Brahma Muni.—*Ed.*: Daśāśrutaskandhasūtram, Lāhaur 1936.—Dasā 8 frequently was commented independently and separately printed. For the 1st ed. by STEVENSON see §1. The Kalpasûtra of Bhadrabāhu ed. with an introd., notes and a glossary by Hermann JACOBI (AKM 7, 1), Leipzig 1879. On p. 25 a survey of the many comm. from the Pajjosavaṇānijjutti onwards. To them we have to add Vinayavijaya's Subodhikā, DLJP 7 and 61, Bo. 1911 and 1923, and ĀGRM 31, Bh.1915.—The text along with Dharmasāgara's Kiraṇāvalī ĀGRM 71, s. 1922. The text alongwith the Kālikācāryakathā DLJP 18,Bo.1914.—The text, illustrated: Śri-Kalpasūtraṃ Bārasāsūtraṃ sacitram. DLJP 82, Bo.1933.—*Transl.*: JACOBI in SBE 22, Oxford 1884.

Kappa. 6 *uddesa.* Rules for the lives of monks and nuns. For the composition see the next work. Often styled Bṛhatkalpa in distinction from the Kalpasūtra mentioned above.

Comm.: Bhāsa by Saṃghadāsa; Cuṇṇi by Pralambasūri (both in 3 recensions); Ṭīkā by Malayagiri, completed by Kṣemakīrti.—*Ed.*: Das Kalpasūtra, die alte Sammlung jinistischer Monchsvorschriften. Einl., Text, Anm., Übers., Glossar von Walther SCHUBRING. Kappasuttaṃ (this text in Nāgarī retranscription by Jivraj Ghellabhai DOSHI). (The Sacred Books of the Jains 4.) Ahm. 1911. Kalpa-Vyavahāra-Niśītha-sūtrāṇi (retranscription of SCHUBRING's editions). (Jaina-Sāhitya-Saṃśodhaka-GM.) Poona 1923.—Bṛhatkalpasūtram (along with Nijjutti, Bhāsa and Vṛtti). Vibh. 1-6, Bh. 1933-42. —*Transl.* into English of the German transl. mentioned by May S. BURGESS IA 39, 257 ff.

Vavahāra. 10 *uddesa.* Contents as in Kappa. Both K. and Vav have flowed together from different sources. In the

AUTHOR's opinion the original K. contained a collection of what was permitted and proper for monks and nuns (*nigganṭha* and -*thī*) and what was not, while the original Vav. was the more differentiated codification of both order of rank and subordination and of the proceedings (*vavahāra*) taken against *bhikkhu* and *bhikkhuṇī* acting contrary to prescripts. Whence it follows that the Vav. rests on the Kappa.

Comm.: Bhāsa; Cuṇṇi, Ṭīkā (Vivaraṇa) by Malayagiri.—*Ed.*: Vavahāra-and Nisīha-Sutta, by Walther SCHUBRING; Leipzig 1918. Nāgarī retranscription along with Guj. transl., by Jivraj Ghellabhai DOSHI. (The Sacred Books of the Jains.) Ahm. 1925.—Vyavahārasūtram (with Nijjutti, Bhāsa and Vivaraṇa). 1-10. Bh. 1926.

Nisīha. 20 *uddesa*. This title appears to be a mixture of *niseha* (interdiction) and *nisīhiyā* (place of study). Udd. 1-19 offer lists of transgressions and their sanctions reaching from 1 to 4 months in which case the punishment either becomes effective immediately and without reduction (*aṇugghāiya*) or else may be suspended or reduced (*ugghāiya*). Thus the text has two different subjects. A third one refers to additional punishment (*ārovaṇā*) when previous transgressions have been concealed or new ones were committed. This is treated in the 20th udd. (20, 1-20= Vav. 1, 1-20). It is this *udd.* that must be meant when Ṭhāṇ. 325a speaks of the fivefold, and Samav. 47b of the 28fold, Āyārapagappa (though in the latter we have but a few terms not contained in Nis. 20). Abhayadeva, it is true, takes the Āy. as being the whole Nis., just as does Malayagiri in his comm. on Vav. 3, 3 and 10, 16 f. Āv. nijj. 16, category 28, gets this number by including the threefold Nis. in the Āyārapagappa=Āyāranga. About the Nis. once having been an appendix (5th *cūlā*) to the Āyāra (§ 45), as state still reflected in the Āyāranijjutti, see LEUMANN, Übersicht p. 22a.

Comm. : Bhāsa; Cuṇṇi; Visesa-Nisīhacuṇṇi by Jinadāsa, ed. by Vijayaprema Sūri. Vol. 1-4. Agra 195f.-60.—*Ed.* See Vavahāra.

§52. *Mahānisīha*. This "greater Nisīha" is very closely linked with the original one in that part of its 7th section, the

Pacchittasutta, which quotes punishments for various transgressions. This is intended to serve as a legitimation for a pretended old date of the Mahānisīha, and there are some more attempts to this purpose. But the language is degenerated and the tradition defective, as was already seen by the copyist of the archetype.

1. Salluddharaṇa. Confession and contrition, 222 śl. except an introduction in prose. *2.* Kammavivāgavivaraṇa, 209 śl., a large centrepiece in prose. The consequences of evil deeds; chastity, sexuality, and moral reflexions. 3. Prose and Gāhās. 200 species of a *kusīla*, ritual and importance of the *panca-mangala* and other formulae; the cult of the Arhats. 4. The story of Sumai and Nāila[1] and the way they behaved towards some *kusīla*, with characteristic details. 5. Navaṇīyasāra. G. and śl. Concerns the Gaccha and the teacher, with kathās of Vaira and Kuvalayappabha. 6. Gīyatthavihāra. 415 śl. The arbitrary dealings of Nandiseṇa, the same of Āsaḍa; confession and atonement; the inaccurate confession of Meghamālā; the intercourse with trained and untrained monks (*gīy'attha* and *agīy.*). The stories of Īsara, Rajjā, Lakkhaṇadevī-Khaṇḍoṭṭhā. The devotion to the life of a monk or a nun must be unconditional. There follow two alleged appendices (cūliyā). *7.* Prose, G. and śl. About atonement; the *pacchitta-sutta* (s. a.); sundry matters. *8.* The story of Sujjhasirī and Susaḍha. The advantages of full confession.

W. SCHUBRING, Das Mahānisīha-Sutta, Berlin 1918.—F.-R. HAMM and W. SCHUBRING, Studien zum Mahānisīha, Kap. 6-8. Hamburg 1951. J. DELEU and W. SCH., the same Ch. 1-5 in the press. Ch. 4 and 5 in: prep. DELEU—Mahānis. 4.5?) in: Sumati Nāgil caritra tathā saṃjatāsamjat ane gaccha-kugacchano adhikār. Ahm. s. 1933.—Susaḍhacaritra: app. to ĀSRM 67 (1918).

There is a close connexion between the Mahānis. and the GACCHĀYĀRA since the latter has borrowed nearly one third of its whole from the former, comp. the AUTHOR, Mahānis. p. 50 f. 137 (138) śl. and G. Description of the qualities requisite for both a teacher and his Gaccha. Occasionally the G. is listed

1. For Nāila and his late successors see LEUMANN Übersicht, p. 28 b.

among the Paiṇṇas, see § 50.—*Ed.*: Gacchācāra-prakīrṇaka along with the Vṛtti by Vānara Ṛṣi. Āg. S. Bo. 1913.

Pancakappa. The contents can be gathered only from the P. cuṇṇi ms. The text originally composed in Gāhās (of which we can see the Pratīkas) refers to the system of monkhood by 5 methods according as the kappa is understood to be 6-, 7-, 10-, 20-, and 40-fold. The Pancakappabhāsa (by Saṃghadāsa ?) apparently is of an age younger than that of the Cuṇṇi.

Jīyakappa. 103 G. dealing with the 10 kinds of punishment and composed by Jinabhadra whose great fame is likely to have caused the Jīy. to be incorporated in the Cheyasuttas if it is not meant simply to fill the gap caused by the loss of the Pancakappa.

Comm.: Cuṇṇi by Siddhasena Gaṇin; Bhāsa (of later origin, see JINAVIJAYA p. 17 f.); Cunṇi-visama-pada-vyākhyā by Śrīcandra Sūri.—*Ed.*: Jinabhadra's Jītakalpa (with extracts from Siddhasena's Cūrṇi) by Ernst LEUMANN, SPAW 1892, p. 1195-1210.—Śrī-Jinabhadra-Gaṇi-Kṣamāśramaṇa-viracitaṃ Jītakalpa-sūtram (along with the complete Cuṇṇi and Śricandra's Vyākhyā), ed. Muni JINAVIJAYA. Jaina-Sāhitya-Saṃśodhaka-GM. 7. Ahm. s. 1983.

Nandī and Aṇuogadārā.

§53. These two texts have no common title as might be expected owing to both being works concerning propaedeutics and both preceding the important group of the Mūlasuttas (see below).

Nandī. The unknown author frequently looks beyond the bars of Jain dogmatics. Hence it is likely that the title was taken from the introductory verses of the Brahman drama (§46). The contents are: cognition (*nāṇa*), its means and sources (including a survey of the canonical texts 262a); 23 *namaskāra*-G.; G. 24-50 a list of the patriarchs from Suhamma up to Dūsagaṇi; 2 fragments: 13 kinds of good and bad pupils indicated by catchwords in one G., and 3 kinds of an audience in 3 G. At the end of the N. we find an uncommented appendix referring to *aṇunnā* or the permission to speak, of which there are 6 kinds with altogether 20 names, and, finally, to knowledge by tradition (*suya*).

No other cognition can be object of teaching. All these items are answers to Goyama's questions.

Comm.: Cuṇṇi by Jinadāsa (printed); Ṭīkā by Malayagiri.—*Ed.* (along with the Tīkā): ĀS 45, C. 1880—Āg. S. 45, Bo. 1924.—JNĀNASUNDARA, Surat V. 2447, (no Ṭīkā).—An Alphabetical Index of the aphorisms etc. occurring in (Nandī, Aṇuog., Āv., Ogh., Dasav., Piṇḍ. and Utt.) along with detailed lists of subjects treated in these seven Āgamas. ĀGS 55, Surat 1928.

Aṇuogadārā(iṃ). Investigations (*aṇuoga*) into the range of knowledge in general and of Jain dogmatics in particular, starting from four different points of entrance (*dāra*). *Suya* as the object of teaching (closely related to the appendix of the Nandī). This leads on to the *āvassaya-suyakkhandha*. The author's purpose to describe all six of the āvassayas (§ 151) has, however, been materialized only in the first one, the *sāmāiya*. Its 4 *aṇuoga-dārā* (in which the *sāmāiya* plays no role whatever) are: approach from without (*uvakkama*, 85b), forming a scheme (*nikkheva*, 250a), penetration (*aṇugama*, 268a), the modes of expression (*naya*, 264a).

Comm.: Cuṇṇi by Jinadāsa (printed); Vṛtti by Hemacandra Maladhārin.—*Ed.* (along with the Vrtti): ĀS 44, C. 1880.—DLJP 31. 37, Bo.—Āg. S., Bo. 1924.—Ātmārām Panjābī, Ajmer 1917 (with Hindi transl.)—Jinadatta Sūri-Prācīna-Pustakoddhāra Fund, 21, Surat 1921.

The Mūlasuttas

§54. *Uttarajjhāyā* (Uttarajjhayaṇāiṃ). 36 *ajjhayaṇa*. In Jiṇac. 147 we are told about 36 *apuṭṭha-vāgaraṇāiṃ*, explanations given by Mahāvīra without being asked (by Goyama, etc.) to do so. Some old authors who took them for our Utt., explaining *uttarajjhāyā* as "last chapters" taught by the Master, were subjected to an anachronism. It rather seems that the work got its name from a group of apparently younger chapters "following" (*uttara*) the old ones. For, on the whole, the Utt. are an ancient chrestomathy intended for the members of the Order. It might be characterized as a mixed variety of catechisms, parables, systems composed in Triṣṭubh, śloka and, occassionally, in other old metres, among which the archaic form of the Āryā (in chapter 8, see § 45) has to be mentioned : there is some prose, too. The Subhikkhu chapter Utt. 15 has a parallel of the same name in Dasav. 10. Dogmatics and duties are exposed in the following chapters: *2*. Parīsahā. 22 kinds of temptations. *16*. Bambhacerasamāhiṭṭhāṇā, the 10 instructions of chastity (comp. Dasāo). *24*. Samiīo. The 5 *samii* and the 3 *gutti* (§ 173). *26*. Sāmāyārī. 10 cases of right conduct. Daily duties. *30*. Tavamagga. 6 outward and 6 inward austerities. *33*. Kammapayaḍi. The nature of Karman, its 8 kinds, etc. *34*. Lesāo. The 6 *lesā*. *36* Jīvājīvavibhatti. The system of both the animate and inanimate world.—*31*. Caraṇavihi, 21 śl., may be the text referred to in the *anga-bāhira* list.

Comm.: Nijjutti; Cuṇṇi (printed); Ṭīkās by Śāntisūri (Śiṣyahitā), Devendra, Lakṣmīvallabha; for others see CHARPENTIER (s. b.) p. 59 f.—*Ed.*: ĀS 42 (Lakṣmīv.), C. 1880.—DLJP 33. 36.41 (Śāntisūri), Bo. 1916-17.—JAYANTAVIJAYA (along with comm. by Kamalasaṃyama), 1-3, Bo. 1923-27.—The Uttarādhyayanasūtra. ed......with an introd.,crit. notes and a comm. by Jarl CHARPENTIER. Uppsala 1922. Rev. by the AUTHOR OLZ 1924, 484 f.—Bikaner 1923.—Lāhaur 1936.—ĀGRM 32 (no year).—Utt. 1-9 in Jainapāṭhamālā, 4. āvṛtti, Ahm. 1921.—Utt. 1 with Guj. transl. in Jainajnānaprakāśa, P. 1, Ahm. 1898.—*Transl.*: JACOBI in SBE 45, Oxford 1895.—For Utt. 12 (Hariesijja) and 14 (Usuyārijja) see CHARPENTIER ZDMG 62 f.; for 13 (Citta-Saṃbhūijja) see LEUMANN WZKM 5 f., ALSDORF, Belvalkar Felicitation Vol.

Dasaveyāliya. According to tradition a compilation of the most important topics arranged by Śayyaṃbhava (§ 22) for his son Maṇaka. This selection considers the practice of the monk's life even more decidedly than is done in Utt. The title means "10 (lectures) beyond (the prescribed study hours)"[1] 2 *cūliyā* at the end bring the number of *ajjhayaṇa* up to 12. Śl.,

1. The AUTHOR in Studia Indologica (Festschrift Kirfel) 1955, p. 280. For the title of Dasakāliya see GHATAGE JBORS 1953, p.432-439, For the chronology of Dasav. and Āyāra II THE SAME NIA I (1938), p.130-13f.

Triṣṭubh, and prose. *4.* Chajjīvaṇiyā. The 6 forms of living beings and their non-violation. The 5 vows and the abstention from eating at night. All chapters of even numbers (incl. the present 4th) deal with monastic life in general, while those of odd numbers do so in particular. *5.* Piṇḍesaṇā. 2 udd. Pure and impure alms. The correct way of collecting alms. *7.* Vakkasuddhi. The allowed and forbidden kinds of speach. *9.* The devotion to right conduct is four-fold (comp. Dasāo). *11.* Raivakka. 18 consolations for a monk in case of temptation.

Ed.: Daśavaikalika-sūtra and-niryukti, nach dem Erzählungsgehalt untersucht und hrsg. von Ernst LEUMANN. ZDMG 46 (1892), 581-662. Comp. the AUTHOR in the article quoted in the preceding footnote. Retranscription into Nāgarī by Jīvrāj. Gh. DOSHI, Ahm. 1912, printed in: Dasaveyāliya Sutta. . . transl. with introd. and notes by Walther SCHUBRING, Ahm. 1932.—Ed. along with the Nijjutti and Haribhadra's Śiṣyabodhinī DLJP 47, Bo. 1918.—With the comm. of Samayasundara, Jinayaśaḥ Sūrijī-GRM 1, Cambay 1919.--Dasav. 1-9 in: Jainapāṭhamālā, 4. āvr., Ahm. 1921. Many more complete prints were published in India. Jinadāsa's Cuṇṇi was printed Indaur 1933.—M. V. PATWARDHAN, The Das. sūtra: a study (with special references to chapters I-VI. VII-XII). Sangli 1933-36.—L. ALSDORF, *vāntam āpātum*, Ind. Linguistics 16, p. 21-28 (concerning Dasav. 2, 7. 8).

§55. *Āvassayanijjutti.* A Gāhā work taking its name from the 6 *āvassaya*, i.e. the formulae to be recited daily and hence called *āvassaya*, i.e. "indispensable").[1] For a great part the contents, however, go their own ways. The Āv.-nijj. being the 1st of 10 *nijjuttis* written by a scholar traditionally called Bhadrabāhu (Āv. 84 ff. of the Āg. S. ed., comp. § 43) is furnished with an elaborate introduction (*uvagghāya-nijjutti*).

The prints of the Āv. contain what may be called the Vulgata recension. As was established by LEUMANN,[2] this recension developed as the last out of four redactions from the original

1. The old text of 1-3 is discussed by LEUMANN, Übersicht p. 6f.
2. Übersicht passim.

work first revised by Sidhasena and then by Jinabhaṭa. Afterwards Jinabhadra wrote an "extensive" Bhāsa; but this Visesāvassaya-bhāsa serves merely the first half of the Nijjutti.

The manuscripts of the Uvagghāya in the Vulgata recension start by rendering the list of teachers taken from the Nandī (§ 53). The printed edition begins with the theory of cognition based upon the 5 *nāṇa* and going back to the Nandī as well. These v. 1-79 are no more than an introduction (1. Pedhiyā)[1], the *sāmāiya* to be dealt with presently being a component part of *suya-nāṇa*. (2. Paḍhamā Varavariyā[2]) (v. 80-242). In the beginning we find "Bhadrabāhu's" programme just mentioned followed by the Sāmāiyanijj. (from v. 87). With respect to the *sāmāiya* it is proposed to explain (137 f.) *uddesa* instruction, *niddesa* special information, *niggama* origin, *khetta* place, *kāla* time, *purisa* originator, *kāraṇa* cause and further subjects, 26 in all. In *niggama* we meet with Mahāvīra's pre-existences (143), the 7 *kulagara* (148) and the *nīti* they exercised, previous lives of Usabha (167), the Karman that predestined him to become a Titthagara (176), his young age (182). The same applies to all Titthagaras (230), the dates of each (up to 337). (*3*. Biiyā Varavariyā) (v. 243-525). The story of Usabha and his people continued (338) with special reference to his grandson Marīci, a pre-existence of Mahāvīra's. The life of the latter (458) up to when he entered into the *kevala-nāṇa*. (*4*). Uvasaggā begins with v. 462 and hence is an excursion to 3. (*5*.) Samosaraṇa (v. 526-590). The place where a Titthagara is going to deliver his sermon: the way how it is prepared and how the audience represented by gods, human beings and higher animals is ranged; the sermon itself and the glory of the Titthagara; the donations of the audience. (*6*). The 11 *gaṇahara* (v. 591-665). (*7*.) The tenfold *sāmāyārī* (v. 666-827). In it the discussion of the methed

1. The divisions given in brackets, as introduced by WEBER and LEUMANN, have been taken from Malayagiri's comm. as far as they appear there. Nothing of it in the verses.

2. *varavarikā*. '*var*. means proclamation of giving the desired object" (Kapadia p. 177, acc. to the Cuṇṇi ?).

of instruction (*puhatta* and *apuhatta*)[1] leads back to the two patriarchs Ajja-Vaira and Ajja-Rakkhiya the latter having played a rôle in it. Then there follows the description of the 7 schisms (778-788). It seems that LEUMANN, when following WEBER'S counting of 20 sections (which was wrong since WEBER took the *uvagghāya-nijjutti* as No. 8), attributed No. 8 to the discussion mentioned. The Uvagghāyanijjutti closes with v. 879.

The main portion deals with the 6 āvassaya in their due order preceded by the (*9.*) Namokkāranijj. (881-1019),[2] (*10.*) Sāmāiya (1020-1062), (*11.*) Cauvīsatthaya (1063-1109), (*12.*) Vandaṇā (1110-1235), (*13.*) Paḍikkamaṇa (1236-1412), (*19.*) Kāussagga (1413-1549), (20.) Paccakkhāṇa (1550-1617). Section *14* to *18* are excursions into *13.* viz.: (*14.*) Jhāṇasaya by Jinabhadra (1-105), (*15.*) Pariṭṭhāvaṇiyānijjutti (1-148) about "leaving aside" animate and inanimate objects, (*16.*) Paḍikkamaṇasaṃghayaṇī, a list of important categories from 6 up to 30, comp. Anga 3, (*17.*) 32 *joga-saṃgaha*, kinds of mental discipline, (1269-1314) and 33 *āsāyaṇā*, see Āyāradasāo No. 3, (*18.*) Asajjhāiyanijj. (1315-1412).

In LEUMANN's words (Übersicht p. 296) the whole of the Āv. nijj. is a manual of fundamental significance. Thanks to introduction and excursions it is far above the Nijjuttis of later composition and rich in legends, myths, anecdotes, allegories and parables, the interpretation of which is left to the commentators since they are presented in the poor shape of catchwords only.

Comm.: Cuṇṇi (printed); Ṭīkā by Haribhadra; the same by Malayagiri; Visesāvassayabhāsa by Jinabhadra; Viśeśāvaśyaka-

1. This calls for a brief explanation. Research (*aṇuoga*) is concerned with practice (*caraṇa-karaṇaṇuoga*), is homiletic (*dhammakahā'ṇuoga*), is calculating (*gaṇiyaṇuoga*), and speculative (*daviyaṇuoga*), comp. Dasav. nijj. 3 (*kāle* to be dropped). Now, if in explaining of one Sūtra all the 4 *aṇ.* are practised, we have "accumulation" (*apuhatta*); if according to contents no more than 1 *an.*, we have "isolation" (*puhatta*), see Dasav. nijj. 4 comm. and Āv. nijj. 762. The Digambaras have the literary divisions of *prathama-*, *karaṇa-*, *dravya-*, and *caraṇa-aṇuyoga*, i.e., world-history, astronomy, philosophy, and ethics, thus indicating a reflex of that old classification.

2. These figures as well as the following have been taken from Māṇikyaśekhara's Āvaśyakaniryuktidīpikā (Bhav. 1929-1941).

ṭīkā by Śīlānka; Śiṣyahitā by Hemacandra Maladhārin.—
—*Ed.*: Āg. S. (along with Haribhadra's Ṭīkā). P. 1-4. Bo. 1916-17. —The same (along with Malayagiri's Ṭīkā). ĀSG No. 56, 60, 85. Bo. 1928-35.—Śrī-Jinabhadra- . . viracitaṃ Viśeṣāvaśyakabhāṣyam (along with Hemacandra's Śiṣyahitā). YJGM 25, 27, 28, 31, 33, 35, 37, 39. Ben. V. 2427-41.—Sri-Viśeṣāvaśyaka bhāṣāntar (the text along with Guj. transl.). ĀSG 38 (1924). 48 and ff.—Viśeṣāvaśyakagāthānām akār'ādi-kramaḥ (along with a summary of the contents) Āg. S. Pariśiṣṭa 1, vibhāga 1.2. Bo. 1923.—Extracts from Vises. in: Pradyumna Sūri, Vicārasāraprakaraṇa. Mhesana 1923.—Hemacandra (-Maladhāri)-Sūri-sūtritaṃ Hāribhadrīy' Āvaśyakavṛtti-ṭippaṇakam. DLJP 53, Bo. 1920.—Many modern prints of Āvaśyakasūtra, Sāmāyikasūtra and, especially, Pratikramaṇasūtra.—The old Pakkhiyasutta is based upon the half month's confession (Pākṣikasūtra. Comm. by Yaśodeva, DLJP 4, Bo. (1911).

Piṇḍanijjutti. A treatise on food (*piṇḍa*) eaten by a monk composed in 671 G., originally part of the Āyāranijj. where now we have a gap after G. 315.[1] In 671 Gāhās we learn to know the mistakes made by an almsgiver (*uggama-dosa* 32b), those made by the receiver (*uppāyaṇa-d.* 120a), further we are told of the wrong way of asking for alms (*gahaṇ'esaṇā-d.* 146a) and the wrong way of using them (*ghās'esaṇā*-d. 170 b), all this in 8 dāra, the last 5 dealing with the fourth item and treated most briefly in 39 Gāhās.

Comm.: Vṛtti by Malayagiri and Vīrācārya.—Ed. (along with Malayagiri's Vṛtti) DLJP 44, Bo. 1918.

Ohanijjutti, "a general explanation" given of subjects and activities in monastic life, viz., examination (*paḍilehā* 12b), food (*piṇḍa* 128a), equipment (*uvahi-pamāṇa* 207 b), how to avoid making mistakes (*aṇāyayaṇa-vajja* 222b), contravention (*paḍisevaṇā* 224b), confession (*āloyaṇā* 225a), and atonement (*visohi* 225 b). In parallel with the Piṇḍ. the first four items

1. LEUMANN, Übersicht p. 22.

take up 1133 G. incl. 322 Bhāsa verses, though at the end the text says to have 1149 Gāhās.

Comm.: Bhāsa; Vṛtti by Droṇa[1]; Avacūri.—*Ed.*: Āg.S. (along with Bhāsa and Vṛtti), Bo. 1919.

§56. We here add those *anga-bāhira* texts which we know to be independent (whereas others, as we have seen above, are preserved as parts of other works).

Isibhāsiyāiṃ. Sentences of certain Ṛṣis (or Pratyekabuddhas, see below) concerning moral subjects. The style, often dark, reminds us of Āyār., Sūy., and Utt. 45 *ajjhayaṇa* for the equal number of Ṛṣis (44 in Samav. 88b. Different other wrong data Ṭhāṇ. 506a and elsewhere).

Comm.: Nijjutti, not yet recovered, see above.—*Ed.*: Śrīmadbhiḥ pratyekabuddhair bhāṣitāni śrī-Ṛṣibhāṣitasūtrāṇi, Indaur 1927, with appendix containing 2 Saṃgahaṇī along with the names of the Ṛṣis and the catchwords.—Ed. by Walther SCHUBRING, Nachr. Gött. Ges. d. Wiss. 1942, p. 489-576; 1952, p. 21-52 (with a Sanskrit Chāyā).

Ṭhāṇ. 506b under the general title of Saṃkheviyadasāo ("Abridged Daśās") gives the names of ten texts of which the third, fourth and fifth will be found with the following three minor products having a common subject. In considering the contents of the latter it seems rather doubtful that they should be identical with the texts of the Ṭhāṇa.

Angacūliyā. Praises the continuous tradtion of, and good instruction in, the sacred texts whence the name of "appendix to the Angas" can be derived. Such considerations are caused by the fact that through negligence bad individuals will penetrate into the Order and that, as to their moral character, the monks are no more than lukewarm. This certainly reflects a picture of the conditions prevailing in those days. A centre portion deals with the teachers as such and with practical teaching. It goes parallel with the Āyāravihi (printed Bo. 1919), but the Sanskrit verses of the same are in Prakrit here.

1. Droṇa also revised Abhayadeva's Vṛtti on Uvav., see LEUMANN, Aup. S. 19 f.

An article by the AUTHOR, following a Berlin ms., in OLZ 1926, 910-913.

Vaggacūliyā, also Vanga-and Uvanga-c. The third name is taken from the colophon in order to explain a relation to the preceding work, whereas the style and the contents speak in favour of the first. Yet a relation exists in that the Angac. towards its end, i.e. behind the words *sāhūṇaṃ hīlanti mamâvi hīlissanti*, refers to the Uvangacūliyā. This "origin of a despite of tradition" is prophesied for the year 1990 after Mahāvīra in the garb of a legend about the 22 lovers (that is, a *vagga*) of a certain courtesan Kāmalayā. The style is that of the canonical *vagga-texts* (see above) Angas 8, 9, 11 and Uvangas 8-12 thus equally allowing for a justification of the title.

See the article just mentioned, the following text, and the analysis in Guj. by KṢĀNTIVIJAYA in: Camatkārisāvacūristotrasaṃgrahaḥ, tathā Vankacūliyāsūtrasārâṃśaḥ, Ahm, s. 1979.

Viyāhacūliyā, wrongly Vivāhacūliyā. In this text, too, we meet with a decay of the Jaina Order. For it is with reference to such a decay that 16 dreams of Piyanandaṇā, wife of Candagutta of Pāḍalipura, are interpreted by Bhaddabāhu, a disciple of Saṃbhūyavijaya[1]. Candagutta resigns the throne to become a layman.—There is another Viyāhacūliyā of 8 *uddesa* where in the form of query and answer Mahāvīra teaches Goyama that idolatry will not lead to salvation.

Ed. (acc. to British Museum Cat.): Vivāhacūlikā. Ed. with Hindi interpretation and paraphrase by Upādhyāya ĀTMĀRĀMJĪ. 2nd ed., Sanjit (Agra) s. 1979.—Comp. also Kiśorīlāl Mu. MADĀYTÂ: Vivāhacūlikā kī Samālocanā aur Vangacūlikā Sūtra. (Ratnaprabhākara-Jnānapuṣpamālā 72.) Phalodi (Marwar) s. 1980. The pamphlet is directed against the Sthānakvāsī or Ḍhunḍhiyā (§ 32). The 22 men mentioned above are said to be analogous to as many representatives of the Ḍh.

Angavijjā. A compendium of divination through man's limbs. This science opens the file of the 8 *mahā-nimitta* (1, 2;

1. In the original (German) edition of this book one line was dropped erroneously in printing.

almost identical Ṭhāṇ. 427 a). Its source is said (1, 10) to be the Diṭṭhivāya whence possibly[1] the expression of *adhā-puvvaṃ* (=*Puvvaṃ* ?) which occurs invariably often. The Angav. calls itself *bhagavaī mahā-purisa* (i.e. *Mahāvīra-Vaddhamāṇa*)-*diṇṇā*. 60 *ajjhāya* in prose and some 4100 śl. (59 f.: G.).

1—7. Anguppattī, Jiṇasaṃthava, Sissopakkhāvaṇa (śl.), Angatthava, Maṇitthava (comp. 9, 1), Ādhāraṇā (presuppositions, starting points), Vāgaraṇopadesa (Disposition and method).

8. Bhūmikamma (Establishment of fundaments, comp. 8, 2, 3). 30 *paḍala* (1326 śl.). 1.2. Saṃgrahaṇī (2: śl.). 3-5. Bh. sattasamuddesa (śl. as in all that follows), Attabhāvaparikkhā, Nemitta-m-upadhāraṇā. 6-10. Divination through the client's mode of sitting, touching the seat, leaning, and from what is nearest to him. 11-16. Divination through his way of looking, laughing, questioning, saluting, addressing, and approaching. 17-27. The same through utterances of grief, indifference and tenderness; 28.29 through rest and activity. 30. Bh. guṇavibhāsā.

9. Angamaṇi (acc. to p. 57, 10=*angāvijjā-maṇi*). Praise of the Maṇisutta with a list of its 270 *paḍala* (1868 śl.). In a motley order the divinations are connected with the limbs of a man, their qualities being natural (e.g. right, left and middle, smooth and rough, curved and straight), subjective (e.g. handsome and ugly, hideous and pleasing, insignificant), abstract (e.g. masculine, etc., present and future, *bambheya, khatteya, vesseya, suddeya*). Finally, limbs are confronted with figures (from 1-10 up to *koḍī* and *aparimita*).

10—58. Prose (śl. in 13, 22 f., 26, 46). The previous qualifications apply to the client's coming, disposition, way of putting questions, and to the locality where this happens to pass (10. 11). Fundamental traits (*joṇī*) in individual human nature beginning with *dhamma, attha,* and *kāma,* and their signs (*lakkhaṇa-vāgaraṇa,* with 69 śl.) (12. 13). Questions of acquisition,

1. This was the view of LEUMANN (VIIth OC; IA 10, 164) who was the first to draw the attention of scholars upon this work.

sexual intercourse, children, health, vitality (*jīvita*), commercial activity (*kamma*), rains (for the crops), and military success, all of them with their negatives (14-21=8 *dāra*). A list of pleasant and unpleasant omina (*pasattha* and *appasattha uppāya*) which allow of respective divinations (22.23, 1 and 3 śl.). Birth as an *ajja* (*bambhaṇa* etc.) or *milakkhu* (*sudda*) and the domiciles as such ones (jātīvijaya 24), gotra and personal name (here 113 śl.) (25. 26). Office, profession, character, residence (*ṇagara*) (27-29). Finery, dress, cropstore, conveyances (30-33). Previous (*vatta*) talks (34). Existence of children and their future fate (Payāvisuddhi 35). *dohala*, *lakkhaṇa*, *vanjaṇa* (36-38). Looking for a wife (Kaṇṇāvāsaṇā 39). Food and drink, festive entertainments (40). Sexual intercourse, partly unnatural (Variyagaṇḍiyā nāma arahass' ajjhāya, Col.: Rahassapaḍala 41). Dreams (42). Journey and coming back (43-45). What one sees on entering the house (91 śl.) (46). Military campaign, victory and defeat (47-49). Diseases (50). Goddesses and gods, nakṣatras, meteoric and terrestrial omina (*uppāta*) (51-53). Precious objects, treasures and where deposited, the same of money ((*ṇidhi*)[1], lost things and persons and where to be detected (54-57). Thought-reading which includes all that the world contains of living beings (*Siddhas* included) and lifeless matter (Cintita 58)

59. Kāla. 27 *paḍala* (709 G., 21, 22 (partly), 27: prose). 5 time units: *muhutta*, *divasa*, *pakkha*, *māsa*, *vassa* (1). *uppāta* referred to *kāla* (U. vidhiparikkhā 2) and to *muhutta* etc. (3-9). The client's reference to most various, though separately grouped, impressions and objects results in predicting the general duration of an *uppāya*, its appearance in a nakṣatra, month and season, pakṣa, tithi[2], night, day and in certain hours of the same (10-19). The precise circumstances (observations, actions) under which the *upp.* came into appearance must be known (20). The aspect of a new-born boy and of a portentous (*ovāta*) human being, animal, plant or lifeless object of both

1. Thus rightly on p. 262, 14 of the Ed. where we find *ṇivvi* and *ṇivvu* (p. 221 f.).

2. The word is not used here nor in 21.

natural sex and grammatical gender with reference to day-times and tithis (21). Increase and decrease of the value (*aggha*) of property (*bhaṇḍa*) with reference to time units on account of what the client has told (Agghappamāṇa 22). Predictions concerning fire and floods (23.24). The time units, increasing in length as they are, referred to actions and objects interrelated and, for their part, increasing in significance (e.g. *muhutta*, *divasa*, *pakkha*, *māsa*=*devāṇaṃ paṇāma*, *vandita*, *thuti*, *namaṃsita*) (25). Similar reflections about *kāla* of an *uppāya*. Its length according to what happened to occur in the client's words (26). Duration and precise term (month, seacon etc.) of an *upp*. as inferred from the client's touching and seizing of his own limbs (Kālappavibhāga 27).

6o. The preceding life of the client as a god, a human being, an animal or a denizen of hell inferred from what he has presently experienced or related (Puvvabhavavivāga Col: Purimabhavavibhāga). The same, in inverse sequence, denotes the client's destiny in the next following life (Upapattīvijaya).

The Angav. is a most remarkable work not only owing to its size and the subject treated but thanks to giving us numerous insights into the daily life of the time. Long lists of individual qualities (as descent, name, occupation), town and house portions, household utensils and public institutions provide a picture of life as led in the early centuries A.D. It follows that apart from stereotype expressions the Jain character of the work is not distinct throughout. The language is near to Jain Śaurasenī.

Ed.: Aṅgavijjā (Science of Divination through physical signs and symbols) ed. by PUṆYAVIJAYA. (Prakrit Text Society, Vol. 1) Ban. 1957.—A detailed review by the AUTHOR ZDMC 109, p. 44f.-459.

IV

COSMOLOGY

§ 57. *The Fundamental Facts.* The word "fundamental fact" is but a fairly liberal version of *atthikāya* which literally means "mass of all that is". As such it represents a mass by the totality of the units (*paesa*).[1] The five fundamental facts are known as motion (*dhamma*), stop (*adhamma*), space (*āgāsa*), souls (*jīva*), and matter (*poggala*), each in combination with *atthikāya*. Viy. 775b renders alleged synonyms which, however, do not hit the point. They simply replace the basic words now in a conventional and then, again, in quite a remote way. Thus e.g. *dhamma* stands for complying and *adhamma* for not complying with the monastic duties.[2]

The five fundamental facts constitute the world, or, rather, the world and the non-world (Viy. 608a). Their qualities are laid down in Viy. 147b. They all share in eternity. The space embraces both the world and the non-world, whereas the remaining four are concerned with the expansion of the world. For the dimensions of parts of the world proportional to motion, stop and space see Viy. 151a ff. and, nearly consonant, 775a. All *atthikāya* except the *jīva* are inanimate (*ajīva*), and, with the single exception of matter, all are immaterial (*arūva*). The last two sentences explicitly represent Mv.'s personal conception (Viy. 324b).[3] Materiality is defined by saying (324b) that

1. *astayaś ceha pradeśās, teṣāṃ kāyaḥ* Sthān. 516a; Prajn. 8b 9a. See also Nemicandra, Davvasaṃgaha 24. From the Attkikāyas KOHL starts in his book, Das physikalische and biologische Weltbild der indischen Sekte der Jainas (Aliganj 1956). Rev. by the AUTHOR, ZDMG 109, p. 226ff.

2. Thus all five *atthikāya* are dealt with in the way described. This speaks against the opinion held by Jagdish Chandra JAIN (IHQ 9, 792-794) saying there here a non-metaphysical outlook on *dhamma* and *adhamma* is being given.

3. Some of the audience had difficulties in understanding this as we are told in two reports (Viy. 323b, 750b). Dissenters led by Kālodāi ask Goyama and the layman Madduya resp. for an interpretation. While Goyama is at a loss for an answer, Madduya declares himself incompetent in the matter,

among all inanimate fundamental facts matter alone is palpable (*poggal' atthikāyaṃsi cakkiyā kei āsaittae vā saittae vā ciṭṭhittae vā* etc.), whereas this does not apply to motion, stop or space, even though they fill the world completely. They are, in fact, as little palpable as are the flames of a thousand candles lighting a closed room (615b).[1] As to *dhamma* and *adhamma* we know them, thanks to JACOBI on T. 5, 1. 17 in their meaning[2] as motion and stop so characteristic of the Jains. It is by their presence only that any motion and any rest become possible at all, so that they themselves are not actually meant[3] (and, for that reason, we ought to speak of stop rather than of rest). Within the realm of souls, *dhamma* and *adhamma* produce all possible conditions of movability and its opposite, on the one hand "coming and going, speaking, moving an eyelid, activity of the inner sense, speech and body" and on the other "standing motionless, sitting, lying, confinement to the acitivity of the inner sense" (Viy. 608a). Concerning space we have to distinguish between the space of the world (*log'āgāsa*) and the space of the non-world (*alog'āgāsa*), the former representing but an infinitely small fraction of the total space (Viy. 151a). It is in the nature of space to give room (*avagāhāṇā*, not *ogāh.*) to any amount of atoms (608a)[4]; but this, of course, applies merely to the space of the world, the space of the non-world being absolutely void (Viy. 151a). Notwithstanding this discrimination i should be observed that both space and motion as well as rest are definitely singular, whereas souls and matter are of an infinite variety, and, moreover, they alone are active. For the

but when pressed he shows by pointing out to the wind, sweet scent particles, fire made by rubbing two sticks, persons living beyond the seas, and gods, all being existent without being visible, that something, even though nothing can be said about it except by a Kevalin, yet may exist. Mahāvīra commends him for not having taught things he does not understand and for thus having evaded giving offence (*āsāyaṇā*) to the sacred law, the Arhats and the Kevalins.

1. Note that the flame as a light is of material nature (§ 60).

2. But the *atthikāya* "*dhamma*" stands next to the *suya*- and the *caritta-dhamma*, Ṭhāṇ. 154 b.

3. This might serve as a reply to SCHRADER's proposal (Festgabe für JACOBI, page 274) to derive *dharma* from a root *dhṛ* "to go".

4. It therefore does not count among the *atthikāya* which "touch world", Ṭhāṇ. 251b.

nature of the soul rests in its intellectual function (*uvaoga*), which by means of will and skill is put to use in all possibilities of intellectual cognition. The matters cause the souls to take possession (*gahaṇa*) of the bodies and to enact bodily functions. They own all qualities of colour (black, dark, red, yellow, white), of taste (bitter, sharp, astringent, sour, sweet), of smell (good, bad), and of palpability (heavy, light, soft, rough, cold, warm, sticky, dry, see also Ṭhāṇ. 422a). The five fundamental facts (see also Ṭhāṇ. 332b, Samav. 10 a) are substances (*davva*)[1]. But the expression *savva-davva* also includes the time (*addhā*[2]-*samaya*) according to Viy. 873 a).[3] With the former it is connected by its eternity and singularity, whereas it is separated from them by being confined in space and by lacking space points. The difference in opinions manifests itself in the conception of T. 5, 38 where time (*kāla*) is being unconditionally acknowledged as matter by the Dig., whereas but conditionally by the Śvet. Just as space consists of units, so does time. One unit of time (*samaya*)[4] forms the present. It then follows that the future owns as many *samaya* as does the past plus 1, and the latter again as many as the former minus 1; the total time comes to twice the amount of the past with a plus, and twice the amount of the future with a minus, and, consequently, the time that has passed makes up half its total with a plus, and the time to come half its total with a minus (Viy. 889a).[5] Even the smallest calculable fraction of time, the *āvaliyā*, consists of as many[6] *samaya* as all

1. *daviyadi, gacchadi, tāiṃ sabbhāva-pajjayāiṃ jaṃ daviyaṃ taṃ bhaṇṇante* Pancatthik. 9.

2. Most certainly it goes back to *adhvan*, but the Sanskrit of the comm. gives *addhā*—(fem.) Viy. 532b; in Ṭhāṇ. 201 a we find *addhā-kāla*, the eternal time as the fourth beside the civil time measure (*pamāṇa-k.*), the amount of life-time (*ahāu-nivatti-k.*), and the time of death (*maraṇa-k.*).

3. F. K. LALANA, The six Dravyas of the Jaina Philosophy. Bombay 1914.

4. Viy. 6, 4, 1 speaks of *paesa* as of time; the soul is *kāl'āesenaṃ sapaesa*, because it has existed since times eternal.—For the atomism of time with the Jains see MASSON-OURSEL, Archiv f. Gesch. d. Philos. 40, 173-176.

5. Both past and future being without beginning and without end are equal in duration. The "plus" and the "minus" are the 1 *samaya* of the present.

6. *asaṃkhejja* (ι)=incomputable as against *saṃkhejja* (x)=computable, expressible by a definite figure; *aṇanta* (∞)=innumerable.

the remaining others which are being recorded (see also Ṭhāṇ. 158a), up to the *ussappiṇī*. When occurring repeatedly their number may increase up to ∞ (Viy. 887 b). For the list of time measures see Viy. 275a, 888a; Jambudd. 89a and also a.o. Ṭhāṇ. 158a. It may suffice to refer to JACOBI on T. 4, 15 and KIRFEL, Kosmographie pp. 337-339, and to note the fundamental difference between those measures that are calculable (*gaṇiya*) and those expressible by way of comparison only (*addho'vamiya*). The latter (see Jambudd. 92b) according to Ṭhāṇ. 90b, 430b are *paliovama, sāgarovama, osappiṇī, ussappiṇī* (§ 12), *poggala-pariyaṭṭa, tīyaddhā, aṇāgay'addhā*, and *savv' addhā*, but that expression will apply only to the first four or five.

§58. *The Units.* Logically the "masses" are preceded by their parts, and these appear as the *desa* and the *paesa*. But while the *paesa* are essential for the structure of the world, the *desa* represent but calculable quantities. So, *e.g.*, the fundamental facts *dhamma, adhamma* and *āgāsa* do not exist in their totalities in the lower, the upper and the higher regions of the world, but only in their parts mentioned (*desa*), whereas in the total world (*loga*) they do not exist in parts but wholly with the exception of *āgās'atthikāya*, which, as we saw, is existent in the world as well as in the non-world (Viy. 522 a). On the other hand (see again Viy. 522a) we may just as well examine a unit of space as to whether it contains the *atthikāya* either completely or in parts (*egammi*[1] *āgāsa-paese*). For other considerations containing the *desa* and the *paesa* see Viy. 149a, 493a, 714a; Pannav. 8a. Let us make it quite clear that it is the *paesa* or the "units" which in their totality, and in their totality only, constitute the "masses". No fraction of either, however large, may replace them, and any deduction is as little admissible as with a concrete object (*no khaṇḍe cakke . . . —sakale cakke . . .* Viy. 148a). With motion, rest and space this comglomeration which lacks both beginning and originator (*vīsasā*) is not a merger, but the units of one and the same mass are strung up like the links of a chain. They do not mix like milk and water (Viy.

1. We ought to expect : *egaṃsi*.

394a incl. comm.). The number of the units is ∞ with the total space as well as with souls and matter, and ṡ with motion and rest (148a) and with the space of the world (421a, 610a, 873b). Moreover there are 8 centremost units (*majjha-paesa*), which, each with motion, rest and space are supposed (acc. to comm.) to exist in the centre of the upper regions of the world, called the Ruyaga, in Rayaṇappabhā (§107), with the souls within their resp. bodies. They will occupy 1 to 6 or either 8, but *vastu-svabhāvāt* not 7 units of space (Viy. 886a, 395b). In the realm of space we meet the 4 main and the 4 intermediate directions (*disā* and *vidisā*) in addition to zenith (*uḍḍhaṃ*) and nadir (*aho*). Their are given as *indā, jāmā, vāruṇī, somā; aggeī, neraī, vāyavvā, īsāṇī; vimalā, tamā* (see Viy. 492b).[1] Acc. to the comm. they are of two-resp. one-dimensional shape.[2] The pole from which they start (Viy. 606a, Thān, 477b) is a square cube[3] of 8 *paesa*.

If the masses constitute the world, they necessarily have to interpenetrate each other, and the units of the one must be touched (*puṭṭha*) by those of the others. Viy. 609a discusses with how many units this will be the case. In doing so, the units of time (*addhā-samaya*) are included. In other words, they are placed on the same level with the others and considered constant. Maximum and minimum figures (*ukkoseṇaṃ* and *jahanneṇaṃ*) mean that a unit in one corner of the end of the world can be surrounded only by 2 lateral units and 1 either above or below, but not by 4 round about and 2 above and below. Both space and time are conditionally, or resp. unconditionally, limited, so that contact will not occur everywhere. The masses interpenetrate each other insomuch that 1 u. motion will coincide with 1 u. rest 1 u. space (*jattha . . ogāḍhe tattha. . og.*). That is to say that e.g. in the minimum of cases the afore-said unit of motion is being touched not by 2 but by 4 u. rest, and not by 6 but by 7 u. But then it coincides (*taiḥ pratyekam antarvyāptaḥ*) with ∞ units of souls, matter and time, as far as the latter is

1. But we find the tripartition above, below and horizontal directions just as well (Ṭhāṇ. 132b).

2. *diśaḥ śakaṭoddhi-saṃsthitāḥ, vidiśas tu muktāvaly-ākārāḥ, ūrdhvâdho-diśau ca rucak' ākāre* Vy. 493b.

3. LEUMANN, Übersicht p. 43b.

concerned. By 1 u. of soul, and, equally, 1 u. of matter, coinciding with ∞ u. of soul and ∞ u. of matter, we are given proof of the greater density of these substances.

Viy. 420b; Ṭhāṇ. 251b say that the individual soul has as many *paesa* as has the space of the world. But this does not refer to the limiting case of the Kevalin as the comm. wants us to believe; it simply says that both have units. One individual soul occupies the room of 1/¿ *ang.* (or either more) of such quantities (T. 5, 15) as are presumed by the part of that or that size acquired through Karman. So then (substantially) the soul of an elephant equals that of a louse, as is explained by the simile of the lamp whose light, as the case may be, will illuminate a large or a small hollow room (Rāyap. 140a, referred to by Viy. 313a). T. 5, 16 in giving this simile its literary expression hereto introduces the conception of contraction and expansion. They stand for different densities within the same number of units, i.e., ¿ in different bodies (Siddh. ref. to T. 5, 8).[1] For the historical importance of the theory (Viy. 365a), according to which the soul equals the body in size, see JACOBI GGA 1919, 17.

Also the units of matter differ in number from 0 up to ∞. The lower limit is the smallest unit of matter, the atom. It is true that, acc. to Kundakunda, the atom has 1 unit (Davvas. 26), but acc. to Umāsvāti it has none. It is one (T. 5, 11 and Siddh. ref. to 5, 11, 14), and thus it coincides with 1 u. It follows that also the word *poggal'atthikāya-paesa* is being applied in speaking of the atom, and its combinations have the word *paesa* added (see below).[2] There is still another difference with regard of the density of these *paesa*: 1 u. space may contain up to ∞ atoms (Viy. 613b). That is to say: 2 units of matter coincide with 1 or 2 u. of space (and as many units of motion and rest), 3 with 1, 2 or 3, and finally ∞ with 1, 2, 3, ... x, ∞ or ∞. For an explanation Siddh. gives a number of similes with ref. to 5, 14.

1. JAINI, Outlines p. 17 speaks of an elasticity of the soul.
2. Comp. also *paramāṇu-poggala-mette vi paese* Viy. 579a.

§59. *The Atom.* *poggala*, the word for atom,[1] is applied in its basic meaning as a "concrete body" in Viy. 176b, whereas in 240a it means the part of an individual. The atom is eternal (Viy. 65b) as is the substance of which it is the ultimate particle and among the fundamental facts it is the only one bearing any physical character (T. 5, 4). Owing to the fineness of its structure by which it eludes observation, it is beyond the grasp of tools and indivisible[2], but it owns the qualities of colour, smell, and taste at either 1 kind or 2 kinds of touch (Viy. 746b. 797a) among the possible 5, 5, 2 and 8 kinds of these four (Viy. 778 a), and such in an endless variety of different grades (*guṇa*). The qualities of touch are cold or warm in combination with smooth or rough.

It is either spontaneously or by means of an impulse from without (Ṭhāṇ. 63b) that atoms by merging constitute aggregates (*khandha*) which, as the case may be, may own a greater number of qualities of colour, etc. (Viy. 748b). According as such a one consists of 2, 3, etc., atoms, we speak, as already mentioned, of a *du-paesiya, ti-p.*, etc. up to *aṇanta-p. khandha*. In connexion with aggregates the atom is called *paramāṇu-poggala*. An aggregate consisting of even-numbered atoms is divisible into halves, but it lacks a middle (it is *amajjha*), whereas conditions are reversed with odd numbers, and both cases are valid with indeterminate numbers, (x, and ¿); it goes without saying, however, that all of them are *sa-paesa* (Viy. 233 a). The way how to decompose an aggregate consisting of 2 and more atoms is demonstrated in Viy. 102b and, more closely, in Viy. 561a. That such a decomposition will result in gaining only complete atoms had to be specifically stressed in 103a. Just as the question of divisibility is being discussed so is the contiguity (*puṭṭha*) between atoms and aggregates by taking as a basis 9 possibilities, either whether it occurs in parts

1. *pūrayati galati ca* Siddh. ref. to T. 5, 10, comp. with 5. 32.—*puggala* is scarcely ever read.

2. This is what the *paramaṇu* has in common with the *samaya* and the *paesa* (Ṭhāṇ. 134b). It appears to be probable that *apaesa* along with *aṇaddha*, *amajjha*, and *avibhāima* equally means only the lacking of parts (see also 233a and others).

(*desenaṃ, desehiṃ*) or completely (*savvenaṃ*) (Viy. 233b). It must be noted, therefore, that the number of atoms constituting an aggregate may divide among one and several *paesa*.

The mergence of atoms and aggregates with atoms and aggregates is brought about (Viy. 102b. 103b) by a *siṇeha-kāya*, though nothing concerning its nature is mentioned.[1] T. 5, 32 introduces the contrasted pair of *snigdha* and *rūkṣa*, 'smooth' and 'rough'.

As is the case with all sensuous qualities, also these two *lukkha* and *niddha* (Viy. 638 b *lukkhī* and *alukkhī*) exist in gradations (*guṇa*), as is presupposed by Viy. 878 a, whereas in Viy. 394 b they are but hinted at by *vemāya-niddhayā* etc. According to T. 5, 33 the lowest grades will not merge because they lack sufficient power to assimilate (*śakti* Siddh.); it takes at least two grades of difference to make this power effective (T. 5, 35), and that is why only equal grades—though only s+r, not s+s (T. 5, 34)—will assimilate, and, accordingly, only the lower grade to the higher.

§60. Thus it follows that the atom, though as a substance it is eternal, is changeable in its conditions. As to Viy. 640 a, colour, smell, taste, and touch are qualified as conditions, (*pajjava*). They are inherent in the substance (*paryāya* T. 5,37). But according to Pannav. 5. (196b) *pajjava* also means the secondary differences of atoms and aggregates within each of the above mentioned four spheres and, moreover, within their size (*ogāhaṇā*). Their number is ∞ , and thus it happens that they coincide with the *pariṇāma*, the "accidental" changes and their results, which constitute the momentary being of an object (T. 5, 41). As such the above mentioned four are referred to by Viy. 420 b along with the shape (*saṃṭhāṇa*, see below). The latter is omitted by Ṭhāṇ. 201a. These five species as existing spontaneously (*vīsasā*) are contrasted with those caused by an impulse from without (*paogasā*) or either by the mixture of both

1. Quite another kind of *suhuma* is the *siṇeha-k.* which acc. to Viy. 83b moves in all directions (*pavaḍai*) and thus dissolves rapidly in contrast to the *bāyara āu-kāya*.

(*mīsa*) according to Viy. 328 a[1]. *pariṇāma*, however, within the realm of the inanimate does not refer to those five only (Pannav. 13, 287b), but also to combination (of smooth and rough), cleavage (s.b.) and sound (s.b.), as well as to motion and the absence of weight and non-weight. Motion may manifest itself by extending either in long or short distances or by either leading to contacts or not.[2] From Viy. 95 b, we learn that neither heavy nor light is a quality of the Karman body § 262), of the tinge of souls (§ 97), the inward sense (§ 71), or of speech (§ 68) which all pertain to the realm of matter.

The transition from one *pariṇāma*[3] to the next is described by synonyms as a process of motion; *paramâṇu-poggale* (and *khandhe*) *eyai veyai calai phandai ghaṭṭai khubbhai udīrai taṃ taṃ bhāvaṃ pariṇamai* Viy. 232 b (after 182b). Aggregates will experience it either totally or partially. T. 5, 26 teaches a.o. that aggregates come about by an amalgamation of atoms as well as by the secreting of atoms (*sāhaṇaṇā* and *bheya*, Viy. 567a), i.e. by giving away atoms. This theory may well go back to Viy. 743b, where it is said that of all *poggala* seized for the purpose of taking in matter (*geṇhai*) a being will retain (*āhārei*) 1/¿ and give away 1/∞ (*nijjarei*), that is to say *seya-kale*, during the vibration as which the transition manifests itself (*grahaṇnântaram* Vy.), for with reference to *eya* all atoms and aggregates are called *seya* and *nireya* (*saija* and *nireja*).[4] The act of motion passes in an incalculably small time, i.e. in 1/¿ *āvaliyā* at the very utmost, which is called *antara* (Viy. 234b, 883b).

In connexion with the theory of motion the *sadda-pariṇaya poggala* are quoted and equated with the atoms and aggregates in motion, whereas the *asadda-p.p.* are equated with those in rest during motion and rest. So that, then, the sound, either *subbhi* or *dubbhi*,[5] is a quality of the matter in its form as an

1. The *paogasā* and *vīsasā pariṇaya poggala* are mentioned by Subuddhi to his prince Jiyasattu (Nāya 12, 174a.)

2. For the *phusamāṇa-gai* Prajn. refers to the act of making a flat stone skip along the surface of water (*bāla-jana-prasiddha*).

3. Acc. to Viy. 638b the new *pariṇāma* comes on when the former is *nijjiṇṇa*. In this connexion *samayaṃ* means "for some time."

4. Vy. is wrong in saying *eṣyati kāle*.

5. Nāyādh. 174a; Pannav. 288a.

aggregate. According to T. 5, 24 the same is true with association, fineness and coarseness[1]), form and decay, darkness, shadow, warmth and light. Of these ten phenomena the first seven are such inherent in the aggregate, whereas the last three are irradiations. The modes of the association, i.e. of the units within the animate and inanimate world, are grouped by Viy. 394b according to spontaneousness (*vīsasā*), impulse (*paogasā*), and finality (*sāiya, aṇāiya sapajjavasiya* and *ap.*). Between the fineness and its opposite there runs the dividing-line which separates this concrete world from the one beyond sensual conceivability, the first being *bāyara*, the latter *suhuma*. Their difference is in the number of atoms: an aggregate consisting of ¿ atoms is equally unsplittable as is the single atom, whereas if consisting of ∞ atoms it can be split, and then it is even combustible as well as it may get wet and be able to float (Viy. 232 b). T. 5, 28 points out that its spectacular appearance results from decay and association, and in order to prove this Devanandin offers a theory[2], though it may simply mean that the object radiates atoms which associate with the organs of sense known to be of material quality. As to the shape of aggregates we distinguish between geometrical and non-geometrical formations, the latter being called *aṇitthaṃtha* "not thus behaving". In circular (*parimaṇḍala*), orbicular (*vaṭṭa*), triangular, square, and linear formations the atoms, or the units resp., are arranged in an either two-or three-dimensional order (*payara, ghaṇa*), in linear formations (*āyaya*) also one-dimensionally (*seḍhi-āyaya*), and, with the only exception of circular formations, they contain atoms in either odd or even numbers (*oya-paesa, jumma-p.*). Their highest and lowest numbers are laid down in Viy. 860a. Decay may manifest itself in the shape of smaller units, lumps, potsherds, leaves, and brookes (Pannav. 266a, 288a). The material quality of darkness becomes evident in the *tamu-kkāya* and the *kaṇha-rāī* of the world (§ 134). Darkness and lightness of night and day are attributed according to Viy. 246b to *asubha*

1. Thus instead of "smallness' and "largeness" (JACOBI for *saukṣmya* and *sthaulya*).

2. JACOBI with ref. to T. 5, 28.

and *subha poggala*, and to the former also the darkness in the different regions of hell (see Ṭhāṇ. 263a). In the legendary story of Jambudd. III the lightness is like scattered matter that lasts. For Bharata (§ 13) at the head of his army succeeds in passing through the long tunnels of both the Timisa-and Khaṇḍappavāya-guhā in the rays of his jewel by forming circles which alternatingly appear on the right and the left walls (Jambudd. 225a). This can but mean that he is anxious not to leave any spot dark, and, actually, no spot remains dark, after he has passed. Each circle lies in the radiant sphere of the other.

§61. *The Substances*. The formations of aggregates, as mentioned just before, result in the substances of, so to say, a second order, i.e., in material masses called *davva* like those of the first order (§ 57). In Viy. 420b we read that one atom and its multiples form whole *davva* or either parts of such (*desa*): from four atoms upwards all eight combinations possible in this connexion will occur. *suhuma* (§60) are the accumulations of colours, smells, and different kinds of taste and palpability which, acc. to Viy. 757 a, are to be found in closely packed density below each region of the lower and the upper world. Material masses of this kind, together with their shapes, come into being spontaneously, whereas all accumulations furnishing the souls in the world with bodies and opportunities of activity—for the inanimate substance is destined to serve the animate (Viy.856a)—result from impulse, i.e., through the working of the Karman. But as those accumulations have concrete qualities, it follows that they represent a mixture of both cases (Viy. 332 a). Now, owing to Karman, matter forms in four bodies, the inward sense, speech and breath (Viy. 567a; Ṭhāṇ. 158a). The infinite variety of matter thus grouped is called *poggala-pariyaṭṭa*[1]. At least in the case of the inward sense matter is divided into *vaggaṇā* (Viy. 222a, 646b), for we hear of the ∞ *maṇo-davva-vaggaṇā* of certain gods. Further proofs for this are missing, but s.b. Of the five bodies existent the body of transmission is

1. Homonymous is the maximum measure of time (Viy. 887b).

equally missing in this connexion, since (comp. Sthān. 158a) it cannot occur along with the body of transformation in the same individual (§ 62). From Viy. 621 a ff. we learn, to begin with, that the inner-sense and speech are of a bodily quality (*rūviṃ*). Concerning the inner sense we may refer to the *vaggaṇā* mentioned above. Speech, however, counts as being shaped like a thunderbolt (*vajja-saṃṭhiya*, Pannav. 255b, comp. § 68), and its atoms are "beyond heavy and light" (*agurulahu*) and thus of a quality (*pariṇāma*) which (comp. Prajn. 389a) is shared by all non-bodily substances including also the inner sense and the Karman. That both speech and the inner sense must be distinguished from the I (ego) (*āyā*) (§ 70), that they are unconscious (*acitta*) and inanimate (*ajīva*), but yet are inherent in souls, adds to establish their bodily nature.

§62. *The Bodies.* During the time of its specific bodily existence the individual possesses more than one body (*sarīra*). Their number is five in all (Pannav. 12. 21; Samav. 216a; Ṭhāṇ. 169b), but their distribution among the different beings differs (§ 67. 104).[1] They all have the Karman body (*kammaga s.*) and the fiery body (*teyaga s.*) life long. All beings pertaining to the upper world, i.e. animal and human beings with one to five senses, permanently own the earthly body (*urāliya* or *orāḷ. s.*). Both the gods and the inhabitants of hell always live in bodies of transformation (*veuvviya s.*),[2] but other beings do so only temporarily, while the body of transposition (*āhāraga s.*) merely applies to human beings and in special cases only. The functions of some of these bodies is as well as their purpose are told in the commentaries which however do not always agree. The established list leading from *orāl.* over *veuvv.*, *āhār.*, *tey.* to *kamm. sarīra* suggests the gradual increase in fineness and, simultaneously, in density of material units (T. 2, 38-40).[3] Apart from the beings already mentioned all higher animal and human

1. Acc. to Viy. 622b. Pannav. 268a we have different kinds due to stages of transition supervening in case the seizure of a new body has not yet been completed.

2. (*a*)*veuvviya-sarīra* ref. to gods= (un)adorned Viy. 746a.

3. In this connexion Prajn. 269b speaks of *vargaṇāsu pradeśa-bāhulyam.*

beings, generated by breeding (§63)—the latter when living in a *kamma-bhūmi* (§117)—own bodies of transformation, that is to say, that a human being may change its appearance (*vikuvvittae*) magically, provided that it be free from sin (*amāī*, § 181). For, so we learn from Viy. 189 a, the prepared food taken by a monk in a sinful way (*māī*) will strengthen his bones and the marrow within, but it will weaken flesh and blood, whereas the accidental food of the sinless will result in the opposite. While the one aids to the development of the bodily organs, the other will transubstantiate into excretions. The capability of transformation therefore depends on bodily pre-conditions. We are not told when and at what point higher animals enter into transformation. Apart from the beings mentioned above the coarse wind-beings equally have bodies of transformation, which appear in the shape of a flag (*paḍāgā*), manifesting themselves either as storms or clouds, yet without changing their minute smallness (1/¿ *angula*) (Pannav. 416a, 417a).[1] Animal and human beings, however, may become either quite small or immensely large (1/¿ *ang.* upto 100, resp. 100,000 *joy.*). The inhabitants of hell and the gods, with the exception of the Gevijja and Aṇuttara (§ 129), are equally able to change their appearance, even though they already live in bodies of transformation. This body of transformation so characteristic of their form of existence and built up without attracting foreign particles of matter (§ 181) is called *bhava-dharaṇijja*, whereas *uttara-veuvviya* is the body deliberately taken.

Pannav. 423a points out that the body of transposition is exclusively destined to serve pious persons in the Karman places (§ 117) who own magic powers (*iḍḍhi-patta*), but who have not yet succeeded in accomplishing self-discipline (*pamatta-saṃjaya*), whereas acc. to Devanandin on T. 2, 37, 49 it is meant to prove those powers, to solve subtile dogmatic questions, and to escape any violation of self-discipline.[2] It is defined by T. 2, 49, and its possession is confined to those who are in

1. *etāvat-pramāṇa-vikurvaṇāyām eva tasya śakti-saṃbhavāt* Prajn. 418a.
2. *sūkṣma-padārtha-nirjnānārtham asaṃyama-parijihīrṣayā ca.*

command of the 14 Puvva, i.e. its occurrence is antedated by Umāsvāti and located in the historical past. We may be allowed to assume that rather than *āhāraka* "attracting"[1] its name should be *ādhāraka* in that the body represents a "vessel" either for him who, for the time of 1 *muhutta* at the longest (T. p. 60, 9), slips into it which is no higher than a *rayaṇa*, or else for the instruction brought home by its bearer from a consultative magic change of place. But it was not before Umāsvāti that the latter purpose was introduced. The body of transposition does not exist simultaneously with that of transformation, as this is neither the case with magic powers by which they are generated. The Karman body is the individual formation given its shape by deeds previously wrought. The fiery body has to be understood as a bearer of potential energies, and by being allotted to all beings the latter are attributed a latent energy which may manifest itself with individual persons on the ground of magic power (*labdhi*). This power will appear a. o. as an radiation of either heat or coolness as an effect of either curse or blessing (comp. the *teya-nisagga* which provides the name for Viy. 15). The teachers referred to by Umāsvāti on T. 2, 43 are wrong in considering only those exceptional persons, as is Devanandin in adding his Sūtra to T. 2, 48. Not enough with the functions mentioned, Siddhasena (T. S. 59) and Haribhadra (T.S. 56), understand the fiery body to cause digestion, but we think it improbable that of all five bodies the finest but one should serve that purpose. All bodies except the earthly one are closely linked with the soul (*jīva-phuḍa*, Ṭhāṇ. 251b).

§ 63. *Physiology*. A being comes into existence physically by three ways; by manifestation, by coagulation, or by generation. Manifestation (*uvavāya*) means creation brought about with lightning-like suddenness without any material basis;[2] thus the gods and the inhabitants of hell spring into life. Caogulation (*sammucchaṇä*) takes place spontaneously out of existing matter; it pertains to all beings furnished with one to four senses. All

1. *āhriyata ity āhārakaḥ* Devanandin 182.

2. *jaha mehāsaṇi-tiyas'indacāva-vijjūṇa saṃbhavo hoi gayaṇammi khaṇena, ahā devāṇa vi hoi uppattī*, Haribhadra, Samaraiccakahā ed. JACOBI, p. 57, 3.

beings with five senses, i.e. all higher animals and human beings, come into existence partly in the same way (s.b.) and partly by generation (*gabbha-vakkanti, garbha-vyutkrānti*). The place where a being comes into existence, is its place of origin (*joṇi*).[1] It is either cold, animated, concealed (*saṃvuḍa*),[2] or the opposite hereof or both. A fourth trinity (Pannav. 227b) is purely anatomical (§ 64). The distribution of these 9 qualities among the beings, as given in Pannav. 9 (comp. Ṭhāṇ. 121a), can be easily understood. The inhabitants of hell, for instance, come into existence in cold and hot places, the gods in temperate ones (*siôsiṇa*). In such as the latter ones generation takes place, and, moreover, they are both covered and open to view (*saṃvuda-viyaḍa*). For according to its position the uterus (*garbha*) is concealed, though yet it is visible in advanced pregnancy. Manifestation takes place in unanimate places: the gods come into being on the throne of gods and in the garb of gods, that is in a covered concealed place, and the same applies to the inhabitants of hell (*nārakôtpatti-sthānānāṃ saṃvṛta-gavākṣa-kalpatvāt* Prajn. 227a. b.). Coagulation takes place in an open place. Of the higher animals the miraculous species of snakes called *āsāliya* exclusively comes into being in this way (Pannav. 46 a), but there are still other beings which may be brought into existence by coagulation, e.g., the *suṃsumāra, mahoraga*, quadrupeds equipped with claws (*saṇapphaga*) and the *viyaya-pakkhi*, birds that never fold their wings (Pannav. 44a, 45a, 46b, 49a), and, finally, the human beings. These all may spring into life from moist human excretions and from uncleanly matter spontaneously[3] (50a), though than they will remain undeveloped (*apajjatta*) and diminutively small (1/¿ *ang.*), and they will stay alive for 1 *muhutta* at the longest. Apart from the *āsāliya* all these beings generated by coagulation are sexless. By development (*pajjatti*) Umāsvāti on T. 8, 12, p. 177, 4ff. asks us to under-

1. With plants we speak of *joṇi-voccheya* when their germinative faculty extinguishes (Viy. 671, 274a; Ṭhāṇ. 123b, 343b, 405a).

2. For *saṃvṛta* JACOBI T. 2, 33 writes *saṃvṛtta*=minimal. Siddhasena p. 191, 19 suggests this version by *saṃvṛtā pracchannā saṃkaṭā vā* (*yoniḥ*).

3. Āyār. 5, 2 distinguishes between the *sammucchima* and the *rasaya* and *saṃseyaya*. For the same list as here ref. to Ṭhāṇ. 385b, 416a.

stand the faculty of assimilating matter to the body and to complete the same along with the sensuous and breathing organs, and, as the case may be, also the speech and the inward sense. In elemental beings, as well as in plants, animal and human beings this development may even be found missing , and then they are *apajjatta*.[1]

§64. The description in the text of embryo-life nearly always concerns the human germ. An animal embryo (*tirikkha-joṇiya gabbha*) exists between 1 *muh*. and 8 years, a human one (*maṇussī-g.*) between 1 *muh.* and 12 years, and a fully developed fruit (? *kāya-bhavattha*) between 1 *muh.* and 24 years. This conception is obviously related to the informations rendered by Viy. 88b saying what evil and good is being practised by a *jīva gabbha-gaya samāṇa*, and of what kind his reward will be when he dies as such a one. Human and animal sperm lives in the womb from 1 to 12 hours (Viy. 433a; Tand. 4b[2]). Cases of getting with child and of its counterpart, negative sexual intercourse, are dealt with by Ṭhāṇ. 312b along with their causes. The first food an embryo (*jīva*) takes after having entered the womb consists in the menstrual blood of the mother (*māu-oya*) together with the sperm of the father (Sūy. II 3, 21); 353b), but later it varies. It is not taken by bits, but by the entire body (§ 96), and while nothing is being excreted, all serves to build up the sensuous organs and the body. Mother and fruit are interconnected by two strings: the one (*māu-jīva-rasa-hāriṇī* scil. *nālī* ?) starts from the mother and serves the fruit to breathe and to transubstantiate the different substances, whereas the other (*putta-j.-r.-h.*) starts from the fruit and serves it in building up the body (*ciṇai*, *uvaciṇai*). While flesh, blood and brain come from the mother (*māiy'anga*, Ṭhāṇ. 170b *māuy' a.*), bones, marrow, hair and nails come from the father (*piy'a.*). These parental gifts (*ammā-piiya sarīraya*) will endure as long as the body of the descendant remains unweakened (*avvavanna*). The main source for the afore-said is Viy. 87a, partly also Tand. 7a, 8a.

1. Acc. to Viy. 852b; Samav. 26b this sums up to 14 kinds of beings.
2. Ed. DLJP 59.

The embryology of the human being is discussed in the first part of the Tandulaveyāliya. In referring to the introductory Gāhās we here but state that the margin of fertility is 55 years with the woman and 75 years with the man (v. 13, comp. Sthān. 313b), and that the fruit remains in the womb for 277½ days on an average (v. 4f). Its stages are listed as *kalala* (7 days), *abbuya* (the same), *pesi*, and *ghaṇa*. Its weight amounts to 3 *karisa*=¾ *pala* in the first month, in the second it gets solid, in the third it rouses lusts within the mother, in the fourth it makes her limbs swell, in the fifth its extremities and its head develop (*panca piṇḍiyāo*), in the sixth its gall and its blood, in the seventh its veins, muscles, vessels, nerves, pores, hairs, and nails, and in the eighth the child is complete. The sex depends on the preponderance of either sperm or blood, in case neither prevails sexlessness will result. A sexless fruit lies (v. 18) in the centre of the mother, but a male on the right, and a female on the left side. Its position and its condition are in accordance with the mother. The word *bimba* (Tand. 14a; Ṭhāṇ. 287a) appears to qualify the result of a miscarriage. Acc. to Viy. 89a. a cross-position will lead to a still birth. A description of the female genitals is rendered by Tand. 4a. From Pannav. 9 (277b); Ṭhāṇ. 121b we learn that the uterus may be either convex, concave, or flat (*vaṃsī-patta*). In Viy. 218 a the role attributed to Hari Negamesi of dislocating the embryo is apparently due to generalising the well-known individual case.

The generated beings are born either in the egg or with the amnion (the chorion), or as living young. Apart from birds, all snakes, fish, lizards, turtles and crocodiles are egg-born (*aṇḍaya*). Most higher quadrupeds and all human beings are born with the chorion (*jarāuya*). Whereas some quadruped like elephants and mammals with digits extended to support a wing-membrane (bats etc.) are born complete (*poyaya*).[1]

1. *poyaya*, Skt. *potaja*, is explained by KOHL (ZDMG 103, p. 153) by "born in a boat", the boat, in his view, being represented by the burst covers developing the fruit when leaving the womb. Though this may well apply to

§65. As coarse as all these conceptions are, so is the human anatomy (Tand. 35b). Apart from the quantities of liquids and other bodily items which can be omitted here, the human being has 700 veins. Starting from the navel 160 each extend upwards, downwards into the legs, downwards into the abdomen, and horizontally; 25 each contain mucus and gall, 10 contain sperm. Furthermore there are 900 sinews, 500 muscles, 900 vessels, 9.9 million hairpores, not counting the hair of the skull and the beard, and 33 million including the latter. Some figures concerning women and hermaphrodites slightly differ in giving them 670 and 680 veins, resp., and 470 and 480 muscles, resp. Moreover, we learn that the male is furnished with 5 and the female with 6 inner organs (*koḍha*), and that with the former we find 9 and with the latter 11 apertures (*soya*).[2] It is but due to a tendency of discrimination that in contrast to the general Indian view, that the left side is qualified as good (*suha-parinama*) and the right side as being unpropitious (Tand. 35b).

With the only exception of the Tand. as concerns the structure of the human body, we meet next to nothing but generalities.[3] Thāṇ. 357 a; Tand. 27b know of 6 different ways of joining the bones (*saṃghayaṇa, saṃhanana*) by means of hooking and pinning: *vajja-risabha* (or *vairôsabha*) *nārāya, risabha-n., n. addha-n., kīliya* and *chevaṭṭha* (Umāsv. on T. 8, 12 gives *sṛpāṭika* instead). For an explanation see a. o. V. GLASENAPP, Karman p. 29, for an illustration see BASTIAN, Ideale Welten I, plate IV (the corresponding sentence on p. 283 is incorrect). From coagulation there results the sixth (and worst) kind, from manifestation none at all, since inhabitants of hell and gods have neither bones, nor sinews, nor veins; with generation all kinds are possible. Acc. to Tand. 27b the *chevaṭṭha*-joint is the only one, however, which now still pertains to human beings.

bats, yet it remains to be asked whether it is equally true of elephants and many more quadrupeds listed in the comm. on T. 2, 34.

1. Umāsvāti on T. 2, 34; Śīlānka on Āyār. 5, 2.

2. Here we have to add the nipples. They are not mentioned by Ṭhāṇ. 450b.

3. But Vivāgas. 42b states the 48 *nāli* and their functions.

The first is the ideal, and as such it is characteristic of the Arhats etc.

The shape of the body (*saṃṭhāṇa*), too may appear in 6 different kinds (Ṭhāṇ. 357a; Tand. 27b). A being is proportioned either all over (*sama-cauraṃsa*), or only above (*niggoha, n.-parimaṇḍala*), or only below (*sāiya*, Comm. *sādi*, Um. *sāci*). It is either hunchbacked (*khujja*), or crippled (*vāmaṇa*), or deformed (*huṇḍa*). The latter refers to the inhabitants of hell (comp. § 109) as well as as to all coagulated beings except those furnished with one sense only, as is described in § 105. While all kinds apply to the generated higher animals and human beings, the first kind only will apply to the gods.

Next to the shape of the body we have to mention its size (*sarīr'ogāhaṇā*). The bodies of elemental beings will not go beyond their diminutive smallness which, as a minimum, partains to all earthly beings. But everywhere else the maximum size is enormous: plants and aquatic animals upto 1000 *joy.*, animals living on dry land up to 6 *gāuya*, and human beings up to 3 *g*. etc. (Pannav. 412b). Beyond the range of the horizontal world the size of the body will increase the more the deeper we go, as it will decrease the more the higher we go : the beings inhabiting the deepest regions of hell measure 500 *dhaṇu*, the Aṇuttarovavāiya 1 *rayaṇī* (Pannav. 417a). For the *siddha* see §187.

§66. We now come to speak of the bodily functions. Breathing is called *āṇamai pāṇamai*[1] *ūsāsai nīsasai*. While the first two words express the inward activity, the last two refer to the outward one (Prajn. 220 b). Unexceptionally all beings breathe (Pannav. 7), but the intervals will be the longer the higher they stand. Thus the inhabitants of hell breathe incessantly,[2] whereas the highest Vemāṇiya breathes every 33 fortnights only; but animals furnished with one to five senses and human beings follow different ways of breathing (*vemāyāe*). As we learn from Viy. 274b in contrast to Tand. 3b, the frequency

1. =*aniti, prāṇiti.*

2. For all tormented beings breathe rapidly, Prajn. 220b.

of breathing is the same with the embryo as it is with the fully developed man , and he will retain this frequency for the whole time of his life, i.e. 3773 in 1 *muhutta*. So, then, respiration (*ussāsa-nissāsa* or *pāṇu*) comes to be a time-measure. While the breathing of beings having two to five senses was accepted as an established fact (*jānāmo pāsāmo*), it seemed problematic with regard to elemental beings and plants, but it is explicitly stated to apply to them as well (Viy. 109a), and, moreover, Viy. 109b continues in saying that "breathing" embraces all possible matter (*davvāiṃ*). This statement is as surprising as is the adjoining and incorrect reference to Pannav. 28 (the Āhāra-paya). A windbody (*vāuyāya*) breathes his own kind, and even though by inhaling its own the same has perished (*uddaittā*) in it a many hundred thousand times, it will yet reappear on and again (*paccāyāi*, Viy. 110a).[1] In some other connexion we are told that the elemental as well as the vegetable beings inhale and exhale each other (Viy. 419b).[2]

The earth- and water-beings are not capable of moving voluntarily, nor are plants. Hence they are called *thāvara*, i.e. stationary, in contrast to all other beings, called *tasā pāṇā*, i.e. movable (comp. e.g. Āyār. 5, 1). The text of Dasav. 4 beg. formed hereafter shows the altogether unobjectionable meaning. But Siddhasena on T. 2, 12 (p. 158, 3) distinguishes between the two groups as such in which both the conditions and the mood of the corresponding being show up externally and such where they do not; for *trasa*, so it is said, originally (*ādau*) means *sukha-grahaṇa*. Acc. to Devanandin *trasa* expresses the possibility of transition into a different class of being which, as was mentioned just before, certain beings are lacking, so that for him all beings having one sense only belong to the *sthāvara*.

All beings brought into existence by coagulation are, without exception, sexless (Jīv. II), and the same applies to the

1. Abhay. maintains that the particles of matter constituting inhalation and exhalation are of finer quality than those composing the "earthly" and the transformation body of the wind-being (110 a).

2. Abhay. without having an opinion of his own follows the "*pūjya-vyākhyā*" and builds up a theory according to which closely connected earthly and other beings mutually assimilate in breathing.

inhabitants of hell, whereas sexless gods do not occur. In correspondence with the sensuality decreasing in direct proportion to the height of the heavenly region, the Gevejja and Aṇuttara gods are short of female deities (see Pannav. 547b ff. and comp. Ṭhāṇ. 105b and T. 4, 8-10). In the dry account rendered by Jīv. 105b, 177a and 198a, we come across three queer similes which originally belong to a more highly styled text: the female sex is compared with a fire for cooking (*phumphuy' aggi*), the male with a forest-fire (*vaṇa-dav'aggi*), and the third kind with a city-fire (*mahāṇagara-dāha*).

§67. The number of different senses (*indiya*; Viy. 223b : *āyāṇa*) amounts to five in all (Pannav. 15).[1] They are unequally distributed among the beings, and that is why the latter are divided into such furnished with one to five senses, as frequently mentioned above, thus forming the fundamentals for approaching the animate world. Beings with one sense own nothing but sensation, those with two have taste added, those with three smell, those with four vision, and those with five the power of hearing.[2] The first four are comprised as beings with incomplete senses (*vigal'iṅdiya*). The immeasurably small particles of earth, water, fire and wind, and, moreover, all plants are counted among the beings having one sense only. The various manifestations of the elements, all plants and such beings furnished with more senses than one are listed by Pannav. 24a ff. without the intention of completeness, and equally by Utt. 36, while Paṇhāv. 1 mentions many of them short of a system. As to the organs of the senses the above mentioned sequence is the reverse, and then, accordingly, the first three senses have 2 organs each,[3] and the latter two one each. For this Pannav.

1. For details ref. to the inner sense see § 15.

2. The Dig. follow Brahman conception by interpolating the teachings of the 10 *prāṇa*, 5 of which are the *indiya-pāṇa*, 3 the *bala-p.* comprising the inner sense (§ 71), speech and body, while the remaining 2 stand for the breath (*āṇā-pāṇa* or *ucchvāsa-niḥśvāsa-prāṇa*) and the vital force (*āuga-p.*). Comp. Gommaṭas. Jīv. 129; Devanandin on T. 2, 14; comm. on Prāyaścitta-cūlikā 4. The latter two state the way in which these *p.* are distributed among the beings furnished with one to five senses. See JACOBI Tattv. for this passage.

3. The one- to three- eyed beings, referred to by Ṭhāṇ. 171b, are so in a metaphorical sense.

312a gives *davv'indiya,* which corresponds to *upakaraṇa* given by Umāsvāti T. 2, 17.

The materiality of the sense causes Viy. 423b to call their bearers, i.e. the *jīva* in itself and all beings in the Saṃsāra, *poggalī*. We have to distinguish between the *uvacaya*, i.e. the accumulation of atoms suited for the purpose, and the *nivvattaṇā*, i.e. the disposition or shaping, which occurs in ¿ *samaya* of a *muhutta*. The *uvacaya* (not mentioned by Umāsvāti) is called *pracaya* by Devanandin (on T. 2, 17). This author distinguishes (see p. 165) between an inner and an outer disposition (*nirvṛtti*), the latter representing the very *pudgala-pracaya*, while the former means the units of the soul with regard of both the extension and shape of the corresponding organ of sense, e. g. the pupil of the eye (comp. JACOBI on the quoted passage). Acc. to Prajn. 294a all that is said about special shapes (*saṃṭhāṇa*) refers to the inner disposition shared by all beings furnished with that sense, and, accordingly, the senses of hearing and smell are shaped like certain flowers (*kalambuya-puppha* and *aimuttaga-canda*), the sense of vision like a lense (*masūra*), the tongue like a knife (*khurappa*), whereas the sense of feeling as not being distinguished into an outer and an inner disposition (Prajn.) appears in different shapes (Pannav. 293b and somewhat divergent Siddhasena on T. 2, 17). Moreover, there are *bāhalla*[1] and *pohatta*[2] the one standing for the thickness and the other for the width of accumulated matter. Both are diminutively small, and only the *pohatta* of the sense of feeling equals the measure of the body. The range (*visaya*) is largest with vision where it goes beyond 100,000 *joy.*; with hearing it goes up to 12, and with all other senses up to 9 *joy.* This certainly must be taken literally, and just as with the size of the body (s.a.) and the allegedly longest duration of life, this conception refers to legendary individuals. With the objects the organs of sense come into direct contact (*puṭṭhāiṃ*—and *paviṭṭhāiṃ*—

1. *bāhalatā=piṇḍatva* Prajn. 293a. The earlier edition of the Pannav. invariably prints *bāhulya* instead of *bāhalya*.

2. Phon.=*pṛthaktva*, but in meaning=*pṛthutva* (*vistara*). Prajn. renders both forms promiscuously.

saddāiṃ suṇei etc., Pannav. 298a, Ṭhāṇ. 253a),[1] though this is not the case with the sense of vision. Acc. to Prajn. 298b hearing, however, manifests itself by a slight touch of the object only (*spṛṣṭa-mātra*), whereas smelling, tasting and feeling contact the object, as it were, by additionally incorporating in the soul (*baddha-spṛṣṭa, baddha=ātma-pradeśair ātmīkṛta*). This is said to be due partly to the greater fineness and the greater number of particles of the sound-matter, and the exceptional position ascribed to the sense of vision is accounted for by its *aprāptakāritva*, i.e. the faculty of perceiving objects without even touching them.[2] Also towards the first impressions the sense of vision behaves differently from the other senses (comp. § 71). It goes without saying that the different effects of the objects on the senses depend on the different qualities of the former (acc. to Viy. 713 the sweetscent particles are called *ghāṇa-sahagayā poggalā*), so that, then, the *indiya-visae poggala-pariṇāma* (Jīv. 373b) is either pleasing or unpleasing (*surūva, durūva* etc.),[3] and it will pass over from the one into its opposite.

All that has been said here about the five senses applies to them in their material respect, i.e. as *davv'indiya*. We shall deal with the *bhāv'indiya*, i.e. the senses in their conditional state, in §71. When germinative life starts, only the latter are existent (Viy. 86b).

§68. Speech, so Pannav. 255b says, originates in the soul, while it becomes manifest in the body in the shape of a thunderbolt, and it ceases to be at the end of the world (*bhāsā jīv'āiyā sarīra-ppabhavā vajja-saṃṭhiyā log'anta-pajjavasiyā*). Most probably the designation of its shape is due to a simile laid down in some other connexion. But what Prajn. actually means is that the world which would be pierced by atoms of speech would then appear in the shape of the *vajja*. All one-sensed beings lack the faculty of speech. For further details see §§61 and 74. Āyār. II 92, 3f. wants to make it quite clear that speech

1. *cattāri indiy'atthā puṭṭhā veenti.* Here *veenti* stands for *veijjanti.*

2. Comp. LEUMANN Übersicht p. 39a.

3. So with *rūva*; with *sadda* it is *subbhi* and *dubbhi* (also Ṭhāṇ. 24a), with *gandha* it is *surabhi* and *durabhi.*

is existent only the moment when being spoken (*bhāsijjamāṇī bhāsā*), but neither before nor after, and this is equally being stated by Viy. 103 b, 621b and 622b. The process of speech as such is dealt with at great length by Pannāv. 260b ff. This process is, to put it briefly, the ejaculation (*nīsarai, nisṛjati*) of substances (*davva*) taken in (*geṇhai*) previously now being ready either for use or on store). They consist of ∞ atoms (*aṇanta -paesiya*), occupy the space of ¿ units, last for 1 *sam.* and own all qualities possible with reference to colour, smell, taste and sensation. Their reception is meant to bring about a close contact (*puṭṭha, ogāḍha*), i.e. with the units of the soul (*ātma-pradeśa*, Prajn.), and to it both fine and coarse particles (*aṇu* and *bāyara*)[1] are subjected which is discussed circumstantially. The reception takes place either with or without interruption (*antara*) in that either reception *or* ejaculation, or both reception *and* ejaculation occur within 1 *sam.*, and then the particle ejected as speech will invariably be the same particle as taken in within the foregoing *sam.*, and, by the way (267a), they will belong to the same content of speech (true, false, etc.) for which they were taken in. Their destiny depends on the intensity of speech. As we learn from Prajn. on Pannav. 262b. and from Vy. on Viy. 612 b, when speaking low the particles of speech leave the mouth in coarse portions (*abhinna*), but they do not reach far and will perish soon, whereas when speaking loud they are finely divided (*bhinna*), and in this case speech will increase infinitely and reach the boundaries of the world.[2]

§ 69. The supposed duration of human life goes far beyond any experience whatever, as has been mentioned before. For together with animals furnished with five senses they may live to reach 3 *paliovama*, thus surpassing the Vāṇamantara-and the Joisiya-Gods by the double. The Bhavaṇavāsi-gods,

1. Prajn. appears to be hesitative (263b) in concluding from *bāyara* that the word concerns *visible* particles, and so the AUTHOR renders but the view of the *mūlaṭīkākāra* that aggregates of a smaller or either larger number of units are being meant.

2. Comp. also Ṭhāṇ. 63a.

however, come up to about 2 *sāgarovama*, and both the inhabitants of hell and the Vemāṇiya even up to 33. The figures referring female gods are lower. One particle of earth will reach 22,000 years, one particle of water 7,000, one particle of wind 3,000, and a plant 10,000. One particle of fire will live for three days and nights at the longest, a two-sensed being for 12 years, if it has three senses for 49 days, and if four for six months. This lifetime (Pannav. 4) is called *ṭhii*, and this word is even used where later authors speak of *bhava-sthiti* in contrast to the *kāya-sthiti* which means the sum of all existences sharing the same characteristic feature following each other (§ 93).

Apart from legendary opportunities, human life has three stages (*jāma*, *vaya*, Āyār. 33, 23; 50, 3 f.b., Ṭhāṇ. 128a), though they do not refer to the physical but to the monastic life. So at least acc. to the comm. where they are said to embrace the time from the 8th to the 30th, from the 31st to the 60th, and from the 61st year until death.[1] For nobody will be a monk before his 8th year (§ 138). The actual stages of life are the ten *dasā* called *bālā*, *kiḍḍā*, *nandā*, *balā*, *pannā*, *hāyaṇī*, *pavancā*, *pabbhārā*, *mummuhī* (*mammuhī*), *sāvaṇī* (*sāyaṇī*) (Tand. 16a, in one Śloka Ṭhāṇ. 519a, in one Gāhā Tand. 16a=Dasav. nijj. 10). The second half of the sequence indicates a decline of the senses, loquacity, bending of the body, expectation of death,[2] and the last bed, though it is frequently interpreted by the comm. in a far-fetched manner. The appointment of these ten stages most certainly goes back to the theory of assuming a maximum age of one hundred years (Tand. 17b. 33a). Half of this time is spent by sleep, and for childhood and old age[3] another 20 years have to be taken into account (Tand. 33a). From the metrical and hence, owing to the position of the words, liberal compound *ṭhiya-jovvaṇa-keś'avaṭṭhiya-naho*[4] (Jambudd. 224b) we

1. Sthān. 128b sees in *jāma* the 4th part of either night or day, though this does not harmonise. The *vayas* (see the same) go up to 16, 70 and 70+x years.

2. With Haribhadra on Dasav.nijj.=*mṛt-mukhī* (*mṛṇ-*, *mṛn-mukhī*).

3. Viy. 699b means physical pain in contrast to psychical pain, the *soga*.

4. In print we find *kesa-avaṭṭhiya*. *avaṭṭhiya-k.-n.* would be grammatically more correct. We have a Veḍha which continues by saying *havai ya savva-bhaya-vippamukko*.

learn to understand that everlasting youthful vigour will go with the non-growth of hair and nails which is one of the special qualities of a Kevalin (Samav. 60b).

One list of 16 different diseases is rendered by Āyār. I 27, 16ff. while another one is delivered by Vivāgas. 40b. Here we come across physicians trying to practise their profession in many different ways. In this connexion we may note that, as Ṭhāṇ. 427 has it, the main subjects of therapeutics are the following eight: the science of children's complaints (*kumāra-bhicca*), the science of internal diseases (*kāya-tigicchā*), surgery both small and large (*salāī* and *salla-hattā*), toxicology (*jangolī*), psycho-therapeutics (*bhūya-vijjā*), the science of cautery (*khara-tanta*), and elexirology (*rasāyaṇa*). They are nearly conform with the eight parts of the so-called Āyurveda (JOLLY, Medicin, Grundriss III 10, P. 13). Medical science (*tigicchiya*), by the way, plainly appertains to the *pāva-suya-pasanga*)[1] (Ṭhāṇ. 451a). As to the causes of diseases Ṭhāṇ. 446a lists the following nine: a sedentary way of living (*accāsaṇā*), bad food, too much sleep, too little sleep, constipation, anury, marching (*addhāṇa-gamaṇa*), sitophobia, and the addiction to sensual enjoyments (*indiy'attha-vikovaṇayā*). The subdivision (Ṭhāṇ. 265a) into *vāiya*,-, *pittiya*-and *simbhiya*-diseases and such in which different factors referred to in this connexion take a share, goes back to the all-Indian system. Viy. 634 a (=Ṭhāṇ. 265a) says that madness (*ummāya*) ensues from being possessed by somebody (*jakkh'āvesa*) or either from the realisation of the so-called Confusing Karman (§ 87),[2] the former kind being more pleasant (*suhaveyaṇatarāga*) and the one to get rid of more easily (*suhavimoyaṇatarāga*) than the latter. The state of being possessed by something is brought about, so the author adds, by a god sending impure atoms (*asubhe poggale pakkhivai*) which are stronger with inhabitants of hell and gods (*mahiḍḍhiyatarāga*) than with elemental beings(!), animals and men. The idea probably is that, in agreement with the conceptions of all primitives, the material body of a malignant individual takes posses-

1. For 25 more all belonging to fortune-telling (see *Samav.* 49a.).
2. This in addition to a concrete sin also in Ṭhāṇ. 360b.

sion of a sound one. In Kappa 6, 12 we find *jakkh'āiṭṭha* and *ummāya-patta* being listed side by side. In this connexion the Yakṣa is not classed as a benevolent being as he is among the Vāṇamantara-Gods (§ 112), but stems from the field of popular belief. That a Kevalin were possessed by a Yakṣa was a contention established by antagonists (Viy. 749a) probably judging by outward appearance and at any rate intending to deprive his maxims of their credulity.

Physical death is scarcely referred to. We are merely told that the soul (*āyā*) leaves (*nijjāi*) the body simultaneously by its feet, its thighs, its chest, its head and all its limbs. Acc. to Ṭhāṇ. 89b and 346a this indicates that the soul henceforth will remain either in hell or among animals, human beings and gods, and that it will enter the realm of the Siddhas (Ṭhāṇ. 346a), though, in fact, it means nothing but a genuinely primitive conception.

§70. *The Soul.* The Theory of matter ought to be concluded by dealing with the Karman. But since, for times eternal, it has been closely connected with the soul, the latter must be dealt with first. The soul as the bearer of life is called *jīva*, and since it is animate, a living being is called *jīva* (beside *pāṇa, bhūya, satta*): this can be concluded from the somewhat playful subsumptions made by Viy. 285a. For the units of the soul and their expansion see § 58. Their total number remains constant for ever, it neither increases nor decreases, while within the different individual grades and classes of beings both equality and either decrease or increase naturally will occur, with the exception of the delivered souls whose number is not subjected to any decrease (Viy. 244a).

We have to distinguish between the soul and *āyā*, the I, though the dividing line is not always clearly discernible, thus when the moral monastic duties serve the *āyā* (*āyā sāmāie* (etc.), *āyā sāmāiyassa* (etc.) *aṭṭhe* Viy. 99a), when, furthermore, all bodily and spiritual doings work out in the I (*n'annattha āyāe pariṇāmenti* Viy. 777a), and, especially, when *jīva* and *jīv'āyā* are explicitly equated with each other (Viy. 723b)[1], The I is

1. The *jīva* is often called *āyā* (*ādā*) by the Dig.

more strongly stressed when the *āyā*[1] as such (*daviy'āyā*) as well as in its connexion with passions, activity, cognition, and other abstracts is quoted as *kasāy'āyā, jog'āyā nāṇ'āyā*, etc. (Viy. 588a), and when all of them prove to occur or either not to occur simultaneously with the individual; comp. also the *ahigaraṇī āyā* Viy. 288b. Cognition, non-cognition, and belief, so it seems, permeate the personality, so that these definitions equal one another: *nāṇe* (nom.) *āyā, annāṇe āyā* (this with one-sensed beings) *daṃsaṇe āyā* (Viy. 588b). In Viy. 621a, 622b we read that speech and the inward sense both mean something definitely different from the I (*no āyā bhāsā, n.ā. maṇe, annā bhāsā, annā maṇe*), whereas this does not necessarily refer to the body (*āyā vi kāe anne vi kāe*) which may be explained by its external and constant working. The same introductory formulation immediately followed the text of Viy. 588b mentioned above (*āyā bhante Rayaṇappabhā puḍhavī annā R. p.* ? Viy. 592b), but it was intended to serve a completely different purpose. Here *āyā* stands in order to express that an object marked by its inherent qualities has a dialectic reality in contrast a. o. to the case that foreign qualities belonging to another object are attributed to it (*Rayanappabhā* . .) *appaṇo ādiṭṭhe āyā, parassa ādiṭṭhe no āyā*. This theory falls into the sphere of Syādvāda (§ 77).

§ 71. The spiritual function, *uvaoga*, is the essence of the soul, though acc. to T. 2,18 *upayoga* also specifically means the functioning of the senses likewise underlying spiritual imagination. Along with the *labdhi*, the faculty of practising, the *upayoga* represents the sense considered as condition (*bhāvêndriya*). Pannav. 308b f. says *laddhi* and *uvaog'addhā* the latter meaning the time during which a sense (to be added: when conceiving) is active. The quickest to react is vision followed by hearing, smell, taste and feeling. Between its quickest and its slowest possible activity there lie the slowest performances of the same row. Both for the *davv'indiya* (§ 67) and for the *bhāv'indiya* the Pannav. (311b-315b) elaborately demonstrates how many of

1. *āyā* is declined as a fem. in the text to be referred to.

each kind were, are and will be existing (*atīta*, *baddhellaga* and *purekkhaḍa*) in the beings during their past, their present and their future. The number of the latter depends on the number of existences still to follow the present one until salvation takes place.

Next to the sensual organs, moreover, the inward sense or either the reason is essential for spiritual imagination. Umāsvāti T. 1, 14; 2, 22 calls it *anindriya*, 2, 25 implicitly *manas*. Pannav. renders *sannā*. It is without any organ. With animals and human beings *sannā* is connected with their coming into existence by procreation, with the gods and the inhabitants of hell with their possessing it in their pre-existence (Prajn. 534a f.). Those who possess the *sannā* are called *sannī* and so the Kevalin is *no-sannī-no-asannī*, since he has come to be beyond the *sannā*. The very brief 31st chapter of the Pannav. is accordingly called Sanni-paya in contrast to Pannav. 8, the Sannā-paya. The latter, as must be mentioned here, deals with the 10 *sannā* (see also Ṭhāṇ. 504a) as the primitive emotions or instincts (*ābhoga* Prajn.) owned by all beings (with the exception, of course, of the Kevalin and Siddha). They are directed towards nourishment, fear, sex, splendour (*pariggaha-s.*), anger, pride, deceit, greed, worldliness and all carnal desires (*loya*-and *oha-s.*).[1] Of the four first fear shows up acutely with the inhabitants of hell, nourishment with animals, sex with human beings, and splendour with the gods (*osannaṃ karaṇaṃ paḍucca*), the remaining being chronic (*saṃtai-bhāvaṃ p.*). Acc. to Ṭhāṇ. 277a (comp. Samav. 9b) the mentioned four depend, apart from depending on the resp. Karman, on imagination aroused by information, on thinking of it independently, and, furthermore, on the concrete causes as cowardice, empty stomach (*omakoṭṭhayā*), too much (*cita*) flesh and blood, and on possession (*avimuttayā*).

§ 72. Acc. to T. 1, 15 imagination, no matter whether it depends on the activity of the five outward senses or on that of the inward sense, proceeds from the primary perception (*avagraha*) over the will to cognition (*īhā*) and ascertainment

1. Sthān. 505a calls the *ogha-saṃjnā* a function (*upayoga*) of belief; the *loka-s.* a such of knowledge; so does Prajn. 222b.

(*apāya* or *avāya*) to the act of imprinting the perception in the mind (*dhāraṇā*)[1]. Though this sequence corresponds with Ṭhāṇ. 281b, 363a; Viy. 571a; Nandī 168a, it does not agree with Pannav. 15, 2. Here we find first the *indiya-ogāhaṇā* (309 a), followed by *avāya*, *īhā* and *oggaha*.[2] That is to say, the sequence is just the reverse, and *ogāhaṇā*[3] rendered in the Prajn. by *avagrahaṇa* without being explained more closely, is replaced by *dhāraṇā*. The author of the Pannav. takes the right to class this genesis of imagination in his chapter about the senses from their having a fundamental share in imagination. But with the *oggaha* this does not apply to all senses as with the other three stages. Here *atth'oggaha* and *vanjaṇ'oggaha* are distinguished from each other, the first constituting a distinct and the latter an indistinct primary sensation towards the object. The sense of vision, however, is not capable of an indistinct primary sensation but of a distinct one only. Nor is the inward sense (*no-indiya*, Pannav. 310 a; T. 1, 18 f.). The reversion of the sequence in Pannav. mentioned above, is due to the fact that the figure of five determined with *indiya-uvacaya*, *-nivvattaṇā* and *-laddhi* could continue to hold good with *ogāhaṇā*, *avāya* and *īhā*, until finally with *oggaha* the sequence ramifies. It was a mistake, however, to maintain it for the *ogāhaṇā* etc. without adding the *no-indiya*. In the Nandī (175 b ff.) this has been done, and the inward sense justly shares in the will to cognition, the act of ascertainment and the act of imprinting the perception in the mind. Here, by the way, we are also told (177a, 184a) that the "primary perception" lasts only 1 *sam.*, while *īhā* and *avāya* remain below 1 *muh.*, whereas the *dhāraṇā* will last for any length of time.

The function of the four stages of perception is the following acc. to Ṭhāṇ. 363a: *oggaha*, *īhā* and *avāya* occur rapidly (*khippa*) and analogically (*dhuva*) in every new case, *dhāraṇā*, however, permanently (*porāṇa*) and intensively (*duddhara-gahaṇa*). But all four are composed of single perceptions

1. Comp. LEUMANN Übersicht p. 38b.
2. In print we read *uggaha*.
3. In the Abhidhānarājendra incorrectly rendered as *uggāhaṇā*.

(*bahu*) or either decompose them (*bahuviha*), they are undoubtable (*asamdiddha*), and they do not occur by virtue of conclusion (*aṇissiya*). T. 1, 16 renders *anukta* for *asaṃdigdha*, and the distinction concerning the *dhāraṇā* is missing, but instead also the reverse applies to the six different functions.

§ 73. Cognition comes on through imagination, and so far as it keeps within the frame of the true teaching, Umāsvāti and his successors generally call it by the name of *mati-jnāna*,[1] whereas in the Canon it appears as *ābhiṇibohiya-nāṇa*. But in connexion with its negation called *mai-annāṇa*, which we shall deal with later (§ 79), it is also defined as *mai-nāṇa*. The other kinds of cognition to which the same assumption pertains, are called *suya-nāṇa*, *ohi-n.*, *maṇapajjava-n.* and *kevala-n.* (Viy. 342b; Ṭhāṇ. 347a; Rāyap. 130a). While the Pannav. (525a) does not deal with it systematically, all five kinds are given their locus classicus in the Nandī (65 ff.) where (144a) the *ābhiṇibohiya*, by the name of *buddhi*, is being subjected to further subdivisions which, however, we abstain from dealing with here.[2] Nor can we do so with the other *nāṇa*. The greater importance lies in its close relationship with the *suya-nāṇa* in its meaning of communication or evidence according to cognition. Both are equal in their relative existence (Pannav. 136b), what is more, they only occur together: *jattha ābh.-n.*, *tattha suya-n.*, *jattha suya-n.*, *tattha ābh.-n.* But this sentence of the Nandī (140a) is immediately restricted by quoting a half-śloka of the *āyariya* according to which the *suya* is preceded by the *mai*, but not the *mai* by the *suya*. Umāsvāti T. 1, 20 and on T. 1, 31 subscribes to this view. There are various ways as to how knowledge from outside the I may be conveyed. But the 14 possibilities of the *suya* as referred to by the Nandī 187a ff. do not exclude one another (comp. 187a 13 f.). They concern articulated, reasonable and spiritual evidences (the latter pertaining to, and corresponding with, the Jain teaching) and such that are contrary to these

1. For synonyms see T. 1 13.

2. For these *uppattiya*, *veṇaiya*, *kammiya* and *pariṇāmiya* ; *buddhi* comp. also Ṭhāṇ. 281 a; Viy. 571a.

qualities. The inward sense serves the transformation of such evidences into cognition, and this seems to be meant in T. 2, 22.

§ 74. As to the "articulated" evidences (*akkhara-suya*) mentioned above they are formed by written (*sann'akkhara-s.*) and oral (*vanjan'akkh.-s.*) ones as well as by such consisting in an object conceived by the senses releasing its denomination (*laddhi-akkh.-s.*).[1] We refer to this simply in order to attach the consideration frequently mentioned in the Canon about the expressive content of language. The earliest comments on this subject appear in Āyār. 11, 4; they are closely related to Dasav. 7.[2] Resting on the monastic discipline they are, to a great extent, based on the primitive distinction between the True (*sacca*) and the Wrong (*mosa*); in between we find what is made up of both the True and the Wrong (*saccā-mosa*), and beyond all three there is what is neither true nor wrong (*asaccā-mosa*) (Āyār. II, 91; Ṭhāṇ. 183 b). They are the four *bhāsājāyā*.[3] Pannav. 11 deals with them, as with speech altogether, more systematically, though, on the whole in a strikingly ill-assorted way on the whole. Of those four contents the first pair is attributed to "distinct" (*pajjattiya*) and the second to "indistinct" (*apajj.*) speech (Pannav. 255b). From their numerous sub-varieties[4] it follows (a.o.) that a mode of speech springing from emotion is by itself understood as *mosā*. Next to true speech a Kevalin (§ 81) avails himself of the *asaccāmosa* only (Viy. 749a). All animals with two to four senses and beings with five senses express themselves in the "neither true nor wrong" way, but the latter will employ the first three modes just as well (Pannav. 260a) provided they have learnt to do so or carry along with them a

1. E.g., *yac. . . .cakṣuṣā āmra-phal'ādy-upalabhy' "āmra-phalam" ityādy-akṣarānuviddhaṃ śabdārtha-paryālocan'ātmakaṃ vijnānaṃ tac cakṣur-indriya-labdhy-akṣaram*, Nandīvṛtti 189a.

2. Dasav. is later than Āyār. If in its ślokas it contains such pādas as are scattered in the prose of Āyār. (Āyār. 93, 2f.=Dasav. 7, 2; 94, 24f. =Dasav. 7, 26) the latter represent an ancient stock, comp. LÜDERS, SPAW 1913, p. 1007.

3. Frequently written *bhāsa-jjāyā*. Acc. to Viy. 622b the four modes also apply to the *nāṇa*.

4. In their discussion Prajn. 257b mentions that in Konkan *piccaṃ* is said for *p ayas* and that by the *gopāla* the lotus is called *aravinda* only. Nearly the same is said Praśn. 117b.

higher ability. The aforesaid fourth mode has twelve cases as address, order, request, question etc. Communication (*pannavaṇī*), too, belongs to the *asaccāmosa*. But the problem was whether such communications were not rather *mosā bhāsā* in case the natural gender of the object was not expressed as in the plural forms *gāo, miyā, pasū, pakkhī*. Pannav. 248b f. denies this and probably dispels even other doubts as to the congruity of grammatical and natural gender and number. Viy. 499b equally affirms that the expression of an intention, e.g. "we want to lie down" (*āsaissāmo*) is a *pannavaṇī bhāsā* and not "wrong". Apart from this kind Pannav. 246b speaks of the *ohāriṇī bh.*, i.e. the statement giving as examples "I mean", "I think" and the like. Such a statement may express any of the four contents (modes) : a true statement will serve (*ārāhiṇī*) the teaching, a wrong one will oppose (*virāhiṇī*) it, etc. It goes with the sphere of *ethics* that all four modes of speech, and consequently the mode of wrong speech as well, are admitted, provided they are employed in a pious way of mind (*āuttaṃ=samyak*), while even true speech coming from a sinner's mouth will count for nothing (Pannav. 268a). It goes with *discipline* that a monk charging himself with abstinence for one month (*māsiyā bhikkhu-paḍimā*, § 157) may express himself by four ways only: by begging for alms, by putting a question, by making a request for lodging and by giving an answer (*jāyaṇā, pucchaṇī, aṇunnavaṇī, puṭṭhassa vāgaraṇī*, Dasā 7 I=Ṭhāṇ. 183b).

§ 75. The *suya-nāṇa*, which we conclude herewith, forms a unity with the *ābhiṇibohiya-nāṇa* thus resulting in indirect or *parokkha* cognition (Nandī 140a; T. 1, 11), indirect inasmuch both rest on outward conditions. In imagination they represent the organic fundamentals. The three modes of cognition following *suya* (Nandī 166 ff.)—we shall deal with them in § 78 ff.—are direct (*paccakkha*) since they are not based on such conditions. Hence cognition is called twofold (*duviha nāṇa* Ṭhāṇ. 49b). Umāsvāti in T. 1, 10 calls *pratyakṣa* and *parokṣa* the two *pramāṇa* or media of cognition. Aṇuogad. 151 a ff. deals with the *pamāṇa*, but of his varieties *davva-*, *khetta-*, *kāla-* and *bhāva-pp.* (also Ṭhāṇ. 198a) only the one mentioned last (210 a) can be taken into consideration here. There the *paccakkha-pp.* (211a)[1] originating partly from the five senses (*indiya*) and partly from another source (*no-i.*)—in the latter case superior forms of cognition are concerned—stands side by side with *aṇumāṇa*, *ovamma* and *āgamma*, i.e. conclusion, comparison and tradition, which altogether might justly have been comprised as *parokkha*. This word, however, fails to appear in the composition of the Aṇuogadāra. Conclusion (212a), to say but this, is *puvvavaṃ* "resting on earlier (sensual perception)", *sesavaṃ* "resting on exclusion" and *diṭṭhasāhammavaṃ* "resting on abstraction", each word being explained by examples.

§ 76. The *nāṇa-ppamāṇa* mentioned in this connexion adds up to the *jīva-pp.* by going together with *daṃsaṇa-* and *caritta-pp.*, and the *jīva. pp.-* again adds up to the *guṇa-pp.* by going together with the *ajīva- pp.* (colours, smell, taste, feeling and shape). The *guṇa-pp.* ranges first among the sub-varieties of the *bhāva-pp.* standing alongside with the *naya-* and *saṃkha- pp.* We pass over the latter, the "number", in order to turn to the *naya* or "modes of contemplation". In Utt. 28, 24 *pamāṇa* and *naya* stand side by side. "The *naya's* are methods intended to represent an object by accentuating of all its different aspects the one only which the teacher has in mind for his special purpose, whereas the others being irrelevant to him remain unconsidered" (JACOBI with ref. to T. 1, 35). *Naya* is known even to Viy. though not in its conventional designation and number (see below). So, when Viy. 302a speaks of the *vocchitti-* and *avvocchitti-nay'aṭṭhayā* (§ 77). The *necchaiya-n.* and the *vavahāriya-n.* (Viy. 748a), i.e. contemplation in theory and praxis , approach the later usage of the word more closely. As to contemplation in praxi a sensual quality of the object stands in the foreground, whereas contemplation in theory starts from all qualities possible. Thus, while a bee, for instance, is black in praxi, it is of all colours, smells, etc. in theory, so that, then, the definition may be supposed to be due to some process of elimination. Along with the *vavahāra-n.* we shall presently

1. A reference to this passage is given in Viy. 221b where it was caused by the word *pamāṇa* in the preceding passage of quite a different character.

come to know also the *ujju-sutta-n.* and others. Probably the Viy. was familiar with the latter, too, for the definition mentioned just before most certainly goes back to the catchword *ujjuya* of the preceding sūtra.

Now, in Aṇuog. 264a ff.; Ṭhāṇ. 390 b; Āv. 754 we come across the seven *mūla-naya* called *negama*, *saṃgaha*, *vavahāra*, *ujju-suya*, *sadda*, *samabhirūḍha* and *evaṃbhūya*.[1] Instead of *ujju-suya* sometimes *ujju-sutta* is being read corresponding to the Sanskrit form. The resp. 100 subvarieties mentioned by Āv. 759 (Sthān. 390b) on account of a certain "main-*naya*" —while according to others their number is said to be but 500 in all— are merely a fictitious conception presumably resting on the fact that in praxi the ways of contemplation are often incomplete and may intercross, etc. The definition of the different ways set forth by Devasūri, one of the later logicians, has been rendered by JACOBI on Sūtra T. 1, 35.[2] As to the *naigama*, it follows from Umāsvāti's Bhāṣya and other passages that this word stands for the so to speak "conventional",[3] though often figurative way of contemplation not distinguishing between qualities of genus and species. The *saṃgraha* has nothing in mind but the generic notion, the *vyavahāra* nothing but the qualities of the species at hand, and the *ṛju-sūtra* nothing but the object in its present state and only so far as it is mine. The *śabda* or *sāṃprata* strictly clings to the sense of the word given to it either by context or convention, that is to say, synonyms are accepted, while the *samabhirūḍha* relies on the etymology of the word contrary to words of the same meaning, and, finally, the *evaṃbhūta* exclusively takes a word as it wants to be taken according to the activity expressed by it. JAINI points out that the modes of

1. Samav. 128b in an incomprehensible way quotes three of the above mentioned names in the alleged table of contents of the Diṭṭhivāya (§ 38). Perhaps this has caused the reference to be made to it concerning all *naya* Āv. 760.

2. Comp. also JHAVERI, The First Principles of the Jaịn Philosophy (1910), p. 53 ff.; JAINI on T. 1 35 (SBJ 2, 45ff.)

3. Siddhasena (on T. 1, 65): explains *nigama=janapada*. Āv. 755 (=Aṇuog. 264a) says *negehiṃ māṇehiṃ miṇai=nega-ma* (!). Others explain by *naika-gama* "having different species". Comp. Satis Chandra VIDYABHUSHANA, Hist. of the Mediaeval School of Indian Logic p. 11 and Festschr. Bhandarkar p. 157 f.

contemplation narrow by steps from 1 to 7.[1] But we also find an internal classification according to which 1 to 3 are concerned with the substances and 4 to 7 with their conditions (*dravyārthika-* and *paryārthika-naya*), and a second one concerning examinations of the object—1 to 4—and its relations—5 to 7—(*artha-* and *śabda-n.*). Finally Umāsvāti offers 5 to 7 subvarieties of the *śabda*, to say nothing of those regarding the *naigama*.

In the Aṇuog., however, all seven enjoy equal rights, save that the last three are comprised as *tiṇṇi sadda-nayā*. We now turn back to the *pamāṇa*-specification rendered by Aṇuog. 222 b ff. where we find the *naya* being illustrated by way of three examples. They strike us by their primitiveness when compared with the subtlety of classic definition. Of all examples the third one, the *paesa-diṭṭhanta*, is the most searching. 1. For the *negama* there exist space units (*paesa*) which pertain to all substances (*davva*) and to any part separated from them (*desa*). Thus, beside the *paesa* of *dhamma*, *āgāsa*, *jīva* and *khandha*, the *negama* quotes as the sixth the *paesa* of *desa*. 2. The *saṃgaha* keeps within the number of five (*pancaṇhaṃ paese*), since the *desa-pp.* pertains to all five substances: if my servant buys a donkey, then the latter is mine, too[2]. 3. The *vavahāra* does the same, though it speaks of the *p.* as being five-fold; for if five men possess something in common, then also a part of it belongs to them in common. 4. For the *ujju-suya* the *p.* is, as the case may be (*bhaiyavva*), one of *dhamma*, of *adhamma*, etc. 5. The *saṃpai-sadda-naya* says: *dhamme* (etc. up to *khandhe*) *paese*, *se paese dhamme* (*adhamme*, *āgāse*, *no-jīve*, *no-khandhe*), the space unit forms the corresponding substance and represents it (save the two last ones owing to the diversity of the *jīva* and the *khandha*). 6. The *samabhirūḍha* maintains that in the words of *dhamma* (etc.) *paese dhamme* may be taken for a loc., i.e. in the nature of a Tatpuruṣa, or either for a nom., i.e. in the nature of a Karmadhāraya. As the first possibility is out of the question since it would qualify *dh.* and *p.* as differing from each other, there remains

1. *Loc. cit.* p. 47.
2. *dāseṇa me hharo kito dāso vi me kharo vi me*, Vyav.bh.IV 25a (quotation).

the second according to which for *dhamme* (etc.) *paese* we have to say *dhamme* (etc.) *ya se paese ya se*, and so forth as in 5. 7. For the *evaṃbhūya*, finally, *desa* and *paesa* are beyond discussion (*avatthu*) since it knows but *dhamm'atthikāya* (etc.) as a whole (*savvam kasiṇaṃ paḍipuṇṇaṃ niravasesaṃ ega-gahaṇa-gahiyam*).

The two examples of the bushel (*patthaga*) and the night-stay (*vasahi*) preceding in Aṇuog. 222b ff. comprise both the *naya* 1 to 3 and 5 to 7, and so they do not give us an exhaustive information about their standpoint. But they compensate for it by distinguishing different grades of quality in a *negama* and, implicitly, in the *vavahāra* coinciding with it. We speak of a genuine (*visuddha*) *negama* when somebody being asked what he is hewing there with his axe, gives an answer by saying: a measure for a bushel (*patthaga*); the *neg.* becomes ever more genuine (*visuddhatarāga*) when, with the same answer given in each case, it is being asked: what are you hewing ? what are you hollowing ? what are you smoothening ? and so on up to the point of carving the owner's name (*nām' āuḍio patthao*). A *neg.* is not genuine (*avisuddha*), however, when the question: where do you go ? is being answered by saying: I am going for a measure for a bushel (*patthagassa gacchāmi*). In the second example the *neg.* is the more genuine the more precisely the question *kahiṃ bhavaṃ vasasi* ? is being answered by pointing out to the upper world, the Jambuddīva, Bharaha, South -Bharaha, *Pāṭaliputra*, the House of Devadatta and, finally, its bedroom (*gabbha-ghara*), whereas the answer: in the word (*loge*) will render a *negama* not qualified as genuine.[1]

§ 77. By means of a *naya* a standpoint is gained allowing of making some statement about an object, though we must be careful in distinguishing from it what is understood as the contemplation of the object as such from different angles. It is in the nature of the matter that the latter is the more original, though it is confirmed by the text. But, to be true, we find it fully developed, along with the *naya*-technique, also only as late as in Aṇuog., and it is even later that it is given the name of

1. Aṇuog. 17 a. For all three examples see also Āvaśy. 378a ff.

nikkheva (e.g. Dasav. nijj. 9). Umāsvāti T. 1, 5 does not refer to it. Acc. to Aṇuog. 250 a ff. *nikkheva* first means nothing but a contemplation more or less comprehensive. Yet we intend to start already here by signifying in this way the technique of discussing an object from four standpoints as is introduced by Aṇuog. These standpoints are called denomination (*nāma*), effigy (*ṭhavaṇā*), substance (*davva*) and condition (*bhāva*). The *āvassaya*, the indispensable, may serve as an example (Aṇuog. 11 b ff.). *Nām'āvassaya* is a denotation saying that a being or a thing is "indispensable". *Ṭhavaṇ'āv.* is the figurative representation of something indispensable. *Davv'āv.* is something indispensable, be it from the standpoint of a monk (the Āvassaya formulae), be it from that of a dissenter (the obligatory religious rites) or be it with regard to worldly activities (the morning toilet). *Bhāv'āv.* says what is emotionally realised as being indispensable: in the Jain Creed the pious fulfillment of the Āvassaya formulae, for the non-Jain epic lectures (*puvvaṇhe Bhārahe, avaraṇhe Rāmāyaṇaṃ*) or either a ritual act practised any time from a religious urge.

The quaternary *nikkheva* is extended by "place" (*khetta*) and "time" (*kāla*), occasionally also by "way of being" (*guṇa*), comp. Viy. 147b. The world, the soul and both the residence of the Siddha and the *siddha* themselves are *davvao* and *khettao* finite but *kālao* and *bhāvao* infinite (Viy. 177b); the souls are in themselves everlasting, whereas with regard to their condition they are not (Viy. 299b). Less uniform than are these disquisitions are statements directly gained from the subject in question: the beings considered as a whole (*avvocchitti-nay'aṭṭhayāe*) are everlasting, while when considered individually (*vocchitti-nay'a.*) they are not (Viy. 302a), or, among others, food and drink (*oyaṇa, kummāsa, sura*), according to their origin (*puvva-bhāva-pannavaṇaṃ paḍucca*), must be called an accumulation of vegetable or, resp., watery substances, and after being heated a community of fiery substances (Viy. 213a). In the latter argument as well as in some others including such that do not reflect on the same object by approaching it from different points of view as *davva* and *bhāva* (e.g. Viy. 65b, 103b, 110b;

also in the Ṭhāṇ.; Jīv. 734a; Dasā 6), the subject is characterised by the words . . . *tti vattavvaṃ siyā*: "from a standpoint it is predicable that. . . .".[1] The word *siyā* standing for itself and occurring in pairs and repeatedly in the from of *siya* (e.g. *neraiyā siya sāsayā siya asāsayā*, Viy. 302a) has become the motto for the theory of the relative validity of any statement. But now, apart from the word *syāt*, the negation *avaktavya* is significant of the seven formulae of the *syād-vāda* which will be mentioned presently. But just as the formula *vattavaṃ siyā* belongs to the sphere of the Syādvāda already so does *avattavva* in the discussions rendered by Pannav. 323b ff.; Aṇuog. 54 ff. From the latter we may take as an example that a mere dual of equivalent elements (e.g. an aggregate consisting of two atoms) eludes observation from the view of the "sequence" (*āṇupuvvī*), i. e. that it lies "beyond what is predicable" (*du-paesie avattavvae*), since this dual is neither a sequence as is the case with three atoms and more nor none as with one atom. While thus the building stones of the Syādvāda are existent in the Canon already, yet the latter is still unaware of the completed building bearing this name or that of the Anekāntavāda. Most certainly the invention of this theory of relativities (as it is frequently called in a somewhat playful manner) goes back to an early time, probably to Mahāvīra personally, but in its fully developed shape as the so-called *sapta-bhangī* it appears only later as an anonymous creation. As to its origin SCHRADER, who noticed the relation with the *vikalpa* of the Ājnānika, pointed to the logics of the southern Indian Digambaras developed in shrewd dialectic argumentations.[2] The *sapta-bhangī* says that an object (a *ghaṭa*, of course) seen from a chosen standpoint (*syāt*) can be signified (1) as existent, (2) as non-existent (i.e. regarded under the aspect of another object) and (3) as both existent and non-existent (the former seen under its own aspect and the latter under alien ones). The three corresponding formulae are : *syād asty eva, syān n̂asty eva, syad asti n̂asti ca*. The two statements of

1. The AUTHOR failed to recognise this in "Worte," p. 25, ann.

2. Philos. p. 51. The reference to the Sūyagaḍanijj. made by Satis Chandra VIDYABHUSANA (Logic p. 8) is misleading.

(3), however, can be made by letting the one follow the other, whereas they cannot possibly be made simultaneously. Under this aspect the object (*ghaṭa*) (4) defies description: *syād avaktavya eva.* The remaining three sentences are identical with the first three by adding *avaktavya.* This means to say in sentence (5) that a thing exists but that, apart from this positive quality with reference to another thing, it has a negative quality as well, and that it is impossible to express both qualities simultaneously: *syād asti câvaktavyaś ca.* Sentence (6): *syān nâsti câvaktavyaś ca* is just the reverse on the basis of non-existence. Sentence (7), finally, expresses that an object as in (3) can be taken either as positive or negative, though not simultaneously but only successively: *syād asti nâsti câvaktavyaś ca.* The wording rendered follows Vimaladāsa's Saptabhangītarangiṇī (p. 2); except for some slight difference it represents the backbone of the Syādvāda literature.[1]

§ 78. Sthān. 347b; Nandīvṛtti 65b and others are correct in defining the name of *ohi*-cognition by *ātmano'rtha-sākṣātkaraṇa-vyāpāra* and by equating *avadhi* with *avadhāna.* The *ohi*-cognition is inherent in both the inhabitants of the world of gods and those of the different spheres of hell owing to this form of existence of theirs,[2] and as such it is called *bhava-paccaiya* (Nandī 76b; T. 1, 22). But the two preceding forms are equally inherent in these inhabitants (Viy. 343b). However, due to a certain behaviour of certain Karman species in the soul, the *khaôvasama*-condition (§ 182), the *ohi*-cognition occurs as *khaôvasamiya* (Ṭhāṇ. 49b) also in human beings and animals with five senses (Viy. 343b). It consists (Nandi 97a) in the

1. Representations and criticisms of the Syādvāda and S.-bh. a.o. will be found in any history of the Indian philosophy, e.g. in S. RADHAKRISHNAN, Indian Philosophy, 1; 302ff. Comp. also the pamphletes Hirachand Liladhar JHAVERI, The first Principles of the Jain Philosophy (1910) p. 34ff; Jagmanderlal JAINI, Outlines of Jainism (1916), p. 116 f; Champat Rai JAIN, Science of Thought (no year) p. 114 ff. First ref. made by R. G. BHANDARKAR, Report 1883-84, p. 95, acc. to which JACOBI SBE 45, XXVII. Most recent books are M. L. MEHTA Outlines of Jaina Philosophy, Bangalore 1954 and THE SAME, Jaina Psychology, ib. 1957.

2 The word for its application by a godlike person is *ohiṃ paunjai.* It draws the object closer by *ohiṇā ābhoei* (*ābhogayati*, Jambudd. 214a).

cognition (*jāṇai pāsai*, comp. § 32) of ∞ [1] up to all bodily substances (*rūvi-davva*, comp. T. 1, 28) in a space ranging from the smallest to the widest possible extension[2] during a time comprising all stages from the smallest up to extremely large extents and, moreover, in the past as well as in the future, and such in ∞ conditions (*bhāva*), though they are all but the ∞ fraction of all preceding conditions.[3] The ohi-cognition is acquired when the teaching of Mahāvīra was conveyed *soccā* (Viy. 432a), but also *asoccā*, if only the Karman conditions mentioned above are fulfilled. The true believer possesses *ohi* wherever he may be always in the same intensity, or either the opposite of both is valid. This results in six possibilities (see JACOBI on T. 1, 23; Ṭhāṇ. 378a) partly explained by Nandī 81a ff. by way of comparisons. The same is done by Umāsvāti and Devanandin (p. 123). What they call *anavasthita* is called *paḍivāi* by Nandī, but while in doing so a certain up and down is presupposed by the former, the latter expresses thus a non-recurring involution (*pratipatati*). As reason for some of those possibilities part of which have even sub-species Siddhasena refers to the corresponding variety of the underlying *khaôvasama* condition, and it may be taken for granted that this goes for all. He who owns the faculty of the "transcendental cognition of bodily things" which represents the *ohi*-cognition (JACOBI on T. 1, 22) is capable of lifting himself up to different mountains, of letting himself down into the deep and of dwelling in the *kamma-bhūi*, just as he is capable of multiplying himself from twice to ten times his size in 1 *sam.* (Viy. 438a). Ṭhāṇ. 393a vividly describes the startling effect of the first occurrence of the *ohi*-cognition on him who comes to behold the earth quite small swarming with tiny beings (*kunthu*), a powerful god, a monstrous serpent living in distant continents or the unclaimed

1. *anantāni taijasa-bhāṣā-prāyogya-vargaṇā'pantarāla-vartīni dravyāṇi; sarvāṇi=bādara-sūkṣmāṇi rūpi-dravyāṇi*, Nandīvṛtti 97b).

2. Also in sections (*khandha*) of the non-world which equal the world in size. For this see also Viy. 437.a.

3. Here, again, it is made clear that ∞ is not more than a very large numerical quantity. For other details see Śrutasāgara on T. 1 10 22, comp. BHANDARKAR, Rep. 1883-84, Notes p. II.

treasures hidden in all possible places. For this, however, so Sthān. says, the blame has to be put on the *mohanīya karman* which is still effective within him who possesses the gift of *ohi*-cognition.

§79. These magic qualities are equally inherent in those who own the negative *ohi*-cognition (Viy. 435a). For the three first kinds of cognition also appear in their negations (T. 1, 32) called the three-fold *annāṇa*: *mai-annāṇa, suya-a.* and *vibhanga -nāṇa* (Viy. 343a). All three of them rest on *micchā-diṭṭhī*, the wrong belief (§168), a word, by the way, not applied by Umāsvāti in the Sūtra (T. 1, 32 f.). As to *mai-* and *suya-annāṇa* (both of which do not occur separately) Nandī gives it in 143a. The erroneous cognition in the field of imagination has the same four stages as has the *ābhiṇibohiya*, which if caused by evidence is based (Nandī 194a; Viy. 343 a) on the non-Jainist philosophy, science and arts.[1] The *vibhanga-nāṇa*, finally, (or *vibhange nāmaṃ annāṇe*, e.g. Viy. 433 a, b) shows up where the teaching of Mahāvīra was not conveyed orally and where, moreover, the Karman condition does not correspond with the above mentioned presuppositions (Viy. 430a). But it is the reward for spiritual preparedness and abstinence in the sense of the teaching, and on account of *sammatta* and its consequences it may even change into *ohi*-cognition (Viy. 433a). Thus Mahāvīra corrects the wrong conceptions of the world view resting on *vibhanga* which the former King Siva had acquired through his chastisements as *disā-pokkhiya vāṇapattha tāvasa* (Viy. 514b), as well as the wrong ideas about gods maintained by the Brahman Poggala (Viy. 551a). And the seven cases of *vibhanga -nāṇa*, listed by Ṭhāṇ. 382b, also refer to questions concerning the teaching. It is not only the wrong view but also the rejection of the true facts which they all have in common, whereas the wrong *ohi*-cognition is being described by Viy. 343a as referring (*saṃṭhiya*) to the most different things beyond the field of belief e.g. localities, geographical dates, places of worship,[2] animals and genii.[3]

1. Comp. WEBER, Ind. Stud. 17, 9 f.
2. *rukkha* and *thūbha*.
3. *kiṃnara* etc., for the Bhavaṇavāsi-gods are known to pertain to the terrestrial sphere.

In this connexion we may omit the calculations following in Viy. in how many different ways and in relation with what kinds of other qualities beings are in possession of either true or wrong cognition (*nāṇī* and *annāṇī*, 343a ff.). In discussing the range of effect (*visaya*) of both kinds Viy. 356a makes us understand that by force of imagination cognition goes back to teaching and by force of evidence to functioning (*āeseṇaṃ jāṇai pāsai* resp. *uvautte j.p.*). Provided that *āesa*, in this case, has not a different meaning, there can be no doubt acc. to § 71 that the two words were changed by mistake : imagination follows from *upayoga*, evidence from *ādeśa*.

§80. Beyond the sphere of the *ohi-nāṇa* there is no longer any wrong cognition, i.e. resting on a non-spiritual basis, but only different grades of infallible orthodox cognition. The *maṇapajjava-nāṇa* following next (Nandī 99b) is the most colourless among all five, while *ohi* and *vibhanga* were the most stimulating for imagination as far as the latter can be spoken of. It occurs only with human beings who in their spiritual career stand on a high level (*saṃjaya appamatta iḍḍhi-patta*).[1] It is inferior to the *ohi-nāṇa* in that it is restricted to ∞ Aggregates with ∞ space units, to the human sphere (*maṇussa-khetta*, §122), to the minute part of a *paliovama* and to the ∞ small fraction of all existing accidents (*savva-bhava*). But it reaches the thoughts (*maṇogaya bhāva*) of the beings with five senses as expressed by the name of *manaḥparyāya* "changing condition of the inward sense".[2] The sub-sections of the two kinds of cognition are named by Umāsvāti T. 1, 25-29, so for instance imperishability (*apratipāta*), not specially mentioned by Nandī. But together with the latter he speaks (T. 1, 24) of two grades of the *maṇapajjava-nāṇa*, the one being achieved by a more simple and the other by a more comprehensive way of visionary thinking (*ujju-mai* and *viula-mai*, Ṭhāṇ. 49b), the latter being more extensive, purer and brighter. For an example the Nandīcuṇṇi speaks of a *ghaṭa* somebody thinks of, and of the different qualities of the same (Nandīvṛtti 108b).

1. Sthān. counts the *avadhi-* up to the *kevala-jnāna* among the possession of an *iḍḍhimanta*.
2. The Dig. in T. 1, 24, 29 speak of *m.-paryaya*.

§81. The conditions under which the *kevala-nāṇa* (Nandī 111 b ff.) comes about belong to the description of the road leading to salvation (§ 186). Here we are concerned with explaining its meaning which is simple enough, as to substantiality, space, time and condition it discloses the cognition of all that is, was and will be, and acc. to Umāsvāti T. 1, 30 it does so with regard to all substances and their conditions. That is why the Kevalin can be called *ega-nāṇī* (Viy. 343a). For his knowledge includes all the other stages of cognition. We are given many proofs for this knowledge of his (e.g. Viy. 216a, 217b, 238b, 567a). Readily and frequently the Kevalin is contrasted with one who stands on a lower stage, *i.e.* with the *chaumattha*, *āhohiya* and *para-m-āhohiya*. *Chauma* means the same as *āvaraṇa*, the "veiling" of the soul, and even the common monk is still subject ot it (*chadmastha, sakaṣāya, niratiśaya, avadhy-ādi-atiśaya-vikala, akevalin* Sthāṇ., Vy.). The *chaumattha* is known by his acting contrary to the five principal rules, by allowing homage to be paid to him and by his not acting according to his words (Ṭhāṇ. 389a). It is but indirectly, not directly like the Kevalin, that a monk becomes aware of his imminent salvation (Viy. 221b), and he also lacks a.o. the Kevalin's high standpoint on which by suffering he gets rid of his Karman in order to give an example to others (Ṭhāṇ. 304 b). He lacks the *ohi* cognition since apart from not perceiving the immaterial basic facts, he neither perceives the free atoms and aggregates of sound, smell and wind (Viy. 342a=Ṭhāṇ. 505b, s. id. 341a, 354a, 427a). But we read Viy. 755a that some *chauṃ.* are capable of perceiving atoms. *ohi*, however, is also the base for the conception of *āhohiya* (Ṭhāṇ. 61a : *ahohi*) and *para-m-āhohiya* monks. The former is said to be (e.g. Vy. 67a; Rājapr. 130b) one whose *ohi* is not yet of the highest grade (*paramâvadher adhastād yo 'vadhiḥ; adho'vadhikaḥ parimita-kṣetra-visayâvadhikaḥ*). That this does not imply the case of one whose cognition is still below the *ohi* level seems to be shown by Rāyap. 129b where the *āhohiya* Kesi is in possession of the *ohi*. The corresponding passages of the text (e.g. also Viy. 65b, 311a, 755b) the *āh.* passes for *chaumattha.*

The *para-m-āhohiya* equals the Kevalin in that he is certain to enjoy salvation even in the same existence (Viy. 311a), and acc. to Viy. 755b his way of realising the objects, as will be discussed below (§ 82), is just the same as well. From our way of spelling the word it already follows how, in our view, it has to be analysed: it concerns an *adhovadhika-para=adhovadhikāt paraḥ* or *paramaḥ*, as we read in Viy. 67a. The reading to *para-m-ohiya* in the same passage expresses the same. Probably *āhohiya* itself goes back to *yathāvadhika*.

The Kevalin, as long as he still dwells on earth, is distinguished as *bhavattha-kevalī* from him who, as *siddha-k-.*, has entered Siddhi. The former[1] is either still active or has ceased to be so: he is either *sajogī* or *ajogī* (§ 186). Just as these two are subdivided in temporal respect according as they are either in the first (or last) *samaya* of their condition or not: (*a*)*paḍhama-* or (*a*)*carama- samaya-* (*s*)*ajogi*, so the *siddha-kevalī* are subdivided temporally into such enjoying Siddhi in the first and others doing so in the further *samaya* of their existence: *aṇantara-s.-k.-* and *paraṃpara-s.-k.* This structure fully corresponds with that of the *kevala* cognition rendered by Ṭhāṇ. 49b; Nandī 111b, and so it repeats also 15 different kinds of the *aṇantara-siddha-kevalī* expressing the origin of omniscience. One owns it by obtaining it from the sacred teaching (*tittha*) or while this teaching is either latent or decays (*atittha*), as a *titthagara* or as monk in general (*a-t.*), by one's own strength (*sayaṃbuddha*) either in order to pass it on or to keep it (*patteya-buddha*) or thanks to another Kevalin (*buddha*), and, moreover, the owner has the physical characteristics of one of the three sexes (*liṅga*, though not their sexual feeling), the external marks of either Jain or alien monkdom or those of laity (*saliṅga* etc.), and, finally, he has acquired them either in company with other true believers (*aṇega*) or by himself.

§82. By concluding this subject we return to its beginning where the spiritual function (*uvaoga*) was designated as the essence and characteristic feature of the soul. The statement

1. For its 34 qualities and marks of distinction (*buddhâisesa*) see Samav. 60b; partly others with the Dig. Śubhacandra on Chapp. 1, 35; 4, 42.

of this fact in T. 2, 8 is followed in T. 2, 9 by the division of the *upayoga* into "formally distinct" and "formally indistinct" imagination. This Sūtra goes back to Pannav. 29. Imagination is *sāgāra* if the object is grasped separately together with its present qualities (*saparyaya*, Prajn.). This happens in cognition, no matter whether it is of the right of the wrong kind, the latter in this case being called non-cognition. Thus it follows that the *sāgāra-uvaoga* is eight-fold and that it comes wherever those two kinds of cognition are recorded, i.e. with all beings. The *aṇāgāra-uvaoga*, however, is given when an object appears without its temporal attributes as an abstract (*sāmānya-rūpatayā*). Prajn. 526 a, b illustrates this by saying that a Kevalin needs for both but 1 *sam.*, whereas any other individual needs for it upto 1 *muh.*, but to become aware of the qualities of the object will take him x times as much as to grasp it as an abstract. The latter is called *daṃsaṇa* meaning "seeing" in a metaphorical sense, and it is four-fold according as it is done either by means of the visual organ, by one or different other organs of sense or else by the inward sense (*acakkhu-d.*), or either whether it comes to happen metaphysically with and without limitation (*ohi-* and *kevala-d.*). All beings own at least one of these kinds of the *daṃsaṇa*. In case, however, a *chaumattha*, by force of *jnāna* and *avadhi-darśana*, should grasp (*jāṇai pāsai*)[1] an object (of ∞ space units), a *sākāra-* and an *anākāra-upayoga* will happen simultaneously. But with the Kevalin it is different: in this case any simultaneity, i.e. any coincidence of the *kevala-jnāna* with the *sākāra-* and the *kevala-darśana* with the *anākāra-up.* is out of the question, and it is this consideration that Viy. 755b and Pannav. 531 a f. are based upon. Prajn. categorically contradicts (532b) Siddhasena who had maintained that a Kevalin grasps an object specially and generally at the same time (*kevālī bhagavaṃ yugapat jānāti paśyati ca*).

The discussion of *uvaoga* in Pannav. 29 is followed by that

1. Thus the process with a Kevalin is rendered (Viy. 221b, 223 b, 888a.) whereas Āyār. 7, 24 does not mean such a one.

of the *pāsaṇāyā* (*paśyattā=prekṣaṇa*). In Pannav. 30 It is equally called *sāgāra* and *aṇāgāra*, but we are given but six kinds of cognition and but three kinds of "seeing". That is to say that among the first both the right and the wrong way of imagination (*mai-nāṇa* and *-annāṇa*) are missing, and among the last the *acakkhu-daṃsaṇa*. For according to Prajn. the *sākāra paśyattā* refers to all three times, whereas the two *mati* are only concerned with the present, and, moreover, the *anākārā paśyattā* is qualified by its distinctness (*parisphuṭa-rūpa*) which is not the case with the *acakṣur-darśana*.

§83. Following the subject of imagination we may proceed to the next paragraph by considering the will. It is represented by the synonyms (Viy. 56b; 149a; 571b; 643; 654a; 657a; 777a; Ṭhāṇ. 19b) *uṭṭhāṇa kamma bala vīriya purisakkāra-parakkama.*[1] By Mahāvīra's coining *atthi*[2] *uṭṭhāṇe i vā*, up to *p.-p.i vā* (Viy. 56b) this sequence has gained a fundamental importance also for the Buddhists (Angutt. 3, 195) causing the *kiriyā-vāī* to be distinguished from the *akiriyā-vāī* and two other so called *samosaraṇa*, i.e. the *s.* of the agnostics (*annāṇiya*) and the *s.* of the ritualists (*veṇaiya*) (Viy. 30), as one acknowledging the free will as a moral principle.[3]

Āyār. 1, 13 renders *kiriyā-vāī* together with *kammā-vāī*, though in this case the inconsistency between a logical prosecution of the Karman idea on the one hand and the principle of free will on the other—the latter being excluded by the former—becomes specifically evident. For the exchange between *kamma* and *kiriyā* comp. § 99.

§84. *The Karman.* By discussing the Karman[4] we return to the field of matter, since the Karman goes back to the fundamental fact of the *poggala*. In the Karman teaching it

1. Another sequence says *iḍḍhi, kamma, paoga* (Viy. 190b, 796a).

2. In earthly life ! Not with the Siddhas (comp. Viy. 657a).

3. SCHRADER, Philosophie, p. 12.

4. Important monography by v. GLASENAPP, Die Lehre vom Karman in der Philosophie der Jainas, nach den Karmagranthas dargestellt. Leipzig 1915. See also Virchand R. GANDHI, The Karma Philosophy, Bombay 1913. Second ed.: 1924.

unites with the other fundamental fact of the *jīva*. The wandering of the souls, a world law (*loga-ṭṭhiī*) among other world laws[1] is exclusively brought about by their being charged with the Karman once and for ever, and this, too, is the primary cause of the world structure (equally called *loga-ṭṭhiī*) (. . . *ajīvā jīva-paiṭṭhiyā, jīvā kamma-p.*; *ajīvā j.-saṃgahiyā, j. k.-s.* Viy. 81a; Ṭhāṇ. 132 b, 213 b, 358 a, 422 b.).

By their merging with matter (*poggala*) the beings are subjected to the Karman (*poggal'āhāra poggala-pariṇāma p.-joṇiya p.-ṭṭhiya kammôvaga kamma-niyāṇa k.ṭṭhiya kammuṇā-m-eva vippariyāsam enti*, Viy. 644 a). If they were not charged with the Karman the souls would lead that existence in the highest possible regions attributed to the Kevalin after his parting from the world (§ 187). This can partly be derived from the names of the Karman; by saying that, among others, it is veiling both knowledge and vision, it follows that when being absent both knowledge and vision are unveiled.

The soul comes to obtain the Karman by means of the binding (*bandha*). T. 8, 2 is clearest in expressing this process: *sakaṣāyatvāj jīvaḥ karmaṇo yogyān pudgalān ādatte.* Hence matter attracted by soul is not yet Karman, but it comes to be so, that is to say by its very penetrating it, while all other matter pertains to the soul but externally. This penetration is of different intensity (i.e. depth); Viy. 34a is careful in distinguishing *siḍhila-bandhaṇa-baddha kamma* from *dhaṇiya-b. b. k.*, and the comparisons given by Viy. 250b help to explain it. A dirty dress is more difficult to clean than a stained one; from an anvil not even the smallest part will come off in splinters, but dry grass is sure to burn up immediately and a drop of water falling on red hot iron will evaporate instantly. Attraction comes about by the soul activating the inward sense and speech activating the body. This is the *joga* (*yoga*, T. 6, 1).[2] By considering that the two first are at work in the four cases of "wrong", "true",

1. They consist briefly spoken, in the unalterability of the facts, though only a few like *jīva* and *ajīva*, *loga* and *aloga*, *tasa* and *thāvara* are mentioned (Ṭhāṇ 470).

2. Related to it is *paṇihāṇa*, the doing (Viy. 750a; Ṭhāṇ. 121a 196a).

etc. (§ 74), that four bodies (the fiery one is missing) form four additional cases and that three mixed kinds (*mīsa*) supervene to the latter, we arrive at 15 different kinds of *joga* (Viy. 854b). Acc. to Viy. 251b the three fundamental kinds together with the Karman are called the "working forces" (*karaṇa*). The obvious question as to the metaphysical way of activity has been dealt with by Devanandin who (on T. 6, 1) denotes the *yoga* as a vibrating (*parispanda*) of the soul units. As to the *yoga* (*joga*) it causes substances which may become **Karman** to flow into the soul (T. 6, 2), a process implied by the word *aṇhaya*[1] (JACOBI: "influence"), and accordingly it follows that speech and inward sense (a.o.) are called *aṇhaya-kārī* and *a.-kāra* (Āyār. II 92, 7; 132, 10).[2] That, however, these substances continue to stick to the soul is due to the work of passions. By the ambiguous word *kasāya* they are, at the same time, attributed a binding power metaphorically.[3] Anger, pride, fraud and greed are denoted as passions (§ 167), and they, for their part, result from Karman (*udaya*, §86). Thus the circle closes. Where passion is absent there the substances fail to have any possibility of sticking. The freedom from passion, however, and hence the purification of the soul leading to *mokṣa* can be realized in life only by the Jain monk (or nun). That is why the *bandha* is twofold (Viy. 383b): it is monastic (*iriyāvahiya*) or profane (*saṃparāiya*). We start by dealing with the former even though its basic conceptions can be discussed only in connexion with the latter. By *iriyāvaha*, *-vahiyā*, and also *īriyā-* Kappa 6,13=Ṭhāṇ. 371a understands the careful walking of a monk, but in a wider sense they also mean his conduct according to the rules. The Karman bound up in such a one is of no duration worth mentioning (§ 85); JACOBI on T. 6, 5 distinguishes it as "momentary Karman" from the "durative Karman." Activity acc. to the rules, so Sūy. II, 2, 23

1. *aṇhaya* "to flow in"=*āsnava* derived from *snu*. Next to it stands *āsava*. In Sanskrit we find *āsrava* and (wrong) *āśrava*. Comp. HULTZSCH ZDMG 72, 149. *aṇhāi* Uvav. § 64ff., however, does not belong to *āsrava* (v. GLASENAPP, Karman p. 11), but is=*aśnāti*.

2. Panhav. 1-5 are the *Aṇhaya-dārāiṃ*.

3. Expressed by Devanandin on T. 6 5.—Also *rajas* is passion, *raya*=*kamma* Ṭhāṇ. 319b.

(316a) says, "is bound in 1 *samaya*, felt in the next and extinguished in the next but one" (comp. also Viy. 183a). The performer of this spiritual Karman is characterised as *saṃvuḍa aṇagāra*, i.e. a homeless man performing a defensive action (*saṃvara*, § 169). But Viy. 309 b adds that he, in doing so, must have released himself of all four passions, i.e. of anger, pride, fraud and greed. Strangely enough this is not mentioned in Viy. 383 b where the *iriyāvahiya-bandha* is reserved but to him who is free from any sexual consciousness (*avagaya-veya*).

Viy. 52a thought it necessary to point out that the Karman operates with the total I on the total object (*savveṇaṃ savve kaḍe*) but not by and on a part of both (*deseṇaṃ dese, d. savve, savveṇaṃ dese*), and that it does so in the past, the present and the future. In this case the process of binding (*kammaṃ karei*) is followed by the accumulation of the Karman (*ciṇai and uvaciṇai*,[1] Viy. 53a), and the ensuing process (§ 86) is furthermore denoted by *udīrei, veei* and *nijjarei*. We find the same as early as in Viy. 23a, though here the author starts from the transformation of particles of substance taken in (*āhāriya poggala*) which, consequently, must be understood as comprising Karman atoms. Comp. also Pannav. 457b (§86). The accomplished fact of binding underlies Viy. 26. This passage thoroughly deals not only with the *bandhī* having already bound the Karman, but also with the possibility or either impossibility (depending on the quality of the soul) of binding further Karmans in either the present or future life of the respective person. If in this Saya as well as in the following and frequently elsewhere the author comes to speak of the *pāva kamma*, he, by this expression, refers both to good and evil doing, whereas its limitation to guilty doing is merely fictitious and caused by the idea that guilty doing forces itself on the natural mind more readily than a meritorious one. The inflow of both merit and guilt is noted by T. 7, 3 as the two consequences of the *yoga*.

§85. We cannot proceed in discussing the problem of binding before having dealt with the way how and into what

1. Or else (*uva*)*ciṇāi*, e.g. Viy. 556a.

different kinds of the Karman, the particles of substances that have flowed in transform within the soul. This transformation becomes apparent as soon as they materialize. There are eight different kinds, and they are called *kamma-pagaḍī* (Viy. 255a etc. ; Pannav. 453a etc.; Utt. 33, 2; T. 8, 5). They comprise the afore mentioned Karman of veiling both knowledge and vision, the Karman to be perceived through the senses, the confusing Karman, the Karman effecting the amount of life, individuality and social standing, and, finally, the Karman obstructing opportunities. Their sub-species (*uttara-pagaḍī* as against the mentioned *mūla-p.*) are demonstrated in Pannav. 23, 1 (§ 87). In dealing with the binding first, we are thoroughly informed by the same in 23, 2 (484b) about the minimum and maximum duration of the different kinds of Karman bound by the individual classes of the beings. So, for instance, with all beings of one sense the Karman veiling knowledge will last for 3/7 *sāgarovama* plus 1/¿ *paliovama*, while with a reasonable being of five senses it will lie between the fraction of 1 *muhutta* and 30 *koḍākoḍī* of *sāgarovama*. Further we are shown (488 b) what soul (*ke* scil. *jīva*) a kind of Karman in its shortest duration has and what sort of being will bind the longest lasting Karman in the eight different kinds (490a). But we cannot go into details here. The d u r a t i o n is called *bandha-ṭṭhiī* and *kamma-ṭṭhiī* in Viy. 255a, whereas Pannav. 475ff. gives but *ṭhiī*, and it consists of the preliminary time of rest following the binding (*ābāhā*) and the time of effectiveness (*kamma-nisega*) which starts with the *udaya* and lasts until the last particle of this Karman is extinguished. The *ābāhā* which amounts to one hundred years for each 1 *koḍāk.* of *sāg.* is included in the *ṭhii*, though, acc. to Vy. 255b, by some it is added to it.[1] For *ābāha* the later literature puts *sattā*, "being existent in potentia" (v. GLASENAPP, Karman p. 43). In the Canon we only find the kindred *santa-kamma* (§ 183). With reference to the mentioned passages and to Viy. 53b; Samav. 147b. *nisega* "ray" is ex-

1. Owing to an erratum in Viy. what follows on 255 b stands on 257b and what follows on 258 b on 256 a.

plained as a Karman particle decreasing in the reaction produced from *samaya* to *samaya*. Thus the duration of the Karman equally suggests the question of its intensity, though but by an indication. Most certainly, however, when speaking of *aṇubhāga-kamma*, the author means intensity. There is only such a one and a *paesa-kamma* (Viy. 65a; Ṭhāṇ. 66a), and Mahāvīra claims the discrimination of this duad to be his own (*mae pannatte*). To this *aṇubhāga* Pannav. 23, 1 (457b ff.) corresponds by giving *aṇubhāva*; Umāsvāti merely has *anubhāva* (T. 8, 4. 22). Apart from the kind, the duration and the power of the binding Umāsvāti, finally, also knows of the quantity (T. 8, 4. 25.). It is characterized by the *pradeśa*. To this there belongs the just mentioned *paesa-kamma*, though nothing in detail is being said as to its nature. We but learn from that passage that it must be perceived through the senses (§ 86) while with the *aṇubhāga*-k. this is not necessarily a must. Acc. to Viy. 421 b *paesa* is synonymous with the *avibhāga-paliccheya*. Each soul unit (*jīva-paesa*) is on all sides surrounded, if at all (for it does not pertain to the Kevalin), by Karman units (*āveḍhiya-pariveḍhiya*). For this comp. T. 8, 25.

In the Canon (Ṭhāṇ. 220 b), different from Umāsvāti, those four points of view appear among the *bandha*, and, moreover, they are being considered with regard to their relative number by asking of what sort of binding, what duration, what intensity and what quantity the relatively least etc. cases will occur. But then the cases mentioned are dealt with in reference to *saṃkama*, *ni(d)hatta* and *nikāiya*. *saṃkama* presents itself when a Karman sub-species different from the one formerly bound materializes. *nidhatta* and *nikāiya* signify different grades of intensity by which Karman particles unite (comp. also Vy. 25b). These explanations as well as those of the following expressions have to be drawn from the commentaries only. For there are still others like *oyaṭṭei* and *uvvaṭṭei* which occur side by side with *saṃkamai*, *nihattei* and *nikāei* (Viy. 24 b, 26 a). They express that the effect and, consequently the consumption of a Karman may become either larger or smaller than is presupposed by its binding. The later authors speak of *oyaṭṭaṇā* and *uvvaṭṭaṇā*, the latter appearing in the Canon in a different meaning (§ 92). Under what conditions the mentioned processes occur is not said there.

§86. By referring to these expression we have already proceded from the binding of the Karman to the way how it works. It starts at the end of the time of rest. A solemnly styled formula (Pannav. 457 b ff.)[1] calls the Karman *jīveṇa baddha puṭṭha baddha-phāsa-puṭṭha saṃciya ciya uvaciya āvāga-patta vivāga-p. phala-p. udaya-p.* The last four expressions contain in *udaya* the common word for the coming-into-life of the Karman. If this comes to pass, the soul is in the state of *udaiya* (§ 182). We must distinguish *udaya* from *udīraṇā*, but in verbal construction we never find *udiya*, but only *udiṇṇa* or *sayam udiṇṇa*; its opposite is then formed by *pareṇa udīriya* (Viy. 57 b; Pannav. 457 b). While *udaya* signifies the so to speak natural beginning of the operative act, the *udīraṇā* or the "initiative" means the premature materialization. Resting Karman is attracted by activity thus awakening it to become effective (*karaṇeṇ' ākaḍḍhiya udae dijjai*, Śivaśarman, Kammapayaḍi, Vy. 24. a). It is only the commentaries that speak of the *udīraṇā* going back to activity, the *yoga*, though they neglect the fact that thus, at the same time, a new Karman is being produced. By *udaya* and *udīraṇā* there begins for the individual the palpability of the Karman (*veyaṇā*). For the different sensations Pannav. 35 gives certain principles of classification parts of which are obvious as, for instance, bodily and spiritual, pleasant and unpleasant *veyaṇā*, and such ensuing from the mixtures of these opposites. In addition we may begin with pointing out the discrimination made between the sensations signified by the words *nidāya* and *aṇidāya*. Though in their varying derivation of these words the commentators betray their uncertainty, it can be said that the first group means "conscious" sensations pertaining only to beings owning reason,[2] whereas

1. For another one see Pannav. 402 a.

2. It seems to be a gerund. Viy. 40 a has *aṇidāe veyaṇaṃ veenti*, Viy 769 b=Pannav. 557 a probably has *(a)nidāyaṃ v.v. for (a)nidāya v.v.*, and in the preceding enumeration *ṇidāya aṇidāya* for *nidāya ya aṇidāya ya.*

it may be assumed that "unconscious" sensations are merely reflexions. Furthermore we may mention that sensation that a monk imposes upon himself and that coming from without (*ajjhovagamiya*—wrongly : *abbhov.*—and *avakkamiyā*) (Viy. 65 a; Ṭhāṇ. 88 b; Pannav. 556 b). Palpability is interconnected both with action and extinction. Towards dissenters Viy. 224 b makes it quite plain that palpability does not always correspond with the produced Karman (*kaḍa kamma*) (*pāṇā* etc. *aṇevaṃbhūyaṃ veyaṇaṃ veenti*). To prove this Viy. 767 b tells us that while with all beings of hell inflow (*āsava*), action (*kiriyā*), and feeling (*veyaṇā*) are strong in comparison with annihilation (*nijjarā*), it is different with the gods where along with extinction also feeling is weak as against the two first. It is simultaneously shown here that palpability and extinction do not correspond everywhere, though this only refers to beings beyond the human range, whereas within this range strong sensation will represent strong extinction and vice versa (Viy. 250a). In any case, however, to feel Karman (*veei, paḍisaṃveei*) means to consume Karman (*nijjarei*), even though the *samaya* of both do not coincide (Viy. 301 a; Sūy. 22, 23). With some kinds of Karman this consumption[1] is accompanied by a special process called *samugghāya* (§ 89). Rhetorically speaking extinct Karman can be signified as good luck (*suha*) as is done in Viy. 314 a. The extinction is irrevocable. In addition to *veyaṇā* it is called *nijjarā* (elsewhere even *khaya*), and the state of the soul prevailing with *khaya* goes by the name of *khaiya*.

§87. Proceeding from these general considerations we now arrive at the different kinds of the Karman. While in the Canon handed down to us the common processes of *bandha* etc., receive next to no definition, most probably owing to the fact that they are supposed to be obvious, we have first-hand information as to its different forms of manifestation (Pannav. 457 b ff., 465 b ff., Comp. also T. 8, 7 ff.). The Karman

The comm. by deriving from *dā*, to give" and *dā* "to purge" take *nidā* either for a subst. (*nidā jnānam* and *aṇidāe* = *anirdhāraṇayā*) or for an adj. (*cittavatī, samyag-vivekavatī*).

1. So far as it is not brought about by ascetic methods it is called *akāma-nijjarā* (Uvav. § 56, p. 61).

o b s c u r i n g k n o w l e d g e (*nāṇ'āvaraṇijja kamma*) obstructs (acc. to Ṭhāṇ. 347 a) cognition in all its five forms. It causes—this is its *aṇubhava* § 85)—the obscuration of the senses as sources of cognition and of all knowledge gained by them (*soy'āvaraṇa soya-vinnāṇ'āvaraṇa nett'āvaraṇa. netta-v.-āv.*, etc.). Insights gained by other than sensual means and their obscurations are not considered. The result is that one does not know what one is to know, wants to know, or else has known. The Karman o b s c u r i n g v i s i o n (*daṃsaṇ'āvaraṇijja* or *darisaṇ'āv. k.*) arrives at the corresponding result for vision. It shows up in nine different kinds (Ṭhāṇ. 447 a; Samav. 15 a), for it obstructs the four-fold vision (§ 82) and furthermore it consists in unconsciousness which, owing to the chosen expressions, gradually deepens by proceeding from normal sleep (*niddā*) to sleeping while walking or standing (*payalā*)[1]—including the intensive stages of both (*niddā-niddā, p.-p.*)—and onwards to acting while sleeping (*thīṇ'addhi*).[2] The Karman which is called the one t o b e p e r c e i v e d t h r o u g h t h e s e n s e s (*veyaṇijja k.*) represents the feelings of comfort and discomfort (*sāyā- and asāyā-v.*). Both are shared by the five senses, the inward sense, speech and body, and, hence, each of them is eight-fold. Next there follows in (52 names, stated by Samav. 71 a, the c o n f u s i n g Karman (*mohaṇijja k.*) producing disturbances in belief and conduct (*daṃsaṇa-m.* and *caritta-m.*), the former manifesting itself supposedly as true belief (*sammatta-veyaṇijja*), erroneous belief (*micchatta-v.*) and as the mixture of both (*sammā-micch. v.*). The *sammatta-vey.* in this connexion is said to be a modification of the *micchatta* (*mithyātva-prakṛti* Prajn. 468 a) (comp. also JACOBI on T. 8, 10.). Perhaps the intention was but to incorporate into the system the fact of orthodoxy being a Karman just as well, and its becoming conscious (hence *veyaṇijja*). The disturbance of conduct is caused by passion

1. This goes with *payalāei*, Viy. 217 b.

2. JACOBI 's "greed in the state of numbness" is based on the *styāna-gṛddhi* of Umāsvāti, etc., for *styāna-rddhi* (T. 8, 8). Sthān. 447 b has both forms.

(*kasāya-v.*) showing up in the four forms of anger, pride, fraud and greed (Ṭhāṇ. 193 a; Samav. 9 a). Each of these passions appear in four grades and each is called accordingly *aṇantāṇu-bandhi*, *apaccakkhāṇa*, *paccakkhāṇ'āvaraṇa* and *saṃjalaṇa*. With the single exception of the last these words are adjectives. Their meaning is the linkage with the Saṃsāra (*aṇanta*), the entire absence and the occasional obscuring of renunciation (*paccakkhāṇa*, § 172), and the sudden eruption, the latter being the weakest form. It thus follows that the form of passion concerning the disturbance of conduct is sixteen-fold (Samav. 31 a). Several moods as laughing, pleasure, fear, grief and loathing[1] do not count among passions and are called *nokasāya* for that reason, and sexual consciousness (*veya-veyaṇijja*) as man or woman or neuter is equally placed into this connexion. So, then, we have altogether nine forms (Ṭhāṇ. 468 b) of disturbance of conduct free from passion, though by disregarding the sub-division their power is five-fold only. For a reason immediately going to be discussed there now follows the kind of Karman invariably ranging last, the obstructing Karman (*antarāiya* k.). It manifests itself as obstructive where the act of giving, taking, enjoying (*bhoga*), using (*uvabhoga*)[2] and volition (*vīriya*) ought to take place. The so far mentioned *kamma-pagaḍī* with the exception of the *veyaṇijja* all share in a more or less strongly pronounced activity, and in that this activity has a destructive influence on the soul they are comprised as *ghāi-kamma* (Aṇuog. 118 b). Together with the *veyaṇijja* they are placed over against the three last kinds as inactive or *aghāi-k.*: first the quantity of life (*āuya k.*) which differs with the beings of hell, animals, humans, and gods (§ 90), and finally, the individuality (*nāma-k.*) and the social standing (*goya-k.*). The latter is either high or low and makes itself felt accordingly, in which case the position within society

1. Causes for laughing (*hās'uppatti*) are given by seeing, speaking, hearing and remembering (Ṭhāṇ. 203 a). Fear concerns both this world and the world beyond, confiscation, something unexpected (*akamhā-bhaya*), pain, death and disgrace (Ṭhāṇ. 389 a; Sam. 12 b).

2. This discrimination acc. to Prajn.

is determined by noble birth (caste, *jāi*) and good family (*kula*), but also by physical strength (*bala*), sacredness (*tava*), erudition (*suya*), costly property (*lābha*) and splendour (*issariya*) as well as by their opposites. All this refers to human conditions, but, though neither text nor commentary gives it, it may naturally, under certain circumstances, apply to non-human beings also. The Karman of the personality or the individuality, at the long last, is built up by very different components which amount to a total of 42 in number. They are physical in both a narrower and wider sense as far as, within one class of beings, they contain: shape of the body, structure and functions of the body as breathing, radiation (*āyava* and *ujjoya*) and locomotion (*vihāya-gai*), and influence on the senses (feeling, smell, taste, and colour). Added to this there are the organic causes of death (*uvaghāya*) and the destination of the new form of existence (*āṇupuvvī*). With individuality there also goes the power of acting upon others: superiority (*par'āghāya*), the presence or absence of the faculty to influence people, honour and disgrace, pleasant and unpleasant impressions. The end is made up of the state of accomplishment achieved by a Titthagara. In comparison with this variety the general activity of the individual Karman is merely distinguished as either being a favourable or an unfavourable one. Each of both these distinctions lists 14 cases based on concrete qualities of the Karman bearer, his reputation and his deeds.

§88. That much about the eight kinds of the Karman and their forces acting in materialization. The general formula for these forces was found (acc. to Pannav. 458 b ff.) by saying *jaṃ vedei poggalaṃ vā poggale vā p.-pariṇāmaṃ vā vīsasā vā poggalāṇaṃ pariṇāmaṃ tesiṃ vā udaeṇaṃ* ... (*kammaṃ vedei*). Although perhaps owing to corruption, it fails to be quite clear, in no way concrete particles, e.g. of wood or earth are being meant, as Prajn. (460 b), wants it thus leading to quite forced results. It rather concerns Karman atoms. We now come to deal with certain notes referring to individual kinds. Viy. 52a, 63 b have the *kankha-mohaṇijja kamma*, and ib. 639 b of the same has the *veyaṇijja* (omitting *kamma*). At first sight they seem to belong to the correspondingly called *pagadi*, but they rather concern general denominations. This follows from the contexts which are of an entirely non-special kind. In a report on the soul the *veyaṇijja* appears as *dukkhī* and *adukkhī*: *aha se veyaṇijje nijjiṇṇe bhavai* (Viy. 639 b).[1] It is the *kankha-mohaṇijja* that with the whole I acts upon the object (§ 84), it makes itself felt in cases of doubt, desire, uncertainty, discordance and defect (*jīva. . . sankiya, kankhiya, viigicchiya, bheya-samāvanna, kalusa-s.*, 52 a), while monks (60a) will experience it as deviations from cognition, belief, conduct and as other irregularities (*nāṇ'antara. . . . ling'antara*, etc.). It is bound (56 b) by force of carelessness (*pamāya*) and activity (*joga*); no soul charged with it is able to get beyond foolish or semi-foolish volition (*vīriyatta*) (62 b). All beings of one to four senses feel this Karman without being conscious of it (69 b). So, then, this concerns entirely general things, and in this context those names may not be taken in a special sense.

§89. By being annihilated several kinds of Karman suffer a special fate by being subjected to the *samugghāya*, i.e. the "ejection" of their particles. Pannav. 36 proceeds systematically in advising us about the *s.*, whereas Umāsvāti does not mention it in his Sūtras. There are seven cases of *s.* (Ṭhāṇ. 409 b; Samav. 12 b), the last of which being reserved to the Kevalin, so that the remaining six are comprised as *chaumatthiya* s. (e.g. Samav. 11 b). This does not mean, however, that it were within the power of monks only to attain it, the fact is, rather, that all beings share in it correspondingly (Pannav. 561 b). For they all have a certain sense of Karman (*veyaṇā*), have passion (*kasāya*), suffer death (*maraṇa*) and thus are in possession of the accordingly called *samugghāya* (1 to 3), in the third case the *māraṇ'antiya s.* As far as they have a body of transformation, a body of transposition and a fiery body they are given the possibility of also attaining the corresponding *samug-*

1. In a counterpart of this passage which, perhaps, is only oratorical the *poggala* is given a *lukkhī* and *alukkhī* (Viy. 638, b comp. § 60).

ghāya (4 to 6) (comp. Ṭhāṇ. 288 a). As to the process concerning the *kevali-s.* we are advised by Uvav. § 141 ff.; Ṭhāṇ. 442 a. To put it briefly, the Kevalin projects his soul atoms still infected with Karman from the vertex and the foot-point from the right and the left side, from the chest and the back in the shape of columns each reaching to the end of the world and then retracts them again. During the time of the 8 *samaya* it takes to accomplish this process, the Karman particles—as must be added logically—disengage from the soul. The *samugghāya* of other beings take a longer time, i. e. ¿ *samaya* within a *muhutta* (Pannav. 561 b), and the space filled up by them is, in proportion, infinitesimally small, i.e. equal to the body of the resp. being, though in the case of the three last of these *samugghāya* columns we have to add up to ¿ *joyaṇa* in one direction. The ejected (*nicchūḍha*) *poggala*· dissipate in the world, and Uvav. § 133; Viy. 740 b[1] discuss the question as to who is able to perceive them, or, as Pannav. 590 a; 496 a f. does, whether and to what degree the ejecting individual has committed actions against other beings to whom they cause an injury (§ 90). The *veuvviya samugghāya*—by differentiating its prefix the appertaining verb is always *samohaṇai*—is equally described (Viy. 153 b) as the projection of a column which, however, reaches no farther than x *joy*. By means of it particles of substance coarse in proportion (*ahā-bāyara*)[2] are eliminated (*parisāḍei*) and others subtle in proportion (*ahā-suhuma*) are attracted (*pariyāei*). This happens twice.[3]

With the *veyaṇā-samugghāya* the *asāyā-veyaṇijja kamma* which comes to be felt as pain is being annihilated, with the *kasāya-s.* the *caritta-mohaṇijja k.* so far as it manifests itself as a passion, while with death the remainder of the *āuya k.* ceases to be. In the case of transformation, transposition and ejection of

1. Here the resp. monk is not called *kevalī* but *bhāviy'appa aṇagāra,* as frequently applied elsewhere, and the name of the disengaged particles is *carima sarīra-poggala.*

2. They cannot to materially coarse since the worlds of gods and their inhabitants are immaterial. This is discussed by Viy. 154 b.

3. *"doccaṃ pi" iti. . . cikīrṣita-rūpa-nirmāṇārtham* Viy. 155 a.

energy (*veuvvivya-*, *āhāraga-* and *teyaga-s.*) which have nothing to do with the Karman directly, the parts of ***nāma-kamma*** becoming effective in the resp. bodies (§ 62) drop out. The whole conception doubtlessly[1] comes from the impression which pain, anger, curse and blessings cause within the onlooker. Pleasant sensations, though they belong to the *veyaṇā* just as well, have no *samugghāya*.

§90. *Āuya* does not mean lifetime, though long (*dīha*) and short (*appa*) *āuya* both depending on moral conduct (Viy. 225 b) are spoken of. It rather refers to some material quantity of life (Viy. 215 b) which materializes as Karman during consumption. In correspondence herewith, except with humans and animals, life painlessly comes to an end by itself. With these humans and animals there may happen a greater consumption, and thus the amount of life may run out more quickly than it ought to do normally. T. 2, 52 calls it *apavartana* by which we have to understand the above mentioned *oyaṭṭaṇa*. It is brought about by the *uvakkama* (Viy. 795 b, specialized Ṭhāṇ. 220 b), i.e. the premature materialization which may be rendered as "cause of death" (JACOBI on T. 2, 52). Its originator is either the being itself or somebody else. Gods and beings of hell are *niruvakkam'āuya*, as has been pointed out before. It need not be explained that the class and the stage of the being is, so to speak, imprinted (*nihatta*, *niṣikta*) on the soul by the *āuya-bandha* and that by causing in it the duration, the dimension, the energy and the occupation of space of the bound Karman it is six-fold for that reason (*jāi-* etc. *-nāma-nihitt'-āuya*),[2] (Viy. 279 b—Pannav. 217 a—Ṭhāṇ. 376 b—Samav. 147 b) nor need it be pointed out that the palpability of the life Karman is strong and uniform from the completed reincarnation onward (Viy. 304 a). Apparently it was necessary to stress that an *āuya* of the future has to be distinguished from such as is consumed in the present. The former is operated in this world (*iha-gaya*), and it is wrong to assume that it should

1. *vedanā-samudghāto vedanā'tiśayāt*, Prajn. 519 b.

2. Viy. 280 a confuses *nāma* with *goya* and *nihitta* with *niutta* which probably goes back to some misunderstanding.

show up in the moment or even after the completion of the reincarnation (Viy. 304 a); it remains untouched before the effective power becomes active (*se purao kaḍe ciṭṭhai*, Viy. 747a). If dissenters hold the view that the soul effects (Viy. 98 a) and feels (Viy. 214 a) the quantity of life of both this world (*iha-bhaviy'āuya*) and the world beyond (*para-bh. ā.*), we are bound to say that the opposite is true in that only the one of both is effected and felt.

The *āuya kamma* takes an exceptional position not only in so far as its effect forms the base for the new existence (comp. Viy. 280 b = Prajn. 218 a = Sthān. 377a = Samav. 148 a) in which now the other *kamma* materializes, but also in that (Pannav. 216 b; Ṭhāṇ. 376 b; Viy. 632 b) its binding is confined to a certain part of life, i.e. to its last. This may be either six months or $\frac{1}{3}$, $\frac{1}{9}$, $\frac{1}{27}$ of the entire *āuya*. The criterion is either the absence or the presence of the cause of death. Hence a person will always effect but the *āuya* of the immediately following life and, consequently, his *ābāha* (§ 85) will be only a very short one. We then read (Pannav. 217 a; Samav. 147 b) that every act of binding does not happen continuously but in stages (*āgarisehiṃ*), of which there are eight and whose intensity diminishes acc. to the commentators. This reminds of the *kamma-nisega*. For comparison we are given the example of the cow repeatedly interrupting itself when drinking water (*bhayena punaḥ punar āghoṭayati* resp. *ābṛhati*).

§91. The *āuya* leads us back to the general consideration following Viy. 422 b dealing with the presence or absence of one or other kind of Karman. The quantity of life, the individuality and the social standing of a person do not show up separately nor are separated from the Karman "to be felt". Where, moreover, there is any "veiling of knowledge", there are equally "veiling of vision" and obstruction. In contrast to these absolute cogencies, the other combinations, except one, are certainly cogent in one direction (*niyamā atthi*), though in their reversion they are but possible (*siya atthi siya n'atthi*); so, for instance, where we have *mohaṇijja*, there must be *veyaṇijja*, but where we have *veyaṇijja*, there may be *mohaṇijja*. The one exception mentioned above are *mohaṇijja* and *antarāiya* which may, though not must, occur together.

Another calculation makes up the contents of Pannav. 24 to 27. 24 is to prove how many Karman kinds possibly can occur with a soul binding one of them. He who, for instance, binds veiling of knowledge (and hence also veiling of vision) is capable of binding either all 8 or but 7 or but 6 kinds. The capability of a soul to bind, however, corresponds but partly with the Karman kinds becoming felt in the same soul. This problem is dealt with by Pannav. 25 where we learn that in a soul binding *veyaṇijja kamma*, either eight, seven or merely four kinds come to be felt.

Pannav. 26 and 27 state how many kinds a soul binding a certain kind is able to bind, resp. to feel at all. The statements given, however, do not confine themselves to the soul and its multiples (*jīvā*), but they also concern the different classes of the beings. On the other hand the proof is given numerically only: we come to know as possibilities the *aṭṭhaviha-bandhaga*, *sattaviha-b.*, *chavviha-b.*, *cauvviha-b.*, *egaviha-b.* and both the *abandhaga* and the *aṭṭhaviha*-etc. *vedaga*. But it is not until we read the commentaries that we learn what we have to understand by it. Besides we find it in the later Karman literature, comp. the columns of *bandha* and *udaya* in v. GLASENAPP's representation of the *guṇa-sthāna*,[1] the canonical fundamentals of which we find in these chapters of Pannav. Their author, most naturally, knew well enough which kinds of Karman dropped out accordingly. If now those Karman specialists state to have taken their subject-matter from the 12th Anga lost to us, then we must conclude that also the Pannav., since it comprises what was at hand, went back to this source.

Finally it is stated (Viy. 257 b) which certain qualities of the soul or of its bearer lead to binding the individual *kamma-pagaḍī*. Physical constitution, as (a. o.) the quality of being

1. Karman, p. 90 ff.

fully developed (§ 63), speech and subtlety, ranges side by side with intellectual constitution, as (a. o) sexual sensation (*veya*), self-discipline, cognition and its formal distinctness (§ 82), and each is multiplied by its negation, its intermediate conditions and its individual cases. To give an example we may refer to the reasonable being (*sannī*) in which case + means *bandhai*, ± *siya bandhai siya no b.* (=*bhayaṇāe b.*) and —*na b.*

sannī:	*vey.*	+,	*āu.*	±,	the remaining	±
asannī:	,,	+	,,	±	,, ,,	+
no-sannī-no-asannī:[1]	,,	±	,,	—	,, ,,	—

A similar representation is given in Viy. 33 (951 b) for all one-sensed beings.

The informations rendered up to here are of a merely general character and correspond with the theoretical character of the mentioned passages of the texts. With the correlation between Karman and action we shall deal in § 167, and we here but mention that (Viy. 574 b=777 b) it is only by force of the Karman that the soul and the world gain their variety. One step in the direction of the concrete is seen being done (Viy. 253 a) in that an insignificant and unsympathetic appearance follows from intensive action and activity, whereas a sympathetic one follows from the conscious abstentation from doing. This directly leads us up to the fundamental fruit of the deeds, the reincarnation.

§ 92. *The Reincarnation.* For want of materiality the soul as such has no gravity, and it is owing to its being affected with Karman only that it stays with in the chain of existence, the Saṃsāra. As soon as it is released from it, it will rush to reach the spacially highest region it is able to gain (§ 187). But "just as the meshes of a net closely following each other by consequently forming in a row without any interval will act up on the next mesh by their gravity, their load, their full weight and their density, thus in every soul in many thousands of reincarnations many thousands of lives by their gravity, their

1. *kevali siddhaś ca*, Vy.

load, their full weight and their density act on their subsequent lives"[1] (Viy. 214 a). But these figures still keep within a modest frame; other texts give only the state of affairs possible with regard to the eternity of the world, its contents and its laws. As a goat pen is filled up with the excrements of the goats, so in every unit (*paramāṇupoggala-mette vi paese*) of the world an incarnated soul has appeared and expired (*jāe va mae va*), so Viy. 579 a puts it in popular language, by continuing (580 a) that, up from times eternal, as has to be added analogously, a soul has been incarnated more than once or endlessly often in any kind of the beings, and, moreover (581 a), has been related by kinship, sovereignty or servitude with all souls more than once or endlessly often. All beings (*pāṇā*, etc.) have lived as parts of a lotus (§ 94) or as other plants more than once already or endlessly often (Viy. 511 b, 513 b). Reincarnation is commonly called *uvavāya*[2] (hence the name of Uvavāiya of the 2nd Uvanga), in the title of Pannav. 6 *vakkanti*. This word covers *uvavāya* and *uvvaṭṭaṇā*, the latter signifiying the rising to a spacially higher stage. Sinking, however, is called *cayaṇa* (Ṭhāṇ. 66 a).

§93. It may happen that several souls come to incarnate simultaneously on the same stage, be it that of the beings of hell (H), of animals (A)—including elemental beings (A)[a] and plants—, humans (M) or gods (G). Hence the statements made by Jīv. 140 a as to such souls which, by proceeding on their way of incarnation, leave nought as their remainder (*nilleva*). The statement made by Viy. 47a is more theoretical *asunna-kāla* stand for the time during which a number or souls remain on the same stage without one of them leaving it nor one adding itself to it; *missa-k.*, however, is the time during which any number, and *sunna-k.* the time during which all of them left it in order to proceed on their way. The four stages are not exchanged indiscriminately, but the change of stages

1. The AUTHOR's Religionsgeschicht. Lesebuch 7, 15.

2. The Śvet. have *upapāta* in a wrong Sanskritization (comp. LEUMANN, Aup. p. 1). The Dig. are correct in giving Tattv. 2, 32. 35. 47 52 *upapāda*.

(*pavesaṇa,-ṇaga.* Viy. 439 b) follows distinct rules. Pannav. 6 (209 a ff.); Viy. 24 (805 a ff.); Ṭhāṇ. 58 b teach (what we may be allowed to express by signs of abbreviation(that HG originate from A^5 M, A^{1-4} from AMG, and A^5M from HAMG. By omitting irrelevant limitations we have but to note that the wind- and fire-beings have no direct pre-existence as gods. But the post-existence following immediately may manifest itself (comp. also Sūy. II 3, 1 ff., 347 a; Pannav. 398 ff.; Viy. 632 b; Ṭhāṇ. 58 b, 445 b) in the following way : H to A^5M, G to A^{1-5}M, T^{1-4} to AM, A^5M to HAMG. In this case the wind- and fire-beings are specialized in that they will not reincarnate into men, whereas gods will not reincarnate into them, as obviously follows from what was said before. As we are taught by the formula quoted above, an A^5M may even repeatedly appear in the same form of existence. In contrast to the *bhava-ṭṭhiī* this is called *kāya-ṭṭhiī* (Ṭhāṇ. 66 a).[1] Pannav. 18 (374 a f.) deals with it. We here but mention the exceptional position taken by the *nigoya* which is that they are able to remain as such for ∞ time. They are those that are refused any higher development (§ 101).

§94. Next to the purely systematical representation Viy. gives a number of more lively informations serving confirmation, a fact from which we may conclude that in those days this assertion was considered a novelty. Expressly it was disbelief that caused the teaching (Viy. 739 b) that an earth-,water- or plant-being in its next existence (*uvvaṭṭittā*) could come to appear in a human shape and gain the Kevala cognition. The phenomenon of the hot spring at the foot of the Vebhāra near Rāyagiha (Viy. 141 a) is brought about by numerous souls destined to have a hot place of origin, and atoms assembling (*usiṇa-joṇiyā jīvā ya poggalā ya*) and forming water (*udagattāe vakkamanti viukkamanti cayanti uvavajjanti*)[2]; rain originates from the formation of water by *udaga-joṇiya*-souls and -atoms; plants live most intensively in summer because then

1. The quantity of life is corresponding called *bhav'āuya* and *addhâuya* (*addhā=kāla*, see the same and 96b).

2. Comp.also Sūrap. 321 a.

many souls enter into plants (*vaṇassaikāiyattāe vakk.* Viy. 300 a). An animal may have experienced the existence of hell, as have the elephant Udāi and his colleague Bhūyāṇanda (Viy. 720 a), who both, however, will find salvation in their next existence. A god, circumstances permitting, may materialize as a serpent, a precious stone or as a tree (Viy. 581 b). To enter into a lower stage of existence (*aviukkantiyaṃ cayamāṇe*) causes shame, discomfort and vexation within him (Viy. 86 a). Viy. in 652 b minutely depicts the next form of existence pertaining to a Sal-tree or -twig, etc. By example of an extensive list of plants, first of all trees, Viy. 21-23 (Viy. 800 a ff.) show that plant souls come from the animal- or man-stage, though it has to be noted that here the emphasis is on the simultaneity of the incarnation partly basing on the fact that certain plants are the bearers of several or many souls (§ 106)—so acc. to Viy. 508 b the *uppala* and others are bearers of as many souls as they have leaves (*patta*)—, and that, acc. to Viy. 800 a, root, branch, bark, etc. each contain one soul. But as is maintained by Viy. 796 b; Ṭhāṇ. 104 b, also all other beings are given the possibility to reincarnate simultaneously and, what is more, to do so by changing their stages (for them .see above). In contrast to those that do so individually (*avvattaga-saṃciya*) those that in a number of x enter into a new stage simultaneously are called *kati-saṃciya*, and those that do so in a number of ¿ *akati-s*. The occurence of groups of six (*chakka-samajjiya*), 12 and 84 is treated with all the delight taken in such calculations, the same that equally shows up in Viy. 31 (948 a f.) from the point of view of the sum (§ 21) of beings.

§95. Other problems related to the question of simultaneity (Pannav. 204 b, 208 a) may be left aside here. Instead we come to discuss the process of reincarnation itself. Released by the *māraṇ'antiya samugghāya* from the particles of the hitherto *āuya-kamma* the soul moves towards the new place in order to take its house there. But this is but the one possibility open to it. The other one mentioned together with it consists in the soul returning (*paḍiṇiyaṭṭai*), performing the *āuya*-ejection once again and then definitely taking its home at the new place destined for it by its deeds—while one-sensed beings may do so at any place.[1] This theory appears in Viy. 272 b only and does not recur in the Pannav. The vehicle by means of which the soul changes its place is the Karman body (T. 2, 26), and it seems that this is its particular and only function. The new place is reached by following either a straight or bent course (Viy. 85 b), and to move on the latter is called *viggaha-gai.*[2] Acc. to Mahāvīra (§ 21) there are seven of such courses (*seḍhi*) of substance particles, aggregates and beings (Viy. 866 b; Ṭhāṇ. 705 b) among which we find the straight one (*ujjuy'āyaya*) and both the one bent once and twice (*egao-vaṃka, duhao-v.* (but see also below). Each straight distance takes 1 *samaya* (Viy. 630 a); *egao-v.* means two, *duhao-v.* three *samaya* time of travel, while one sensed beings may partly need even four. This is (Viy. 630 a) still a speed leaving behind all earthly comparisons. In this connexion we must know that the upward- and downward-movement takes place within a shaft (*nālī*, Viy. 957 b) measuring 100,000 *joy.* in diameter which goes through the whole world perpendicularly and confines the places of existence of most beings. As far as the starting point and the place of destination within this shaft, called *trasa-nāḍī* by later authors, are situated on one level it takes the soul but 1 *samaya* to cover the straight course (*ega-samaiya viggaha*). If, however, we have a different level the soul first will move either up- or downwards in 1 *sam.* and then horizontally to its place of destination (*du-s. v.*). If the place of destination does not lie, as was assumed above, within the range of a main direction but in that of a side direction, first the one (by a *sama-śreṇī*) and then the latter (by a *viseḍhī*, *viśreṇī*) has to be gained (*du-s.-v.*, ti-*s. v.*). Now, if, as is the case with all one-sensed beings known to be spread world-wide in unrestricted numbers, the starting

1. *atthegaie tao paḍiṇiyaṭṭai, tao paḍiṇiyaṭṭittā iha-m-āgacchai, iha-m-āgacchittā doccaṃ pi māraṇ'antiya-samugghāyaṃ samohaṇai, . . . samohaṇittā* (. . . (. . . *neraiyattāe* etc.) *uvavajjittā* (thus instead of ⁰*ttae*) *tao pacchā āhārejja* etc. Viy. 273 a.

2. But Viy. 955 a also gives (*ega-samaiya*) *viggaha* for the straight one (see below).

point lies without the *nālī*, then it follows that the soul can equally enter it from a main direction only, and not until doing so by an intermediate direction will the soul be able to gain it (*ti-s. v.*, *cau-s. v.*). Indeed, in case it should happen that the place of destination equally lies in an intermediate direction, the soul would need another fifth *sam.* (Viy. 287 b), as is the opinion of some authors, though Abhayadeva professes (Sthān. 177 b) it to be his own. But the text does not go beyond 4 *sam.* and confines them to the one-sensed beings.[1] For this comp. Viy. 287 a, 632 a and Saya 34, 954 b ff., but especially Vy. offering details on these passages, and Ṭhāṇ. 177 a.

§96. The *samaya* dealt with above form an intermediate time (*antara*) between the existences. The *antara* is taught by Viy. 439 a=Pannav. 207 a and Viy. 632 b, and it is obvious that the beings are both *santara* and *nirantara*, the latter being the case when they are able to avail themselves either of the *ega-samaiya*-or the *ujjuy'āyaya*- course. In contrast to this it is not clear why there is explicitly no intermediate time given for the one-sensed beings since we know them to move in 4 *sam.*[2] With the last of all travel-*samaya* there begins the taking in of matter, the *āhāra* (Viy. 287 a). That is why the souls on the way are considered to be *aṇāhāraga* as follows from Pannav. 512a. It happens, though, that the intake of matter precedes the change of place (Viy. 729a, 789 a), i.e. when an earth-, water- or wind-being has performed the *maraṇa-samugghāya* imperfectly (*deseṇaṃ*). We are not told why and when this happens. The intake of matter is understood to be an activity, *joga* (Viy. 854 a), and the *joga* of two beings in the first *samaya* of reincarnation (*padhama-samaôvavannaga*) is unequal in kind when the one has arrived without and the other with a change of direction. By starting earlier the one is ahead of the other (*abbhāhiya*). *āhāra* (acc. to Ṭhāṇ. 120 a one of the movements of the *poggala* happening without a force acting from without means) both the

1. Umāsvāti in T. 2, 31 does not know of any *catuḥ-samayika*, whereas Devanandin does.

2. By comparing § 187 it is equally striking that the Siddhas *sijjhanti* both with and without *antara* (only Pannav. 207 a).

intake of matter for the purpose of reincarnation (comp. Viy. 701 b) and the attraction of atoms on the whole, especially for eating. This in the first line follows from the Āhāra-paya Pannav. 28 (498 b). The theory distinguishes between the *āhāra* in *ābhoga-nivvattiya* and *aṇābhoga-n.* (498 b), i.e. between the *āhāra* which, or, rather, the satisfaction of a demand for being supplied with matter (*āhārattha*), rests on intention (*ābhoga*) (comp. also Pannav. 544 b), and the one that happens unintentionally. In the first case we find a.o. the omission of the meal in the fast of the *cauttha-bhatta* (§ 156). The attracted mass is called *avīci-davva* acc. to Viy. 644a when being complete, and *vīci-d.* when lacking one or more *paesa*; but we hear nothing more in detail about it. Moreover the *āhāra* is *lom āh.* (first mentioned in 506b) and *pakkhev'āh.*, and we are tempted to understand by it either continuous or dosed supplies. But the *loma* concerns undifferentiated appropriation, whereas the *pakkheva* concerns the taking of food through the mouth.[1] In addition to these two ways of taking in matter (*oy'āhāra*)[2] there is the quality of *maṇa-bhakkhi* pertaining to gods who attract matter by mere wishing.[3] Regarding the remaining contents of Pannav. 28 we may but mention that those beings owning a body of transformation take in inanimate matter only, while those having an earthly body take in both animate and semi-animate matter (*mīsa*) additionally (498 b). The beings take in such matter as is found within the range going to be occupied by their bodies, at least this may be supposed to be the meaning of *atta-māyāe* and *āya-sarīra-khetta* (Viy. 286a). Any more closely or more distantly neighbouring ranges are out of the question, and thus for special magic cases it is always being expressly stressed that it concerns *bāhirayā poggalā*, so Viy. 189a, 190a, 282b. The actual process of reincarnation, however, appears to be described, in the beginning of Pannav. 34 (534a—Samav. 145b), as follows: "(beings of hell and five-sensed

1. In this sense Ṭhāṇ. 263 b describes the *āhāra* for the 4 stages of beings partly in the way of comparison.

2. *oja utpatti-deśe āhāra-yogyaḥ pudgala-samūhaḥ*, Prajn. 510 a.

3. Comp. Charlotte KRAUSE Z I I 71, 272. Comp. Sūtr. 342 b ff.

beings) start on their way by taking in matter immediately after having reached the place (*aṇantar'āhāra*). Then they are busy with developing the body (*tao nivvattaṇā*), then they let the stages of development follow one another (? *tao pariyāiṇayā*), then they produce the details (*tao pariṇāmayā*), then they allow their faculties to act (*tao pariyāraṇayā*),[1] then, finally, they convert what has been acquired into individual materiality (? *tao pacchā viuvvaṇayā*)"[2]. As to gods the two last stages have changed places. The place where this process happens is, of course, the resp. place of origin (§ 63). From here the soul once again starts on its course. As (Viy. 927a) the monkey (*pavaga*) swings from one place to the next, so the soul wanders from one existence to another, and like the monkey it does so on its own determination (*ajjhavasāṇa-joga-nivvattieṇaṃ karaṇôvāeṇaṃ*). It enters into the new life as a whole (*savveṇa savvaṃ uvavajjai*), real (*santo*), independent (*sao*), by itself (*sayaṃ*), on its own responsibility, and through its own Karman (*ā'iḍḍhīe, āya-kammuṇā*), by force of good (*subha*), evil and mixed deeds (Viy. 84a, 454a, 796a, 927b).

§97. *The Colours of the Soul.* The Karman does not only effect the fate of the soul; but it equally supplies it with a conditional quality reflecting the moral level , and as such is called by the name of *les(s)ā=leśyā*. We are of opinion that this word has to be derived from *lesa*[3] which, on its part, has not been explained etymologically as yet. By means of the *lessā* the Karman imprints (s.b.) a character upon the soul by qualifying it with colour, taste, smell and feeling. Since these qualities are of a material nature, this possibly expresses a relation to particles (*lesā*), and we have reason to assume that an adjective *leśyā* was changed into a substantive. The corresponding

1. On account of this word the phrase was placed in the Pariyātaṇāpaya Pannav. 34.

2. See the AUTHORS's Religionsgesch. Lesebuch 7,, 21. Comp. the sequence *āhārenti pariṇāmanti sarīraṃ bandhanti* ("build") Viy. 762a, 773b,

3. In accordance with CHARPENTIER Festskrift Johansson p. 38 38 JACOBI derived the word from *kleśa* (SBE 45, 196). When putting (e.g. Prajn. 330a) *liśyate=śliṣyate* the commentators might refer to *laṇha* aside with *saṇha=ślakṣṇa*. But that is all there is to it.

feminine noun may well have been *chāyā* "light, brilliancy, colour", for this is the non-technical meaning of the word *lessā*.[1]

The *lessā* or the "type of the soul", as LEUMANN (Aup.) named it, is represented (Ṭhāṇ. 361b; Samav. 11b, 145b) by the six colours of black (*kaṇha*), dark (*nīla*), grey (*kāu*), yellow (*teu*), pink (*pamha*) and white (*sukka*) each of them being determined in the Lessā-paya (Pannav. 17 (360b) by a number of comparisons which, however, are said not to reach up to "reality". The same is done with taste (*āsāya*, 364 a), and moreover, the first three are considered as evil smelling and unpleasant, the last three as good smelling and pleasant (266b; Ṭhāṇ. 175a). Gradations in each of the qualities—of which taste, smell and feeling range far behind colour—are calculated by subdividing them by three into minimum, medium and maximum up to 3^5, and atoms (∞), their categories (*vaggaṇā*,∞) and space volume (¿ units) are determined (367b). Thus it follows that we are fully concerned with a material product of the Karman, that is, so T, 2, 6 says, with a product of its realization (*udaya*). Likewise there is no doubt that we have the insertion of the primitive idea[1] of the moral qualification of the soul by colour being adapted to Jain dogmatics. By ascribing the second effect to the Karman the juncture becomes clearly visible. Moreover, this gives proof of the secondary character of the *leśyā*- theory that it might stay out of the system without leaving a gap in its composition.

§98. Together with the infinite variety of actions it is also its resplendence that changes continually,[3] just as the soul is accompanied into the beginning of its new existence by those *lessā* only that it had in its hour of death (Viy. 188 a). But it

1. The usage of *lesa* in the sense of *maṇa* follows a different course; we find (Āyār. I) *abahi-lese* aside with *a.-maṇa* in the meaning "of not allowing one's thoughts to be distracted" and with the object of female distraction (Ṭhāṇ. 331 b) *nigganthīe bahil-lesa*.

2. The Ājīvikas equally have it, comp. Sumangalavilāsinī on Dīgha-Nikāya II 20. There we have *abhijāti* for *lessā* in connexion with a colour. The *sukkâbhijāya* is also found in Viy. 656b where Vy., however. explains it as *parama-śukla*°.

3. And also with its annihilation. The beings, so Viy. 39b teaches, have a lighter *lessā* when being older, a darker when being younger (*puvvôva-vannaga* and *paccho' tav.*). Only with gods it is the other way round.

is in the nature of the grades and classes of the beings that their behaviour is limited, and correspondingly their *lessā* moves within certain ranges (Pannav. 343 b; Ṭhāṇ. 115a, 237b), so that beings of hell, fire, wind and lower animals will not reach beyond the third (grey) *lessā* and all remaining one-sensed beings not beyond the fourth (yellow). It may be noted that even female gods will not reach farther, whereas their male partners have all six and those of the highest standing but the last three. Also humans and five-sensed animals are capable of all *lessā*.[1] The way how a *lessā* passes over into another one (*pariṇamai*) is explained by comparisons in Pannav. 358 b.

The qualities determining a *lessā* are represented in Utt. 34 along with the whole of their theory. We need not quote from Pannav.17 in which way the five kinds of cognition divide among the bearers of the six *lessā* (Pannav. 357 a), but we have to point out that though the Kevalin during his stay on earth (*sajogī kevalī*) still has the white *lessā*,[2] the Siddha has no longer any of it. That is why in the canonical expositions, e.g. Viy. 40b, the *salessā* are particularly mentioned wherever circumstances ask for it. The *ohi*-cognition so characteristic of the beings of hell extends the farther the brighter the *lessā* is, just as from the top of a mountain we see farther than from any point in a plain (Pannav. 355a). Things are different with the Karman: as said by Viy. 300b, a being may have a darker *lessā* with a lesser Karman and a brighter one with a stronger, i.e. when the owner of the darker *lessā* has annihilated his Karman stronger in itself down to a remainder smaller than the whole Karman of the owner of a brighter *lessā*. So in Vy. the explanation of the text words *ṭhiiṃ paḍucca*.

§99. *The Actions.* In the passages above the word *kamma* signified the "action"' in a metaphysical respect. We can

1. Thus Ṭhāṇ. 175 a distinguished the act of dying as a *ṭhiya-*, *saṃkiliṭṭha-* and *pajjavajāya-lesa*, according as in the existence to come the *lessā* remains the same, grows dim or brightens (v. KAMPTZ, Sterbefasten p. 15.)

2. That is why the favourable *lessā* becomes still purer (*pasatthāo lesāo visujjhamāṇio*) when Mallī attains the highest grade of cognition (Nāyādh. 152 b).

(Viy. 768a) distinguish the beings as *mahā-* and *appa-kammatarāga* according to the more or less of Karman (and, equally, of influence —*āsava*— and sensation —*veyaṇā*). Thus (Viy. 228b) a freshly lit and a dying fiery body are called *agaṇi-kāya* according to their greater and smaller activities. So, where Viy. 767b compares action, sensation and annihilation on the different stages, we should, correspondingly, expect to find the word *kamma*, but what we find is *kiriyā*. This word is preferred when thinking of concrete actions even when abstract fundamentals are concerned. Such is the case with the *saṃparāiyā* and *iriyāvahiyā kiriyā* (Viy. 106a and elsewhere), and, moreover, with the statement (Viy. 79b) that an offence against the main commandments—by which offence however, we but have to understand the specialization of a general law—goes back to contact and to one's own doing (*pāṇāivāeṇaṃ kiriyā... puṭṭhā kajjai, kaḍā k,*) and follows a course (*āṇupuvviṃ k.*). It is also common opinion that an action even while being performed equals one completed.[1] This is stated immediately at the beginning by Viy. giving a selection of the most different kinds of activities (13b); we repeatedly come across it in the course of the book (86a, 582b, 706b), and it is even maintained against contradicting teachers (102b f., 379a).

Just as these questions occupied the minds (to which degree, it is shown by the various antitheses Ṭhāṇ. 39b ff.), so the classification of the actions was a problem. Sūy. II 2 gives and supports by examples 13 cases of activities (comp. also Sthān. 316b; Samav. 25a): 1 to 5 are called *daṇḍa-samāyāṇa* thus being characterised as acts of violence, while 6 to 13 stand for activities of an otherwise blamable kind, though, to be true, the list ends up by kind to be observed by the monk (*saṃparāiya*). They all are based on offences against the fundamental commandments as far as they are involved, i.e. the first, second and third underlie the cases 1 to 7, and the four passions of anger (10), pride (9), fraud (11), and greed (12), though it has to be observed that anger appears in the shape of an offence against

1. Comp. the AUTHOR's Worte Mahāvīras p. 24 f. In the German translation p. 24 read "nach Konsonant und Vokal" instead of "nach Klang und Schrift."

friends (*mitta-dosa*). 8 is the (evil) state of mind (*ajjhattha*). Ṭhāṇ. 316a leads the discussion over into the field of theory and sets up actions in groups of five the first three of which appear here only and, partly, also in Ṭhāṇ. 39b f. The *first* of these groups—provided the interpretations prove true—concern an activity for the purpose of seeing (*diṭṭhiyā kiriyā*), touching (*puṭṭhiyā k.*), on the ground of certain outlooks (*paḍucciyā k.*), of the conform judgment of persons closely concerned (*sāmantô-vaṇivāiyā k.*) and performed by one's own hands (*sāhatthiyā k.*). The *second* group calls the *kiriyā* a *nesatthiyā*, *āṇavaṇiyā*, *veyaraṇī*, *aṇābhoga-vattiyā* and *aṇavakankha-v.*, by which an action may be understood resting on an order,[1] on communication, on permission, and brought about without thinking and willing participating in it. The *third* group refers to an action strictly confined to humans which may go back (*-vattiyā-k.*)- to affection (*pejja*), antipathy (*dosa*), plan (*paoga*), going for alms (*samudāṇa*) or wandering (*iriyā*). Nearly everywhere the commentary (Sthāṇ. 42a ff., 317a) is uncertain, and, partly, no doubt goes wrong. The sub-division can be omitted here.

§100. Two further groups must have come to gain a more distinct canonical significance since they are dealt with exclusively on the ground of the Viy. in the Kiriyā-paya 22 of the Pannavaṇā. They also appear in Ṭhāṇ. 316a, 284a and Samav. 10a. Viy. 228a teaches the following. A vendor who follows up a stolen object in any case commits an *ārambhiyā k.*, possibly even a *pariggahiyā k.*, a *māyā-vattiyā k.*, an *apaccakkhāṇa-k.*, or a *micchādaṃsaṇa-k.* The text carries on the casuistry by saying that, according to the situation, now all five and then again but the first four actions are either with the buyer or the seller. The interrelation is represented by Pannav. 446a. The action is either committed for a set purpose, for intentional appropriation, or emotionally, or it rests on non-renunciation[2] or on heterodoxy. In humans they correspond in the following

1. *nesatthiya* cannot belong to *sṛj*, but rather to *śās*. Umāsvāti, however on T. 6, 6 gives *nisarga* similar to Sthāna.

2. About this comp. also Viy. 101 a.

way either necessarily (*niyamā*), +) or possibly (*siya*; *bhaijjai*, ±):

	tassa ār.	*p.*	*m.-v.*	*ap.*	*mi. kajjai.*
jassa ār. kajjai		±	+	±	±
„ *p.* „	+		+	±	±
„ *m.-v.* „	±	±		±	±
„ *ap.* „	+	+	+		+
„ *mi.* „	+	+	+	+	

Hence, e.g. every purposeful action is emotional, but not every emotional one is purposeful.[1] In such statements we are able to discern an approach to psychology for which in the first mentioned groups we are looking in vain.

The group of the *kāiyā*, *ahigaraṇiyā*, *paosiyā*,[2] *pariyāvaṇiyā* and *pāṇâivāiyā kiriyā* is of a still greater importance which follows from the conception in Pannav. 436 ff. It is proved in Viy. by quite a number of examples (91b; 697a; 717a; 720b f., also 377b; 491b; 703b). We here but mention 91b, where a man hunting game makes himself guilty of the first to the third, the first to the fourth, or of all five of those actions, according as his intention is directed merely to the means of killing (*uddavaṇayāe*)[3] or to catching the animal or even killing it. Or take Viy. 229b, where an archer from the preparation of the bow and the arrows up to his shooting them into the air commits all five actions in case he hits a being by doing so.

And what applies to the archer, applies as well to the bow, the arrow, the sinew, the arrow-feathers, etc.[4] If, however, beings are injured by the arrow falling down on them from the air, then the above mentioned objects have committed but the first four actions, whereas those beings catching up the falling arrow (? *uvaggahe ciṭṭhanti*) have committed all five. As is shown by Viy 181a; Ṭhāṇ. 39b; Pannav. 435a and also by the sub-division (which may be left aside), it concerns physical, instrumental, hostile, tormenting and murderous action. Here,

1. This, however, contradicts the passage of Viy. where the *māyāvattiyā k.* was not obligatory beside the *ārambhiyā*.

2. Frequently written *pausiyā*.

3. This is the substantive for *miyassa vahae kūḍa-pāsaṃ uddāi* at the same place.

4. Obviously the weapon is supposed to be animate, comp. § 101.

too, acc. to Pannav. 443b a table of the mutual relativity might be drawn up. But we dwell on it as little as we do on the bridge which (439a) is thrown for binding the *kamma-pagaḍi,* and on other statements. The five groups of 5 each as presented above, reappear as the 25 *kriyā* in Umāsvāti's Bhāṣya on T. 6, 6, though partly in a different composition which may, perhaps, be ascribed a greater logical coherence than presented by the passages of the Canon.

§101. The technique of monachism is touched by the special action called *anta-kiriyā.* This name is connected with the frequently (e.g. Sūy. II 2, 83; Uvav. § 56 (p. 62) recurring solemn phrase speaking of "to reach the last goal, to wake up, to become free, to fade away and to put an end to all pain", i.e. *savva-dukkhāṇam antaṃ karittae.* Thus *anta-kiriyā* is equal to *mokṣa,* salvation.[1] It, too, is represented systematically in Pannav, 20 (369a ff.), and by learning (396b) for which kind of beings it is either *aṇantar'āgaya* or *paraṃpar'āgaya,* i.e. taking place either in the immediately subsequent existence or in a later life, we are confirmed (§ 93) that in his pre-existence a man may belong to any stage of being. Man and man alone is given the possibility to "put and end" and to reach the highest goal. But from this we have to distinguish the other possibility of coming within the range of hearing the sacred teaching (*kevali-pannattaṃ dhammaṃ labhejjā savaṇayāe*), of taking delight in it, and of acting according to it in all fundamental things. All five-sensed animals are equally given this opportunity (Pannav. 398b), and they can advance to the *ohi* though, to be true, they are not able to enter into monachism. This reminds us of the frog, as an example among others, who dies by uttering the formula of veneration *namo tthu ṇaṃ* (Nāya 13).[2] This, of course, implies that the corresponding Karman has been formerly bound, and it expressly

1. In persons of the sacred legend Ṭhāṇ. 180a distinguishes four kinds of the *a.-k.* according to the greater or smaller amount of Karman they possess and to their longer or shorter monastic lives.

2. An example from the later legend is the tigress in the story of Sukosala (v. KAMPTZ, Sterbefasten p. 37).

concerns (Pannav. 402a) the hero- and Tīrthakara-ship (§ 13). A Titthagara in his immediate pre-existence may have dwelt in hell (though in its upper regions only)—his Karman has now turned him into a superman. Pannav. 403 b gives corresponding examples with regard to world emperors, heroes and high dignitaries— including the Queen Consort (*itthī-rayaṇa-*), to state-animals (*āsa-r.*, *hatthi-r.*) and, most remarkably, also to seven certain crown jewels (comp. § 13) which count for being one-sensed, as we know from Jambudd. 260b; Ṭhāṇ. 398 a.

Anticipating the style of the successive comments the Antakiriyā-paya of the Pannav. begins by saying (369a): *atth'egaie (jīve anta-kiriyaṃ) karejjā, atth. (j. a.-k.) no karejjā.*[1] This means that not all souls are able to find salvation. It was Viy. 285b that had expressed it: a being of the one stage or the other may be capable of salvation, but this does not apply to every being of this or that stage. While the canonical word is either (*a*)*bhava-siddhiya* or *-siddhīya* (Samav. 2b, 8b, etc. 45b, 47b), Umāsvāti speaks of (*a*)*bhavya*. Acc. to him (T. 2,6) this quality pertains to the qualities inherent in the soul (*pāriṇā-mika*) (§ 60). What is said by Viy. 557a is but seemingly contradictory to it. While the former says that the capability of salvation is *sabhāvao*, not *pariṇāmao*, the latter makes us understand that it is not an acquired, but a natural quality, All souls that have it (so it is continued to be said) will come to enjoy salvation, but never will the world be void of souls capable of salvation. From this contention of Mahāvīra's (which Jayantī hears with amazement[2], and which he substantiates by a comparison with the atoms) we understand that the *bhava-siddhiya* replenish themselves on and again. In order to grasp its proper meaning we obviously—though the text does not say so—have to anticipate the theory of the *nigoya* (§ 104). These plant souls distributed throughout the world in ∞ number constitute the inexhaustible stock of souls, as far as they are subtle (*suhuma*) and undeveloped (*apajjatta*). As soon as in

1. Viy. 49a refers to it.

2. "*se keṇaṃ kh'āi ṇaṃ* (print: *khāieṇaṃ*) *aṭṭheṇaṃ bhante, evaṃ vuccai*..."

such souls development starts causing to participate in the world course proper, there appears the possibility of salvation: if once *pajjatta*, then they are partly *bhava-siddhiya*, partly not. By what impulse the development and the capability of salvation are being brought about, is not said in the texts of the Canon.

This class of the *nigoya* form the polar contrast to the Siddhas. Of both there exist innumerably many, but while the *nigoya* fill up the entire space of the world, the Siddhas are confined to its highest region (§ 187). The former will not live longer than for 1 *muhutta*, the latter for ever. The former represented the lowest possible stage of development of a being, the latter the highest that can be thought of. In both of them we see the foot and the head of the ladder formed by the occupants of the world. The undeveloped, subtle *nigoya* are not yet subjected to the Karman law, whereas the Siddhas have left it behind.

V

COSMOGRAPHY

§102. The "cosmic system"—by which name we intend to comprise both the general plan of the cosmos and the organization as well as the activities of its occupants—is, in contrast to renunciation and world conquest (see Chapters VI and VII), a given fact just as is the "world course" (see Chapter IV). The great amount of details ask for an individual treatment of the subject which, however, as to the cosmographic plan will be restricted to the more important items (of which there will be still enough after all), since, on the one hand, we have more or less comprehensive descriptions at our disposal already,[1] and since, on the other, vagaries not based on ethical grounds and hence being empty are not attractive to dwell upon. In order not to overcharge our text we, therefore, frequently disregarded to deliver detailed proofs, all the more since the passages in question can easily be traced from chapter III. The main sources are Pannav. 1. 2; Jīvābh. III with the Dīvas.; Jambudd. and the cosmographic sections of Ṭhāṇa and Samavāya.

§103. There is (Ṭhāṇ. 1 b; Samav. 1 b) but one world (*loga*) and beside it but o n e non-world (*aloga*). The latter surrounds the world on all sides like a hollow sphere (Viy. 522a) and is out of reach, since beyond the boundaries of the world the medium of motion is absent (Viy. 717 b). The extension of both is illustrated (Viy. 525 b) by describing the speed of divine personalities and the distance they are able

1. The cosmographic plan has been described in all general representations, of the system , first of all in those by Mrs. STEVENSON, v. GLASENAPP, GUÉRINOT (§ 4.6). KIRFEL in his Kosmographie der Inder (Bonn 1920), pp. 208-339—reviewed by the AUTHOR ZDMG 75, 254-275—and in the Bilderatlas zur Religionsgeschichte (Lpf. 1928), No. 12a (ill.) deeply goes into details. Comp. also PULLÉ in La cartografia antica dell' India. P. 1 (SIFII 4, 1900); BARNETT, Antag. pp. 137-141. and, finally BASTIAN, Ideale Welten, vol. 3 (Bln. 1892), A. C. Sen IHQ, 8, 43-48,

to cover by it; in figures the world measures ¿ times 10^{14} *joyaṇa*[1] in all directions (Viy. 579 a). Seen in its vertical cross-section it narrows from below to the centre and then widens again in nearly the same degree to above (Viy. 248a; 616 b). Both the summit and the base are built up in a convex shape. To make it plain we may compare it with an 8 of equal halves rotated round its axis. Canonically, however, the three sections (Ṭhāṇ. 126a)—we call them by the names of the lower, the centre and the upper world[2]—are compared with a bed to rest on (*paliyanka*), a so-called thunder-bolt (*vara-vaira*), and an upright standing drum (*uddha-muinga*)—this following the teaching of Pāsa (Viy. 248 a); acc. to Viy. 522a the lower and centre section are even illustrated by a couch (*tappa*[3]) and a cymbal (*jhallarī*), resp. For the whole Viy. 522 a; 616 b apply the comparison with a *supaiṭ-ṭhaga*, i.e. a "broad-bottomed" vessel. By these concept-tions it is demonstrated as good as certain that the horizontal cross-section was thought to be circular. The calculations, however, drawn from the Lokaprakāśa of the Śvet. (composed 1708 A.D.) by KIRFEL[4] prove that its author imagined the world as three pyramids one upon the other each having a square base and rising in steps on all sides, the centre one of which standing on its top surface, whereas the description given by the Dig.[5] shows three roof-like bodies of the same unchanging length but of a steadily de-, resp. increasing width. In the Canon we read of these details as little as we do of the unit of measure of *rajju*, "rope", by means of which the proportions of the parts is being expressed.[6] With the height of the whole

1. 1 *koḍākoḍī* (Jīv.: *koḍikoḍī*) $= 10^{14}$.

2. Acc. to Ṭhāṇ. 171 b the upper world causes the least, the lower world the greatest difficulty for understanding (*abhigama*). (The passage is a fragment.).

3. *talpa*, not *tapra* (*uḍupaka* Vy.).

4. Kosmographie, p. 210 f.

5. Comp. Brahmaveda on Davvasaṃgaha, 20 (SBJ 1, 47 ff.) Vīrasena in Ṣaṭkhaṇḍāgama Vol. 4, p. 11 f. and Introd. p. II gives *tala-rukkha-saṃṭhāṇa* as the shape of the world.

6. The *rajju* which is nothing but a proportional number has also been made to be some kind of an absolute quantity. (Comp. COLEBROOKE, Misc. Essays III. 1983.).

world measuring 14 *r.* the upper and the lower world each come to 7 *r.* (the centre world is not considered). The width of its base decreases from 7 *r.* down to 1 *r.* in the centre world, in order to increase again to 5 *r.* (§ 129) and then to decrease once more down to 1 *r.* A third non-canonical conception refers to a world of human appearance[1] (as *loka-puruṣa*). This easily makes itself clear by the mere outline of the whole which, moreover, certainly accounts for the name of the Gevejjaga or "neck" regions (§ 129) and the expression of *loga-matthaga* (Dasav. 4, 25).[2]

§104. Along with the shape and the organization of the world and its different sections we shall equally consider the beings they contain, and we feel entitled to do so by the fact that the tabular treatment they receive in the dogmatic texts ascends in stages through all three worlds; the inhabitants of hell are followed by those appertaining to the classes of gods which belong to the uppermost stage of the lower world and the upper world, they again are followed by the prestages of the animals and their lower classes, by the higher animals and men, and, finally, by the gods of the upper world and the Siddhas on a still higher stage. Outside dogmatic teaching the entity of all beings is called by the words of *pāṇa bhūya jīva satta*, certainly without making any discriminations by doing so, as the commentators want it.[3] According to the number of their senses all animals (*tirikkha-joṇiya*) down to their most simple forms are called one- to five-sensed (§ 118). As is the case with all beings, they are either fully developed (*pajjatta*) or not (*ap.*), to which we ask to comp. § 63. The one-sensed beings (*eg'indiya*)—so called since they have nothing but feeling—are the animate smallest particles of earth, water, fire, wind, and plants. As occupants of these particles or accumulations of matter (*kāya*), their souls and equally the beings them-

1. But by no means of an expressly female app. as GRÜNWEDEL, Alt-Kutscha I, 47 gives it. The interpretation of the corresponding figure 20 (see also KIRFEL, Bilderatlas) is certainly very doubtful.

2. The AUTHOR ZDMG 75, 260 f.

3. In a frequently (e.g. Jīv. 305 b; Prajn. 131b; Ācār. (old ed.) 80, 15) quoted verse; but comp. Ācār. 162a 12.

selves are called *puḍhavi-* etc. *-kāiya.* Their number in any of their kind is ¿, as is the case with all beings in the Saṃsāra, with the only exception of the plant souls whose number is ∞ (Pannav. 179 a). The one-sensed beings occur both in a form so fine that no sense is able to conceive it (*suhuma*) and in a concrete (*bāyara*) shape. In their fine form we find them, indifferentiated within their kinds, all over the world (*savva-loya-pariyāvannaga*, Pannav. 71. b).

Among the plant souls or *vaṇassai*[1]*-kāiya* we also find the *nigoya* or *nioya-jīva.* Jambūdv. 171 a; Vy. 309 a explain *nigoda* by *kuṭumba*, which makes us think of *nyoka(s)*. As mentioned above, the *nigoya* (Viy. 889 b—Jīv. 423b; Viy. 764 b; Pannav. 381 a) are both fine and concrete. Originally, however, the name is certain to have belonged to the former (*suhuma*) only. This is explained not so much by the word of *nigoya* (without an adjective) standing side by side with *bāyara-n.* (Pannav. 381 b) than by an objective exceptional position. The above mentioned ∞ number of plant souls goes to the debt of the fine ones among them; they alone may stay for an infinitely long time in the same form of existence, whereas the remaining fine elemental beings (to say nothing of the higher ones) can leave it, at the latest, after an indeterminably long (¿), i.e. after all a measurable time (Pannav. 377a, 381b). This is the so-called *kāya-ṭṭhii*, the uninterrupted sequence of existences having the same form (§ 93), i.e. existences each of which ends within one *muhutta* in a fine form in the elemental beings and plants regardless of either their complete or incomplete development (Pannav. 171b). Hence the fine undeveloped *nigoya*, though it pertains to the Saṃsāra, yet does not take part in the up and down within it, until it starts to develop. By this way it is the intellectual and actual counterpart of the Siddha (§ 101). The Canon does not supply us with any detailed information about a certain way as to how the *nigoya* fill up the entire world. It is most probably a post-canonical conception acc. to which these *nigoya*

1. Also *vaṇapphai.*

form in ¿ numbers into ¿ minute balls (*gola*) each having ∞ souls—which for their part permeate all and everything.[1] Pannav. 39a speaks of an *aya-gola* only by way of comparison.

§105. The concrete (*bāyara*) elemental beings do not occur in the same way everywhere in the world, but we find them in all of its three sections. They represent the palpable occurrence of the elements, and, to mention but some of them, they appear in the forms of earth, minerals, metals; of water, clouds, snow; of flame, coal, lightning; of breath, wind, storm. Their concrete shapes are, resp., those of the lens, the drop (*thibuga*), the quiver, and the flag (Ṭhāṇ. 234b; Jīv. 11a, 24b, 27a; 29a; Pannav. 410b). The animate elements of earth, water, and wind[2] appear in a concrete shape (Pannav. 71b ff.) except in the centre world at all obvious places also within the sphere of the subterranean and heavenly dwellings and, naturally, also in the structure of the hulls enveloping the lower world (§ 107). In the watery hulls there are also concrete vegetable bodies with their souls; acc. to Viy. 278 b clouds come into existence also in the lower world and in the upper world as a work of gods (*deva, asura, nāga*). Fire only is confined to the centre world as far as it is inhabited by men. It comes into being at a fire-place (*ingālakariyā*), but it comes to glow (*ujjalai*) only when joined by the wind (*vāuyāya*) (Viy. 696 b). The lower (two- to four- sensed) and the higher animals (*pancendiya tirikkha-joṇiya*) occur in the lower and centre world at places where, according to their kind, they belong (*tad-ekka-desa-bhāe*). We shall consider them when dealing with the centre world (§ 113).

§106. The concrete plants, acc. to Pannav. 30a ff. (in prose and nearly 100 Gāhās), fall into individual plants (*patteya-sarīra*) and group plants (*sāhāraṇa*-s. Viy. 762a), the latter a.o. lichens and mosses, without any subdivisions, but very rich in

1. Comp. the Nigoyachattīsi incorporated by Abhayadeva in his Vy. vṛtti (528a ff.). Nig. 12 appears in the Kālaka legend, comp. AUTHOR OLZ 1933, col. 451.

2. Wind caused by walking, blowing, pressing, etc. is inanimate (*acitta*). Hence as to this statement Ṭhāṇ. 334b ought to have *vāu-kāya* instead of *vāu-kāiya*.

variety. The more highly developed individual plants are divided twelve-fold acc. to their habit into trees, bushes, shrubs, creepers, grasses, etc. Trees are subdivided into two groups, the mono-kernels (*eg'aṭṭhiya*) and the multi-kernels (*bahu-bīyaya*). On grasses (*taṇa*) it has been observed that they bear seeds at the top, at the roots, at the stalk, and at other places (Dasav. 4, introd., Ṭhāṇ. 186b, 322b, 354b). The five classes of *rukkha, ajjhāroha, taṇa, osahi,* and *hariya* (Sūy. II, 3) joined by a sixth bearing no name of its own, look older than the duodecimal classification. Both classifications are now crossed by one classifying according to the number of souls within a plant. With its quality to have more than one soul the plant stands alone in the realm of living beings[1]. The seats of these souls are the roots, the bulb (*kanda*), the stem, the bark, the branches (*sālā*), the twigs (*pavāla*), the leaves, blossoms, fruits and seeds (*mūlā mūla-jīva-phuḍā* etc. Viy. 300a). Acc to Sūy. this refers to the five classes mentioned above, acc. to Pannav. to the trees, acc. to Ṭhāṇ 520b to the *taṇa*. The taking in of matter and its transubstantiation starts (Viy. 300a) with the souls of the roots which are near to the souls of the earth (*paḍi-baddha*) from whom they take what substance they need. From there it is taken by these of the bulb, from here by those of the stem, a. s. o. As to this theory concerning the growth of plants (the text of which suggests the wrong conclusion that the resp. former were decaying in favour of the resp. succeeding ones) it may be pointed out that this growth decreases in proportion to the sequence of the starting of the rainy season— the main rainy season[2]— autumn– winter— spring—, and summer. The opposing vital force which manifests itself in the general bloom is explained acc. to § 94-.[3] Now, the number of the souls in trees is either x, ¿ or ∞ (Viy. 364a; Ṭhāṇ. 122b), the quantity of ¿ pertaining to the roots, etc., whereas the first pertains to the blossoms (Pannav. 31a) and one to each leaf. ∞ souls

1. Discussed by KOHL, Ztschr. f. Ethn. f8 (1953), p. 91-95.

2. *pāusa-vāsā-ruttesu*. This bipartition reoccurs in the monastic lif., see § 146.

3. *gimhāsu ṇaṃ bahave usiṇa-. j. j. ya p. ya vaṇ.assaikāiyattāe vakkamanti* etc.

are attributed (acc. to Viy. 300 a) to a number of certain specified plants. The *uppala* and other plants are discussed by Viy. 508 b ff., while Viy. 800 a deals with useful plants for the most part. Pannav. gives many details especially of the *sāhāraṇā-sarīra*.

§107. *The Lower World* (*ahe-loga*). In the lower world there are seven regions (*puḍhavī*, Umāsvāti gives *bhūmi*). Their names are Rayaṇappabhā (*imā R.*, see § 113 footnote), Sakkarappabhā, Vāluyappabhā, Pankappabhā, Dhūmappabhā, Tam(appabh)ā, and Tamatamā or, commonly, Ahesattamā (Mahātamaḥprabhā).[1] This is their sequence from above to below. In between them there are spaces of unmeasured extension,[2] and a space of that kind separates also the lowest region from the non-world (Viy. 651 b). For each region is enveloped by hulls which, in succession, consist of viscous water, viscous wind[3] and light wind. The last and most remote is followed by an intermediate space (*uvās'antara*), Ṭhāṇ. 177a,388b; comp. Viy. 152a and also Ṭhāṇ. 152b). Below each region these hulls are very wide: the water hull amounting to 20,000, the remaining to ¿ joy.; to their sides, where they are ring-shaped (*valaya*), they are quite thin: measuring 6, 4½ and 1½ *joy.* in the Rayaṇappabhā, increasing evenly up to 8.6 *joy.* in the remaining regions and measuring 2 joy. in the Ahesattamā. Beyond the light wind hull, at the sides, the world ends (*loy'anta*); thus the intermediate part of space lies below the regions only. The hulls of the uppermost region include the centre world and, partly, also the upper world (§ 129).

§108. The regions are determined in respect of their depth only, but not as to their width. Of the latter Viy. 604 b (=Jīv. 306a) merely says that it increases downwards. The

1. Other names for all seven regions are given by Ṭhāṇ. 388b, acc. to which the Bhāṣya ref. to T. 3, 1 in the edition (p. 90) must be partly rectified. Ṭhāṇ. 440 also counts Īsīpabbhārā (§ 135) as *pudhavī*.

2. Any concussion of these hulls (*guvie samāṇe*) is conveyed by the water hull to the earth and causes a general earthquake (Ṭhāṇ 161b).

3. By entering a minute distance from above into the space below the Rāy. (and naturally horizontally in the centre) we come to the centre of the world (Viy. 606a) and, equally, to the centre of its three sections—§ 103—, that of the centre world called Ruyaga (§ 58).

depth decreases from 180,000 *joy.* in the Rayaṇappabhā down to 108,000 in the Ahesattamā which is the number of the places of hell it contains (*niray'āvāsa*), 8.4 mill. in all, and in the 1st to the 5th region from 3 mill. down to 300,000. Tamā has 99,995, Ahesattamā but 5, though especially extensive, places. While (Pannav. 79b) the layers of the 1st to the 6th region lie between every two unoccupied layers of 1,000 *joy.*—the upper one in the Rayaṇappabhā equals the thickness of Jambuddīva (§ 113)—, these layers in the 7th region amount the 52,500 *joy.*, so that the occupied is but 3,000 *joy.* in depth here. In the Rayaṇappabhā we have three special layers: Khara-kaṇḍa, Pankabahula-k. and Āubahula-k. of 16, 000, 84, 000 and 80,000 *joy.* These names indicate the transition to the water hull which follows accordingly. The former on its part has 16 layers of 1,000 *joy.* each, the uppermost being called Rayaṇa-k. (Ṭhāṇ. 525a; Samav. 89b f., 92b, 104b).

Another arrangement in layers—though not represented in the Canon itself- goes by the way of *patthaḍa.*[1] In the 1st to the 7th region there are 13, 11, 9, 7, 5, 3 and 1 of such layers tiered one beneath the other, i.e. 49 in all. From the central hell of Sīmantaga in the uppermost layer of the Rayaṇappabhā measuring 4,5 mill. *joy.* in diameter[2] a succession of 49 hells leads off in every main direction, and a succession of 48 hells in every intermediate direction. In the second layer the numbers are 48 and 47, etc., up to 49, which is identical with the 7th region where the medium one is surrounded by 4 only. More extensive hells at certain places in these successions are called something like "eccentric" (*avakkanta-mahāṇiraya*) (Ṭhāṇ. 365b). So far as these hells appear in successions they are either circular or quadrangular, while in other cases they may be of any shape possible. In the lowest region four triangular hells, called Kāla, Mahākāla, Roruya,

1. Sthān. 366 b *patthaḍa* is *prastṛta*, though it is rendered as *prastaṭa* exclusively. Abhayadeva here refers to the *Vimānanarakendrak'ākhya grantha*, presumably the Vimāṇa-and Naraya-Pavibhatti, comp. AGRM, 24, 1924.

2. Because it is as large as Samayakhetta (§ 122), the Uḍuvimāna in Sohamma (§ 129) and Īsipabhārā (§ 135) (Ṭhāṇ. 125a, 250b).

and Mahāroruya, with their vertex pointing outward form a frame round the 5th circular one, called Appaiṭṭhāṇa.[1] The latter measures 100,000 *joy.* in diameter.[2] The different hells in the Rayaṇappabhā are 3,000 *joy.* in depth, and they are something like egg-shaped. Within them it is dark.[3] except for a glow of fire,[4] slippery with fat, pus, blood and filth, evil smelling as if of decay, and a touch causes pain. In the descriptions given by the Sūy. and Utt. (except the reference of Utt. 19, 48) the hells are considered hot only; in the Jīv. their three uppermost regions are hot, whereas the two lowest are cold; in the 4th and 5th we have both in the extreme; heat prevails in the former, cold in the latter.

§109. The earlier conception—already mentioned above—still represents the beings occupying the hells as humans who, in these hells, partly at certain designated places, rivers and the Veyāliya mountain, suffer the most exquisite punishments by cruel warders (Sūy. 1 5; Utt. 19, 47 ff.). Acc. to later conceptions the hells are populated by beings (*neraiya*)[5] totally different from humans. They look black and ghastly, they resemble plucked birds; they are sexless, emanate a smell of decay and cause pain when being touched. They greatly vary in size, the maximum being in each region twice that of the preceding and reaching up to 1,000 *dhaṇu*. They suffer from hunger and thirst, heat and cold, and even though they themselves cause terror, they live in constant indescribable fear of mutual persecution in the most different shapes into

1. Less accurate are the earlier statements made by Sūy. II 2, 66 f. = Dasā 6, 15 f.—Pannav. 79b; Jīv. 102b; *te ṇaṃ naragā anto vaṭṭā, bahiṃ cauraṃsā, ahe khurappa-saṃṭhāṇa-saṃṭhiyā.* They must not be referred (as JACOBI does in Sūy.) to the inside and outside of the various hells. Comp. § 111.

2. This it shares with the Jambuddīva (§ 113), the Pālaga-jāṇa-vimāṇa in Sohamma and Savvaṭṭhasiddha (§ 129) (Ṭhāṇ. 250 b) Comp. the *nālī* § 95.

3. For its motivation see Ṭhāṇ. 263 a.

4. *nicc'andhayāra-tamasā. . . kāū* (or *kāuy*'; Sūy. wrong *kaṇhā*) *agaṇi-vaṇṇ'ābhā.*

5. Acc. to Viy. 230b the world of hell is covered with hell-beings down to a depth of 400 to 500 *joy.* (*samāiṇṇa*).

which they change.[1] All these torments increase in proportion to the increasing depth of the region to which they are doomed according to the measure of their wrong-doing (Viy. 596a, 604b, 606b). But also the animate elemental and plant-particles to be found in the different hells or either building them up, have much to suffer after they have been transferred there by their Karman (Jīv. 127b; Viy. 606a).

§110. However, the lower world is not only a place occupied by hell-beings, but its uppermost region, known as Rayaṇappabhā, is also the seat of gods, the Bhavaṇavāsī and the Vāṇamantara, though we shall see that both kinds are not confined to the lower world, but are at home to a great extent in the centre world, too. Of the Bhavaṇavāsī (or -vai; Pannav. 84b) there are 10 different kinds: the Asura-, Nāga-, Suvaṇṇa-, Vijju-, Aggi-, Dīva-, Udahi-, Disā-, Vāu- and Thaṇiya-[2] kumāra. By the denomination they have in common they are characterized as youthful appearances with all exterior virtues, and in dogmatic passages they are described mainly as male, though elesewhere some of them are female[3] according to their root-word. The size of these gods is 7 *rayaṇa*, and they differ in colour; the Asurak. are black, the Nāga- and Udahik. whitish (*paṇḍura*), the Suvaṇṇa-, Disā- and Thaṇiyak. golden, the Aggi-, Dīva and Vijjuk. orange, and the Vāuk. dark (*piyangu-vaṇṇa*).[4] These colours contain indications as to their activities and their seats, and so do, in parts, also their emblems (Uvav. 34= Pannav. 85a)[5] and, above all, the offices assigned to them consequent on the *logapāla* (§) 132). The Asurak. are mere gods of the lower world. But just as they may go down

1. Viy. 314 a=Ṭhāṇ. 505a quotes 10 general painful sensations of the hell-beings.

2. JACOBI, Utt. 6, 225 wrong Ghaṇika. The sequence above rendered by Viy. and Pannav. is the normal. In Dev. it is: 1. 2. 3. 6. 7. 8. 9. 10. 4. 5. For another different sequence see Umāsvāti on T. 4, 11.

3. *kumāra* and *-rī* only Viy. 3, 7; 4, 1-4. Exclusively *disākumārīo* Jambudd. 383 ff.; *disākumārī-* and *vijjukumārī-mahattariyāo*. Ṭhāṇ. 198b, 222 b, 418b. The grammatical gender of *diś* and *vidyut* obviously excludes masculine princes.

4. Partly different in Umāsvāti on T. 4, 11.

5. Those of the Udahik. and Vāuk. are exchanged by mistake in the text.

into the deep beyond the Rayaṇappabhā, they are able to reach both the centre- and the upper world.[1] The Nāgak. are water gods in general and as such are connected with the rain clouds[2] while the Udahik. seem to command over the sea.[3] to water must apply to the Udahik, just as well. The Suvaṇṇak. having their seat also in the Māṇuss'uttara mountains (§ 122)[4] go back to the idea of the Suparṇa-Garuḍa,[5] the Disāk. to that of the world elephants. The latter female dignitaries share in the consecration of a Titthagara for the purpose of which they come running from the centre world as well, for these *disākumārī-mahattariyā*[6] have their seats also on the Ruyaga mountains (§ 123) and in the tree tops of the Nandaṇa forest (§ 115).[7] The meaning of the *Dīvak.* with a lion as their attribute[8] is not clear. The *Vāuk.* occupy submarine caves (§ 121), and they cause the movement of the wind bodies (Viy. 212 a) which is either a normal or an abnormal one (*ahā-riyaṃ riyai, uttara-kiriyaṃ* r.). Following the same passage (211b) the theory of the wind may be added here. There are winds of the 4 kinds or grades *īsiṃ-purevāya, patthāvāya, mandā-vāya, mahā-vāya*, and in the sections of the compass-card opposite each other winds of the same character are simultaneous, whereas winds blowing over continents (*dīviccaya*, comp. Nāya 11) are not simultaneous with winds blowings over oceans (*sāmuddaga*), since the wind turns back on the sea-shore (*tesi ṇaṃ vāyāṇaṃ vivaccāseṇaṃ Lavaṇe samudde velaṃ nâikkamai*).

1. For the motives see Viy. 169b, 180b.
2. Viy. 278b; Jambudd. 238 b f.
3. *velaṃ dharanti* Dīvas. 308a.
4. Dīvas. 342a.
5. Hence it is wrong to render it by Suvarṇak. in Prajn. Comp. Āyār. II, 15 XII f. and the comm. on Samav. 155b. Their fight with the Nāgak. may be the cause for a partial earthquake (Ṭhāṇ. 161 b).
6. See ALSDORF's instructive essay New Ind. Ant. 9, 105-128. The author complains that his essay abounds in misprints.
7. They therefore are called *ahelɔga-vatthavva* as well as *uḍḍhaloga-v.* (Jambudd. V, (383ff., 388b) comp. Ṭhāṇ. 436 b and Sthān.) since in this altitude the upper world has begun already.
8. The lion of the so-called Dvīpakumāra may go back to the animal of the *dvīpa* kat' exochen, Siṃhaladvīpa. But the neighbourhood of *aggi* and *vijju*, perhaps even the princely names of Puṇṇa and Vasiṭṭha (Avaśiṣṭa) are indicative of *dīpa* instead of *dvīpa*.

§111. With regard to both kinds of gods the Rayaṇappabhā region is horizontally divided into a southern and a northern half, being void, however, above and below in a layer measuring 1,000 *joy.* in depth both of hells and places pertaining to gods. These places (*bhavaṇa*) are bright,[1] sumptuously furnished and pleasant in every respect. Those situated on the edge are circular, those situated inside are square shaped, the nethermost layer is merely circular (Jīv. 94b). the total number is 77.2 mill., the number of the individual kinds differs from 6.4 mill. with the Asurak. up to 9.6 mill. with the Vāukumāra.[2]

Each of the two halves, of which all southern ones contain some more places than the northern ones, is governed by a prince. These pairs of princes in the above quoted sequence of the kinds are: Camara and Bali Vairoyaṇa, Dharaṇa and Bhūyāṇaṇḍa, Veṇudeva and Veṇudāli, Harikanta and Haris(s)aha, Aggisiha and Aggimāṇava, Puṇṇa and Vasiṭṭha, Jalakanta and Jalappaha, Amiyagai and Amiyavāhaṇa, Velamba and Pabhanjaṇa, Ghosa and Mahāghosa. It is but in the case of Camara and to a smaller degree of Bali that we come to know more than the mere names of these princes, while the remaining pairs stand back completely, and it is only by their surnames (Viy. 200b) that we are, partly, informed of their origin. With regard to Camara and his Asurakumāras (and equally with Sakka, § 131) we can speak of something like a mythology (comp. Viy. 169b ff., 319b, 752a, etc.) His residence—it is called Camaracancā as that of Bali bears the name of Balicancā—is described in Viy. 144a, 617a, though it is added that it does not serve him as a dwelling but simply as place of entertainment.

§112. The transition to the centre world is formed by the Vāṇamantara- (or Vantariya-) gods, for their seats are partly (Pannav. 95a) subterranean (§ 110), partly in the groves (Jambudd. 31a) summarized in § 116—in the so-called

1. Viy. 246 b.

2. Viy. 770a, where also the places of Vāṇamantara and Joisiya are mentioned.

Long Veyaḍḍha hills (Jambudd. 72a) (§ 114) and (Jīv. 145a) on the intermediate continents (§ 116). In the acknowledged sequence they range between humans and star gods who belong to the centre world. In them we find the dogmatic reflection of popular spirits, ghosts and demons,[1] and it is characteristic, that in the Canon nothing special is being said as to their activities and numbers (¿ × 100,000, Viy. 601a). There were two sequences of Vāṇamantara kinds known, though at least by Umāsvāti T. 4, 12 one of them got the preponderance over the other. It is (Ṭhāṇ. 442b; Pannav. 95b) that of the Pisāya, Bhūya, Jakkha, Rakkhasa, Kinnara, Kiṃpurisa, Mahākāya (Ṭhāṇ, 161b 442b, Mahoraga), and Gandhavva with two princes each (Pannav. 97b). The other sequence has the Aṇavanniya, Paṇavaṇiya, Isivāiya, Bhūyavāiya, Kandiya, Mahākanduya, Kohaṇḍa (Ku-) and Payaga, and here equally two names of princes[2] for each were invented (Pannav. 95b, comp. also Ṭhāṇ. 85a). Umāsvāti mainly quotes these Vāṇamantara as sub-groups of the former sequence (differently classified by him). That at least the Aṇavanniya enjoyed popularity is clearly proved by Viy. 498a. As to T. 4, 12 we also find specifications regarding their outward appearance which, except for the Rakkhasa, is a pleasing one; the colour is mostly of a dark shade (*śyāma*). The dwellings (*bhomejja-nagara*) are in the uppermost layer, the Rayaṇakaṇḍa, of the Kharakaṇḍa of Rayaṇappabhā, and, what is more, within the 800 *joy.* left both above and below after deducting 100 unoccupied joy on either side. The largest among these dwellings are as large as is the Jambuddīva, the medium ones as large as Videha (§ 113), and the smallest are *khetta-sama.* Within them the Vāṇamantara lead a happy life, free from care and ageless (Dev. 75 f.).

§113. *The Centre World* (*tiriya-loga*). The centre world rests on a disc the thickness of which we may say to be 0. For the 1,000 *joy.* beneath the surface into which the mountains

1. Thus also Ṭhāṇ. 141b quotes the *deva, nāga, jakkha,* and *bhūya* as either sending or refusing rains.

2. Dev. 72 has none but these, quoted by Pannav. 98a.

penetrate (usually with the *uvveha*, a fifth quarter of their visible elevation[1]) are identical with the 1,000 *joy.* which, in the Rayaṇappabhā, are void of places pertaining to either gods or hells. The surface of the centre world consists of the circular continent of Jambuddīva surrounded by other continents and by oceans in concentric rings.[2] We shall deal but with the former first.

The diameter of the Jambuddīva[3] measures 100,000 *joy.* Its centre point and therewith that of the whole centre world, is the Mandara mountain (s.b.). To the south of it—from S. to N.—we have the different parts of the world (*vāsa, varisa, vassa*)[4] called Bharaha, Hemavaya, Harivāsa, and to the north—from N. to S.—those of Eravaya (Erāv.), Hiraṇṇavaya (also Her., Er.),[5] Rammaga, They, however, do not occupy the entire disc. It its centre there lies the continent called Mahāvideha or Videha. It divides into Puvva-Videha east and Avara-Videha west of Mandara, whilst to the south and to the north of it we have the countries of Devakurā and Uttarakurā[6] (*-kuravaḥ*). In the latter we behold the world tree of Jambū from which the whole continent derives its name. It measures 8 *joy.* both in thickness and height, and it is the seat of the god Aṇāḍhiya. In *Devakurā* the tree Kūḍasāmalī inhabited by the Veṇudeva Garula corresponds to it.

These seven parts of the world are separated from each other by world mountains (*vāsadhara-pavvaya*) extending from east to west, so that in the south between Bharaha and

1. This is shown by the distances measured in *joy.*, and the astronomical distances (comp. Jiv. 376 ff.) counting from a *bahusama-ramaṇija bhūmi-bhāga* in Rayaṇappabhā. Hence the reason why it is merely called by the name of *imā Ray.*

2. We shall see (§ 123) that their number is limited, though by the term of *asaṃkhejjāiṃ diva-samuddāiṃ* we might suppose the reverse. Also Umāsvāti on T. 3, 7 calls them countless, yet at the end of his Jambudvīpasamāsa he gives a specified list.

3. For a plan not true to scale see Antag. ed. BARNETT, p. 138.

4. Umāsvāti T. 3, 10; *vaṃśa, varṣa vāsyā iti c'aiṣām guṇataḥ paryāyanāmāni bhavanti*; *vaṃśadhara* on T. 12. In the Prakrit of the Dig. we read *vaṃsa.*

5. *Viy.*, Thāṇ. and Samav. write Eravaya and (H)Eraṇṇavaya, Jambudd. has Erav. and Hir., also Nelavanta except in Jambudd. V. Comp. § 119.

6. Pl. *-kurāiṃ* corresponding to *Bharahāiṃ* etc. Viy. 791b.

Hemavaya we have Cullahimavanta (Himavan), between Hemavaya and Harivāsa: Mahāhimavanta, between Harivāsa and Mahāvideha: Nisadha; in the north between Eravaya and Hiraṇṇavaya: Sihari, between Hiraṇṇavaya and Rammaga: Ruppi, and between Rammaga and Mahāvideha: Nīlavanta.

As to the ratio of size of these continents and world mountains, it is of a kind that towards the centre each of the succeeding is twice as wide as the preceding. The width (*vikkhambha*) of Bharaha and Eravaya measures 526 $\frac{6}{19}$ *joy.*—i.e. two quite narrow segments—, that of Cullahimavanta and Sihari 1,052 $\frac{12}{19}$ *joy*, etc. By taking Bharaha as 1 we may imagine the Jambuddīva as consisting of 190 units (*khaṇḍa*). From the width there follows the length of the chords (*jīvā*) representing the boundaries of the continents and world mountains, of the pertinent arcs (*dhaṇupaṭṭha*), and of the arc sections between the chords (*bāhā*). The northern edge of the Cullahimavanta, for instance, is a little longer than 24,932 $\frac{1}{38}$ *joy.*, and the arc above it embracing both the mountains themselves and Bharaha measures 25,230 $\frac{4}{19}$ *joy.*

§114. The world mountains—JACOBI calls them by the appropriate term of "banks" (on T. 3, 11)—have 100, 200 and 400 *joy.* in height measured in pairs towards Mahāvideha, and they show 11, 8 and 9 summits (*kūḍa*).[1] These summits rising to an individual height of 500 *joy.* sit upon the mountains. In the centre of these mountains we find the longish lakes (*maha-ddaha*) from which the large rivers spring (Ṭhāṇ. 72b). From those of the Cullahimavanta and Sihari there flow three each, i.e. into Bharaha eastward the Gangā, westward the Sindhu, northward into Hemavaya the Rohiyaṃsā; into Eravaya eastward the Rattā, westward the Rattāvaī, southward into Hiraṇṇavaya the Suvaṇṇakūlā. From the remaining lakes spring two rivers each to flow southward and northward. Thus from the Mahāhimavanta there come the Rohiya in Hiraṇṇavaya and the Harikantā in Harivāsa from the Nisaha ibd. the Harī and the Sīoyā in Mahāvideha. They

1. Ṭhāṇ. 70 a ff. counts 2 each.

correspond to the Ruppakūlā in Hiraṇṇavaya flowing northward and the Narakantā in Rammaga flowing southward from the Ruppi, as do the Nārīkantā and the Sīyā in Mahāvideha flowing from the Nīlavanta ibd. These rivers start by flowing on top of the mountains in the above mentioned directions to leave it in a leap (called *jibbhiyā* for its tongue-like shape). At their foot they cross a lake (*pavāya-kuṇḍa*, *p.-daha* or *salila-kuṇḍa*) and turn off into their definite direction before the uplands (soon to be mentioned) in order to fall into the Lavaṇa Sea either to the east or to the west. Those mountains lying in this course are crossed by flowing beneath them. The medium continents are divided by the rivers into two equal halves. All rivers of the continents that start by flowing to the south end up in the east, all others end up in the west. A chord standing perpendicularly on them and its ends coinciding with those of the Nisaha and Nīlavanta forms the boundary of an arc 2,923 *joy.* wide which is filled by the "estuary forest" of these rivers (*muha-vaṇa*).

Each of the two rivers in Bharaha and Eravaya has 5 tributaries (*antara-naī*, Ṭhāṇ. 351a, 477b). Those of the Gangā are called Jamuṇā, Sarayū, Ādī, Kosiyā and Mahī, those of the Sindhū: Sayadū, Vivacchā, Vibhāsā, Erāvai and Candabhāgī. Both the Sīyā and the Sioyā have three tributaries each of which springs from lakes on the slopes of the southern and northern world mountains.

The mountains of the different continents, with the exception of Mahāvideha, are known by the name of Veyaḍḍha, (T. 3,11: Vaitāḍhya, Jambūdv.: Vijayāḍhya or Vijayārdha; comp. end of § 115).[1] The Veyaḍḍha mountains which divide Bharaha lengthwise into equal parts are exemplary. They measure 25 *joy.* in height and 50 *joy.* in width, and they culminate in 9 summits. These mountains to which, naturally, there are corresponding ones in Eravaya, are called long (*dīha-V.*), whereas the other Veyaḍḍhas (bearing special names), are called round (*vaṭṭa-V.*). The latter are situated in the four

1. For the etymology (*vedyardha*) see ALSDORF ZDMG 92, 485f.

remaining continents on the S.-N. Middle axis and are hemispherical in shape with 1,000 *joy.* in diameter and height. Other characteristics of Bharaha and Eravaya are (a.o.) the Usabhakūḍa on the slope of the Cullahimavanta or, resp., the Sihari between the two rivers.

§115. The mountains in Mahāvideha are called *vakkhāra-pavvaya.* They are grouped round the Mandara mountain which forms the centre point of the Jambuddvīa. This mountain which, apart from 14 other names (Samav. 31b),[1] bears the name of Meru—preferred by later authors—reaches below the earth surface by 1,000 *joy.* and rises above it by 99,000; at its visible foot in measures 10,000 and on its top 1,000 *joy.* in diametre. On its slopes we have four forest districts (*vaṇa*). On the earth surface there is the Bhaddasāla forest extending over a distance of 22,000 *joy.* from east to west, but of not more than 250 *joy.* from south to north, with eight directive summits (*disāhatthi-kūḍa*) rising from it up to a height of 500 *joy.* (Ṭhāṇ. 436a). On the side of Mt. Mandara, at a height of 500 *joy.* we have the flat terrace of the Nandaṇa forest, and at a height of 62,500 *joy.* that of the Somaṇasa forest, both measuring 500 *joy.* in width. The former has ninesummits (Ṭhāṇ. 454a). At a height of 36,000 *joy.*[2] above the latter there follows the Paṇḍaga forest with four sacred places (*abhisega-silā*) for world-emperors (*cakkavaṭṭi*) (s.b.) and Titthagaras (Ṭhāṇ. 224a). From its ring 494 *joy.* broad the headpiece (*cūliyā*) on the top level of the mountain measuring 12 *joy.* in diametre juts up. It is 40 *joy.* high and 4 *joy.* wide at its top. From the Mandara four mountain ranges stretch in the intermediate directions to the Nisaha and Nīlavanta, their height decreasing on their course from 500 down to 400 *joy.*, whilst their width increases from a minimum up to 500 *joy.* They embrace the countries of Devakurā in the south

1. Jambudd. has but 12 in all, whereas Sūrap. 5 and 7 has 20. The Meru is desci ibed by the name of Sudaṃsaṇa in Sūy. I, 6, 10 to 13. Comp. also Dasav . 11, 16.

2. The figures (500+62,500=) 63,000 and 36,000 acc. to Jambudd. Samav. 75a gives 61,000 and 38,000 for these parts (*kaṇḍa*).

and of Uttarakurā in the north. Either country has five lakes with 20 mountains of gold each, i.e. 200 mountains of gold (*kancaṇaga-pavvaya*) in all; in Devakurā we have, furthermore, the mountains of Citta- and Vicittakūḍa corresponding to the two twin mountains (*Jamaga-p.*) in Uttarakura. In their western, resp., eastern part we have the world trees referred to above. Moreover, there are four times 4 parallel mountain chains;[1] stretching from the world mountains by which Mahāvideha is bounded, they hit the two rivers a right angles, and it is here that they have their maximum height in correspondence with the case mentioned before. Between every two of them there flow the 12 tributaries quoted above following their course. As in all other world continents, the mountains consist of one kind of noble metal each or either of precious stones. Merely the nethermost 1,000 *joy.* of the Mandara, hidden in the earth, consist of common rook.

The mountains and rivers, as well as the estuary forests of the Sīyā and Sīoyā form, in equal distances, the boundaries of the empires (*cakkavaṭṭi-vijaya*) under the rulership of a world-emperor (*cakkavaṭṭi*). By including Bharaha and Eravaya there are 34 of them in all (Ṭhāṇ. 435 b). The empire of Bharaha with its Veyaḍḍha,[2] with its Gangā and Sindhū and other geographical details is merely copied by the remaining ones, and so are these names. There we also find a great number of cities with an imperial residence in each case, and countless villages.

§116. At the point where the mountains of Cullahimavanta and Sihari touch the edge of the Jambuddīva, we find four intermediate continents (*antara-dīva*) protruding into the sea in the four intermediate directions for a distance of 300 *joy.* and six more following each in the same directions always for a distance of 100 *joy.* So that, then, each of the mountains ends up in 14 promontories, whilst their total number is 56.

1. They are listed with the other *vakkhāra-pavvaya* in Ṭhāṇ. 224a, 326a.

2. Since they halve the empire, Umāsvāti's Jambūdvīpasamāsa (Appendix to Tattvārhādhigama Bibl. Ind. 1905), also gives Vijayārdha owing to a wrong etymology (see end of §114).

In rendering a description of the geography of the Jambuddīva we have confined ourselves to dealing with its major points only, and we shall continue to do so in dealing with the rings surrounding the J. In this connexion it may suffice to mention summarily that, just as is the case with the J. itself, "all hills, hill tops, summits, lakes, forests, estuary forests, spring ponds, sacred places, water courses, etc."[1] are surrounded by an enclosure (*pauma-vara-veiyā*) and a grove (*vaṇa-khaṇḍa*). The respective descriptions follow a certain conventional pattern. Here we also but mention the palaces, gates, lotus ponds, sanctuaries and residences of gods on mountains and in islands.[2]

§117. Though the dwelling place of man is not confined to the Jambuddīva but extends beyond it also to the continent of Dhāyaīkhaṇḍa and the inner half of Pukkharavara (§ 122), we may yet discuss it already here. The quasi political classification of men is done according to their dwelling quarters, i.e. to the *kamma-bhūmi*, *akamma-bhūmi* and *antara-dīva*. Karman places of a kind, where the Karman is acquired and annihilated, are found on the 2½ continents in the world parts of Bharaha, Eravaya and Mahāvideha, except the two Kurā; the latter, the remaining world parts and the intermediate continents are free from Karman (Viy. 791 b). At the Karman places there live (*kamma-bhūmaga*) Aryans and Barbarians. Among the different classifications of the former (Umāsv. on T. 3, 15; comp. Ṭhāṇ. 358a) the *khett'āriya* range first. We are given 26 towns in 25½ countries as native places of Jinas, *cakkavaṭṭi*, *baladeva* and *vāsudeva* in that one section (*Kekaya*) is considered non-aryan. With the *bhāsāriya* the Ardhamāgadhī and the "holy script" (*bambhī livī*) serve as a criterion,[3] the latter being distinguished into 18 provincial and technical scripts. The Barbarians (*milakkhu*, also *meccha*) greatly vary in kind; Pannav. has more than 50 names of different peoples.

1. Umāsvāti, Jambūdv. 4.

2. For examples concerning their description see LEUMANN, VI OC III, 2, p. 495 ff

3. Umāsvāti, being a Sanskrit author, expresses himself in general terms only.

Unfortunately these names as well as the others are given next to no support by the commentary. We but mention the Saga, Javaṇa, Cilāya, Pārasa, Hūṇa, and Romaga. The list of the royal household which, next to some curiosities, includes even ladies of foreign nationalities, is much shorter (Viy. 457a, 557a; Nāyādh. § 117; Pannav. 14a; Uvav. § 55). About the places void of Karman and their people we are told next to nothing (§ 119). The inhabitants of these intermediate continents (*antara-dīvaga*) are strangely shaped: they are one-legged, they do not speak, they have tails and horns, the ears and mouths of horses, elephants, cattle, etc., radiant teeth, etc. etc. Their 28 different kinds on the southern continents—each bearing one—repeat themselves on the northern. Their cultural state is that of paradise. They are vegetarians and eat but every second day. They live in trees and know of no communal life. Their character is the best one can think of. They have neither masters nor servants, neither parents nor children, neither enemies nor friends, no harmful animals and nothing evil from whatever side. Their outward appearance (they are 800 *dhaṇu* tall) is of every possible excellence, and as to the mentioned abnormities, they apparently do not stand in its way.[1] The beauty of their wives is most extraordinary.

The mountain-banks as well as the different mountain ranges and hills are considered not to be inhabited by humans, and to get there or to the oceans of Lavaṇa and Kāloya (§ 122) they can only do so by transposing themselves (Umāsv. on T. 3, 12).

§118. All over the centre world we find the animals of any shape. The one-sensed kinds have been mentioned above already, since the smallest particles of earth, water, fire, wind and plants occur in all parts of the world, no matter whether they are solid or subtle. The two-sensed kinds which are

1. The description in Jīv. 350a ff. equals on the whole that of Mahāvīra's Uvav. 16, but since it concerns beings of common standing, it goes in the opposite direction, i.e. from below to above (just so Āyār. 2, 23 ff.). In either case the procedure is contrary to Brahman usage.

capable of sensing and tasting, the three-sensed which, in addition, are capable of scenting, the four-sensed which are gifted with seeing, and the five-sensed which are even able to hear, all these kinds vary greatly; Pannav. 41 a ff. without having the intention of being exhaustive, counts up to 40 species.[1] The informations given in Utt. 36[2] are less complete. And yet the classification is crude. Worms appear side by side with shells, many lower insects as having three senses, and bees, scorpions, crickets, flies, etc. as having four. The highest class is formed by the higher animals, though, strangely enough, we are but insufficiently informed concerning their habitats (Pannav. 78 b f.); for merely to say that all two-sensed animals live about water places of the most different kinds, is but relatively true, and yet this statement is repeated for all three- to five-sensed animals, for the latter even twice (Pannav. 84a). The habitats equally serve for the classification of the higher animals, though only secondarily, for their being called water-, earth- and air- animals, or, more precisely, such that move in the corresponding element (*jalayara*, *thalay.*, *khahay.*, Sūy. II 3, 22 ff.; Utt. 36, 171 ff.; Pannav. 43 b ff.) goes back to the fundamental discrimination between voluntarily movable and immovable beings, the *tasa* and *thāvara pāṇa*[3]— the latter comprising the earth- and water- beings and the plants[4] (a. o. Ṭhāṇ. 134a). The medium or the way of locomotion further leads to speak of the land animals as solid- and multi-

1. Many animals are quoted in a more than one context. Pannav. 7b f.

2. The two- to four-sensed do not occur as *suhuma*. Hence the translation of Utt. 36, 128, 137, 146 SBE 45, 219 f. has to be rectified.

3. The *tasa pāṇa* are divided (Āyār. 5, 1 f. (=Dasav. 4, 1 intr.) acc. to their physical creation into such coming out of eggs, being born ready made, being brought forth with the amnion, into such coming into existence in moisture, in sweat or by coagulation, and others that spring from the womb of the earth or from the nil. We have dealt with the sixth case in § 63 already. It is mentioned by Ṭhāṇ. 114a where it is claimed that the first and second case (*aṇḍaya* and *poyāya*) pertain to fishes, birds and the afore quoted crawlers. For an attempt made by KOHL (ZDMG 103, p. 151-155) to explain *poyaya* by "born in a boat" see above, p. 142.

4. It is improbable that the five *thāvara-kāya* called *inda*, *bambha*, *sippa*, *sammai* and *pājāvacca* together with their consonant *ahivai* (Ṭhāṇ. 292 a) have anything to do with it, even though Sthān. insists on it. In the Dig. 2, 13 f. also fire and wind are *sthāvara*.

hoofed, as equipped with claws, and as such crawling either breast- or armwise (*ura-* and *bhuya-parisappa*). In Sūy. II 3 we are systematically informed of the first and the later food taken by these creatures as well as by men and lower animals down to the elemental beings and plants.

§119. The conception of the circular shaped Jambuddīva is obviously due to that of the segment Bharaha as which the Indian peninsula seemed to show. We may further assume that the conception of the intermediate continents goes back to an ancient knowledge of Indo-China and the Malacca peninsula which was symmetrically enlarged later on. *Bharaha* (or *Bhāraha vāsa*) is called after the king bearing this name and whose capital Viṇīyā lay in the centre of the country to the south of the Veyaḍḍha. He gained the rule over the entire continent, as we are told by Jambudd. III, and thus became *cāuranta-cakkavaṭṭi*. Of *Eravaya* we hear nothing except the precise repetition of this legend where, naturally, the king is given the name of Eravaya. In *Mahāvideha* we find the happy conditions prevailing in the *susama-susamā* period (s. b.). In the following pairs of Karman-free continents the conditions are of the *susama-dūsamā* or, resp., the *susamā* kind. The names of *Hemavaya* and *Hiraṇṇavaya* have been explained by the rich occurrence of gold, and this certainly goes back to the gold found in Tibet. As to the form of the latter Eraṇṇavaya it is, of course, of a secondary character.[1] In *Harivāsa* the people are of a yellowish or reddish colour (*aruṇ'ābha aruṇ'obhāsa*), by which it is intended to define the name. *Rammaga* needs no explanation regarding its name.

§120. The periods we have just come to mention have been connected with the ever turning time-wheel in a rather clumsy way.[2] The most happy period of *susama-susamā* (Jambudd. 97a; Viy. 276a) is followed by the *susamā*.[3] Both and two thirds of the succeeding, the *susama-dūsamā* are essentially

1. For its occurrence in later texts comp. LEUMANN, Übersicht 44a.

2. Comp. F O. SCHRADER, Philosophie p. 60 ff.

3. The following after Jambudd. II.

equal; their conditions correspond with those of the inhabitants of the intermediate continents, and they differ but in certain physical qualities of the human being and the regions, where they are reincarnated. Their want of food, for instance, manifests itself in the three periods after four, three and two days.[1] In the last third of the *susama-dūsamā* the change for the worse makes itself felt, it increases in the *dūsama-susamā* and *dūsamā* to reach its climax in the *dūsama-dūsamā*. The birth of Mahāvīra fell in the end of the *dūsa ma-susamā*;[2] 75 years and $8\frac{1}{2}$ months later the *dūsamā* came on. Towards its end it brings the corruption of all religious and social order (comp. Ṭhāṇ. 398a),[3] and with the *dūsamā* the order of the Jains, too, ceases to exist. With their names changing, her last representatives are with the Śvet. the monk Duppasaha, the nun Viṇhusirī (Phaggusirī) and the lay-couple of Jiṇadatta (Nāila) and Phaggusirī (Saccasirī).[4] In the *dūsama-dūsamā* (Jambudd. 164a; Viy. 305a) all disaster aggravates beyond all bounds; the moons radiate detrimental cold, the suns scorching heat, and evil comes raining from the clouds. The earth is red-hot and impassable so that people have to hide in caves which they dare not leave but at sunrise and sun-set in order to feed on the water animals jiggering on the dry banks of the retreated rivers. These six periods or spikes (*samā*, Ṭhāṇ. 120a; 357a) are unequal in length. They measure 4, 3, 2 times 10^{14} *sāgarovama* (1 *s.* = $8{,}400{,}000^{19}$), 10^{14} minus 42,000 and two times 21,000 years.[5] They form an *osappiṇī*, i.e. the descending half of the time wheel. Then they are followed[6]—again beginning with a *dūsama-dūsamā*—by the ascending half, the *ussappiṇī*, with the same

1. They are *aṭṭhama-*, *chaṭṭha-* and *cauttha-bhatta*, comp. § 156.
2. Āyār. II, 15, 2=Jinac. 2.
3. The signs by which to recognize the approach of the *dūsamā* are (Ṭhāṇ. 398a) untimely rainfall, tribute paid to discreditable persons, ineffectiveness of instruction, and bad thinking and doing.
4. The AUTHOR, Mahānis. p. 18, 42 (here also quotations). The Daṃsaṇasāra of the Dig. Devasena calls (48) Vīrangaja as the last one having the name of *jai*.
5. Comp. also Viy. 274b.
6. For the reverse sequence in later literature comp. LEUMANN, Übersicht p. 43 b.

periods. By calling them both *samā*, Ṭhāṇ. 47b may well have thought of the adj. *sama*.

After the *dūsama-dūsamā* has come to its end, the cloud of Pukkhala-saṃvaṭṭaga[1] appears in the *dūsamā*. It is as big and thick as is Bharaha, and in a tempest lasting for seven days it extinguishes the fire. Now for the same time rains fall from the cloud of Khīrameha thus producing colours, smells, etc. potentially. With the Ghayameha there comes fertile humidity (*siṇeha-bhāva*), the Amayameha causes plants to grow, and the Naraṃsameha gives them flavour. Now all people come to light again and greet the reborn earth. Then the remaining periods up to the *susama-susamā* follow. This sequence pertains to Bharaha and Eravaya only, whereas in the other continents the conditions mentioned last for ever. Chronology is unknown there (Viy. 791b).

§121. The Jambuddīva is surrounded on all sides by an enclosure (*jagaī*) with numerous window-like openings. It measures 8 *joy.* in height and its width decreases from 12 to 4 *joy.* From the centre of its surface a pinnacle (*veiya*) stands up ½ *joy.* high and 500 *dhaṇu* wide, and a grove (*vaṇa-saṇḍa*) extends in front of it. All measurements are made by starting from the outermost edge of this pinnacle. In the four main directions the enclosure is breached by a gate which, again, is 8 *joy.* high and 4 *joy.* wide. The rivers Sīyā and Sīoyā fall into the eastern and western gates, since they form the entrances leading to the Lavaṇa sea. There are three other entrances of such a kind to the east, south and west of Bharaha and Eravaya. They are the *tittha* we find in the legend of Bharaha (Jambudd. III).

The Lavaṇa sea has a width of 200,000 *joy.* Its maximum depth is 1,000 *joy.* with a mean strip of 10,000 *joy.* down to

1. Also Viy. 232 b. In another context this word stands for a generic name, where (Ṭhāṇ. 270b) the rain-power of clouds is being described. A single rainfall from the *pukkh.* lasts for 100,000 years, from the *pajjunna* for 1,000, from the *jīmūta* for 10, while many showers from the *jimha* do not mean a real rain for certain.

2. Thus the comm; acc. to the text the *jagaī* is enclosed by a *jāla kaḍaga.* The following *veiyā* we mentioned in § 116 already.

which the bottom descends evenly, the enclosure being left out of consideration. This slanted bottom is called by the name of *go-tittha.* Nor is the water-level a plane surface, since—owing to an optical illusion—it ascends from the shore up to 700 *joy.* to where the maximum depth begins, above which, however, it rises up to 16,000 *joy.* This section above the deepest channel is the *sihā.* Ebb and flow, which occur twice within 30 *muhutta,* here cause a difference of ½ *joy.* as compared with the mean sea-level. This is due to the existence of submarine caves (*pāyāla*) which equally account for the spring-tides on the 8th and 14th and at new moon and full moon. For in the main directions of the compass card, 95,000 *joy.* distant, there are four vast spaces below the sea. They are 100,000 *joy.* deep with a width of 10,000 above and below and 100,000 *joy.* in between, so that they nearly have the shape of hollow spheres with walls of diamonds 100 *joy.* thick. It is in them that the Vāukumāras Kāla, Mahākāla, Velamba and Pabhanjaṇa reside, the latter two of which we have mentioned already as princes of this species of gods. Apart from these four large caves we have 7,880 smaller ones with a ḍiametre of 100 *joy.* above and below, and 1,000 in between. The contents of all caves gradually changes from below to above from wind into water. Heavy winds blowing out of them cause the spring-tides, while their being emptied of, resp., filled with water account for ebb and flow.

The god of the Lavaṇa sea is called Suṭṭhiya, and he lives in an island, Goyamadīva, 12,000 *joy.* distant from the Jambuddīva to the west. Equally distant to the east (§ 128) we find the two islands of the moons of the Jambuddīva, Candadīva, and opposite to them—though the island of the Suṭṭhiya is said to lie there already—those of the suns, Sūradiva. The four moons (s. b.) of the Lavaṇa sea have two islands lying 12,000 *joy.* off its easternmost point, and two others equidistant from the Jambuddīva to the east; this in correspondence with the four suns in the west. All these islands have a surface slanting from a height of 90 *joy.* in the east to ½ *joy.* in the west. The position of the moon- and sun-islands of the remaining continents and seas is the same, though they are level. At a range of 42,000 *joy.* from Jambuddīva in the main directions there are, in the Lavaṇa sea, the hills (*āvāsa-pavvaya*) of the Velaṃdhara-Nāga prince, and in the intermediate directions at the same range those of the Aṇuvelaṃdhara. They are 1,000 *joy.* wide and 1,721 *joy.* high. Like all other continents and seas, so the Lavaṇa is also enclosed by a *veiyā* with four gates bearing the same names as that of the Jambuddīva. But no other sea is inhabited, nor has it any up and down as to its surface or any cloud formation (Jīv. 320b). Now, that the Lavaṇa remains within its bounds without flooding all and everything, this is due to the sacred and benevolent human and superhuman inhabitants of Jambuddīva, "and, moreover, it is a world-law" (*ad-uttaraṃ ca ṇaṃ loga-ṭṭhiī logāṇubhāve*, Jīv. 324a).

§122. Just as the Lavaṇa sea is twice the width of the Jambuddīva, so the ring-shaped adjoining continents (*dīva*) and the oceans (*samudda, oya*) lying in between are twice the width of the preceding. The continent beyond the Lavaṇa is Dhāyaīkhaṇḍa.[1] Two mountain ranges in the north and the south, bearing the name of Usuyāra (Iṣvākāra), divide it into an eastern and a western half, and within each we find a perfect copy of the geographical conditions prevailing in the Jambuddīva even including the names and with the only exception that here the world trees standing for the Jambū tree are called Dhāyaīrukkha and Mahādhāyaīrukkha. The world mountains run in a radial course towards the Mandara of the Jambuddīva, and the two Mandaras naturally lie strictly to the east and the west of it. Instead of 100,000 they measure but 85,000 *joy.* in total height and but 9,400 *joy.* in width at their foot (Samav. 92a; Sthān. 167b; Umāsvāti on 3, 11). Beyond the Dhāyaīkhaṇḍa there follows the Kāloya[2] sea with black and thick water, and behind it the continent of Pukkharavara. Its two halves with the Paumarukkha and Mahāpaumarukkha in the place of the Jambū, are an interior and an

1. Jīv.: °saṇḍa.
2. Jīv. frequently has Kāloyaṇa.

exterior one, i.e. each of them is ring-shaped measuring 800,000 *joy.* in width each. The interior one—that much is clear—repeats the design of the Dhāyaīkanda. Behind it and to separate it from the outer ring there rise the Māṇussuttara mountains with one summit in every main direction measuring 1,721 *joy.* in height and 1,022 *joy.* in diametre at their foot. They form the boundary of the world inhabited by men, the Samayakhetta or Maṇussakhetta, beyond which men as such are not able to reach. Where it terminates, all human institutions which include chronology (*samaya*) come to an end, and so do the atmospheric phenomena of lightning, thunder and rain; fire, metals in the earth, lakes, darkness and other astronomic occurrences do no longer show (§ 128).

§123. Scarcely anything characteristic is being said about the continents and oceans beyond the Pukkharoya. First there follow the continents of Vāruṇavara (Umāsvāti : Var.) Khīravara, Ghayavara, Khoyavara (Ikṣuvara) with their seas of Vāruṇoya (Var.), etc.[1] Beyond the Khooya (Ikṣuvaroda) there lies the Nandissaravara-dīva. At every cardinal point we have an Anjanaga mountain measuring 84, 000 *joy.* in height, 1,000 *joy.* in depth and 10,000 *joy.* in diametre at the foot decreasing down to 1,000 *joy.* at the top. Its surroundings include a Dahimuha hill of circular shape. In the intermediate directions this continent has four Raikara hills 1,000 *joy.* high, 1,00 *gāuya* deep and 10,000 *joy.* in diametre. The continents following on the Nandissaroya nominally belong together in threes each. For to the *dīva* Aruṇa, Aruṇavara and Aruṇavarohāsa there correspond three Kuṇḍala, Ruyaga, Hara, Addhahāra, Kaṇaga, Rayaṇāvalī, Muttāvalī, Āiṇa and Sūra at a time, and it goes without saying that each of them has a sea: Aruṇoya, Aruṇavaroya, Aruṇavorohāsoya, etc.[2] On the Kuṇḍalavara

1. Of the seas hitherto quoted Kalôya and Pukkharôya taste of pure water (*udaga-rasa*), and so does the outermost sea to be mentioned. The Lavaṇa sea, Varuṇoya, Khīroya and Ghaoya are *patteya-rasa* (*samudràntaraiḥ sahâsādhāraṇa-rasaḥ*). The remaining are *khoya-rasa* (Dīv. 371 b).

2. Thus after Dīv., where Addhahāra to Āiṇa are quoted only in the comm. as the insertion for a *jāva*. Umāsvāti on T. 3, 7 has Nandīśvara-(vara) and the Nandiśvaravarôda followed by the Aruṇavara and its sea. and presently, by ṡ continents and seas up to the Ṣvayaṃbhūramaṇa. But at

and Ruyaga there are the circular mountains all bearing the same name (*maṇḍaliya pavvaya*, Ṭhāṇ. 166b) following the pattern of the Māṇussuttara. They are 42,000 and 84,000 *joy.* high and 100 *joy.* deep and their diameter decreases from 10,000 down to 1,000 *joy.*[3] The Ruyagavara has 4×8 summits.[4] The last five continents are simple again. Their names are Deva, Nāga, Jakkha, and Sayaṃbhūramaṇa and they are washed by seas called by their names.

§124. Of the gods belonging to the centre world it is only the stars that are quoted in the acknowledged quaternary number, though, apart from them, we have numerous local deities. The superior gods in the Jambuddīva and the Lavaṇa sea haven been mentioned already. Even individual places of the Jambuddīva have a god of their own bearing their name and for us mostly leading a wholly vague existence. With a few exceptions only he appears as the second answer to the question as to why a country, a hill, etc., bears his name, in that this name, e.g. of the Mandara, is referred to as transmitted from that of the god to the resp. locality. The lakes from which the great rivers spring belong to the goddesses named Sirī, Lacchī; Hirī, Buddhī; Dhiī, Kittī. The reservoirs at the foot of the mountains have islands inhabited by the deities of these rivers the names of which they bear. Apart from these and many other individual deities we have different kinds of localized gods. On the Long Veyaḍḍhas in Bharaha and Eravaya measuring 25 *joy.* in height—as well as in their copies

the end of his Jambudvīpasamāsa he is in conformity with Aṇuog. 90a by quoting after the Aruṇābhāsa (sic Aṇuog.): Aruṇavara: Kuṇḍala, Rucaka, Aruṇa (Aṇuog. correctly Ābharaṇa), Vastra, Gandha, Utpala, Tilaka, Pṛthivī, Nidhāna (Nihi), Ratna, Varṣadhara, Hrada, Nadī, Vijaya, Vakṣāra, kalpa, Indra, Pura (Kuru), Mandara, Āvāsa, Kūṭa, Nakṣatra, Candra, three Sūrya, etc. as above. The separation of these names is not quite certain. To each of these continents there pertains a sea of the same name. The comm. on Aṇuog. discusses some more deviations from the Cuṇṇī.

3. The Dīv. contain nothing as to these mountains. The statements made above follow Ṭhāṇ. and Samav. In the verses rendered by Sthān. 167a the diametres differ, thus 1,022 to 424 with the Kuṇḍalavara, 1022 to 4,024 with the Ruyagavara. Sthān. 480b notes these deviations. Ibd. partly even other continents are quoted, so that Kuṇḍalavara is the 11th and Ruyaga (sic) the 13th.

4. Ṭhāṇ. 436b.

in Mahāvideha—we find (Jambudd. 71b) at an altitude of 10 *joy.* both to the south and the north a so-called *vijjāhara-sedhi*, i.e. a line of seats (*nagar'āvāsa*) numbering 50 in the south and 60 in the north reserved for this human species gifted with magic power (§ 181). 10 *joy.* above there are two equal lines for the *ābhiog(iy)a deva*, and another 5 *joy.* higher, on the top level, there follow the residential quarters of many Vāṇamantara gods. Equally located on the Long Veyaḍḍhas as well as on the Citta- and Vicitta-Kuḍa, the two twin hills, and on all 200 mountains of gold in Devakurā and Uttarakurā we have the seats of the Jambhaga gods (Viy. 653b) who devote themselves to pleasure, play and lust. Their contentedness grants glory, their anger infamy. So it is they who, equally as servants of the Vesamaṇa,[1] greatly add to the riches in Mahāvīra's parental home.

§125. Among the acknowledged gods those of the stars (*joisiya deva*) are considered to belong to the centre world. The star gods are (acc. to Ṭhāṇ. 302a) the moons, the suns, the planets, the Nakṣatras and all fixed stars (*tārā-gaṇa*). Cand-(im)a and Sūr(iy)a are considered their princes. All these gods, however, scarcely show any personal traits.

Acc. to Sūrap. 285b there were people[2] who supposed the moon and the sun to be incarnated souls or either both dead and soulless, as solid or hollow, as morally (by *uṭṭhāṇa*, *kamma*, etc.) or materially (by lightning or thunder) effective or uneffective. In the face of these assumptions, however, it is more correct to say that, in fact, they are powerful and magnificent gods, individuals that take an active part in the up and down of the sequence of existences (comp. Sūrap. 17).[3] Their names of Sasi aud Āicca are defined (Viy. 577b=Sūrap. 291a) as

1. *Vesamaṇa-vkuṇḍadharā* Jiṇ. 89. 98 (*kuṇḍa* in the comm.=*āyattatā*, *ājñā*). Preferably *Ves.-kuṇḍaladhara* Āyār. II, 15 IV, though apparently this is said of the Logantiya gods (§ 134); in the Jiṇac. they go by the name of *tiriya jambhaga*.

2. Rational definitions as the following arc by no means sporadic among the *paḍivatti* of the Sūrap.

3. When their life has come to an end, they are replaced by 4 or 5 gods of the next lower rank until their likes will incarnate (Jīv. 346b).

saśrī and *āditya*: "making the begin" (of chronology). With Rāhu it is similar (Sūrap. 286b). Some take him for a black mass (*poggala*) of which kind there are said to be 15 and all after the moon and the sun, while others take him for an ordinary god who either seizes or releases them below (*buddh'-anteṇaṃ*) or at their head *muddh'ant.* with his right or his left arm. But Rāhu is (Viy. 474a=Sūrap. 287a) also a powerful god with 10 names and with palaces of five colours; by penetrating (*vīivayai*) he passes over to the side vis-à-vis of his advent, he then stands to the side, he withdraws, he passes right through, or, finally, he obscures the moon and the sun completely. Such observations prove spectacularly plain when compared with the popular belief saying (as is mentioned) that Rāhu has either seized or swallowed the moon and the sun, resp., that by doing so Rāhu's belly explodes, etc. Viy. 575a=Sūrap. 288a distinguishes between the *dhuva-R.* causing the moon to wane and the *pavva-R.* causing lunar and solar eclipses, the former occurring every 42 months at the most and the latter every 48 years at the most. The waning and the waxing of the moon, however, are explained by Rāhu's *vimāṇa*, which invariably accompanies the moon at a distance of 4 *angula* below, successively obscuring the moon by $\frac{4}{62}$ of her disk for 15 days (*kiṇha-pakkha*)— with $\frac{2}{62}$ remaining free at its uppermost part—and releasing it at the same rate for another 15 days (*sukka-p.*). Those $\frac{4}{62}$ of the disk of the moon come up to $\frac{1}{15}$ of the *Rāhu-vimāṇa*.

Both the god of the moon and the god of the sun bear the emblem of their qualities in their diadems. They measure 7 *rayaṇa* (Ṭhāṇ. 405b). Their palaces (*vimāṇa*) have the shape of half a *kavittha* fruit measuring $\frac{56}{61}$ in diameter with the moons, $\frac{48}{61}$ *joy.* with the suns, $\frac{1}{2}$ *joy.* with the planets, 1 *kosa* with the Nakṣatra, and $\frac{1}{2}$ *kosa*[1] with the fixed stars (i.e. $\frac{1}{4}$ and $\frac{1}{8}$ *joy.*). Their thickness is one half of it. They do not move of their own strength, but 4,000 gods are pulling the moons and the suns[2] in all directions, 2,000 are doing so with the

1. Up to 500 *dhaṇu* Umāsvāti on T. 4, 14.
2. As to the pl. see below.

planets, 1,000 with the nakṣatras, and 500 with the fixed stars; those in the east have the shapes of lions, those in the south such of elephants, those in the west of bulls, and those in the east of horses. The speed is in inverse proportion to these tractive powers, whereas the importance (*iḍḍhi*) is in direct proportion to them. This movement, however, only occurs within the field of Samayakhetta, while the stars beyond the Māṇussuttara mountains—their dimensions are half of those on this side—are fixed and do not move.

§126. As now to this movement itself, it is said to continue above the Jambuddīva as with a lion's roaring (*ukkiṭṭha-sīha-nāya-bola-kalakala-saddeṇa*) right round the Mandara (Sūrap.: Meru), and it does so in a normal course (Viy. 206b; Jīv. 346a; Sūrap. 278b). The moon accomplishes it in 15, the sun in 184 circles (*maṇḍala*) which widen and narrow in the course of a year. The advance from a narrower to a wider circle (*nikkhamai* as against *pavisai*) is not by leaps (*bheya-ghāeṇaṃ*) but by forming a spiral (*sūrie. . . kaṇṇa-kalaṃ nivveḍhei*[1]) as is explained by Sūrap. 48a with regard to the sun. The process of widening and narrowing results in the solar year of 366 days (Sūrap. 11a), and it causes the length of the day decreasing from 18 down to 12 *muhutta* and again increasing up to 18 as compared with the length of the night. Every further circle produces a day shorter by $\frac{2}{61}$ *muh.*, shorter, since of the 184 circles but 65 go above the Jambuddīva—i.e. their innermost, as with the moon, 180 *joy.* distant from its edge—whereas the remaining go above the Lavaṇa sea (Jambudd. 434a). With the moon it is 5 of the 15 circles. She stands 880, the sun 800 *joy.* above the earth surface, the fixed stars stand lower than the latter with 790, the nakṣatras with 884 higher than the former, and the planets at a height of 888 up to 900 *joy.* The shortest (but invariably constant) distance of a star (*joisa*) from the Mandara is 1,121 *joy.* (Jīv. 376b; Sūrap. 259b). All these

2. *kaṇṇa-kalaṃ*, acc. to the comm., is an adverb and should be analysed by something like *karma-kalā yathā bhavati tathā*. *karṇa*, however, is the most acute angle forming by the emergence of the new circle from the preceding.

stars represent the retinue of a princely couple, the moon and the sun, consisting (Jambudd. 521b) of 88 planets, 28 nakṣatras and 66,975 times 10^{14} (i.e. 1 *koḍakoḍi*) of fixed stars. Among all of them we shall see but the nakṣatras stand out, since they are important for dividing up the year. The planets (*gaha*) with Ingālaga ranging first are enumerated but annexwise by Sūrap. 294b, while Jambudd. 532b does so in a more casual way. Six of these planets, i.e. Sukka (Venus), Buha (Mercury), Bahassai (Jupiter), Angāraga (Mars), Saṇiccara (Saturn), and Ketu are comprised by Ṭhāṇ. 354a as *tāraggaha*, to which Sth. remarks that the common number of nine is made up by adding the moon, the sun, and Rāhu.[1] Of the different fixed stars, the polar star in special, we hear nothing. Now, acc. to Jambudd. 495b, the 28 nakṣatras are called as follows: Abhiī, Savaṇa, Dhaṇiṭṭhā, Sayabhisayā, (5) Puvva-Bhaddavayā (Potthavayā); Uttara-Bh. (P.), Revaī, Assiṇī, Bharaṇī (10) Kattiyā; Rohiṇī, Magasira (Sūrap. 132a: Saṃṭhāṇā), Addā, Punnavvasū, (15) Pussa (Pūsa); Assesā (Asilesā), Mahā, Puvva-Phagguṇī, Uttara-Ph., (20) Hattha; Cittā Sāī, Visāhā, Aṇurāhā, (25) Jeṭṭhā; Mūla, Puvv'Āsāḍhā, Uttar' Ās. The beginning with Abhiī in the first month of the rainy season is expressly stated by Sūrap. 93b (96a is correct) as against other authors who start with Kattiyā, Mahā, Dhaṇiṭṭhā, Assiṇī, or Bharaṇī. In the Sūrap. we are told the design formed by each individual nakṣatra as well as the number of its stars which is between 1 and 7 (this partly also in Ṭhāṇ. 99a, 178a, 289a, 351b, 379b, 414b), and that each has a deity and a gotra of its own. Important occurrences in the life of a Titthagara happen in the sign of one and the same nakṣatra, comp. Āyār. II, 15, 1; Jiṇac. 149, 170, 204; Ṭhāṇ. 307a. By consulting also some later Śvet.—and Dig.—writings KIRFEL in his Kosmographie, p. 278 ff. has given a detailed description of the Jain Astronomy.[2]

§127. If the altitude of the sun (and of all different kinds

1. Those just mentioned go together with moon and sun as *mahaggaha* (Ṭhāṇ. 429 b).

2. Comp. also S. R. DAS IHQ 8, 30-42.

of stars in general) is invariably the same, so Viy. 392a=Jambudd. 458b wants to make it clear[1] why at sunrise and sunset we see him *dūre ya mūle ya,* while at noon (*majjh'antiva-muhuttaṃsi*) we see him *mūle ya dūre ya.* Acc. to the comm. *mūle* means "near". Owing to the atmospheric obstruction of light (*lesā-padighāeṇaṃ*), so we are told, the sun is easily visible in the morning and in the evening and, hence, is considered to be near, whereas owing to his blazing heat at noon (*lesā'bhitāveṇaṃ*) which by blinding our eyes makes him invisible to us, he is considered to be far off. It may be doubted if by giving this explanation the comm. has grasped the actual meaning. The range of solar radiation measures (Viy. 392b) 100 *joy.* up- and 1,800 *joy.* downward including the depth mentioned in § 111, while horizontically it has 47, 263 $\frac{21}{60}$ *joy.* Contrary to differing opinions terrestrial warmth, however, results from the circumstance (Sūrap. 92b)[2] that in the intervals between the *lesā* radiated by the residences (*vimāṇa*) of the gods of moon and sun other and separate (*chinna*) *lesā* are formed (*sammucchanti*) which for their part warm their neighbourhood. Viy. 77b and 392b render detailed information also about the visibility, the radiation field, etc. of the sun.

§128. Even where both the moon and the sun are spoken of in the singular—e.g. also in the contemplation of the red morning sun with Mahāvīra (Viy. 656a)—it should always be remembered[3] that either exist in duplicate over the Jambuddīva (Sūrap. 175a, 268b). The one follows the other at an angle of 180°. The "scientific" argument, however, is that in the course of 24 hours the sun can complete not more than half of his circle round Mount Meru. When it is day over the southern half it is equally day on the same longitude over the northern, while in the meantime it is correspondingly night to the east

1. The question having this in view begins in Jambudd. by: *kamhā ṇaṃ,* in Viy. by: *keṇaṃ kh'āi aṭṭheṇaṃ.* This form is more archaic.

2. The question: *tā kati-kaṭṭhaṃ* ("how long") *te sūrie porisi-cchāyaṃ nivvattei āhie ti vaejjā ?* is erroneously anticipated from 94a.

3. Comp. THIBAUT in this Grundriss p. 21 f.—"Each season has its sun" (*nānālingatvād ṛtūnāṃ nānā-sūryatvam*) Taitt. Ār. 1, 7, 6, comp. OERTEL, Dativi finales etc., Munich 1941, p. 35.

and the west of the Mandara.[1] The celestial bodies produce time (T. 4, 15) in a way that its periods—and Viy. 210a gives full particulars of them up to the largest time units—enter simultaneously in the south and in the north, while in the east and in the west they do so 1 *samaya* later (*aṇantara-purakkha-ḍaṃsi samayaṃsi*). Now the duplication of the two princes also involves the duplication of the afore mentioned retinue, and, hence, acc. to Sūrap. 268b we have 56 nakṣatras, 176 planets, 133, 950 fixed stars over the Jambuddīva. Since, however, each single star completely equals its counterpart in shape and activity (Sūrap. 197o) and since nobody on earth sees a star twice at the same time, the matter is practically of no importance. As was pointed out in § 21, it may be a assumed that here we have an analogy to doubled dimensions of the continents and ring seas, though outside the Jambuddīva this analogy soon comes to an end. It is true, the Lavaṇa sea still has 4 moons, 4 suns and the corresponding other double numbers, but over Dhāyaīkhaṇḍa there stand 12, over Kāloya 42, and over Pukkha-ravara 72, and the remaining stars are multiplied correspondingly (Sūrap. 268 ff.). The course of a celestial body circling over sea of course lacks a centre point which on the continents is given by the Mandaras. Over Pukkharoya up to the Kuṇḍalavarobhāsa sea there are x stars each of the different kinds, and from Ruyaga on ¿ stars each (Sūrap. 282), but, as was said before, they are fixed and do not wander (*cāra-ṭṭhiīyā, no gai-raiyā*; Sūrap. 278b; Jīv. 345f, more plainly Sūrap. 278a), for beyond the Maṇussa- or Samayakhetta there is (or either for that very reason) no longer any division of time (§ 122).

§129. *The Upper World* (uḍḍha-loga). The upper world begins at an altitude immeasurably high over the stars. There, again separated from each other by intermediate spaces of *i joy.*, its different sections lie one above the other by stories. These interspaces are partly formed by the hulls enveloping the Raya-

1. The word "half", as already noted by Abhay. is not quite correct. Since all 4 directions are inquestion we are concerned with quadrants.

2. For a survey see KIRFEL, Kosmogr. p. 337 ff.

ṇappabhā together with the centre world. The idea represents itself as follows: the nethermost celestial regions (*kappa*), Sohamma and Isāṇa, lie on the same level above the viscous water hull; above them and beyond the viscous wind hull there follow the heavens—if we may say so—of Saṇamkumāra and Mahinda, and above the latter one after the other: Bambhaloga, Lantaga, Mahāsukka and Sahassāra.[1] Following Sahassāra we have the light wind hull and an interspace supporting the 4 uppermost heavens of Āṇaya and Pāṇaya, Aruṇa and Accuya in twos each one above the other. Hence, from the fact that obviously the viscous wind hull is more concave than the viscous water hull and the subsequent hulls more than the preceding ones, it follows that we come to have the spaces for the above mentioned regions. By Aruṇa and Accuya the group of the 12 *kappa* ends. Above them there lie first the lower, the intermediate and the upper Gevejja places each again consisting of a lower, an intermediate, and an upper part, then on one level the 5 Aṇuttara regions, and above the highest point of their centremost (we shall deal with the details later) the region of Īsipabbhāra, the place of the Siddhas, above which the world ends. In consequence thereof, those *kappa* that lie on one level in twos are crescent shaped with their diameters either in the north or in the south. Acc. to Umāsvāti, on T. 4,20, however, we never come across a side by side position, but each region lies above the preceding, i. e. Īsāṇa (Aiśāna) above Sohamma (Saudharma). The Aṇuttara region of Savvaṭṭhasiddha measures 100,000, that of Īsīpabbhārā 4, 5 mill. *joy.* in diameter. The circles of the remaining have radii of an infinite length. But the Bambhaloga is considered the largest[2], most certainly because it includes also the so-called Black Fields and the Logantiya places (§ 134). At the same time the Bambhaloga is qualified by having the greatest curvature (*viggaha-viggahiya*, Viy. 616a)[3]. This can

1. The Dig. in T. 4,20 again render pairs by noting Brahman and Brahmottara, Lantava and Kāpiṣṭa, Śukra and Mahāśukra, Satāra and Sahasrāra.

2. Than. 166 b.

3. That is to say at the *viggaha-kaṇḍaga* (scil. Brahmalokasya) Viy. 616a.

only be understood by casting a look at the world profile (comp. § 103). Above the narrow waist representing the centre world[1] the upper world increases horizontally and tapers off capwise above, as was just mentioned above. At the place of its widest extension we have to imagine the Bambhaloga.

§130. Just as the regions of the lower world count by layers, so do those of the upper world, and they, too, are called *patthaḍa*. They are but sporadically mentioned.[2] In the 4 first pairs there are 13, 12, 6, 5, in Āṇaya up to Accuya 4 times 4,[3] in the Gevejja 3 times 3[4] and with the Aṇuttara 1.—The number of the places occupied by gods (*vimāṇa*) decreases from below to above. In Sohamma and Īsāṇa, for instance, they amount to 3,2 mill., is Sahassāra to 6,000, in the Gevejja to 318 altogether, and in the Aṇuttara to 5. Their total number is about 8, 497 mill.[5] The southern halves contain a greater number than the northern. Their downward depth and their altitude[6] invariably add up to 3,200 *joy*. From Sohamma and Īsāṇa measuring 2,700 *joy*. the depth decreases in pairs as far as Sahassāra, then by 100 *joy*. each as far as the Aṇuttara down to 2,100, while the height increases in proportion. The arrangement (Dev. 208 to 218) is either by sequences or at will, and, accordingly, the shapes are either circular, quadrangular or triangular (Ṭhāṇ. 144 b), or else they vary. Only

1. This part is conceived as two layers of (comparatively) insignificant height (*khuḍḍāga-payara*, comp. Ṭhāṇ. 477b) one resting upon the other (*uvarima-heṭṭhilla*). The world profile is completely even (*bahusama*) here and not bulging (probably *savv' aviggahiya* instead of *savva-vigg.*, Viy. 616a).

2. In Pannav., where they ought to be expected, they are but mentioned relative to the Gevijja places (104b); Ṭhāṇ. 367b is the only one to name the 6 of the Bambhaloga. The details above follow the comm. on this passage.

3. *terasa bārasa chap panca c'eva cattāri causu kappesu* Sthān. 368a must probably be understood as above, since the total number is said to be 62 here. Hence we have to suppose that Bambhaloga is thought to lie on *one* level *together* with Lantaga, Mahāsukka with Sahassāra, while Āṇaya, etc., *each* lie on a level of their own.

4. For their names see Ṭhāṇ. 452 b.

5. Comp. JACOBI ZDMG 60, 322.

6. *vimānaṃ mahānagara-kalpam, tasya coṭari vanakhaṇḍa-prakara-prāsād'-ādayaḥ*. The *vimāna-pṛthvī-bāhalya* concerns the former, the altitude to the latter (Jīv. 397b).

some 7,900 places are arranged in sequences. Towards the end of the passages the Samav. mentions numerous places by their names. Of the Aṇuttara the place of Vijaya faces the east, Vijayanta the south, Jayanta the west, and Avarāiya the north. They are in the shape of a triangle, and the centre is occupied by the circular Savvaṭṭhasiddha. It need not be pointed out that the different adamantine places equalling palaces with enclosures and gateways are radiant with all possible beauty and by their own illuminating power. All five colours blaze in Sohamma and Īsāṇa, in every following pair one of them vanishes, until at last, above the merely white Āṇaya etc., the Gevejja and Aṇuttara glisten in a still higher purity of white.

§131. The gods of the upper world are called Vemāṇiya according to their places of residence, and they are distinguished into such that reside in the *kappa* (*kappôvaga*), and such that have gone beyond them (*kappâīya*). With them, too, the place is marked by emblems. Moreover, their outward appearance is such of paramount beauty and immaculate radiance (Pannav. 100a). Their size, however, decreases with the height of the region. In Sohamma and Īsāṇa it still amounts to 7 *rayaṇa*, in every successive pair there is one less, until the Gevejjaga measure but 2 and the Aṇuttara not more than 1 *ray*. The 12 *kappa* are commanded by princes (*inda*). In Sohamma his name is Sakka whose capital seat, the *Suhammā sabhā*, gives the whole its name, in the Bambhaloga most naturally Bambha, in Āṇaya and Pāṇaya Pāṇaya, in Āraṇa and Accuya Accuya. The remaining are called according to their regions.[1] Further up there are neither princes, nor are there any distinctions of rank being observed any longer (s.b.), and anyone may call himself a prince.[2] As among the Bhavanavāsī it is but Camara, the ruler of the first kind, and Bali, that come into prominence personally, so among the Kappa gods it is scarcely but Sakka

1. This would mean 10 princes. Later there are 12 since as against Pannav. 103b f., Ṭhāṇ. 85a the 4 highest *kappa* have 4 princes of the same names (Dev. 167; Umāsvāti on T. 4, 20).

2. *Ahamindā nāmaṃ te deva-gaṇā pannattā*, Pannav. 104b, etc.

and Īsāṇa that do so. Their attributes are, according to tradition, the thunderbolt and the elephant as a draught-animal with Sakka (*vajja-pāṇi erāvaṇa-vāhaṇa*),[1] the spear and the bull with Īsāṇa (*sūla-p. usabha-v.*). As a prince of the south Sakka is superior to Īsāṇa (Viy. 168 a). For the way he punishes the Asurakumāra comp. Viy. 3, 1, and for the way they have a squabbel with Sakka see Viy. 3, 2. We are also told of Sakka's pre-existence (Viy. 737b). Other details (Viy. 633b, 405b with ref. to Rāyap., see LEUMANN VIth OC III, 2, p. 495 ff., 644b) concerning his faculties, his palace, etc., are not characteristic of him alone, but they give proof of his popularity. Saṇaṃkumāra is placed above both him and Īsāṇa since both appeal to him as an umpire in points of controversy (Viy. 168a), and just as much the princes of every higher region may be supposed to be the superiors to those of the lower. So, then, it is Sakka who inaugurates the consecration of the new-born Titthagara, whereas it is Accuya who executes it (Jambudd. 395a, 410a).

§132. It is this the place where to deal with the distinction we observe among all gods, whether it be Bhavanavāsī, Vāṇamantara, Joisiya, or Vemāṇiya, under the rulership of their princes. They are followed in rank by 4 chiefs of the four districts orientated towards the main directions, the *logapāla* (Viy. 194b, 203a). Acc. to Viy. 3, 8 they are of nearly equal rank with the *inda*. Their names in every northern half do not only equal those in every southern, but they also reappear in all *kappa*; they are Soma (E.), Jama (S.), Varuṇa (W.), and Vesamaṇa (N.). A great number of related gods is subordinate to those in the upper world including altogether all different kinds of the Bhavaṇavāsī of either sex, and they, for their part, again control an obedient retinue. They all are bound to watch carefully the most manifold occurrences of importance happening within their world-half either on the earth or in the stellar world. So Soma and a.o. the Vijju-, Aggi- and Vāukumāra are entrusted with supervising all possible

1. The traditionally accepted description of Sakka, Jiṇac. 14.

disturbances of the peace by the stars, all meteorological phenomena and all terrestrial conflagrations, Jama and the Asurakumāra with supervising all wars and epidemics, Varuṇa, the Nāga-, Udahi- and Thaṇiyakumāra with supervising all floods, and Vesamaṇa including the Suvaṇṇa-, Dīva- and Disākumāra with supervising the metals and their divine rain at important events. The Vāṇamantara and Joisiya do not know of any *logapāla*, nor do they know of the class of the 33 highest officials (*tāyattīsa*)[1]. Everywhere we have the same number of corps (*aṇīya*) and their commanders (*aṇīyahivai*), i.e. 7 each. Proportionate to terrestrial conditions we find infantry, cavalry (*pīḍhâṇīya*), elephants, bulls, chariots, dancers, and musicians. The infantry consists of 7 army-groups (*kaccha*) each twice as strong as the preceding. The first is formed by the *sāmāṇiya* gods, the third by the so-called body-guards (*āyarakkha*) in full armour.[2] We may skip the names of the commanders except that of Hari Negamesi who is in command of Sakka's infantry while, at the same time, he appears as his messenger.[3] He is taken over from the Brahman mythology[4] as is *Pajjanna*, Sakka's official rainmaker (*kālavāsī*, Viy. 634b; Isibhās. 33, 4). The number of gods who, as it were, are members of the Crown Council (*parisā*) is equally large. Arranged in three gradations this council is called an "inner" ("secret"), a medium, and an outer one, or with the Bhavaṇavāsī and Vemāṇiya it is known by *samiyā*, *caṇḍā*, and *jāyā*, with the Vāṇamantara by *īsā*, *tuḍiyā*, and *daḍharahā*, with the Joisiya by *tumbā*, *tuḍiyā*, and *pavvā parisā*, denotations which we are

1. For a story explaining their origin see Viy. 500 a.

2. It is true that in the traditional division of the state of the gods into: *sāmāṇiya*, *tāyattīsa*, *logapāla*, *agga-mahisī*, *parisā*, *aṇīya*, *aṇīyahivai*, *āyarakkha* (e. g. Pannav. first 98b), we must distinguish the *sām.* and *āy.* from the *aṇīya*, and acc. to JACOBI ZDMG 60, 317 the *sām.* are considered by the later authors to be gods of princely rank. But their numbers equal those given for the first *kaccha*, Ṭhāṇ. 406 a, and, moreover, they are very large. Camara, for instance, has 64,000 and Sakka 84,000. There are always four times as many *āyarakkha* as there are *sāmāṇiya*.

3. For the *aṇīya*, *kaccha* and commanders see Ṭhāṇ. 406a ff. For the special part played by Hari Negamesi comp. Jiṇac. 21. 30 (§ 17) where (see also Āyār. II 15, 4) he is called (*hiyānukampanta* (*-paga*) *deva*. He is represented by the head of an antelope (comp. JACOBI SBE 22, 227).

4. Comp. WINTERNITZ JRAS 1895, 149 ff.

partly able to interpret differently or either not at all (Ṭhāṇ. 128a; Viy. 202a; Jīv. 164b). It would take extensive tables to render the figures both relating to these gods and to the *sāmāṇiya*, and we may content ourselves with saying that the outer council is the largest and that all three of their kind are also shared by goddesses, though to a comparatively small extent only.[1]

In the afore mentioned sequence traditionally acknowledged we also find the chief Queen Consorts numbering 4 to 8 (though from Saṇaṃkumāra onward they disappear) together with their attendants, whereas we miss the ministering gods so frequently listed elsewhere (*ābhiogiya*), their absence being apparently due to their being classed with the centre world.[2]

§ 133. The activities of the godly princes and their heavenly hosts have been sufficiently explained by the description concerning their state organization faithfully reflecting human living conditions and involving their terrestrial shortcoming, i. e. rivalries and struggles. The range of power (*iḍḍhi*, Ṭhāṇ. 172a) of a god goes beyond four to five godly places pertaining to his class; beyond it he requires support (*paṛ'iḍḍhi*)). Of two gods possessing the same amount of power he will lose the battle who fails to be on the alert (*pamatta*). Circumstances permitting trickery (*vimohittā*, Viy. 498b, 637a, 751b) is employed, e. g. the producing of darkness. To a sinful heretic god it may happen that he attacks a spiritually advanced monk (*majjhaṃ majjheṇaṃ viivayai*, Viy. 636b), most certainly because in exercising magic (§ 181) he thinks him to be his like.

The life of the gods passes in a state beyond time (Viy. 522a)—since the stars dividing time merely pertain to the centre world—in the unearthly radiance of the figures with their jewelry and their princely residences (Ṭhāṇ. 263a).[3] They pass in luxury and pomp and in the enjoyment of sensual

1. With Camara in the *samiyā* 350 against 24,000.

2. Viy. 634b, also on the gradation of the three *parisā*. Comp. also LEUMANN, VIth OC III, 2, p. 491; Jambudd. V; Utt. 36, 263.

3. The decrease of this radiance indicates that the godly life in soon going to some to an end (Ṭhāṇ. 144b).

pleasures which, however, decrease in intensity according to the height of the divine abode, since it must be remembered that the mutual intercourse of the sexes is executed in ever nobler ways, until beyond the Kappa regions all desires have come to cease (Ṭhāṇ. 302a; Pannav. 547b; T. 4, 8 to 10).[1] When the gods make their appearance in the centre world it is to serve the veneration of the Titthagaras in the great moments of their lives. For the Titthagara rules the worlds : just as his birth, his departure into monkhood, his inspiration by supreme knowledge, all lighting up the whole world (*lo'ujjoya*) —while his decay and that of his teaching bury it in darkness (*log'andhayāra*)—, so they shake the seats of the gods and cause them to send rains (Viy.634b) and to draw near in veneration. Comp. Ṭhāṇ. 116a ff. Jambudd. V. In the same way the future *cakkavaṭṭi* on his campaign of conquest acts on the local deities, comp. Jambudd. III. By sympathy and apathy a god remains attached to the world (Ṭhāṇ. 144b). In the beginning of his career also private inclinations lead him back to the centre world : his gratitude towards his former teacher, his veneration for an ascetic, the display of pomp in front of his family, an appointment with a friend (Ṭhāṇ. 142b, 253a).[2] As to his faculty of crossing the world a god knows of no limits, but his interest in doing so dwindles the more the higher he is seated (Viy. 752a; comp. Umāsvāti on T. 4, 22). In order to make their appearance in the centre world the gods betake themselves to the continent of Nandissara to the south-eastern Raikara hill (Jambudd. 402a). The place where Camara manifests himself is the silver mountain of Tiricchakūḍa which does not taper off but, narrowing at half of its height, offers a plane on its top measuring about three quarters of the width of its base. It rises to 42,000 *joy.* from the Aruṇa sea to the south of the continent bearing this name (Viy. 144a). From the

1. Gods have intercourse (*saṃvāsaṃ gaccchai*) with Asuras, Rakkhasas, humans and beasts of either sex. This discrimination pertains to the popular belief, not to dogmatics. Humans (*māṇusa*) as well as beasts seem to be called *chavi* (Ṭhāṇ 193a, 274a).

2. Both passages also contain the cases where the celestial enjoyments arrest him in spite of such a natural desire.

same sea there also rise the *uppāya-pavvaya* of the Nāga and Udahi princes, those of the remaining Bhavaṇavāsī rulers partly on the Aruṇa continent and partly elsewhere.[1]

§ 134. Before we come to the end of this chapter we shall deal with some classes which, though relating to space they stand near by the hitherto mentioned Vemāṇiya, are not included by them, and to do so we have to be somewhat circumstantial. Darkness is conceived as being of a material quality (*tamu-kāya*), and this matter is supposed to be an aggregate not of earth, but of water. In the centre world, 42,000 *joy.* distant from the continent of Aruṇavara into the sea bearing the same name, darkness rises (Viy. 267b; comp. also 246b) as a wall, which, hence, must be ring-shaped, having the thickness of a space unit (§ 58) and reaching up to 1,721 *joy.* Above this height its extension increases to fill the four nethermost heavens up to the Riṭṭha region (s. b.) in the Bambhaloga.[2] As far as it extends the darkness is so intense that even a god would like to escape. Among its 13 names[3] we find the one of Aruṇodaga.[4] The upper continuation of the darkness-matter is represented by the 8 Black Fields (*kaṇha-rāī*).[5] They lie above Sanaṃkumāra and Mahinda in the Riṭṭha region of the Bambhaloga, and there are two of them in every direction, an inner and an outer one. Furthermore that much is clear that in between there are intermediate sections of the same number. That absolute darkness so characteristic of those regions does not reign there, but these sections contain the 8 abodes of the Logantiya gods (Ṭhāṇ 61b,[6] 432a, 452b; Viy. 267b: Āyār. II 15, V). They comprise Sārassaya and Āicca, 14 Vaṇhi and Varuṇa each, 7 Gaddatoya and Tusiya each,[7]

1. Dev. 46 ff.

2. *tao pacchā tiriyaṃ pavittharamāṇe* 2 . . . *cattāri vi kappe āvarettaṇaṃ* (comp. also Ṭhāṇ. 217a) *uḍḍhaṃ piya ṇaṃ jāva Bambhaloe kappe Riṭṭha-vimāṇa-patthaḍaṃ saṃpatte* Viy. 268a. For the gods as originators of a *tamu-kāya* see Viy. 634b.

3. 3 times names, Ṭhāṇ. 217a.

4. *Aruṇodaka-samudra-jala-vikāratvāt,* Vy. 270 a.

5. Incorrect JACOBI SBE 22. 195.

6. Here the *maruyā devā*, acc. to Sthāṇ. a group of the Log.

7. Ṭhāṇ. 405b, 452b.

and 9 Avvāvāha[1] and Aggicca each with each having a retinue of 100 or, resp., 1,000. In the centre of this circle forming out of Black Fields alternating with Logantiy a abodes there lies Riṭṭhābha whose gods (again 900 in number) are equally counted among the Logantiya.[2] The qualities of all these abodes correspond with those of the Bambhaloga, and as does the latter they, too, of course rest upon the hull of viscous wind.

Analogous to the Logantiya in the Bambhaloga, the Kibbisiya gods (*deva-kivvisiyā* Viy. 488b; Ṭhāṇ. 162a) in different Kappa occupy special places corresponding to their lower[3] rank already expressed by its name. According to the time their lives are supposed to last they are grouped into three classes. Those of the lowest dwell in the lower region of Sohamma and Īsāṇa, those of the middle on in that of Saṇaṃkumāra, and the uppermost in that of Lantaga.[4]

§ 135. Both the position and the kind of the place representing the abode of the Siddhas are known from Uvav. 163 to 167.[5] 12 *joy.* above the highest point of Savvaṭṭhasiddha measuring 10,000 *joy.* in diameter we find the circular shaped region of Īsipabbhārā 4.5 mill. *joy.* wide, thus extending over it like an open umbrella. Its central thickness measuring 8 *joy.* decreases towards its edge until it is even thinner than the wing of a fly. Hence it owes its name to the small inclination of its surface. Its radiance is of an immaculate white. One *joy.* above it the world comes to an end. In the uppermost part of this *joyaṇa*, or, more correctly, in its last twenty-fourth, we have the place of the Siddhas (§ 187).

1. The Avvābāha gods owe their name to their performing plays on the eye-lids of a man without giving him any physical trouble by doing so (Viy. 653b).

2. Subodhikā p. 273 (ref. to Jiṇac. 110). Here the differing forms of Aruṇa and Tuḍiya. For Aruṇa see also ZDMG 60, 323. Both the 8 Logantiya and the Riṭṭha are called 9 *deva-nikāya*, Ṭhāṇ. 516b.

3. Acc. to Sthāṇ. they are untouchable as are the *caṇḍāla* (162b).

4. The *prakīrṇaka* gods mentioned T. 4, 4 do not appear in our passages.

5. Pannav. 130b to 132b; Ṭhāṇ. 440a; Uvav. 168 to 188—Pannav. 132b to 137b=Dev. 278 to 299.

VI
RENUNCIATION

§136. The mode of life practised in the monastic community[1] is called *kappa*. While the late Pancakappa knows of up to 42 different *kappa* divided among five different methods (§52), we have but six according to the old tradition (Ṭhāṇ. 167b, 371b; K. 6, 14). Thus the monastic order, the *kappaṭṭhii*, is sixfold. Before his consecration the monk lives in the state of the *sāmāiya-* (or *s.-saṃjaya-*)*k.-ṭṭhii* (§ 138). It also includes the followers of Pāsa (§ 16) who do not take the vows. The monks of the *cheovaṭṭhāvaṇiya-k.-ṭṭh.* are exclusively followers of Mahāvīra. They have gone through with the process of taking the vows (*uvaṭṭhāvaṇa*) thus ending either their state as pupils or their membership of the *Pāsavaccijja*, unless it be that, as a punishment of the *cheya* (§ 16), they were forced to repeat it. Another pair are the *nivvisamāṇa-* and the *nivviṭṭhakāiya-k.-ṭṭh.* of those monks that were sentenced to disciplinary punishment (§ 161). The teaching of right conduct (§ 177) which starts with the two mentioned first comprises the last two by a special name. A third pair is, in a certain way formed by the *jiṇa-* and the *thera-k.-ṭṭh.* for qualifying such monks that, for the purpose of some extra self-castigation, have withdrawn from the community (§ 142), and such following the general rules. (§ 140).

All that a good monk practises or from what he abstains (*samācāra*) adds up to the *sāmāyārī*. In its special sense, however, the word applies to 10 deportments[2] of a monk referred to by Ṭhāṇ. 499a; Viy. 920b; 102 b; Utt. 26, 1-7; Āv. 7; they comprise the compliance with a wish, the admission of one's being guilty (§ 159), assent (*icchā-kāra. micchā-k., taha-kk.*),

1. For many details taken esp. form the Nijjuttis and Bhāsas the reader is referred to Sh. B. DEO, History of Jaina Monachism from inscr. and lit., Poona 1956. Rev. by ALSDORF JAOS 1959, p. 319 ff., the AUTHOR ZDMG 109, p. 225 f.

2. Thus LEUMANN, übersicht. p. 9b.

formulae for either leaving or entering (*āvassiyā*, *nisihiyā*, § 151), a request for instructions as well as for confirmation—either a question concerning oneself and someone else (*āpucchaṇā*, *paḍipucchaṇā*), placing something at somebody's disposal and giving a promise (*chandaṇā* and *nimantaṇā*), and, finally, entering upon a new novitiate (*uvasaṃpayā*). For *nimantaṇā* we also have *abbhuṭṭhāṇa*=service.

The canonical sources for what concerns monastic life are, in the first place, the Cheya- and Mūlasuttas along with Āyār. II and a number of scattered notes in Ṭhāṇ. and Viy., whereas for all question concerning laymanship the Uvās. are the main text. The late Mahānisīha holds a special position, and as to its deviations we can refer to them in a few cases only. It may suffice to refer to the AUTHOR's treatise on this work (§ 52). Rather young Dig. texts which for us take the place of the Cheyasutta or, more precisely, that of the Jīyakappa, are the Chedapiṇḍa (Cheyapiṇḍa, Chp.) of Indranandin, allegedly the 4th section of the Indranandisaṃhitā, and the anonymous Chedāṇaudi (Chṇ.), called Chedaśāstra in print In the following some few details will be pointed out to.

§137. The adherents of Mahāvīra's teaching constitute the community (*saṃgha*). It comprises both monks and nuns as well as both male and female representatives of laymanship, and hence at is called fourfold (Viy. 792 b; Ṭhāṇ. 281b).[1] The name for the monk is, partly, rather epithetic in speaking, for instance, of *cāī*, *jai*, *niyaṇṭha*,[2] *māhaṇa*, *samaṇa*.[3] The Viy. mostly speaks of *aṇagāra* and *samaṇa nigganṭha*. In the texts purely concerned with disciplinary questions the monk is called

1. When Chapp., a Dig. work, in 1, 18 states that *linga-darisaṇa* is confined to monks and both laymen and law women (called *ukkiṭṭha* and *avara-ṭṭhiya sāvaya*) and that there is no fourth group, this cannot mean that there were no Dig. nuns. For Chp. 278, 289, 258 and Chṇ. 71, 93 call the community by the name of *cauvaṇṇa* and they provide regulations for the *samaṇī*. This is also done in the Mūlācāra and by Indranandin in the Nītisāra.

2. Viy. 112b calls the layman Pingalaga (§ 17) by this name.

3. *samaṇa* and *māhaṇa* in connexion with individuals in want of help to whom the monk gives precedence—comp. gloss. on Āyār. I and the *vaṇīmaga* of 5 kinds Ṭhāṇ. 341b—probably apply to non-Jain beggars. But a *tahā-rūva*, i.e. obviously distinguishable as such, *samaṇe vā māhaṇe vā* is, in this connexion (Viy. 140b, 289a, 373a), a *nigganṭha*.

nigganṭha, *bhikkhu*, *samaṇa nigganṭha*, later *sāhu*. He is addressed by the words of *āusanto samaṇa* and *samaṇ'āuso*. Fellow-believers go by the names of *sāhammiya* and *sāhammiṇī*. The nun is called *nigganthī*, *bhikkhuṇī-*, and *sāhuṇī*.[1] There are various reasons for devoting oneself to monkdom, i.e. the *pavvajjā*, which actually mean the departure from homely life into the state of homelessness (*agārāo aṇagāriyaṃ*). The motives for doing so differ widely. They may be found either in extrinsic reasons or in some inner urge just as they may be either of a more noble or a more vulgar character, comp. Ṭhāṇ. 128b, 276a, 473a—passages which, partly, give the impression of holding up a mirror to the monks. It is certainly true that in many cases the former life of a person made itself felt also later, since we are told of nuns who are *aṭṭha-jāyā*, i.e. who are the object of some claim or other. Against inopportune elements, however, the community guards itself by means of strict rules. There is no entry (K. 4, 4) for sickly persons (*vāiya*) or such with sexual defects (*paṇḍaga*, *kīva*). The prohibition is extended (a. o. Sthān. 165a) to persons being either too young or too old, being either of a vicious nature or unqualified, being previously convicted, suffering from bodily infirmity or else not being master of themselves, e.g. on account of being involved in debts (*aṇ'-atta*). Furthermore there are the *guvviṇī* and the *bālāvacchā*. In other respects any person is free to enter and may do so even as early as a child of seven years and a half,[2] though, to be sure, at this age there can hardly be the question of voluntariness. *pavvāvettae* consists in the act of handing over the outfit, and it may be performed both by a nun and a monk.[3] It deserves mentioning that acc. to Ṭhāṇ. 56b this act as well as those immediately succeeding and, later, the studies, the confession, and the fasting-death, must be "orientated" towards the east

1. For shiftings in the usage of these words comp. the AUTHOR, Vav. p. 8.

2. The little monk Aimutta who makes a boat swim in the rain (Viy. 219a. comp. the AUTHOR, Worte p. 19) is scarcely much older.

3. Comp. the *nigganthī-pavvāviyaya* Ṭhāṇ. 314b. Haribhadra as Yākinī-dharmaputra was such a one.

and the north. The novice's head is shaved clean of hair (*muṇḍāvettae*). He is now *muṇḍa*, i.e. "bare", a word equally applied to the state following the suspension of the five senses and the four passions (Ṭhāṇ. 334b; 496a). From now on the hair may not grow to a length longer than cow-hair, and this, too, only during the rainy season. Every half month it is alternately cut by scissors (*khura*) or altogether removed by shaving; every six months or every year what of hair has grown is torn out (Pajj. 57; Nis. 10, 44). This is the act of the *loya*, comp. the *lūya-siraga* Dasā 6 XI. In the legend we read of the *panca-muṭṭhiya loya*, the act of tearing out 5 handful of hair, being performed right at the beginning of one's becoming a monk, e.g. for Mahāvīra Āyāra II 15 § 22 (a),[1] for Subhaddā Pupph. 32a, and thus it is done up to this day. This process certainly goes back to an ecstatic eruption.

§138. The beginner is given into a teacher's tutelage (*sikkhāvei, sehāvei*) and remains in the state of a novice or pupil (*seha, sehatarāga*) for at least one week, for six months at the longest, but on the average, as seems to be the case, for the time of 4 months (Vav. 10, 15=Ṭhāṇ. 129b). The novice is not yet subject to the whole austerity of the regulations; thus he is allowed to partake of alms, as a monk is not, when offered to him by the latter, provided that it does not contain anything living (K. 4, 13). The novitiate comes to an end by the novice's taking the vows for becoming a monk (*uvaṭṭhāvaṇā*, later: *dikkhā, dīkṣā*). This may not be done (Vav. 10, 16f.) before his having reached the end of the 8th year of his life.[2] A post-ponement beyond the date up to 10 days is admissable (Vav. 4, 15-17). A candidate who turns out to show the above mentioned deficiencies is granted neither admission (*uvaṭṭha-vettae, -ṭṭhā-*, Mahānis. : *dikkhettae*) nor the subsequent tutelage

1. Mahāvīra naturally follows the example of his predecessors 2-22, Usabha (1) on Indra's request abstaining from the fifth *muṭṭhi* (Hemac. Triṣ. 1, 3, 69-71).—In the Muṇḍaka-Upaniṣad which, acc. to its title, postulated the removal of the hair, HERTEL (comp. his ed. 1926, p. 65ff.) saw "distinct allusions to the teaching of the Jains."

2. This date minus the longest possible novitiate of half a year, even when no direct statement is made, results in the above mentioned seven years and a half.

nor is he made a novice (K. 4, 4). The admission implies the taking of the five vows. From here there dates the spiritual rank (*pariyāya*) commanding the relation towards the equals and, for this reason, shortened in case of offence (§ 161). He who ranges in this sequence of age is called *rāiṇīya*[1] (Vav. 4, 24f.); that it is being observed, a.o. by the younger monk (*oma-rāiṇīya* Ṭhāṇ. 240a) giving precedence to the older and by obliging him, is expressed by the word of *āhārāiṇiyāe* or *ahā-r.* (K. 3, 19-21; Vav. 4, 24-32). A monk's age of 20 years represents the *pariyāya-thera* (Vav. 10, 14).

§139. The companionship of monks and nuns in the *saṃgha* is characterized by either side observing strict retinence. It is in cases of emergency only that they are allowed to share the same quarters (Ṭhāṇ. 314a), i.e. in the very centre of the forests, at the cult place of a Nāga- or Suvaṇṇakumāra,[2] when endangered by robbers or persecutors, and, finally, in case of them should not have succeeded in finding shelter. They may speak to each other (Ṭhāṇ. 216 b) only for the purpose of asking their way and of showing it, for exchanging food and for asking it to be taken along for an equal, and as to touching a nun for the sake of assisting her (Ṭhāṇ. 327b; K. 6, 7-12) a monk may do so only in order to protect her against harm of different kind. In spite of these restrictions monks and nuns go together in forming groups called *saṃbhoga* (Uvav. 30 II, Utt. 29, No. 33; Nis. 5, 63; comp. also § 25). Sthān. 139 a defines it as a community practising in joint action the acquisition and consumption of the monk's outfit (and, probably, of the alms as well).[3] In exacting the duties of con-

1. The comm. is as wrong in deriving this word from *ratna* as is PISCHEL Gr. § 132 in tracing it from *aratni* (="ell" as a measure for fixing the time of the day by the length of a shadow). It goes back to *rayaṇi* "night" (="day") in the sense of "date". That is why the Mūlācāra of the Dig. in 1, 25 calls *rādi* (*rātry-adhika*) him who precedes in the spiritual rank.

2. This reference made to the Jain pantheon (comp. § 109) by the word of *kumāra* is, or course, secondary. We are concerned with pre- or non-Jain Nāga-stones and resp. places of the Suparṇa cult.

3. Hence the word has a wider meaning than was supposed by the AUTHOR, K. 4, 18-20. It appears that also *saṃbhunjittae* K. 4. 4; Ṭhāṇ. 56b; 164b alludes to the *saṃbhoga*, whereas by *saṃvasittae*.. (or *saṃvās.*) a different and closer living community is being meant.—BUHLER WZKM 3, 237; 4, 316 along with LEUMANN understood by *saṃbhoga* a "district-community" in the kind of the *maṇḍala* known among the Dig.

fession and service it remains within its frame (Vav. 5, 19f.). The cancellation of membership (*saṃbhoiyaṃ*—for this comp. a.o. also Vav. 6, 19f.; Āyār. II 66, 12; 106, 20. 24—*visaṃbhoiyaṃ karettae*, Vav. 7, 2-5; Ṭhāṇ. 139a; 300a; 444a) follows from reasons of discipline as is treated in detail by the Vṛtti 22bf. in the light of the twelve-fold *sāṃbhoga* Samav. 21a. As follows from Vav. 7, 1, a person becomes a member of the *saṃbhoga* by being admitted to it; this admittance is repeated when changing over to a new *s.* in case one should come from a different gana. For the *gaṇa*, as we know, is the superior unit embracing several *saṃbhoga* (comp. K. 4, 18-20). This name was already known in the early communities, since Mahāvīra's eleven disciples were called "group leaders" (*gaṇahara*) (Ther. 1). Their successors have propagated the teaching by branches and schools (*sāhā* and *kula*, Ther. 5 ff.). Hence the *gaṇa* denotes both a conception regarding the history of the teaching (§ 22) and a technical term. The same applies to the *gaccha* by which the former was replaced in the later parts of the Canon, e.g. in the Paiṇṇa (incl. the Gacchāyāra[1]) and the Mahānisīha. The branches of the Śvet. are known to call themselves *gaccha* (§ 34). Uvav. § 31 speaks of the *gaccha*, if only in the phrase of *gacchāgacchiṃ gummāgummiṃ phaḍḍāphaḍḍiṃ*. but it is not likely that they are allusions to actual groups, even though the comm. subordinates the *gaccha* to an *āyariya*, the *gumma* to an *uvājjhāya*, and the *phaḍḍa* to a *gaṇāvaccheiya* (§ 140). There may be different personal reasons (Ṭhāṇ. 381 a) for changing the *gaṇa* though this may be done once only in the course of six months (Dasā 2, 8) unless one risks to be called as *gāṇaṃgaṇiya* (Utt. 17, 17 along with comm). For leaving it needs the permission of the superior, and even a teacher who wants to do so because as a teacher he does not fill the requirements, or because he is in love, or else because he should not like to part from others leaving (Ṭhāṇ. 331b; 385b), is bound to give up his office (K. 4, 15-20). To remove obstinate from a *gaṇa* (K. 4, 25) or to refuse his admittance (Vav. 2, 6-17) is called *nijjūhettae*.

1. In the Gacch. we have *gaccha* alternating between masc. and ntr.

Among the different reasons for which a monk leaves his *gaṇa*, we also find his wish for performing an *egalla-paḍimā* (also Ṭhāṇ. 171a), i.e. one of the ascetic exercises to be described in § 157. With Vav. 1, 25-27 where his return to the old *gaṇa* is settled, there are connected (1, 28-32) similar regulations regarding his temporary withdrawal owing to his wish for seclusion, though acc. to Dasav. 12, 10, this wish must not be granted for a time longer than one year. Here as well as elsewhere (a.o. Viy. 501a, in the Nis. not before 4, 28-37) the monks are called *pāsattha*, *ahacchanda*, *osanna*, *kusīla*, *nitiya*, and *saṃsatta*.[1] These names express different kinds of displeasure and spiritual weakness. We also find the cases of an undisciplined "escape" (*ohāvai*, *ohāṇa*, Vav. 1, 33; 2, 25; 3, 18-22; 4, 14; Dasav. 11 beg.), i.e. of a monk's return to civil life.

§140. Both monks and nuns are under the command of superiors, in the first line under that of the *āyariya* and the *uvajjhāya*, to whom we have to add the *pavattiṇī* for the nun (Vav. 3, 11 f.). General expressions for subordination are *purao kaṭṭu* (*kāuṃ*) *viharai* (K. 3, 14; Vav. 4, 11; Pajj. 46. 48) and *disaṃ* (*aṇudisaṃ*) *viharai* (Vav. first 1, 22-24; Nis. 10, 11 f.). The superiors are enumerated in the order of *āyariya*, *uvajjhāya*, *pavattī*, *thera*, *gaṇī*, *gaṇahara*, *gaṇāvaccheiya* (K. 3, 14; 4, 15-23; Āyār. II 66, 33; 67, 7; 80, 31 etc.; Nandī 252b etc.), In this order of succession the *thera* is followed by the leaders for the exterior formation. The *gaṇī* by way of his name is the head of the *gaṇa*. The qualities by which he has to distinguish himself are, most naturally, eminent qualities of the mind manifesting themselves by knowledge, exemplariness, and a high proficiency in teaching, as well as such of the body represented by physical efficiency and an engaging appearance. They all go together as the 8 *gaṇi-saṃpayā* Dasā 4, 1-8=Ṭhāṇ. 422b. The duties of the *gaṇī* are dealt with by the Gaṇivijjā based on considerations concerning both the calendar and the horoscope. Here we see the

1. Examples are the nuns named Kālī (Nāyādh. II 1), Subhaddā (Pupph.), Bhūyā (Pupphacūl.) The *kusīla* of allegedly 200 different kinds is treated by Mahānis. 3.

gaṇa being summoned by him for certain ceremonies (*gaṇa-saṃgahaṇaṃ kujjā* first 27) apart from the *gaṇi*'s performing the *seha-nipphedaṇa, s.-nikkhamaṇa, vaôvaṭṭhāvaṇa* and other duties which, as will presently be shown, is the task of the *āyariya*. The *gaṇin*, however, is—to speak with Sthān. 140—*gaṇ'ācārya*. Acc. to Gaṇiv. 37 the (common) *āy.* is explicitly meant to be the object of an act performed by the *gaṇī*, and he, too (*Gaṇiv.* 40. 76), commands the *gaṇahara* and the *gaṇāvaccheiya*. The latter, being of a lower rank (see later) as is indicated by his designation presides over a part of the *gaṇa* nominally.[1] A nun occupying this office is called *gaṇāvaccheiṇī* (Vav. 5, 3f. 7-10. 16).[2] He who is pious, honest, intelligent, learned, efficient and sociable is qualified for *gaṇaṃ dhārettae*, i.e. the profession of the *gaṇahara* (Ṭhāṇ. 352b). The monk himself volunteers to take over this office, and his *thera*, provided that they can do without him, are bound to give their permission (Vav. 3, 1f.). At any rate the word of *gaṇahara* has lost much of the meaning it had in the times of the early communities.

§141. Parallel to those mentioned above the spiritual leaders in this sequence range on a descending line according to their rank.[3] At the top we have the *āyariya* who by his person embodies both the teacher and the master (*dhamm'-āyariya*), though he, too, directs the act of admitting and instructing the disciple or pupil (*antevāsī*) (Vav. 10, 11f.—Ṭhāṇ. 239b). Moreover he is bound to inspect the objects of the outfit obtained as a present and the alms that have been accepted (K. 1, 39; Dasav. 5, 1, 90; but Nis. 14, 55; 18, 25 says something the like of the *gaṇī*). The office held by the *uvajjhāya* consists in his task of instructing in the reading of the teaching's text. Where there is a discrimination being made between the text (*sutta*) and its deeper meaning (*attha*), it is the task of the *āyariya* to instruct in the latter and that of the *uvajjhāya* to do so

1. Contrary to this, however, Ācār. 322b describes the *gaṇadhara* as being the head of a group living separate from the *gaṇa* and acting for the *gaṇin*, and the *gaṇāvacchedaka* as *gaccha-kārya-cintaka*.

2. 5, 16 read *gaṇāvaccheiṇittaṃ* with the Sthānakvāsī print Haidarabad instead of *gaṇāvaccheiyattaṃ*.

3. The transl. in K. is to be corrected correspondingly.

in the former, comp. Sthān. 140a. Standing between either we have the *āyariya-uvajjhāya* (also *āyariôvajjhāya*) by whom the comm.—they might refer to Vav. 4, 11f.—mostly understand (comp. Sthān. 329b; Vy. 232a) two persons, and this may apply to the few cases where the word is in the plur., e.g. Vav. 1, 34. But thanks to what we are told (Vk. 7, 15f.; 3, 3-8) there can be no doubt that, apart from being otherwise qualified, the *uvajjhāya* in order to meet the demands of his position must have been a monk for three years running and hence, on the ground of the syllabus (Vav. 10, 20ff. § 39), must at least command the knowledge of the Āyārapakappa, while the office of an *āy.-uv.* asks for five years and the *suyakkhandha Dasā-Kappa-Vavahāra*, and that of an *āyariya* for eight years and the Ṭhāṇa-Samavāya.[1] The K. and Vav. frequently refer to the *āy.-uv.* (Ṭhāṇ. 444a to both the *āy.* and the *uv.*) in connexion with the *gaṇāvaccheiya* whom he preceds in rank since he is allowed either five or seven privileges (*aisesa*), while the latter may enjoy but two (Vav. 6, 2f.; Ṭhāṇ. 329a; 403b). He himself suggests his successor in office to be promoted (*samukkasaṇā*) (Vav. 4, 13f.), the appointment is called *aṇunnā* (Ṭhāṇ. 139a), whereas the monk on his part[2] may change the *āy-uv.* only with the consent of his superiors and by giving the reasons for doing so (K. 4, 21-23). It is a matter of course that by any culpability the qualification for teachership (*āyariyatta*) is postponed, interrupted or either altogether cancelled (Vav. 3, 9. 13—29; 4, 17; 5, 15f.),[3] unless the *kula* to which the person concerned belongs enjoys an exceptionally good reputation. *kula*, however, means a school having formed around an outstanding teacher and his followers, and two schools of such kind, when being related with each other, constitute a *gaṇa* (comm. on Ther. 5). As to the duties of a *pavattī* the texts

1. Acc. to Vav. 3, 7 the 8 years entitle to the *āyariyatta jāva* (in the Sthānakvāsi print rendered by *pavattitta theratta gaṇitta*) *gaṇāvaccheiyatta*. This does not correspond with the order of precedence, and possibly the words of *jāva gaṇ.* (and their resp. renderings) have but crept into the text after the model of other passages. Equally so in the comm. on Uvav. 31 (above § 140).

2. This does not fully harmonize with the *gaṇāv.* and least of all with the *āy.-uv.* (4, 22f.).

3. For merely pretending the virtue of an *āyariya* see Nis. 17, 132.

fail to provide us with detailed references, though acc. to Ācār. 322 p. this "promotor" is known to deal with matters of practical concern and not with instruction. His female counterpart, the *pavattiṇī*, acc. to K. 1, 41f. (and 3, 13f.) holds the position of the *āyariya*, acc. to Vav. 5, 1f., 5. f., 13f. (as compared with 4, 1f., 5f., 13f.) that of the *āy.-uvajjhāya*. To rise to the rank of an *uvajjhāya* it takes a nun 30 years and even 60 years before she is able to become an *āy.-uv.* (Vav. 7, 15f.). Acc. to Viy. 375a the *pavattiṇī* stands parallel to the *thera*. As mentioned before, *thera* (Ṭhāṇ. 516a) or *therī* does not only mean a monk or a nun with a 20 years' seniority but equally (Vav. 10, 14) any sixty years old believer (*jai-th.*) and anyone knowing both the Ṭhāṇa and the Samavāya (*suya-th.*). The facilitations referred to by Vav. 5, 17f.; 8, 5 doubtlessly apply to older people. With regard to the expression of *thera thera-bhūmi-patta* Vav. 5, 17f.; 8. 5) it appears that the quality as *thera* must be explicitly acknowledged.

§142. By force of the fifth vow (§171) the monk is unpropertied. The objects he needs do not pass for *pariggaha*; he uses them and has them for himself for reasons of piety and decency (Dasav. 6, 20f.). He receives them as alms, but he may not ask for them except within an orbit not exceeding 1-2 *joy.* (Āyār. II 96, 10; 102. 5), nor may he accept them other than in bright daylight (K. 1, 45f.). It goes without saying that he is forbidden to buy, to borrow, to barter or, least of all, to steal them (comp. Nis. 14, 1-4; 18, 21-24; 16, 25-29). The outfit (*bhaṇḍaga* Āyār. II 54, 18. 21) comprises with novices[1] in the beginning three (with females four) unmended garments, a hand-broom, an alms-bowl and a brush (*rayaharaṇa-paḍiggaha-gocchaga* K. 3, 15f.). After his being admitted the novice has as few and as bad clothes (*ahā-pariggahiya*) as may be the case. The common formula *vattha, pāya, kambala, pāya-puṃchaṇa* (e.g. K. 1, 39-41; Āyār. 1 32, 26f.; Dasav. 6, 20) has a cloth instead of the brush. Neither sequence means to be exhaustive since also other objects (s.b.) are being quoted. In making

1. This is the *tap-paḍhamayāe saṃpavvayamāṇa* K. 3. 15.

allowance for the accessories of the alms-bowl Ohaṇijj. 668 ff. (comp. also a.o. Ācār. 251a) quotes 12 or 14 different parts for the monk and 25 for the nun. The former difference explains itself by the discrimination made between *jiṇakappiya* and *therakappiya*. They are two of the six stages (*kappa-ṭṭhii*, K. 6, 14—Ṭhāṇ. 167b; 371b; § 136) pertaining to the career of a monk. While the *therakappa* stands for the traditional membership of a *gaccha*, the monk of the *jiṇa-k.* of his own free will stands outside it living for himself and observing certain rules (comp. Sthān. 169a). This certainly goes back to the idea of imitating the *jiṇa* which, however, is no longer intact at the time of our sources, since acc. to them the *jiṇakappiya* wears clothes (s.b.).

§143. The clothing (*vattha, cela, cīvara*, Ohaṇijj. 669 etc.: *pacchāga*) may be either of wool, hemp, linen, cotton or *tirīṭa* (Symplocos racemosa)-bark (K. 2, 29; Ṭhāṇ. 138a); Āyār. II 96, 2; 97, 15 does not refer to the fifth kind and divides the fourth into *khomiya* (allegedly *kārpāsika*) and *tūla-kaḍa* (*arkatūl'ādi-niṣpanna*).[1] Nothing is being said as to the colour of the material which later comes to play an important part in the history of the Order (§ 26. 36). Under certain conditions even furs (*camma*) are admissible (K. 3, 3-6; Nis. 2, 22; 12, 5 (at variance with K. 3, 4); Vav. 8, 5; Āyār. II 106, 8 (comp. 77, 32). In this connexion we hear of *camma-(pali)ccheyaṇaga* and *c.-kosaga* which, acc. to the comm., stand for strap or needle and respectively, shoes or pouches. Traces owing to wear and tear, rents, patches (*paḍiyāṇiya*? Nis. 1, 47f.) of stains, of furs with the hair worn off in places, may not be repaired (K. 3, 7-10:Nis. 2, 23f.; Āyār. I 29, 19; 35, 26, etc.; II 96. 16). For further details concerning careful treatment see Āyār.II 5; Nis. 18. The *cela-ciliminiyā* or *-liyā* (K. 1, 18) serves for protection, whereas the *cilimilī* means a curtain for the nuns' quarters (K. 1, 14).

The monk, including the *jiṇakappiya* (Ohaṇijj. 669), is allowed to have three garments (K. 3, 15, the so-called *kalpa-traya*; Āyār. I 35, 26), two of linen and one of wool (Sthān. 393b;

1. On the other hand *khomiya* (96, 25) ranges among the material forbidden for usage since it is too fine.

Ācār. 251a). A young monk of a strong physical constitution will content himself with one only (Āyār. II 96, 4) and an older one may confine himself to two, but in any case he will have to stick to the number chosen (ibd. I, 36, 15; 37, 4). In the warm season he puts off his worn out clothes and goes, as the case may be, either as *santar'uttara*, as *oma-celiya* or simply with the *sāḍa*, a cloth worn about the loins (ibd. I 36, 1, etc.). The *therakappiya* monk, finally, is bound to wear also the *cola-paṭṭa* (Viy. 374b; Ohaṇijj. 721f.) which conceals his genitals.—The nun wears the *saṃghāḍī* of which she has four in all (K. 3, 16) to be worn on various occasions (Ācār. II 176, 5, comp. SBE 22, 157[2]), and all of different width (Āyār. II 96, 6; Ṭhāṇ. 186b). She is well secured by means of 11 pieces of clothing listed by Ohaṇijj. 676f. (comp. Sādh. 23-36), while in older texts only some of them are referred to. They comprise 1. the boat-shaped bandage *oggaha*[1]*-ṇantaga* and 2. the *oggahaṇa-paṭṭaga* covering it (see also K. 3, 11 f.), 3. the two *addho'ruga*, loin cloths, 4. the *calaṇiyā* a length of cloth reaching down to her knees, 5. the *abbhintarā* and 6. the *bāhirā niyaṃsaṇiyā*, the former reaching down to the middle of her thighs and the latter going about her loins to be tied up, 7. the unsewn *kancuya* for covering her breasts, 8. the *okacchiyā* covering her breasts and her back on her right side and fastened by a button on her left, 9. the *vekacchiyā* which covers the two preceding pieces, 10. the above mentioned four *saṃghāḍī* measuring from 2 to 4 *hasta* in length, and 11. the *khandhakaraṇī* to cover the shoulders held by means of the *khujjakaraṇī*.—A wollen cloth which may be worn by either sex, is the *kambala* (Dasav. 6, 20: 8, 17).

§144. The alms-bowl is called *paḍiggahā(ga)*[2] or *pāya*, two names which are mutually exclusives.[3] In the *jiṇa-kappa* there is but one (Ohaṇijj. 679) as is for a young strong monk (Āyār. II 102, 3). Where (as in the *thera-k.*) we have two, the other one is called *mattaga*, and Ācār. 368a shows

1. Simplified form of *oggahaṇa. ṇantaga* also in *sikkaga-ṇ*. Nis. 1, 13.

2. Skt. frequently *patad-graha*, but Pkt. never *paḍaggaha*.

3. Comp. Āyār. II, 102, 1-103, 22 and 103, 23 ff. (26 *-hagaṃ* Mss.) along with Nis. 14 and variants.

that both are carried one on top of the other (in the *saṃghāṭaka*) as is still the case to-day, the one intended for solid and the other for liquid alms. Anyone destitute for one reason or the other may have a third bowl (Nis. 14, 6). These bowls either consist of a gourd (K. 5, 41f.) or else they are made of wood or clay (Āyār. II 102, 2; Ṭhāṇ. 138a; Nis. first 1, 39). Accessories are (Ohaṇijj. 668; 676; 693 ff.): *bandha*, the cord by which to carry the bowl, *ṭhavaṇa*, its foot (or its saucer ?), *kesariyā*, the dish-cloth,[1] in certain cases (K. 5, 53f.) with a handle, *paḍalāiṃ*, according to the season, 3, 5 or 7 linen cloths to cover both the bewl and the shoulders, *raya-ttāṇa*, the lid, *gocchaga*, the above mentioned brush (which acc. to Utt. 26, 23 also serves for cleaning the clothes). Nis. 1, 41f. refers to the *tuṇḍiyā* of the alms-bowl. It would, however, lead too far to give the measurements of the objects mentioned and of those to be mentioned presently.

A *mattaga* different from the one mentioned and existing in three types serves both monks and nuns for their excrements and as a spittoon during the rainy season preventing them from going out (K. 1, 16f.) It probably equals the *kamaḍhaga* attributed to them by Ohaṇijj. 675. Finally Ohaṇijj. 713 f. refers to a *mattaya* as a means of fetching and carrying away things of sorts, though a *jiṇa-kappiya* will not use it.

§145. The hand-broom, invariably referred to as *raya-haraṇa* or *pāya-puṃchaṇa*,[2] serves for clearing from living beings those places where something is to be laid down or where one wants to step on. Acc. to Ohaṇijj. 710 it represents a specifically characteristic part of the outfit. It has (K. 2, 30= Ṭhāṇ. 338b) fringes of either sheep or camel wool, hemp, *balbaja* grass (Eleusine indica)or read, while its handle is made of wood to be covered with a different material (Nis. 2, 1-8 generalized as compared with K. 5, 45f.). This cover consists of two strips of fabric called *niṣadyā* (Sthān. 339b). Acc. to Ohaṇijj. 26 the *pāya-*

1. Explained by *pātraka-mukhavastrikā*.

2. This word appears to have been formed with *madhyama-lopa*, i. . *pāda-nyāsa-pronchana*. In considering the character of the text nothing is proved by Paṇhāv. 123 thewordsapplyinga side by si de in the same comm.—For *rajoharaṇa* comp. ZACHARIAE WZKM 16, 35ff.

lehaṇiyā made of different kinds of wood is used instead of the *rayaharaṇa* during the rainy season (Sthān. 356a).

Significant as is the hand-broom so is the napkin called *muha-pottiyā* (*-patti, -pattiyā*), *m.-ṇantaga*; *mukha-vastrikā*. Acc. to Ohaṇijj. 712 its purpose is first (and in accordance with its root *pū*) to wipe insects and dust which we know to be animate, off the face—this the old teaching after Droṇa's comm.—and, second, when occupied with cleaning within the house to prevent such beings from entering into both the mouth and the nose. It is characteristic of the Jains' dependence on Brahman models that the face-cloth unknown to the latter is not referred to in the sequences mentioned § 142, nor that it appears frequently at other places (Viy. 139a=Uvās. 77; Vivāgas. 38a; Paṇhāv. 123a; Utt. 26, 23; Nis. 4, 24). At any rate we are not told that it should be used when talking with a superior, as is done by the Sthānakvāsī to-day, nor, since cultic customs are not being dealt with, that it should be applied towards the sacred figure.

As to such objects not necessarily pertaining to the outfit, the *uvaggaha* as against the *oha* (Ohaṇijj. 671, 23 ff.), the *camma, c.-kosaga, c.-cchevaṇa*, and the *cilimilī* have been mentioned above already. Of the four *uttara-paṭṭa* admitted two are the above mentioned *nisejjā* on the hand-broom, while the remaining two serve as blankets on the bed (*saṃthāra*, § 147). A further *paṭṭa* is defined as *yogapaṭṭaka* indicating that it was used for meditation or for ascetic positions. The passage referred to deals more widely with the *daṇḍaga* and the *vidaṇḍaga*, the travelling-staffs for either the dry or the rainy seasons, and with the *laṭṭhi* (Āyār. 1 43, 4), *laṭṭhiyā* (Āyār. II 77, 31; Viv. 8, 5) and *vilaṭṭhi*, which are applied differently and serve for protection, etc.

§146. Equipped with these objects monks and nuns are fit for participating in the life of the community. The rhythm of this life is controlled by the seasons. The rainless season (*uḍubaddha-kāla*) comprising winter and summer each lasting for 4 months (*hemanta-gimhāo*) is opposed to the rainy season (*vāsāvāsā*, or *-sa*) (comp. Uvav. 29). It obliges both monks and nuns to abstain from travelling from place to place (*gāmâ-*

ṇugāmaṃ dūijjittae) and to remain at a permanent residence (K. 1, 36f; Nis. 10, 40-43). The Pajjosavaṇākappa which name is more precise than Sāmāyārī give the regulations concerning this 4 months' stationary life, the *pajjosavaṇā*. According to an alleged custom of Mahāvīra's and the early community they come into power within the time of one month and a half after the rains (Pajj. 1-8) since then the prepared houses are already damaged by occupation. This licence sanctioning a belated observation of the rainy season is not in harmony with the regulation referred to by Ṭhāṇ. 308b; Nis. 10, 40f. saying that travelling *paḍhama-pāusaṃsi* is forbidden unless exceptional cases—danger, famine and other afflictions of an outward nature—enforce it. By this word we are to understand the first month of the *prāvṛṣ* consisting of Āṣāḍha and Śrāvaṇa which, again, means the first half of the rainy season altogether. Travelling in this time (see again Ṭhāṇ. 308b) is allowed but for reasons of some inner spiritual need, e.g. instruction failing to take place, etc. Walks may not exceed a certain distance (Pajj. 62). These restrictions expire 5 or 10 days after it has stopped raining (Āyār. II 82, 20, 25; Nis. 2, 50).[1] This secluded way of living is necessary owing to the abundance of life which springs up in nature and which must not be damaged (Āyār. II 82, 1). For the same reason at all times greatest care must be taken when walking, and it is this care which, as a duty, takes the foremost place among the five circumspections (*samii*, § 173). In poetry the circumspect traveller appears in various characterizations (Āyār. 1 24, 9 ff.); he must not run (Dasā 1, 1) nor is he allowed to be out at night or at dusk (K. 1, 47). In this respect Āyār. II 3 provides most accurate prescriptions. We here but mention the way of how to behave when on water (see also Nis. 18) along with the manner of resting on river banks (K. 1, 19) and of crossing great streams (K. 4, 27; Nis. 12, 42; Ṭhāṇ. 308b). Unsafe and politically disturbed dis-

1. The end of the rainy season was celebrated acc. to later sources Bhādrapada sudi 5, and tradition referring to the Jiṇacariya (JACOBI, Kalpasūtra p. 114 ff.) calls it an exceptional event that Kālaka (§ 24) antedated this celebration by one day. Comp. also § 213.

tricts should be avoided, and this warning may well be connected apart from others with the regulation that one should avoid visiting too often ten individually mentioned capital towns (Nis. 9, 19). Hence we see both monks and nuns leading a life of constant travelling, and we know of no permanent settlements. Nuns may not stay in close living communities (villages, etc.) for longer than four, monks not for longer than two months (K. 1, 6-9). We may assume that in most cases the time of their stay was much shorter, comp. the words *gāme ega-rāiyā, nagare panca-rāiyā viharanti* in Uvav. 29. Busy places like a main street, a square or a bazar and public localities as, for instance, a guest-house, the roots of bamboo and trees (comp. Ṭhāṇ. 157a), may be chosen for quarters by monks only (K. 1, 12f. 2, 11), and it goes without saying that the two sexes are not allowed to stay together in one house (K. 1, 27-30; exceptions Ṭhāṇ. 314a). For further regulations see Āyār. II 2; K. 1, 14 f. 31-34).

§147. By a certain formula, so it seems (Āyār. II 78, 8;[1] 106, 15; 108, 6), the monk introduces himself as a guest and asks the proprietor *sāgāriya*, occasionally *sāriya*) for a accommodation. This request concerns the *oggaha* of the host, i.e. the room of which he is the master.[2] So this word gave the name to the user granted by him for a limited time, the expression *ahâlandaṃ* denoting the shortest space in question. Several special cases are referred to by K. 1, 39-42; 3, 28-33; 35; Vav. 4, 20ff.; 7, 20. 23; 9, 43; the basic rule and a detailed casuistry in Āyār. II 7. Here we learn that the monk is bound to ask for the *oggaha* even for objects to be used temporarily only. The accommodation (*uvassaya*, Āyār. 1 34, II: *āvāsaha*) does not merely serve for resting (*sejjā*) but equally for ascetic exercises (*ṭhāṇa*) and either for meditation or studying (*nisīhiyā*). The resp. passages in Āyār. II 2, therefore, refer to all three cases; for the first and the third comp. also Āyār. II 8 and 9. For many reasons the quarters may not be shared by the host

1. Read *kāmaṃ*.

2. Comp. the *ogg*. of celestial and terrestrial princes and proprieors Viy. 700a.

(*sāgāriya, sejjāyara*), his family and his servants, nor may they be visited by his animals,while, at least as far as nuns are concerned, they must not lie beyond the reach of his command (K. 1, 22ff.; Āyār. II 72 ff). They may not contain any paintings (K. 1, 20 ff.), and their hight must allow for standing in them either erect or at least somewhat bent (K. 4, 28-31). Supplies of grain, meat etc. which are kept there, must be locked up; quarters in which there are pitchers containing certain beverages or where either fire or light is burning at night may be taken up in cases of emergency only (K. 2, 1-10). It is doubtful whether during the rainy season the monk was allowed two supplementary quarters as a makeshift apart from his permanent one (comp. Pajj. 60).

The resting place (*sejjā*) consists in a shake-down (*saṃthāra, -raga*) of either dry grass or hay (Āyār. II 53, 1; *dabbha-s.* Viy. 126b),[1] the above mentioned *uttara-paṭṭa* serving as a cover.[2] As is the case with some other objects (Nis. 1, 31-34; 5, 15-24), this *sejjā-saṃthāraga* is either lent to the monk for taking it away with him (*pāḍihāriya*, also *paḍi-*) or else it remains with the host (*sāgāriya-santiya*), K. 3, 25-28; Nis. 2, 53-58; Vav. 8, 7-10, and it probably applies to the first case when the *s.* is counted among the additional outfit (§ 145). Before being placed back it has to be shaken up afresh (*avigaraṇaṃ kaṭṭu* K. 3, 26). Though we are not informed as to how the *s.* was transported, it follows from Vav. 8, 2-4 that it may be light enough to be carried by one hand for five days and for one day at least during the rainy season. This difference in weight is probably due to the monk's then using a bench (*pīḍha*) or a plank (*phalaga*) instead of the *sejjā-s.*, and, accordingly, Pajj. 53 does not speak of a *sejjā.-s.* but of a *sejjâsaṇiya.*[3] Ṭhāṇ. 157a the "resting litter" is a stone or wooden plate used for self-castigation.

§148. Utt. 26 supplies the description of a monk's routine duties, and by it of all others we shall let ourselves be

1. Here as well as in the Paiṇṇas the word has also the meaning of "death-bed".

2. This may account for the comm. giving *kambal'ādi* (a. o. in Utt. 17, 7) as an explanation.

3. Read *sejjasaṇiyāṇaṃ* in 53 with AB.

guided in the course of the following. Day and night are divided into four equal parts (*porisī*, *porusī*),[1] their length changing according to the length of the day which, hence, has either 2, 3 or 4 *paya*. On days of rest and in the night the first and fourth *porisī* are for studying the sacred texts, the second is for meditating, whereas in the daytime the third is reserved to the monk's making his round for collecting alms and in the night to sleeping. Travelling is done in the first and second *por.* of the day. Such is the ground-plan into which different duties of different kind are incorporated. As to the confession of offences, if any, committed during the night, we shall deal with them in § 159. Apart from it the beginning of the day and the morning hours, comp. Utt. 26, 22 ff., are devoted to examining both the utensils and one's own body, i.e. the monk most carefully examines (*paḍilehai*) if anything animate (in the broadest sense and, hence, including dust particles) adheres to them, and what is found he removes (*pamajjai*). This examination extends even to places where something was put off (comp. K. 4, 11-13; 5, 11f., and as far as objects are concerned it is certainly not confined to those hours but is done at all times, especially so before using them (comp. Uvās. 77; Viy. 139a). While the monk is very punctilious in carrying out all this, he takes no heed of physical culture. The regulations concerning the act of dejection referred to by Āyār. II 10 cannot be counted among this point of the matter since they do not relate to the cleanliness of the performer, but to that of the locality. Acc. to Nis. 3. 4. 6. 11. 15. 17 the monk is forbidden both to oil and to wash his limbs,[2] he must abstain from treating wounds or eczemae, nor is he allowed to rid himself of vermin, to cut either his nails or little hair, and to brush his teeth. He may not even have these benefactions carried out on him by a fellow monk, let alone by a dissenter or any profane person, as little as he may carry them out on him. So then, as indicated by Āyār. II 74, 13., the presence of a monk may be scarcely

1. Comp. JACOBI ZDMG 74, 256 etc.
2. Comp. the nun Bhūyā Pupphacūl. 77a and Utt. 2, 3 f.

bearable.[1] Curiously enough Āyār. II 13. 14 is more indulgent in this point in allowing such favours being done by someone else (*para*) or, mutually, by two monks, provided that the receiver of such favour neither asks for nor refuses it—though a mutual service of this kind is difficult to imagine. K. 5, 50f. accordingly fails to refer to such cases, and the restrictions given lie in a different field.

Among the duties starting the daily routine we have, furthermore, the monk's reporting to his superior who, in cases, gives his orders. For the monk is bound to serve him as well as anyone superior to himself (*thera*), comp. K. 3, 21, if it be only by assisting him in rising from a seat or sitting down, in cleaning his things or in removing garbage (comp. K. 4, 26). This equally applies to the countenance he lends to the sick (*gilāṇa*) (comp. Nis. 10. 38f.) or to those weakened by castigation (*tavassi*). On the other hand the master and teacher is equally bound by obligations towards his pupil (*seha*). Thus the members of the community are interconnected by services (*veyāvacca, veyāvaḍiyā, kiikamma*). This is expressed not only by the personal kinds of the *vey.* mentioned above but also by the impersonal ones of the *kula-*, *gaṇa-* and *saṃgha-vey.* All 10 are referred to by Uvav. 30 III; Vav. 10, 34; Ṭhāṇ. 473b.

§149. The modes of deportment which may be added here, are attuned to the note of decency, sociability and consideration. Even a slight indication of harshness is punishable (Nis. 2, 18; 13, 13-16; 15, 1-4). Ebullitions are called *asamāhi*, disrespectfulness is known as *āsāyaṇā*; of the former we have 20 kinds, of the latter 33 (Dasā 1 and 3). The monk is obliged to behave in a strictly reserved and unobtrusive manner; when found singing, dancing, making music, imitating animal voices, laughing and disguising himself he is liable to prosecution (Nis. 4, 27; 11, 64-70; 17, 134-138). The reserve he exercises towards dissenters and profane persons (*annautthiya* and *gāratthiya*) quite naturally goes back to different causes. No more

1. The filth (*mala*) on the body of the *ācārya* Hemacandra brought him and his sect the honorary name of Maladhārin. PETERSON, Third Report p. 274 (See HERTEL, Pāla und Gopāla p. 150).

than he may call in their help is he allowed to render them a service or any other kind assistance, comp. Nis. at various places. This also applies to laymen (§ 163).

His behaviour towards the teacher is determined by the *viṇaya.* According to Uvav. 30 II; Ṭhāṇ. 407b the *viṇaya* concerns both something abstract and concrete to a wide extent; as deference, reverence and respect it is of a positive quality, whereas as restraint from and rejection of bad profane things (*apasattha*) it is negative. The way how to deport himself, and especially so in front of his teacher and master, is plastically demonstrated by Dasav. 9. The tribute externally paid to him is the *vandaṇa* which has been given its place also among the resp. formulae necessary (*āvassaya,* § 151)[1] It comprises two bows accompanied by a certain phrase as well as by certain movements and it has to be performed in the monk's normal outfit. This is obligatory for some acts, especially so for the act of confession and during instruction, and, what is more, four or, resp., three times, though it may equally be exercised on other occasions. LEUMANN Übersicht p. 11 ff. refers to it in detail by the name of the *kiikamma* which acc. to Āv. 12, comp. also Samav. 21 b, means the same.

§150. As mentioned above and acc. to Utt. 26, 12 the the first and fourth *porisī* at day and at night are assigned to instruction (*sajjhāya*). The statements made by Nis. 19, 8; Ṭhāṇ. 213 b. are more detailed and yet less accurate. They forbid lessons at dawn and at dusk, at noon[2] and at midnight, and Ṭhāṇ. allows them in the morning and in the afternoon (*puvvaṇhe* and *avaraṇhe*), at or probably until—nightfall (*paose*) and at—or probably from—daybreak (*paccūse*). Holidays are constituted by the festivals (*maha*) in honour of Indra and Skanda, of a Yakṣa or a Bhūta (Nis. 19, 11). Acc. to Ṭhāṇ.

1. In the Mahānis. (the AUTHOR p. 82f.) we are told of monks who owing to offences were unworthy for some time of accepting a salute (*avanda, avandaṇijja*). This obviously applies to the salutation of monks among themselves.

2. *majjhaṇhe* with Ṭhāṇ. Nis. has *avaraṇhe* which is obviously incorrect since in Ṭhāṇ. this means an allowed time. *puvvaṇha* and *avaraṇha* are supposed to be the first or, resp. the last *prahara* (=*paya,* § 148) of the day.

213b the *pāḍivaya* of the Inda-maha is the full moon-day in Āśvina; further *pāḍ.* are those of the Āṣāḍha, Kārttika and Sugrīṣma (Caitra); Nis. 19, 12 has the *pāḍ.* of the Bhādrapada instead of the Inda-maha referred to in 11. The hours assigned to the *sajjh.* must be punctually observed and hours not assigned to that purpose (*asajjhāiya*) may not be used for it (Vav. 7, 10-14; Nis. 19, 8. 13-16). Acc. to Ṭhāṇ. 475b an *asajjhāiya* may also be caused by certain phenomena, e.g. thunder and lightning, northern lights=aurora borealis (*disi-dāha*), dustfall (*raya-ugghāva*), lunar and solar eclipses and the miraculous appearance called *jakkh'ālitta*, but just as well by the death of a person of high standing (*paḍaṇa*), war (*rāya-vuggaha*), a dead person within the house or else by lumps of meat, blood, bones, and excrements lying close by thus adding the spacial to the temporal point of view.[1] The place of instruction is called *nisīhiyā*, and its requisites referred to by Āyār. II 2 (§ 147) are in conformity with those pertaining to the quarters as such. As demonstrated by Āyār. II 112, 11 the pupils go there in groups but careful of not coming too close to one another. From the way the instruction is performed (*sajjhāyaṃ uddisittae, samuddisittae*) we learn that the pupil—occasionally called *sissa, sissiṇī*—recites the text (*vāyaṇā*), puts questions about it (*paḍipucchaṇā*) and repeats it (*pariyaṭṭaṇā*), whereupon it is examined for its deeper meaning (*aṇuppehā*, comp. Utt. 29, 22), and finally we have some exemplary or theoretical considerations regarding the Dharma, the *dhamma-kahā*, see Uvav. 30 IV; Ṭhāṇ. 349a (not in Nis. 5. 5-11). Āyār. II 55, 9 etc. has *dhammaṇuoga-cintā* instead, a reflection on the Dharma, whereas *dhamma-kahā* stands for the sermon delivered by the teacher. From Ṭhāṇ. 210a we know that as *akkhevaṇī* it develops the teaching from within itself,[2] that as *vikkhevaṇī* it contrasts it with non-Jain teachings, that as *saṃvegaṇī* it promotes piety, and that

1. In Āv. 18 the *asajjhāiya* is given a special treatment.

2. Āyāra, Vavahāra, Pannatti (i.e. Viy.) and Diṭṭhivāya represent the Canon. Acc. to another conception the first three words do not mean texts but notions. But comp. Dasav. 8, 49.

as *nivveyaṇī* it effects melancholy. Rhetorical means of the sermon are the narrations of similes or *naya*. Their theory represented by Ṭhāṇ. 253b; Dasav. nijj. 53-88 was treated by LEUMANN ZDMG 49, 602 ff.[1] The *vāyaṇā* (as is equally said of the whole) is directed by the *uvajjhāya*, though Vav. 10, 12 speaks of the *uddesaṇ'āyariya* and the *vāyaṇayariya*. The words *heṭṭhilla* and *uvarima* used in connexion with portions of the texts (Nis. 19, 17f.) may, perhaps, show that a manuscript served as a base for instruction referring to its passages by "see above" and "see below". Reciting must be done with understanding, with accuracy, and by strictly observing the right sequence; want of self-possession and reliability is detrimental to the qualification for teaching; the teacher must be just in calling up pupils who may not speak without being asked to do so, and they are allowed but a limited number of questions (Vav. 5, 15-18; Nis. 19, 19-24). Outsiders an such having isolated themselves are not admitted to instruction (§142; Nis. 19, 25-28), nor are unsociable and inattentive monks (K. 4, 5=Ṭhāṇ. 165b—comp. § 156—, extended 246b). He who commands a portion of the text is given the permission by the teacher (*aṇunnā*, *aṇujāṇei*) to pass it on to others.

§151. In later texts we find the *porisī* assigned to studying being distinguished into *sutta-porisī* and *attha-p.* according as a text is treated by the *uvajjhāya* relative to its wording and by the *āyariya* with respect to its deeper meaning. Hence in the Mahānis. and outside the Canon we frequently read about the *gīyattha* in the sense of a thoroughly instructed monk. As now concerns the subject of instruction we have already mentioned (§ 40) the regular (*kāliya*) and irregular (*ukkāliya*) line of texts. This is the discrimination made with works not pertaining to the Anga (*aṇangapaviṭṭha* or *anga-bāhira*), provided they are no Āvassaya. By it, however, we understand, as indicated by the name, certain formulae which "necessarily" have to be known, and, what is more, from the very moment a monks start on his monastic career, since the novitiate is

1. The subject was taken up by the AUTHOR in Studia Indologica (Festschrift KIRFEL 1955) p. 297-319.

characterized by the name of the first Āvassaya (§ 136). This 1st Āv. is called *Sāmaiya,* a short vow to be brought to one's mind repeatedly during the day (§ 170) for promising to shun for life all that is blamable in thoughts, words and deeds as well as in all one has presonally caused and approved of. The 2nd Āv., called *Cauvīsatthava,* is a hymnical prayer of seven stanzas to the 24 Titthagaras. The 3rd place is taken by the *Vandaṇaga,* the formula of respectfully addressing a superior by touching his feet with one's hands followed by a humble request for indulgence (*khamemi*) towards offences committed during the day or the night. This formula contains the words of *āvassiya* and *nisīhiyā* (mentioned § 136) by which a monk unobtrusively announces his due leaving and entering to the place and those being present.[1] The 4th, called the *Paḍikka-maṇa,* is the formula used at confession. The 5th, the *Kāussagga,* introduces the low devotion (§ 161) and demands an attitude of complete immobility for the duration of one Namaskāra except for unvoluntary and insignificant movements like breathing, coughing and physical secreting. Finally and 6th we have the *Paccakkhāṇa,* expressing different modes of refusing food and drink.[2] Owing to individual versions of the 1st and the 4th laymen equally share in the *Āvassaya* (§ 164), and this is likely to account for the *agāra-* and *aṇagāra-sāmāiya* (Ṭhāṇ. 64b). As profusely the Āv. was treated in later literature (for which LEUMANN, comp. § 4, rendered an eloquent testimony,[3] as scantily it is referred to in the Canon. We have its wording not otherwise than embedded in the explaining works; Utt. 29 No. 8-13 gives but the names and Viy. 466b.; 758b but the Āvassaya group as a whole.

§152. The time devoted to studies is followed by meditation (*jhāṇa*) to be dealt with in § 180. So far as either draws upon the night, we read about the *dhamma-jāgariyā* (K. 1, 19 v. 1). To be awake (*jāgariyatta*), as says Mahāvīra Viy. 557b,

1. LEUMANN, Übersicht p. 9b f. where also the derivation from *ni-ṣīd*—with abnormal aspiration—is being made probable.
2. For *pacc.* in its ethical respects see § 173.
3. Comp. also his lecture Xth OC II, 1, 125.

is good for those that have the *dhamma*; all others should rather apply themselves to sleeping (*suttatta*), since in this state—as well as in that of weakness and sloth—they will do nothing bad. The life of the pious layman equally includes wakefulness as is demonstrated by the episode with Sankha (Viy. 552b). His wakefulness (*sudakkhu-jāgara*) goes together with that of the monk (*abuddha-j.*) and of the Arhat (*buddha-j.*).

§153. The third *porisī* of the day is reserved to the monk's round for collecting food and drink (*bhikkhāyariyā*). It does not take place—nor do rounds for other purposes—in case of heavy rainfall, fog, or dust-wind or when insects are swarming (Āyār. II 54, 25), just as it may be dispensed with if certain reasons ask for doing so (Utt. 26, 35). For his round the monk is allowed a range (*oggaha*) of 1½ *joy.* in radius, though in the rainy season this range will be limited by a larger river (K. 3, 35; Pajj. 9-13). What of alms he receives must be consumed within ½ *joy.* (K. 4, 11; Viy. 291b—Nis. 12, 30: comp. Utt. 26, 36). Newly occupied villages, especially such where metal is being hammered, must be shunned (Nis. 5, 34). Only respectable houses in contrast to the *ṭhavaṇa-kula* (Nis. 4, 22) may be visited (Āyār. II 51, 26). As to the order in which these visits have to succeed one another there are 6-8 different methods; accordingly the way may be chosen by either walking it in a quadrangle, in a zigzag line or in a spiral, etc. (Dasā 7, 1 4: Ṭhāṇ. 365b; Utt. 30, 19. 26)[1]. But the monk may just as well go from house to house, and thanks to such a *ghara-samudāṇa* Viy. 139a) he may receive a *samudāṇiya* (or *sām.*) *piṇḍavāya* (Āyār. II 53, 26. 29; Uvas. 77).[2] He is obliged to display a modest behaviour and to give precedence to other receivers (Āyār. II 57, 25; 52, 10), in Mahāvīra's praxis even to animals[3] (Āyār. I 44, 8ff.). Once turned away from the door he may not return there for a second time (Nis. 3, 13).

1. The word of *vii-pantha* occurring only in Viy. 495b equally seems to refer to the round for alms as a way going forwards and backwards like that of a wave.

2. For an explanation see HOERNLE's ann. 146. But his spelling of *samuddāṇiya* is unacceptable.

3. Comp. also the *sāṇa-vaṇīmaga* Ṭhāṇ. 341 b.

He must never stay long at one place nor stand in a lax way, and he is not allowed either to be inquisitive or to recite long quotations from the texts (K. 3, 22-24; Āyār. II 58, 28; 59, 1).[1]

Āyār. II 1 and Dasav. 5 contain many more details to which we cannot refer here, and it is especially in the latter section that we gain an insight into the deficiencies of human nature.[2] The cleanliness and, for this reason, the edibility of the alms (*phāsuya*[3] *esaṇijja*) have been treated in summarizing representation of the Piṇḍaṇijjutti. The different qualities making them to become unacceptable—and they are so even in case of doubt (Āyār. II 54, 13)—are there indicated as 15 or 16 *uggama-dosa* or mistakes on the side of the giver, 16 *uppāyaṇa-d.* or ill-gotten acquisition of the receiver, 10 *gahaṇ'esaṇā-d.* and as either 4 or 5 *ghāsa-* or *paribhog'esaṇā-d.* or unclean condition and application.[4] For these expressions compare Ṭhāṇ. 159a, 320a, 487a; Piṇḍaṇijj. v. 129ff. Some of the 46 (Piṇḍaṇijj. 659; Sthān. 159b)[5] appear in the following on the ground of the earlier texts. Viy. 291 b already says that greedily eaten food is called *saingāla*, food eaten in a state of anger *sadhūma*, and food improved by admixtures *saṃjayaṇā-dosa-duṭṭha*. These are three of the *ghās'esaṇā-dosa*.

§154. The person of the giver—mostly a woman as may be concluded from Dasav. 5, 28, etc.—is in the first line affected by the prohibition of the *sāgāriya-piṇḍa*. He who accommodates a monk may not equally treat him to food and drink (Āyār. II 78, 12; Nis. 2, 46-48; Dasā 2, 11; Viy. 231a; Dasav. 3, 5), though what of alms he gives may be accepted for the benefit of one who is ill or otherwise prevented from doing his begging round, and also for the teacher acc. to Viy. 374a (*dāvei*, K. 2, 19-28; Vav. 9, 1-30, 36-39; Pajj. 14-16). Weak and ill monks

1. The beggars in general (*bhikkhāga*) owing to their swarming in all directions are compared with fishes (Ṭhāṇ. 341 b) and owing to their obtrusiveness of different intensity with worms (*ghuṇa*) (ibd. 185 b) eating up the outer or inner bark of a tree, its wood or its pith.

2. Comp. the AUTHOR, Dasav. p. VII.

3. *sparśuka* (LEUMANN), not *prāsuka*, as tradition will have it.

4. Comp. JACOBI SBE 45, 131 ff. after the Dīpikā on Utt. 24, 12.

5. Guṇaratna in his comm. to Haribhadra's Ṣaḍdarśanasamuccaya speaks of 32 *antarāya* and 14 *mala* (ed. SUALI p. 112. 1).

are treated with consideration not only in point of food (K. 5, 49-52; Ṭhāṇ. 138a) but also in general respects (K. 3, 22; 5, 47f.; Vav. 2, 6; Nis. 10, 36-39; Āyār. I 36, 22). Nor is a monk allowed to accept any alms given by a prince or his retinue, the *rāya-piṇḍa* (Āyār. II 54, 53)[1]; Nis. 9, 1-6; 8, 13-15; Viy. 231a; Dasav. 3, 2). As is demonstrated in detail by Nis. 4, 1-6; 9, 7ff. the monks must not enter into relations with potentates, and, accordingly, Āyār. II 83, 16; K. 1, 38; Nis. 11, 71 forbid their come and go in anarchic provinces and times in order that all complications be avoided.[2] Some exceptions are referred to by Ṭhāṇ. 311b. Even he who lives in the woods or passes them in travelling may not contribute to their sustenance (Nis. 16, 12), and this probably accounts for the *kantāra-bhatta* (Viy. 231a; Uvav. 96 III). The alms, above all, must not be prepared in advance, neither for receivers of alms in general (*āhākamma*[3]) nor for him personally who is expected to ask for them (*uddesiya*), no more than they may be sent for (*abhi-haḍa*) or bought (*kīya-gaḍa*) or set aside from one's own meal (*ceiya* K. 2, 25-28; Dasā 2, 4; Nis. 10, 4; Āyār. I 36, 20; II 50, 20; Dasav. 3, 2). There is danger of such alms being offered when the monk calls on relatives or acquaintances (*nāya-vihiṃ ei*, Vav. 6, 1; Dasā 6 XI; Āyār. II 55. 30; 65, 10) or when attending a public feeding (*saṃkhaḍi* Āyār. II 52, 19; Nis. 3, 14). Nor may he visit a house where he is sure to get some (*nitiya piṇḍa*) or a certain part of the meal (Āyār. II 61, 6; 56, 16; Nis. 2, 32-36). The substance of the alms—in correspondence with the component parts of a modern Hindu meal—may consist (comp. Ṭhāṇ. 219b) in a main course (*asaṇa*), liquids (*pāṇa*), sweets (*khāima*) and spices (*sāima*). As a matter of course it

1. Comp. against this ibd. 51, 28.

2. For the expressions of *verajja-viruddha-rajja* etc. comp. N.N. LAW IHQ 1, 383-397.—Talks about the public procession and the display of power by princely persons (*rāyā-kahā*, Ṭhāṇ. 201 a) pertain to this subject, but partly also to the general talks (*vikahā*) about women, food and drink, and about the morals of other countries (Ṭhāṇ. 209 b; extended in 403b). They do not help the monk or the nun to profit by them, but, on the contrary, they help to bring them off the right path (Ṭhāṇ. 221 a).

3. Acc. to LEUMANN ZDMG 37, 495=*yāthākāmya*. The Skt. transcription invariably has *ādhākarma*. For the Karman sequence regarding the eating of *āh.* comp. Viy. 101 b=314 b.

must be of course free of life[1] (comp. Āyār. II 50, 1; 63, 5; K. 1, 1ff.; Nis. 15, 5-12; 16, 4-11; Dasav. 5, 2, 14-24). These passages and others refer to vegetables and fruit only, but it is evident that meat and fish in a live state were not less forbidden. Whether or not they were allowed to be eaten in a lifeless condition is a matter of interpretation. The vegetarian standpoint is strongly maintained.[2] Thus the words *bahu-y-aṭṭhiya maṃsa* and *bahukaṇṭaga maccha* or *aṇimisa* are meant to indicate a "flesh" of fruit and fish interspersed with kernels and stings. On the other hand we learn from Āyār. II 65, 33 (=II 1, 9, 3: Ācār. 321a) that in the interest of a sick monk or nun some meat or fish just being prepared for a guest may be asked for by a monk passing incidentally. In the case of Āyār. II 67, 23 (=II 1, 10, 5) acc. to the Cuṇṇi (344b) a layman or a lay woman must not rebuke a monk asking for meat or fish for the same medical reason. And Dasav.-cuṇṇi (184 b) as well as Haribhadra (Dasav.-ṭīkā 176 b) would not have justified Sūtra 5, 1, 73 by referring to peculiar circumstances (*kaṃci kālaṃ desaṃ paḍucca*, resp. *kāl'ādy-apekṣayā*) if cases of non-vegetarianism were considered to have been totally excluded in those remote times. But, of course, the old scholiasts are anxious to put aside the literal meaning of *maṃsa* and *maccha* in favour of the metaphorical one as fruit or trees, and Śīlānka (Ācār. 323 b) goes to the length of taking them as prescribed by an able surgeon for exterior application (!) to cure a cutaneous eruption.

As follows from Sūy. I 2, 2, 18-20; 3, 3, 12; 3, 4, 1-4; 7, 12; Āyār. I 3, 20-23, etc. the monk may neither drink nor use cold water, i.e. water in its natural state. It must be boiled and is then called *udaga-viyaḍa* (K., Nis., Āyār. II, etc.). Even externally no live matter may adhere to the food, comp. Āyār. II 49, 1, and it must not stand on natural ground (Āyār. II 61,

1. Hence *maḍāi* (*mṛtādin*) *niyaṇṭha* Viy. 110 b.

2. KAPADIA Rev. Phil. Rel. 4 (1933), 2 p. 232-239 apart from his own scholarly deductions reproduced a letter of JACOBI's trying to solve the problem in a most ingenious manner.

10, 28; 60, 5; Nis. 17, 126-129). Another important question is whether the vessel or the hands of either the giver or the receiver of the food or the beverage are moist (*saṃsaṭṭha*, Āyār. II 59, 5; Dasav. 5, 1, 31-36) or not. This leads to establish 7 different ways of how the monk must have alms being given to him (*piṇḍ'esaṇā, pāṇ'es.* Āyār. II 69, 7; Ṭhāṇ. 385 b).

§155. What food has been received on a round for alms (*piṇḍavāya*) must be shown to the Guru (Āyār. II 67, 4; Dasav. 5, 2, 31) and it must be sufficient for the needs of a healthy person, while only he who feels weak (*no saṃtharai*) may repeat the round (K. 5, 54; Dasav. 5, 22), as a nun may a when having received but very little, a *pulāga-bhatta*, as the figurative expression has it. 32 bits (*kavala*) of egg size are considered a normal quantity (Viy. 292a—Uvav. 30 II—Vav. 8, 18). As was pointed out above, the round may be done but once in a day, during the 3rd *porisī*, and what has been received must be consumed within a certain spacial and, hence, also temporal limit.[1] To receive food in the dark is forbidden by K. 1, 43, and it is out of the question to consume it as *rāi-bhoyaṇa* (§ 171), comp. K. 5, 6-91, nor is it allowed to keep it for the next day (K. 5, 49) except in cases of heavy illness. But yet K. 4, 11—Nis. 12, 30 and Viy. 291b refer to food received during the 1st *porisī*, i.e. in the morning. It remains but to assume that in this case it was brought to the monk[2] and this must equally apply to such food as was accepted before sunrise and consumed after it (Viy. 291 b). That there is an early meal is also demonstrated by calling certain fastings by the name of *cauttha-bhatta* and the like (§ 156).

§156. Uvav. § 30 III; Sūy. II 2, 72; Ṭhāṇ. 296a f. quote a large number of different methods as to how food may be asked for and taken by a monk. The acceptance of either the one or the other of these methods appertains to the province of a s c e t i c i s m or self-castigation to which we now proceed. Physical asceticism (§ 178) is known to concern, for its greater

1. It is not said that what has been received must be eaten while standing. This is the case with the Dig. (*sthiti-bhojana*; also *ubbh'asaṇa* etc. Chapp. 1, 14 = *ūrdhvâśana*, comm. erroneously *udbha-bhojana*).
2. This is implied by *ānīta* Sādhudinakṛtya 277 (§ 201a).

part, eating and drinking. There are but few methods occurring apart from those quoted in the texts. The *saṃkha-dattiya* confine themselves to a certain number of ways regarding the reception (*datti*,[1] Vav. 9, 40) of food and drink. Those among them observing the *java-majjhā* and the *vaira-majjhā canda-paḍimā* (Vav. 10, 1; Ṭhāṇ. 64b) follow the example given by the waxing and waning moon. Starting with 1 *datti* on the 1st day of the bright half of the month the former take 1 *d.* more every day for a fortnight's time proceeding up to 15 *d.* taken on full moon day and then to decrease the d. in the same way. In the *vaira-m. c.-p.* the number of *d.* increases during the dark half of the month to decrease during its bright half, so that here the lowest point or the state of contraction fall on full moon, while there it is the highest point or the state of expansion that do so, and hence the names. *paḍimā* in the frequent usage of the word[2]—as Samav. 96a wants it there are 92 *paḍ.* in all—is explained by *abhigraha*. By Ṭhāṇa 64b; 195a we come to know them as interior (*samāhi-p.*) and exterior (*uvahāṇa-p.*) ones. Other exercises do not proceed from day to day but at a much slower pace. They take 7 times 7, 8 times 8, 9 times 9 or 10 times 10 days and are accordingly called *satta-sattamiyā* etc. *bhikkhupaḍimā* Vav. 9, 31-34; Ṭhāṇ. 385b; 440a; 518b. During the first 7, 8, 9 or 10 days 1 *datti* is taken daily, during the second 2 daily, etc. so that all *d.* sum up to 196, 288, 405 or 650. All these methods already positively concern the quantity and would therefore, come under the *omoyariyā* or the restriction of food. Uvav. § 30 II=Viy. 292a=Vav. 8, 16 here quotes that instead of 32 morsels one takes but 31, 24, 16, 12 or 8, or that either one diminishes each figure by 1. As against that the *aṇasaṇa*, as far as it is only temporary (*ittariya*),[3] consists in the dropping of the meals. If one half of the day remains without a meal being taken we have the *egâsaṇa* fasting, and in case it be the first half we have the *purim'aḍḍha* (comp. § 161).

1. *dattiḥ sakṛt-prakṣepa-lakṣaṇā*; *eka-kṣepa-bhikṣā-l*, comm. In doing so *bhikkhā* Vav. 9. 31-34 is unprecisely equated with *kavala* Sthān. 65 b.

2. And equally so with the 91 *para-veyāvacca-kamma-paḍimā* Samav. 95a.

3. For fasting leading to death (*āvakahiya*) see § 165.

cauttha-bhattiya, *chaṭṭha-bh.*, *aṭṭhama-bh.*, etc. is called he who refuses to take food until the 4th, 6th, 8th, etc. meal, i.e. who spends 1½, 2½, 3½, etc. days by fasting, though he may take certain drinks differing as the case may be (Ṭhāṇ 147a). The *moya-paḍimā* (Vav. 9, 35; and comm. Ṭhāṇ. 64b; Uvav. 24) as a "small one" lasts 6½ as a "large one" 7½ days; for both of them the drinking of urine (*mokaṃ kāyikī*) was obligatory.[1] Either was reserved for monks of a strong constitution at the beginning or the end of the hot season. The *cauttha-* etc. fastings are arranged in artificial systems and sequences. We find their names in Uvav. 24; Ṭhaṇ. 292a, while the ways as to how most of them and some others are being practised are referred to in Antag. 8.[2] The *kaṇag'āvalī*, for instance, appears as follows: 4 (abbreviation for *cauttha*, the following accordingly); 6; 8; 8 times 8; 4 up to 34; 34 times 8; 34 down to 4; 8 times 8: 8; 6; 4. This sums up to 522 days in all. Moreover we have the "short" *savvaobhadda-paḍimā* of 100 and the "long" *s.-p.* of 245, the "short" *sīha-nikkīliya* of 187 and the "long" *s.-n.* of 462 days apart from several more up to the *rayaṇ'āvali* of 472 days. In all cases, however, the individual fastings are interrupted by times of recreation (*savva-kāma-guṇiyaṃ pārei*). The female ascetics of the Antag. carry out such fastings four times each in succession and in connexion with the changes as to the contents of the meals allowed to them (see below). By ascetic positions (§ 157), however, the *guṇarayaṇa-saṃvacchara* cycle of 16 months' duration is intensified, and the way they act upon the fasting Khandaga is illustrated by Viy. 123b, comp also Antag. in BARNETT on p. 56. The third aspect of asceticism in eating, and drinking is the change of food, of which Uvav. § 30 IV gives nine different kinds (comp. also Ṭhāṇ. 296a) by the name of *rasa-pariccāga*. We here point out the abstention from the 10 *vigai*, i.e. milk and its products *dahi*, *sappi*, *navaṇīya*, *ghaya*, oil, fat, honey, meat and marrow (Ṭhāṇ. 204 b; 450 b). Accordingly we speak of the *nivvīya*.[3] We are

1. Malayagiri's *āḍātavyam* in the AUTHOR'S ed. of Vav. p. 32 ult. is wrong for *āpātavyam* (=*āīyavve* of the Sūtra).
2. Comp. also BARNETT, Antag. p. 98ff.
3. For *nivviiya*=*nirvikṛtika*.

told that he who is not able to brace himself upto this abstention (*vigaī-paḍibaddha*) may attend lessons no more than he who is illmannered (*aviṇīya*) or unsociable (*aviosaviya-pāhuḍa*, K. 4, 5). But *vikṛti* here certainly stands for "ill-humour", and what is meant is a monk of moods easily getting out of tune. The *āyaṃbiliya* owing to his disposition to sourness has to content himself with eating the sour porridge called *āyambila*.[1] The words of *panta* and *lūha āhāra* are, so it seems, expressions of general meaning denoting old and, hence, dry leftovers.

§157. According to their time of duration we have 12 different *bhikkhu-paḍimā* referred to by Samav. 21b and illustrated by Dasā 7. The first seven last 1 to 7 months (*māsiyā*, *dom.*, *tem.*, *etc. bh.-p.*), the 8th to the 10th 7 days, the 11th is *aho-raiṃdiyā*, the 12th *egarāiyā*. For the seven month's *paḍimā* the principle of *jettiyā māsā jettiyā dattīo* (§ 156) as to solid and liquid food prevails. For the one month's *p.* we have an additional number of complicating regulations. The shorter they are the more the strains grow in that certain ascetic positions (see below) preceded by a *cauttha-* to an *aṭṭhama-bhatta* become obligatory. For doing so the monk (see also Ṭhāṇ. 147b) who carries out the 12th *paḍimā* after a 3½ days' fasting without taking any liquid food, i.e. continuing outside as village for one night with his body slightly bent forward (*īsiṃ pabbhāra-gaeṇaṃ kāeṇaṃ*), his eyes fixed on an object, his feet close together, his arms hanging down, is rewarded with attaining the three supersensual forms of cognition (§ 78), while if he fails he is doomed either to madness, long illness or apostasy. Anyone performing one of these *paḍimā* does not take part in the life of the Gaṇa, he is an *egalla-vihāri* (Vav. 1, 25-27). It goes without saying that only a deserving monk will have the teacher's permission for doing so (Ṭhāṇ. 416a). For the modes of expression he is allowed to apply see § 74.

The repeatedly quoted positions are listed in Uvav. § 30 V; Ṭhāṇ. 387b among the *kāya-kilesa* which form another component part of asceticism. The general expression applied

1. For derivation see BARNETT, Antag. p. 99 PISCHEL, Gr. §137.

by Āyār. II 2 preceding *sejjā* and *nisihiyā* is *ṭhāṇa* (*ṭhāṇaṃ ṭhāi, ṭhāṇaiya*). The positions are 1. lying: *uttāṇaya, uttāṇa-sāi* stretched out on the ground, *pāsillaga* sidewise, *daṇḍ'āyaiya* with feet outstretched, *lagaṇḍa-sāī* with hollow back. Then follows 2. the squatting position with the *vīr'āsaṇiya* and *ukkuḍuya*. Acc. to Ṭhāṇ. 300b the latter is a sitting position, i.e. one of the 5 kinds of the *nesajjiya* among which we have also the *godohiya* (Dasā 7). The above mentioned performer of the 12th *padimā* and others mortify their flesh in standing erect as do those who stare into the sun with one foot lifted up and both arms raised (K. 5, 22). *āyāvaṇāe āyāvettae* here refers to one exposing himself to the blazing sun,[1] comp. *āyāvaga* Uvav. and Ṭhāṇ. The *avāuḍa* exposes himself to the cold, the *akaṇḍuyaga* to insects (comp. Āyār. I 41,21). and the *aṇiṭṭhubhaga* refrains from spitting, a habit probably popular already in those days. The nuns (K. 5, 19-34) are allowed to exercise physical asceticism to a very small extent only. When exposing themselves to the blazing sun they may do so only by wearing not more than 1 *saṃghāḍi* and by standing on a level ground within the enclosure of their quarters.

§158. Voluntary asceticism has some points of contact with the compulsary forced upon a monk for punishment. Punishment is the consequence of guilt, and guilt, as § 168 will show, is something leaving the path of truth, hence being called *māyā*; *māī* he who has made himself guilty, *saṃphāsai māiṭṭhāṇaṃ*.[2] A monk caught in three *māi-ṭṭhāṇa* in the course of one month and in ten in the course of one year makes himself guilty of *sabala* (Dasā 2, 20). We have 21 *sabala* which, acc. to Dasā 2; Samav. 32a, range among gross offences, whereas the 20 *asamāhi* (Dasā 1; Samav. 37b) are considered acts of rashness rather than of calculation. Improper behaviour towards an older monk is gathered up in 33 cases called *āsāyaṇā* (Dasā 3; Samav. 58b). A sin not confessed is a *salla* (§168; Mahānis. 1, 16; comp. Utt. 26, 24).

1. The translation K. 5, 22f. must be corrected.

2. i.e. *māyi-sthānam*, neither *mātṛ-sth.* (Śilānka on Āyār. II, 53, 27) nor *māyā-sth.* (JACOBI on Sūy. I, 9, 25).

For instituting further proceedings every offence committed by oneself (*akicca-ṭṭhāṇa, paḍisevaṇā*) must be reported (*āloettae*; comp. Viy. 498a) to the teacher (*thera*, resp. *pavattiṇī*). This asks for self-victory as developed by breeding and instruction (Ṭhāṇ. 423b; 484a). In the motives inducing a monk not to confess we are shown the deficiencies of human nature (Ṭhāṇ. 137a; 417a), thus when saying to himself "it cannot be helped" or for fear of slander, or in the reasons for yet confessing his guilt for fear of the verdict of the teacher and of his fellow monks, of the Karman consequences and of his own conscience, and finally 10 *dosa* (Ṭhāṇ. 484a; Viy. 919a) in the way he makes his confession, i.e. with reservations within and tricks without. Insincerety, however, adds to the punishment (Vav. 1, 1-20 = Nis. 20, 1-20).

§159. The qualities of him who accepts the confession is demonstrated by Ṭhāṇ. 423b; 484a. He must be pious, attentive, experienced in practical affairs, gifted with the power of inspiring trust (*ovīlaga*), energetic (*pakuvvaga*), discreet (*aparissāī*), convincing (*nijjavaga*) and ready to allow extenuating circumstances (*avāya-daṃsī*). If by force majeure the monk was prevented from seeing the teacher—in which case he becomes an *amuha*—he is not liable to reproach (Viy. 375a). Hence, when the teacher is absent he is (acc. to Vav. 1, 34) represented by a number of substitutes i.e. by a member of the same *saṃbhoga* (§ 139), by one of another *s.*, by a layman going through the (temporary) career of a monk (*sārūviya*, § 163) or by one of the common kind (*sammaṃ-bhāviya*). When even one of the latter is not at hand, the monk makes his confession under the open sky in the spiritual presence of the Siddhas. Performed in this way, however, the act has no further consequences, whereas in the normal case it entails the criminal procedure.[1] The same applies to the confession made by a monk before his death (§165). It is equally requisite (Vav. 1, 25-32; 6, 10 f.; 7, 1) when a monk enters into a new *gaṇa* or when he returns to his former after having gone through an

1. Yet this is also maintained in the Sūtra referred to.

ascetic exercise. Self-accusation (*āloyaṇā*) is invariably bound up with one's confessing one's guilt (*paḍikkamaṇa*), and only if both go together we come near to the western act of confession. The word applied for it signifies the return, and in the fivefold *paḍikkamaṇa* relative to "influx" (§ 167 f.), heresy, passion, etc. (Ṭhāṇ. 349a) it has the meaning of "conversion." Its literal meaning is intermixed with the sixfold *p.* (Ṭhāṇ. 378b) as far as reference is being made to one's return from having relieved nature or either from sleep (*uccāra-p.*, *pāsavaṇa-p.*, *somaṇ'antiya-p.*). The confession which, now, concerns us here and which, like that formula, culminates in the words of *tassa micchā me dukkaḍaṃ* is made at certain appointed times: in the early morning for offences committed during the night (*rāiya* p.), in the evening for such committed during the day (*devasiya* p.) and for the purpose of confirmation and also for making good in a more solemn way at the end of each half of a month (*pakkhiya p.*—hence the name of Pakkhiya Sutta (§ 55)—, after a lapse of 4 months (*cāummāsiya p.*) and after 1 year (*saṃvacchariya p.*). So then also in this respect the *p.* is fivefold. The proceeding is demonstrated in the comm. by Yaśodeva (p. 82) in the words of the Pakkhiyacuṇṇi and the Āvassayac. important mainly for the lecture delivered by the Paḍikkamaṇa-Sutta[1] (§ 55) and the prayer for remission (*khāmei*, *khamāvei*) directed not only by a younger monk to an older according to seniority but also by the teacher (*guru*) to his group and, what is more, to the youngest first.

§160. What lies between the confession of guilt and the acceptance of the penalty inflicted upon the confessor (*ahā' rihaṃ pāyacchittaṃ paḍivajjittae*) is rendered by the texts (e.g. Viy. 375a; Ṭhāṇ. 56b; K. 4, 25) in the words of *ninditae garahittae viuṭṭettae visohettae akaraṇ(ay)āe abbhuṭṭhittae.* The first two say that the delinquent reproves himself in front of himself and his teacher,[2] the second pair expresses the process of the

1. Literally printed from a ms. by WEBER Verz. II, 739-741. All sentences throughout start with *icchāmi paḍikkamiuṃ* to end with *tassa micchā mi dukkaḍaṃ* (a Śloka-pāda).

2. In verses Caus. 50-54 *garahai* between *udīrai* and *saṃvarai*, see Viy. 57b; theorizing Ṭhāṇ. 43b; 112b; 213b.

inner purge from ill-doing, and the last two the will to amendment. The further proceeding (*vavahāra*) is theoretically, as the case may be, determined by superior cognition (*āgama*), traditional prescriptions (*suya*), a commission sent over a long distance (*āṇā*), a regulation (*dhāraṇā*) or by a habit legitimated by the qualified (*jīya*) (Vav. 10, 2) in that always the following comes in with the absence of the preceding (Ṭhāṇ. 317b; Viy. 383a; comp. LEUMANN, Jīt.p. 1196). In praxi we have but the *suya* (K. 5, 25) as a necessary evidence for the execution (*paṭṭhavaṇā*), *paṭṭhavei*), while the *vavahāra* is merely mentioned as a "lightest possible procedure" (*ahā-lahusae nāmaṃ vavahare*, K. 5, 53; Vav. 2, 6-17).[1]

§161. The frequently quoted[2] stanza Āv. 19, contains 10 different forms of atonement, an enumeration probably going back to Uvav. § 30 I (also Ṭhāṇ. 484a; incomplete 355b; 423b; 453a), where atonement (*pāyacchitta*,[3] frequently also *pacchitta*) is coordinated with inward asceticism. The first two forms are report (*āloyaṇā*) and confession (*paḍikkamaṇa*). Now, certainly, there are offences which by merely reporting them are atoned for, whereas there is no confession possible without *āloyaṇā* or else both must go together (*tad-ubhaya* or *mīsa*, the third form). Hence to count *paḍikkamaṇa* individually comes up to mere schematism. The sequence continues by giving (4.) *vivega*, the renunciation of the corpus delicti, and (5.) *viussagga*, standing motionless with one's arms hanging down. Under the name of *kāussagga* this is (so also Ṭhāṇ. 212b)part of the ceremonial observed in the act of confession etc. and may be called "low devotions", particularly as its duration is determined by the time it takes to say one or several *namaskāra* formulae.[4] In the Jīy. the time is a measured

1. The classification into 3 times 3 *vav.* communicated by the AUTHOR, Kalpasūtra p. 14 footnote is obviously a mere construction.

2. LEUMANN, Jīt. p. 2. For a Dig. analogy see Chp. 174 (§ 136).

3. This in the case of an offence and of a combination of such, and it is decreed as an additional punishment (§ 162) as well as for insincerety in confessing (Ṭhāṇ. 199a).

4. *namo arihantāṇaṃ, n. siddhāṇaṃ, n. āyariyāṇaṃ, n. uvajjhāyāṇaṃ n. loe savva-sāhūṇaṃ.* Then there follows the presentation of this formula in the famous Śloka: *eso panca-namokkāro savva-pāva-paṇāsaṇo, mangalāṇaṃ ca sa-*

by breaths, and we there read of *viussagga* which have to last for 8, 25, 100, 108, etc. up to as many as 1008 *ūsāsa*. If in Ṭhāṇ. 64b both *vivega* and *viussagga* are called *paḍimā*, it may be assumed that the former word stands for the spiritual and the latter for the physical "position". (6.) *tava* is the food either reduced, dropped or changed. The forms previously mentioned as well as those ranging from 7 to 10 (*cheya*, *mūla*, *aṇavaṭṭhayā* and *pāranciya*) are dealt with by the Jīyakappa (§ 52), while in the older disciplinary collections we meet but with concrete cases of the last four. In K. and Vav. the *cheya* mostly appears in connexion with the *parihāra*. In this book we must, however, deny ourselves the discussion as to what offences ask for what atonements, but it deserves mentioning that in the non-disciplinary parts of the Canon there is no reference whatever being made to punishments of this kind.

§162. (7.) *cheya* means the reduction of the monk's age (§ 138). Among the Śvetāmbaras as well as among the Digambaras this punishment gave the name to one group of disciplinary texts each, comp. the Cheyasutta, Indranandin's Chedapiṇḍa and the Chedāṇauḍī (§ 136). Where we are able to make out the duration of an offence we find that with a common monk the *cheya* amounts to the fivefold, with the *uvajjhāya* to the tenfold, and with the *āyariya* to the fifteenfold of it (Cuṇṇi on K. 5, 5), and it may well be that this is what in the Sūtra is expressed by the word *s'antarā* (=*sva-kṛtād antarāt*). The *parihāra* means a "special position" mainly with regard to diet. Sthān. 168b gives the differences in diet fasting according to the different seasons. Acc. to Jīy. the restrictions concern the constituents mentioned § 156, they merely allow of *nivvīiya*, *āyambila*, *egâsaṇa* or *purim'aḍḍha*.[1] For other regulations regarding alms see K. 4, 26; Vav. 2, 28-30. They rest on the

vesiṃ paḍhamaṃ havai mangalaṃ (printed along with other formulae in the ritual books). Canonical only Mahānis. 3 II (the AUTHOR p. 14). For a dispute concerning the wording (*havai* or *hoi*) see WEBER, Kup. p. 811.

1. For the 3rd and 4th word Chp. and Chn. have *ega-ṭhāṇa* and *purimaṇḍala*. There all four words and, additionally, *khamaṇa* (=*upavāsa*) are called the 5 *kallāṇa*.

fact that the *parihāra-kappa-ṭṭhiya* is obliged to render service to the *thera* from which he is released only temporarily (K. 5, 53; Vav. 1, 22-24). Strictly speaking he stands outside the *gaṇa* (comp. Vav. 2, 6), and he joins the others neither in their obligatory rounds nor in their travelling (Āyār. II 50, 7=Nis. 2,40—42; Nis. 4,112). If several monks of a closer companionship have committed an offence and, hence, are under *p.*, always one of them is except from it and considered *kappāga* (= *kappa-ṭṭhiya*, § 136), to be served by the others. He will atone for his guilt (*nivvisai*)[1] after them (Vav. 2, 1-4). By the same word the *nivvisamāṇa* is distinguished from the *nivviṭṭhakāiya* (K. 6, 14=Ṭhāṇ. 167b; 371a). The principle of inequality which governs the life within the Order is complied with by alternately dividing such a group into *parihāriya* (also *pāri-*) and *aṇuparihāriya* (for which see Vav. 2, 5) with the latter serving the former (Dīp. on Utt. 28, 32).

The *parihāra* is pronounced in two ways according as a reduction is admissible or not (*ugghāiya* or *-ima* or *aṇuggh.* K. 4, 1=Ṭhāṇ. 162b; 311a).[2] In K. and Nis. (comp. Nis. 1 end etc.) the duration is either one or four months, Vav. 1-20 has all numbers upto six. For the distribution of the restrictions on one, four or six months and their calling them *lahu* and *guru* comp. the Cuṇṇi on Jīy. 61 and Kalpasūtra p. 14 footnote. Though for an individual offence the *p.* does not extend over a period longer than six months, yet its duration will be extended if within this period a new offence is being committed (Nis. 20, 21-53). Then an additional *p.* (*ārovaṇā*) is due amounting to 20 or, resp. 15 days if the new offence is subject to a *p.* of two or, resp. one month. As to additional *p.* charged for new offences of three to six months the Nis. cuṇṇi (fol. 650ff.) gives the following extra charges: with 3 months 25 days, with 4: 30, with 5: 35, and with 6: 40.

As we have seen the *cheya* reduces the spiritual age of a

1. In his translation of K. 3, 13 this word was misunderstood by the AUTHOR.—Comp. also Vav. 1, 17.

2. Chp. 204 (*aṇ*)*ugghāḍa*.

monk. If reduced without a remainder the monk is punished with the (8.) *mūla*, i.e. by repeating the act of consecration he starts right "from the bottom." The comm. attach some importance to the *mūla* (Chp.: *mūla-khidi*, *m.-bhūmi*), whereas the Canon neglects it altogether. From this "new start" the (9.) *aṇavaṭṭhappa* (K. 4, 3=Ṭhāṇ. 162b)—adj. to *aṇavaṭṭhayā*—distinguishes itself in that the offender has to temporize for an interim till the act of consecration can be once more performed on him. Since during this interim, acc. to the comm., fastings have to be exercised, it may be assumed that it is limited according to the case. However, the offender can be re-consecrated only when, in the meantime, he has conducted himself like a layman (as opposed to a profane person), provided that the *gaṇa* he is to belong to categorically asks for it (Vav. 2, 18f., 22). The same applies (Vav. 2, 20f. 23) to the (10.) *pāranciya* (K. 4, 2=Ṭhāṇ. 162b; an abstract subst. is missing).[1] He is excluded from the community of the monks, and no reference is made as to his being re-admitted. Yet his readmittance is possible, as we learn from those Sūtras. But we have to consider that it is not offences but qualities of character that make a *pāranciya*: he is bad, frivolous or of a homosexual disposition (*anna-m-annaṃ karemāṇe*). That is why in praxi his classification as a *par.* comes up to his permanent exclusion, all the more since his subsequent conduct as a layman does not necessarily imply his re-consecration.

§163. The *saṃgha* is constituted not only by monks and nuns but by laymen and lay women as well (§ 137). The latter two are called *samaṇovāsaga* and *-siyā*, abbreviated *uvāsaga* and *-siyā*. Other names are *sāvaga* and *sāviyā* (along with the preceding pair Āyār. II 92; Viy. 221b), *saḍḍha* (e.g. Āyār. II 69, 15; 75, 22) and *gihī* (e. g. Vav. 2, 18-23). The *sāgāriya* which in itself means the same (Vav. 4, 18f.; 9, 1-30 *sāriya*) is the host (§ 147), the *gāratthiya* and the *gāratthiṇī* are complete strangers to the community of true believers by whom

1. In Chp. 174. 262 ff. the 9th and 10th form are comprised as *aṇupaṭṭhavaga* and *pāranciga* under (9.) *parihāra* (comp. also Mūlāc. 5, 165). Here the *saddahaṇā* leading through *nindaṇa* and *garahaṇa* (comp. § 160) to the *sammatta*, i.e. to righteousness, is considered as the 10th form of the *pāyacchitta*.

they are even avoided (§ 148). An expression for the layman taken from the ethics (§ 168) is *desa-viraya*, i.e. "he who observes but part of the main regulations" (Bhattap. 29, 34; Āurap. 7; Caus. 57) as opposed to the *savva-v.*, the monk.

Ṭhāṇ. 242b says that a layman may wave to and fro like a flag, that he may either offer resistance like a picket or else be provocative like a thorn-bush (*khara-kaṇṭaya*), while on the other hand he may reflect the picture like a mirror. All this certainly goes back to his attitudes taken towards the wishes or the instructions on the part of either the monk or the nun. He is bound to grant them shelter, food, equipment and, in certain cases, to nurse them (comp. Uvās. 58 where, at the same time, it is emphasized that monks and nuns should observe a reserved attitude towards heretics and profane persons), and this certainly explains why, in the passage quoted, he is compared with father and mother, brother, friend or wife (*savattī*). For the hospitable welcome of a monk comp. Vivāgas. 2, 1. The moral value of giving alms is demonstrated by Viy. 289a; 373a. Nothing, however, is said in the Canon regarding the services rendered by a layman for the general welfare, i.e. nothing regarding the foundation of local meeting- and rest-houses resembling the *dharma-śālā* and *upāśraya* of our days,[1] let alone temples or Jina statues (§ 25). The scene of instruction—as a return made by the monks (Viy. 141a), though also laymen among themselves ask for it (Viy. 550a)—is represented by the *ceiya*. The layman approaches the teacher in simple clothing without having anything on him containing life, and he does so with concentration and with his hands uplifted for the *anjali* from the moment he comes in sight of the teacher (Viy. 137a; Uvav. 54).

The morality of the layman is involved in his vows to be treated in § 170. Horizontally expanded as it were, these obligations are projected into the vertical by the ladder of the the 11 *uvāsaga-paḍimā* (Dasā 6; Samav. 19a).[2] 1. *daṁsaṇa-*

1. The words *samaṇovāsagassa*. . . *samaṇovāsae* (*-ovassae*) *acchamāṇassa* Viy. 288b 367a seem to speak of a layman who is staying at his own house.

2. See also HOERNLE Uvās. footnote 127, for which comp. the comm. vol. I, p. 27ff.

sāvaga is one who approves of the regulations for laymen in theory without having realized them in praxis yet.[1] This having been done on the 2nd step, the layman is a *kaya-vvaya-kamma*,[2] though he does not yet practise the *sāmāiya* (acc. to Dasā 6 II also the *desavagāsiya*) to its full extent. On the 3rd step he is *sāmāiya-kaḍa*, but he still lacks the *posahôvavāsa*. The (4th) *pos.-niraya*, on the other hand, neglects the *ega-rāiyā uvāsaga-paḍimā*. Apart from various externals the latter is chiefly characterized by the observance of sexual moderation according to which the layman is called (5th) *diyā bambhāyārī rattiṃ parimāṇakaḍa*. In this state of life he remains from 1-3 days upto 5 months.[3] On the 6th step he is continent even at night up to 6 months. Also with the further *paḍimā* their longest duration in months corresponds with their numbering. On the 7th step he starts with renouncing any food containing life (*sacitt'āhāra*), on the 8th and 9th he altogether ceases doing harm to living beings by either his own or foreign actions (*ārambha* and *pess'ārambha*), and on the 10th he gives up any diet ready for him (*uddiṭṭha-bhatta*, § 154). Here, moreover, the layman's head is clean-shaven except for a lock of hair (*khura-muṇḍaga chihāli-dhāraga*). When being asked questions[4] he must speak the truth by saying frankly whether he is able to answer or not (*kappanti duve bhāsāo bhāsittae, jahā jāṇaṃ "jāṇaṃ"*[5] *ajāṇaṃ vā "no jāṇaṃ"*.[6] By this we find ourselves in the very centre of the monastic ethics to which the preceding *paḍimā* came conspicuously close already, and it is small wonder that on the 11th step equals the monk for as many months (*samaṇa-bhūya*). The only

1. In the description Dasā 1 (*tassa ṇaṃ bahūiṃ sīlavvaya-guṇa-veramaṇa-paccakkhāṇa-posahovavāsāiṃ no sammaṃ paṭṭhaviya-puvvāiṃ bhavanti*) the *aṇu-vvaya* are missing, but comp. Abhay. Samav. 19b.

2. These and the following word only Samv.

3. Abhayadeva lists (Samav. 20b) a.o. a sequence wherein the 5th *paḍimā* renounces eating in the dark and the following range in the order of 7, 5, 6, while 8 und 9 go together as one *p*.

4. Acc. to the Tikā *ābhaṭṭha* and *samābh*. =(*sam*)*ābhāṣita*. They accordingly belong to PISCHEL § 564.

5. =*jānāmi*, This and more such forms were registered from archaic Ms. (the Vasudeva-hiṇḍi) by ALSDORF BSOS 8 (1936), p. 321.

6. Comp. also HOERNLE loc. cit.

difference is that he still acknowledges relatives and close relations, and that on his round for alms he is allowed to call on them (*nāya-vihiṃ ei*) though he has to observe the regulation forbidding him to accept food prepared in advance—we hear of *cāulôdaṇa* and *bhilanga-sūva*. In any case, however, when asking for something he is bound to introduce himself as a layman.

The texts (comp. Uvās. 71 and others) are anxious to make it appear credible that a layman performs the 11 *paḍimā* one after the other.[1] But this, certainly, is not meant, whereas the idea rather implies partly a gradation of a more theoretical kind and partly the opportunity of making a selection. On step 1-4, as we have seen, the layman does not yet fully comply with the demands, and if Āṇanda (loc. cit) after 14½ years of laymanship would charge himself with all *p.* he would have to re-descend to their lower grades.

§164. The ancient sources fail to provide us with details concerning this temporary monastic life, and only K. 2, 13 in speaking of *pārihāriya sāgāriya* can be taken as doing so.[2] In case this does not hit the point, i.e. if the word *sāgāriya* rather refers to the layman leading a normal life, then even such a one would be subject to disciplinary measures. This would correspond with the statements made in the Saḍḍhajīyakappa (141 G.) of Dharmaghoṣa (13th century), a later counterpart[3] to the above mentioned Jīyakappa. Since (in spite of Ṭhāṇ. 240a) there is, at least in the strict acceptation of the word, no "seniority" for a layman he can be punished only by restrictions imposed upon his food. These punishments extend from the *nivvigai* up to the *aṭṭhama bhatta*. A layman can make himself guilty either by acting contrary to his vows or by not observing the regulations concerning the condition and the acceptance of the alms. Confession (*āloyaṇā*) takes place in the middle of every month, but we also know of corresponding

1. Comp. also HOERNLE loc. cit.

2. The German and English translations rendered by the AUTHOR are in any case wrong.

3. WEBER, Verz. II, 881f.

ceremonies taking place every four months and every year (Saḍḍhaj. 10), whereas acc. to the older Saḍḍhadiṇakicca of Devendra[1] confession is made every evening (stanza 233). Acc. to Saḍḍhaj. 12 the layman chooses a confessor from among the *āyariya*, *uvajjhāya* or *pavattī*, and they are replaced by others in a way similar to that set down by Vav. 1, 34 for the monk, though here the *sammaṃ-bhāviya* is called *pacchā-kaḍa*, and corresponding to the changed times the last instances next to the Siddhas are the figures of the Titthagaras (*devayā-paḍimā*). A Saḍḍhapaḍikkamaṇa-Sutta of 50 G.[2] reflects the act of confession of a layman. Among the *āvassaya* this act is referred to by Sāmāiya and Paḍikkamaṇa rendering it in a separate version. As long as the layman practices the *sāmāiya* Saḍḍhad. 231 expects him to be respected equal to the monk.

§165. As indicated by the Uvās. reporting on Āṇanda it certainly happened more often than not that by practising the eleventh monastic mode of life the layman also came to practise the monastic mode of death, since the monk no less than the layman can form and carry out the resolution of ending their lives by fasting themselves to death. For the true believer this is the only possible kind of suicide[3] unreservedly acknowledged and even recommended, and that is why in the way of a feeling of sympathy (*ārāhaṇā*, comnonly "loyalty") it is added (as *saṃlehaṇā*, *sallehaṇā*) to the solemn act of a layman taking the oath of allegiance (§ 170). This subject is treated in a study delivered by K. v. KAMPTZ[4] on which in the main the following is based. Theory (Viy. 118a; 624a; Ṭhāṇ. 93b; 175a; Āurap.) distinguishes between a fool's (*bāla*) way of dying and a wise man's (*paṇḍiya*) manner of death[5] by adding a third category in between. All those untouched by Mahāvīra's teaching or disregarding his postulations die the fool's

1. Śrāddhadinakṛtya aur Āt. bh. the latter (in Hindi). Benares 1876.

2. WEBER, Verz. 883 ff.

3. The natural death is discussed (*vīsumbhai*) are discussed in K. 4, 24; Vav. 2, 26; 4, 11f.; 5, 11f.; 7, 17.

4. Comp. p. 75.

5. For the discrimination made also with the *tiriya* see Viy. 63b and for that made with the personality in general see Viy. 90b; 102a.

death, whereas the semi-wise death (*bāla-p.*) comes to the layman who is "befallen by him unexpectedly and suddenly, without any preceding fasting, but after having confessed and on a death-bed recognized as such."[1] In the description (Viy. 118a; Ṭhāṇ. 93b; Nis. 11, 92) the execution mixes with the motives among which we find the desire for post-existence (with the *niyāṇa-* or *tabbhava-maraṇa*) or, provided we do not misinterpret them, weariness and incapability (with the *vdlaya-* and *vas'aṭṭa-m.*). In all cases we are, of course, concerned with voluntary dying. It is unconditionally disapproved of by Mahāvira when executed in the form of putting an end to one's life by drowning, burning, poisoning oneself, by using a weapon or by hurling oneself down a precipice, whereas in certain cases he is not blamed (*kāraṇeṇa appaḍikuṭṭha*) who hangs himself or allows himself to be lacerated by vultures, i.e. who dies the *vehāṇasa-* or *giddha-paṭṭha*[2] *-maraṇa*. There is reason to assume that such a tolerant attitude is explicable only by the idea that the latter kind of suicide does not injure earth, water, and fire-beings by his fall. Over against this the suicide of the sage (*paṇḍiya-m.*) is the result of a fasting which as a lifelong fasting (*āvakahiya*) pertains to the system (§ 178). There are two different kinds: *bhatta-paccakkhāṇa*[3] and *pāôvagamaṇa* with subdivisions for either kind. The renunciation of food expressed by the first word equally applies to the second, and the aim expressed by the second equally applies to the first. The difference consists in maintaining a posture without moving, and that is why, at least among the Śvetāmbaras, there has been since long the tendency of a wrong[4] derivation from *pādapa*. This tendency may have been encouraged by the role which the tree is known to play in Indian religion in general and in both the Buddhist and Jain teaching (§ 18) in particular. Occasionally (Samav. 33a; Utt. 5, 32; and others) a third category is placed between the two mentioned above, the *ingiṇi-maraṇa*, which

1. v. KAMPTZ, loc. cit. p. 15.
2. Preferably = *gṛdhra-spṛṣṭa* in the sense of *g.-bhukta* (loc. cit. p. 16).
3. Viy. 650 a appears to refer to a recidivous *bhatta-paccakkhāyaga*.
4. LEUMANN, Aup.

allows of a limited freedom to move, and after all it is probably these three that are described by Āyār. 38, 20 leaving out their technical names. The actions serving for the preparation have been represented by v. KAMPTZ on the authority of the Paiṇṇa. We here but talk of the act of confession, the atonement for publicly confessed offences and the new subjection to the great or smaller vows, the solemn renunciation of the threefold, i.e. the solid food, the taking of a soft laxative drink (*samāhi-pāṇa*) and the renunciation of the fourfold food, i.e. liquid food as well. The diffierent acts are performed in the presence of the community fellowship attending in an attitude of devout attention and accompanied by a sermon (*aṇusaṭṭhi*) delivered by the Guru. Gn the whole this corresponds with rhe description of Khandaga's death-fasting supplied by Viy. 126ff. As may be concluded from the expressions *māsiyā saṁlehaṇā* and *kāla-māsa*, death is expected to come in the course of a month.[1] The corpse is cremated, as was the rule (comp. Sūty. II 1, 15; Isibhās. 20 end) and as is equally said (comp. §15) of the Titthagaras.

1. HOERNLE, Uvas. footnote 161. The expression *kāla-māsa* is equally applied for the death of profane persons (e.g. Vivāgas. 41b; Rāyap. 131a) though probably only out of habit.

VII

THE VICTORY

§166. As mentioned in § 5 a great number of catchwords obviously representing the core of the parables delivered by Mahāvīra have been handed down to us. Their similes are concerned with the character of human nature and with human ways and doings. Yet Mahāvīra did not couch his practical experiences in parables only but in forms enumerative and otherwise as well. All these forms may be observed in Thāṇ. 4, and one case of each referred to in Ṭhāṇ. 3 and 5 (Ṭhāṇ. 113a; 341b) has its prototype there already. Hence with these exceptions the subject is considered fourfold. In the *simplest* type an x which later is equated with man[1] has the attribute a or b or c or d. Thus man (*purisa*) retaliates in different ways, just as the bud (*korava*) of a mango is synchronous with the twig from which it springs, as the bud of a palmtree develops late, that of a liana quickly, while the bud of the *meṇḍhavisāṇa* tree ripens into an inedible fruit (185a). Just as trees can—at the same time—have leaves, flowers and fruit, and, partly,[2] offers shade, so man—and this is probably meant—acts differently on his equal (113).[3] A *second* type says that an x has the attribute a but not b (1st case) or, vice versa, b and not a (2nd case), or that it has both the attributes a and b (3rd case), or, finally, neither a nor b (4th case). Human beings, like bulls, differ in descent, strength and beauty (207b), like elephants they differ in temper (208a), like warring armies in being either successful or not (218a), like song- and pleasure-birds (234b) or flowers (239a) in the preference they are given, they differ in that some are sociable and others are not

1. *purisa* may be translated this way although sometimes the simile applies also to women, s.b. Even teachers and monks are subject to treatment in similes.

2. This last one only in Ṭhāṇ. 4 (235 b).

3. *pattŏ (pupphŏ, phalŏ) vā-rukkha* contracted from *ŏvaya* (=*ŏpaga*).

(197 a), in their faculty of either causing or healing wounds (264 b), in the way a kernel is different from its shell (265 b), etc. A *third* type is concerned with mutually exclusive opposites like erect and bent (trees; 182a), clean and soiled (clothes; 184a), straight and crooked (ways; 315b), full and empty (pots; 278b), stallion and mare (248 b), friend and foe (284 a), etc. etc. Here the contrasted pairs are linked by *nām'ege* or *nāma-m-ege*: *cattāri kanthagā* (horses) *pannattā*, *taṃ-jahā*: *āinne* (stallion) *nāma-m-ege āinne* (1st), *ā. n.-m-e. khalunke* (mare) (2nd), *kh. n.-m-e. ā.* (3rd), *kh. n.-m-e. kh.* (4th), *evaṃ cattāri purisa-jāyā* (248 b). Such antitheses probably will concern the contrast between pretence and reality, rule and exception, and perhaps even between formerly and now. The subject presumably takes the second place. The same may be supposed to be the case with a *fourth* type formally associated with the third and giving the opposite (b) to the first attribute a along with the uniform extension of a and b: *cattāri saṃbukkā* (shells) *p.*, *t.-j.*: *vāme nāma-m-ege vām'āvatte*(a), *v. n.-m-e. dāhiṇ'āvatte*(b). *dāhiṇe n.-m-e. vām'āv.*(c), *d. n.-m-e. dāhiṇ'āv*,(d), *evam cattāri purisa-jāyā* (216 a). Loc. cit. the same with regard to whirling smoke, fire, and wind[1] and in numerous other cases. Its meaning probably comes up to what was supposed above. It is with regret that we miss the exemplifications which in former times the living speech is certain to have offered to the edification of the audience.

§167. The heterogeneousness of human beings[2] results from their Karman. Karman penetrates into the soul through the activity of body, soul and inward sense, the *joga* (Ṭhāṇ. 106b; T. 6, 1), and this process stands for what is understood by "influence" (*aṇhaya*, more frequently *āsava*, § 84). For the determination starting which certain spiritual or physical process produces a certain kind of Karman in the soul comp. T. 6, 11ff. Here partly also the conception that the effect equals the cause in kind: contempt for knowledge causes the Karman

1. These three are applied to women as well (*agga-mahisī, itthī*).

2. Their acting as *sumaṇa* and *dummaṇa* is documented by Ṭhāṇ. 130 b on the ground of many examples following the normal pattern.

obscuring knowledge, killing results in the "unpleasant", respectable conduct in the "pleasant" Karman, wheras Viy. 304b teaches that the *assāyā-veyaṇijjā kammā* spring from actions causing pain, grief, depression, etc., while, on the other hand, the *sāyā-v. k.* follow from abstaining from them. Previous to this Viy. loc. cit. quotes the *kakkasa-v. k.*, an expression missing in the traditional sequence. They are caused (by virtue of sensual perception, Viy. 571a) by the different passions (*kasāya*) of anger, pride, fraud, and greed,[1] by love (*pejja*) and hate (*dosa*), by quarrel, calumny, tale-bearing, and slander, by discomfort and comfort (*arai-rai*), by cheating and lying (*māya-mosa*), and, finally by heresy (*micchatta*).[2] They all are preceded by the five main vices, i.e. damage done to living beings, untruthfulness, appropriation, dissipation, and possession.[3] These 18 will be discussed in a different context (§ 170). There is no common name for them, but in Mahānisīha they are called the 18 *parihāra-tthāna.*[4]

The texts frequently refer to posthumous retaliation for defects of character. In Ṭhāṇ. 274a we seem to be concerned with such of a monk, since *avaddhaṃsa* "apostasy" presupposes the prescribed good conduct. After the mental disposition (*bhāvanā*, Sthān.) inderlying it or after the reward to be expected in the future existence the *av.* is called either as *āsura*, *ābhiog(iy)a*, *sammoha* or a *deva-kibbis(iy)a*, expressions reflecting the names of lower classes of gods (§ 134). The remarks, however, saying what defects—along with occupations and performances like *nimitt'ājīviya*, *bhūi-kamma*, *kouya-karaṇa*—will result in what forms of existence generally refer to the *jīva* and not exclusively to the monk. Acc. to Viy. 49a the reward in the shape of either a higher or lower heavenly existence is listed in a sequence strangely composed of spiritual and temporal conceptions and placing next to those of a more or less disciplined character

1. But acc. to Ṭhāṇ. 195a they all take a share in all 8 kinds of the Karman.

2. This sequence a.o. also Uvav. § 56. 87. 123.

3. They all refer either to oneself or to somebody else (Ṭhāṇ. 92a).

4. The AUTHOR, Mahāṇis. p. 66, where the sequence slightly departs from the rule.

(*saṃjama*, § 177) the *asannī*, *tāvasa*, *kandappiya*, *caraga-parivvā-yaga*, *kibbisiya*, *tericchiya*, *ājīviya*, and *ābhiogiya*.

§168. The different passions[1] have been dealt with before in § 21 and 87. They are recorded in Ṭhāṇ. 193a; Samav. 9a where their motives (*uppatti*) are said to be space, object, body and some piece of the outfit. Their effects are demonstrated in detail by Dasav. 8, 37-39. They depend on impressions made by all colours, different kinds of taste or smell, and the four sensations warm, cold, soft and rough (the latter acc. to Vy.), and this they have in common with the central offences and all other sins (Viy. 571). However, we are not told why the 8 sensations possible (§ 57) are confined to these 4. In a somewhat far-fetched way they are compared with a whirl (*āvatta*, Ṭhāṇ. 288a) which according to the passions listed in the traditional sequence is either violent (*khara*), high, concealed, or fleshy (*āmisa*).[2] In any case they result in an existence in hell (also Thāṇ. 284b). With anger their violence resembles the line drawn with stone, earth, sand or water (Ṭhāṇ. 234b), with pride a pole of stone, bone, wood or a Dalbergia tendril, with fraud a curved handle[3] made of bamboo, horn, *gomuttiya* or a chip, with greed the scarlet spot (*kimi-rāga*)[4] wet and the dry dirt, and the spot caused by curcuma (Ṭhāṇ. 218b). The similes try to come near to the character of what is being compared: strength, height, crookedness and spreading are pictures suggesting themselves with anger, pride, fraud, and greed just as does the vision of "white" with glory and laughter. The latter two represent a delusion of a friendly, the former of a hostile nature: a distinction is made between a *pejjavattiyā* and

1. For synonyms of *koha*, *māna*, *māyā* and *lobha* see Viy. 571a; Sūy. 1, 1, 4, 11f.; 1, 2, 2, 29; 1, 9, 11.

2. Examples provided by Abhay. are a.o. waterwhirl (horizontal), windwhirl (vertical), ball of thread, and the circling of birds of prey above the flesh (?).

3. Thus Abhay. exactly defines the crooked object which he compares with fraud which in poetry is said to form a zigzag line on the ground. *gomuttiyā* in this connexion cannot be the urine of a cow itself, but it must rather be a textile named after it and cut in that way.

4. The comm. (219a) has two opinions of how this dye-stuff came into being.

a *dosa-v. mucchā* (Ṭhāṇ. 98a) thus causing *pejja* and *dosa* to be placed over the *kasāya.* All details offered with regard to the passions (except *greed*) derive from the sphere of the monk, *Anger* arises with the experienced or anticipated confiscation of pleasant things or with the act of supplying someone with unpleasant ones, and it is aroused by one's self-satisfaction wounded by the teachers (Ṭhāṇ. 472b). *Presumption* (*maya,* acc. to Viy. 571a a synonym for *māṇa* "pride") is entertained (*ahaṃ antī ti thambhejjā*) towards one's ancestry and family, physical strength and handsomeness, erudition and asceticism, gifts, and prestige, visits by gods and goddesses, and finally, towards one's standing above the average of the masses by one's knowledge and faith (Ṭhāṇ. 424a; Samav. 13b; Ṭhāṇ. 473a).[1] *Fraud* means all that contradicts truth. Since the concrete prescriptions offered by Mahāvīra's teaching serve the truth their violation comes up to *māyā,* the offender is *māī,* and the single case *māi-ṭṭhāṇa* (Āyār. II 1, 5, 1 and at frequent other places). Thus we come to understand the connexion between the consumption of forbidden food and the incapability of transforming oneself or of perceiving the proper thing in magic television. Only an *amāī* is capable of either (Viy. 189a—already § 62—191b; 627b; 747a—here a god). That sinfulness goes hand in hand with *heresy* is shown by the combination of *māī* with *micchā-diṭṭhi* (Viy. 636b; 746b). According to the points of view of either approving of what is wrong or failing to recognize what is right the *micchatta* can be divided tenfold (*adhamme dhamma-saddā, dhamme adhamma-s.,* etc. Ṭhāṇ. 487a), less distinctly (Ṭhāṇ. 153a) into *akiriyā* (probably *duṣkriyā*), *aviṇaya* and *annāṇa,* each of which being divided still further. Apart from the large sequence of the 18 sins (§ 167) *māyā* and *niyāṇa,* the desire for reward (§ 180), along with the *micchatta* belong to the smaller sequence of the 3 "pricks" or "thorns" (*salla,* Ṭhāṇ. 147b; Samav. 8a) sticking in the heart.

1. Seven of these ten showed up as early as with the *goya-kamma* § 87. Acc. to the comm. on Ṭhāṇ. 538b objects of pride also include the 6 things that will do harm to an *aṇattavaṃ* (*anātmavat*), but will add to the benefit of an *attavaṃ*: monk's ranks followers, knowledge, asceticism, reception of alms, and respect.

By its pertaining to the causes of the *kakkasa kamma* (s. a.) the *micchatta* is a form of the *aṇhaya* or "influence". But it is equally and expressly called one of the 5 gates[1] of the same (*āsava-dāra*) (comp. Ṭhāṇ. 316a: Samav. 10a). The remaining are: disregarding the commandments (*avirai*), negligence (*pamāya*), the passions and the performance (*joga*). Acc. to Umāsvāti T. 8, 1 the same represent the causes of the binding. He continues the teaching of the *asrāva* in 8, 6.

§ 169. The Paṇhāv. since they call the devotion to the cardinal vices by the name of *aṇhaya-dāra* contrast them with the *saṃvara-d. saṃvara* stands for the "stoppage" against the influence of Karman. It is man's task towards each of the five outward senses and the inward sense, to speech and to the body (Ṭhāṇ. 322b; 355b; 422a; also 472a). As to the technique of salvation it is practised by a number of means referred to further below (§ 173). These means include the observance of the cardinal commandments, and that is why they constitute the 2nd part of the Paṇhāv. Acc. to Ṭhāṇ. 316a; Samav. 1a the *saṃvara-dāra* are, furthermore, the counterparts to the actions referred to above and quoted by the same texts; in this case the *sammatta* corresponds with the *micchatta*. In the Karman teaching *sammatta* stands for the condition of one who has deprived his *mohaṇijja kamma* of its effect (§ 183). "Righteousness"—this is the common meaning (JACOBI on T. 2, 3)—included the true faith called *sammad-diṭṭhi* or *-daṃsaṇa*. The Sammatta-paya of the Pannavaṇā (19) teaches that *sammad-d.*, *micchā-d.*, and *samma-micchā-d.* occur differently with all beings from which we here but conclude that with rational beings all three possibilities occur. In the field of practised religion we meet the *sammad.-d.* less often than the *rui* (Ṭhāṇ. 151 a) and the *saddahaṇā* (*saddahaṇayā* Ṭhāṇ. 355 b), and in the formula applied for confessing one's conversion this corresponds with *saddahāmi pattiyāmi roemi*

1. *dāra* "gate" fits in with *aṇhaya* only. Combined with *saṃvara* it means the "case".—In commencing to render our positive representation of Jain ethics we refer to the lectures delivered by Charlotte KRAUSE: An Interpretation of Jain Ethics, Bh. 1929 and The Heritage of the Last Arhat, Bh. 1930.

(Viy. 99b). The objects of the creed, however, are the 9 „ethical fundamentals" (*sab-bhāva-payattha*, Ṭhāṇ. 445b), i.e. souls and all that is unanimate, merits and guilt, influence and stoppage, annihilation, binding, and salvation. Umāsvāti, T. 1, 4 did not add *puṇṇa* and *pāva* to these "truths" (*tattva*) by which name they continued to be represented in the course of the centuries.

§170. We started our description by dealing with man in general as appearing in Mahāvīra's similes, and we now proceed to him in whom the teaching has taken root even if without leading him to monkhood. It is the layman. He charges himself with a number of restrictions, and paradoxically enough, they exceed in number those accepted by the monk. This is due to the larger diversity of the civil life in which the layman still stands, and this also accounts for the texts specifically, naming several exceptional cases which, according to the subject, are contained in the fundamental commandments. The duties a layman is bound to observe must be derived from those observed by the monk. They divide into three groups of lay restrictions: (a) the small vows (*aṇu-vvaya*), (b) the additional vows[1] (*guṇa-vvaya*), and (c) the strengthening vows (*sikkhā-vaya*).[2] Their number is twelve in all, and hence the texts speak of the *duvālasaviha agāra-dhamma*. We gain this tripartition from Uvav. 57, the wording, at least as far as it concerns the first, is shown by Uvās. § 13ff., and offences are quoted by Uvās. 45ff.[3] The Small (*aṇu*) Vows Ṭhāṇ. 290a; Samav. 10a) are called thus as compared with the Great Vows taken by the monk (§ 171),[4] and they remain in force lifelong as do the latter. While the Great Vows are unconditional, they are reduced for laymen to their abstaining 1. from gross

1. Called "meritorious v." by the AUTHOR RL 7, 22. But the expression above is, perhaps, more to the point since it concerns exceptional cases of the *aṇu-vvaya*.

2. This is=*śikṣā-vrata*, not=s.-*pada* as LEUMANN Aup. writes.

3. This is followed by Haribhadra, Samarāicc. p. 49f.

4. Both together are the *mūla-guṇa* as compared with the *uttarag.* by which the texts (e.g. Viy. 295b) understand first of all the additional and the strengthening vows.

(*thūlaga*) offences against live matter leading to death (*pāṇâi-vāya*), 2. from gross untruthfulness (*musā-vāya*), from gross appropriation (*adinn'ādāṇa*), 4. from adultery by contenting oneself with one's wife (*sa-dāra-saṃtosa*), and 5. from greed by restricting one's striving after possession (*icchā-parimāṇa*). *thūlaga*[1] in the first line concerns the action expressed by the prohibition, but (Uvās. 45ff.) different others, i.e. five in each case, are equated with it.[2] That it concerns merely a selection—taken especially from agriculture and commercial activities—is indicated in Uvās. 45 by the word *peyāla* "typical" which, however, is missing in later texts. Gross offence against live matter is understood by fettering, beating, wounding, overloading and disregarding the urge of appeasing one's hunger and quenching one's thirst, all this most probably with a view to domestic animals. Gross untruthfulness is understood by falsely accusing[3] a person either directly or indirectly, by compromising one's wife by indiscretion,[4] by passing on wrong informations and by forgery. Gross appropriation consists in receiving of, or dealing in, stolen goods, in the instigation to theft, in illegally entering a country, in using false weights and measures, and in the adulteration of goods. The offences against matrimonial faith need not be mentioned (Uvās. 48). As to self-restriction we are referred to gold, cattle, real estate, carts and carriages as well as to a long list of possessions, jewelry and luxuries. The five Small Vows are followed by the three "Additional" Vows: 1. refraining from useless actions which may cause damage (*aṇaṭṭhā-daṇḍa*), i.e. from worries and desires, from doing foolish and dangerous things, and from instigating others to do them,[5]; 2. the commandment directing the layman to confine himself to an area of a certain extension in either direction which he may not leave in his undertakings

1. Umāsvāti T. 7, 2. 15 does not use the word.
2. They partially somewhat differently in T. 7, 19ff.
3. He who does so (*abbhakkhāṇa*) will be done so himself, no matter where it be (Viy. 231 b).
4. Even a truthful statement is not allowed if by it somebody else is hurt (§ 171).
5. In civil life *aṭṭhā-d.* is distinguished from *aṇaṭṭhā-d.* Ṭhāṇ. 47b.; Samav. 7b.

(*disi-vvaya*), and 3. the commandment of observing moderation in eating and drinking as well as in all furnishings along with the prohibition of practising certain trades (*uvabhoga-paribhoga-parimāṇa*). In a concrete sense the latter was already listed among the fifth *aṇu-vvaya*. That is why here, first of all, fundamentals are referred to, i.e. the consumption of things containing life. They are followed by the trades or by activities affecting live matter of which fifteen different kinds are listed, e.g. charcoal burning, ivory- and lacquer-trade, pressing of fruit kernels, drainage of swamps, etc. This prohibition accounts for the fact that up to this day the Jains are found but in a restricted number of occupations. According to this view also b 3 along with b 1 represents but a special formulation of the commandment asking for the preservation of life a 1, though in Uvās. the demand to restrict one's striving after possession 5a is immediately followed by b3 and b 1. In any case, however, the *guṇa-vvaya* prove to be special forms of the *aṇu-vvaya* in which b 2 equally follows a 5. As compared with those mentioned up to now the Strengthening Vows are of a positive nature. By them the layman temporarily comes near to the monk and his conduct of life. 1. By *sāmāiya* the comm. understands the state of an inward balance without adding that it concerns an act of devotion to be repeated several times every day (§ 151).[1] 2. *desavagāsiya* stands for the self-limitation of one's dwelling- and occupation- area which may not be transgressed by messengers, calls, signs, nor by the way of throwing objects across. 3. By the *posahôvavāsa* certain fasting days combined with night watches (*posahaṃ paḍijāgarettae*) are observed at least every fortnight in a special room called the *posaha-sālā* (comp. Viy. 553a; Jambudd. 3). 4. *ahā-* or *atihi-saṃvibhāga* means the distribution of gifts in which a.o. tricks of any kind excluding their acceptance are forbidden. To these twelve duties of a layman the texts (also Samav. 119b), and in conformity with them Umāsvāti in T. 7, 17, add the fasting leading to death which by its name

1. Umāsvāti in commenting on T. 7, 16 explains *sāmāiya* to be a regulation stating how long the layman is willing to keep the Great Vows.—It strikes the eye that in Dasā 6 II *sāmāiya* and *desavagāsiya* are treated as one subject: *se ṇaṃ sāmāiyaṃ desavagāsiyaṃ no sammaṃ aṇupālittā bhavai.*

of *apacchimā māraṇantiyā saṃlehaṇā jhūsaṇ'ārāhaṇā* indicates the high esteem it enjoys. This addition explains itself by the fact that in the *saṃlehaṇā* (or *sallehaṇā*), too, the layman puts himself on a par with the monk. It could not be admitted among the formal duties since, by its nature, it is voluntary (§ 165). A man carrying loads stops in his way by placing his burden from one shoulder on to the other, by relieving nature, by resting at a shrine (*nāga-* or *suvaṇṇakumāra-vāsa*), or by retiring from active life for good. Ṭhāṇ. 235b compares these ever increasing breathing-spaces (*ussāsa*) with the interruptions in the increase of Karman which occur when the layman undertakes responsibilities, in which case *sāmāiya* and *desāvagāsiya* are considered more effective than the remaining[1] except for the fasting vow which, again, is more effective than those two, while the *saṃlehaṇā* effects the ultimate goal of ending.

§171. The formula of the layman has: *jāvajjīvāe duvihaṃ tiviheṇaṃ: na karemi na kāravemi maṇasā vayasā kāyasā* (Uvās. 13ff.). In other words, the layman renounces not only all directly but also all indirectly forbidden activity so far as it consists in one's actively causing it. Nor is it possible in the frame of civil life to adjure the approval (*aṇujāṇai* or *samaṇujāṇai*) of what others are forbidden to do, though in monkhood this is obligatory. Hence the monastic vows (*maha-vvaya*, Ṭhāṇ. 290a; Samav. loa) have the phrase of *tivihaṃ tiviheṇaṃ*, and moreover, they equally pertain to what is done by "heart, mouth, and hands." With regard to their subject they are no less unconditional and comprehensive. They are quoted by Āyār. II 15 end and are repeated by Dasav. 4 beginning.[2] For a brief treatment of the same see Dasav. 6, 9-26. The 10th Anga (Paṇhāvāgaraṇāiṃ) is a monography not only on these five self-restrictions but precedingly also on their

1. *sīlavvaya-guṇavvaya-veramaṇa-paccakkhāṇa-posahôvavāsāiṃ*. *guṇa-vv.* are the above b 6-8. *sīla-vv.* possibly stands for the *sikkhāvaya*,, above c 9-12 *veramaṇa* (*-paccakkhāṇa* ?) a 1-5. Inaccurate as is this mode of expression so is the inclusion of the *posahovavāsa*, and the more so since the (*paḍipuṇṇa*) *posaha* follows immediately.

2. Comp. also Uvav. § 87.

five counterparts (*pāṇi-vaha*, *aliya-vayaṇa*, *adinn'ādāṇa*, *abambha*, and *pariggaha*). With the latter we confront the ethical fundamentals of monkhood. The vow asking for the preservation of life (*pāṇaivāyāo veramaṇaṃ* Dasav.) comprises life manifesting itself in any form or shape, either immaterial or material, either of a superior or inferior kind. The sermon by which Āyār. 17, 16 starts is a counterpart to the explanations commenting on the acts of consecrating laymen, since here the performance of power suggested to be exercised by the Kevalin is described fivefold. Practically parallel to them, however, are the *bhāvaṇā* (Samav. 44a), instructions for right understanding, which in Āyār. II 15 follow every vow.[1] We find the same in Paṇhāv., though here some Bhāvanās have changed places, and several ones have a different, if cognate, content. Apart from demanding the highest possible care to be taken in all monastic affairs they ask for abstention from malevolent thinking and speaking. The "reverence towards life" (as Albert SCHWEITZER has put it) by which the realm of life was so immeasurably extended, permeates the discipline of Mahāvīra's Order in a way no other ethical prescription does. We can observe its entering into the field of sexual abstention which alone equals it in importance.[2] 2. The vow of truthful speech (*musāvāyāo ver.*) discovers sources of untruthfulness in the main passions represented by anger, pride, fraud, and greed along with fear and joy and asks for a considerate mode of expression. Truthful speech causing pain must be equally avoided. It is treated in detail along with the allowed modes of expressing oneself by Āyār. II 4 and hereafter by Dasav. 7. For what is being understood by "true" and "wrong" comp. § 74. 3. The vow of non-appropriation (*adinn'ādāṇāo ver.*) comprises all that is not expressly given as a present (*adinna*) regardless of its kind and size and wherever it be. Since a monk is not allowed possessions of any kind (s. 5) this merely refers to his outfit and to alms. The exemplifications concern the monk's

1. They are presupposed by K. 3, 24.

2. The AUTHOR, Mahānis. p. 73.

quarters (§ 147). 4. The vow of chastity (*mehuṇāo ver,*) has, as was mentioned above, an extremely vast effective range. The prescriptions cohering with it do not refer to normal sexuality only, but they frequently also indicate events of sexual pathology. Among the cases resulting from frustrated desires we find the apparitions of godly persons of opposite sex to which either monks, or nuns surrender (K. 5, 1-4). 5. The vow of being void of property (*pariggahāo ver.*) concerns the abandonment of all one's belongings down to the smallest item including even the preservation of food for later use. The outfit necessary for monks and nuns is not considered as property (Dasav. 6, 20 ff.). The desire for possessing something is roused by pleasant impressions forcing themselves on the five senses. That is why the five interpretations of this vow demand indifference towards them as well as towards their negations which on their part naturally rouse desires, if only in the direction of warding off temptations.[1]

To these five vows Dasav. 4 adds a sixth which, however, instead of *maha-vvaya* is called *vaya* only. It is the *rāi-bhoyaṇāo veramaṇaṃ*, the abstention from taking food and drink after darkness has set in , resulting from the consideration that an insect or either any vegetable or other living substance might drop into the food to perish there. Dasav. 6, 22-26 in treating the subject of taking food at night rather concerns itself with the subject of going out at night, and especially so for the purpose of asking for alms (*esaṇīya*), which certainly is quite out of the question, whereas to be out at night is indeed strictly forbidden (K. 1, 4 ff.). The reason for this is, of course, that in the darkness something living may escape one's notice and be injured. The *rāī-bhoyaṇa* is actually a special case of the *pāṇâivāya* accentuated by several teachers, so that along with Dasav. 4 we see Uvav. § 57; Utt. 19, 30 refer to it. Acc. to Dasav. 2, 2, however, it is not differentiated (as *rāi-bhatta*) within the great number of individual prohibitions. Principally this . conception is the

2. For the development of five vows from four thanks to Mahāvīra comp. §16.

older one, nor are the old collections of disciplinary texts at variance with it.[1]

§172. Details have been considered here only so far as they were necessary to describe the fundamental commandments according to their essential contents. The way they work in praxi is represented in a special paragraph (§§ 136 ff.). As was shown by JACOBI[2] the monastic vows originate from Brahman asceticism and, as there and with the Buddhists, their selection rests on the ethical feeling. Umāsvāti's Sūtras T. 7, 4-7 produced by him with regard to the five principal commandments and weak as they are in this respect are not supported by the Canon. Hence, acc. to JACOBI's conjecture[3] 7, 5, and 6 are borrowings from Patanjali's Yoga-Sūtra i.e. the consideration that killing, lying, etc. are, in the main, nothing but sorrow (*duḥkha*), and the demand "for benevolence (*maitrī*) towards all beings, joyful reverence (*pramoda*) towards those who are better, compassion (*kāruṇya*) for sufferers and indifference (*mādhyasthya*) towards all that are incorrigible". Sutra 7, 4 renders the standpoint of utility and 7, 7 the frame of mind as means for avoiding what is forbidden.

In § 168 we briefly dealt with the *avirai*, i.e. the contempt for the commandments, and it is this offence that causes the souls to suffer and to act (*ahigaraṇī* and *ahigaraṇa*, Viy. 698a). In it the poor and the rich, the largest animal as well as the smallest (*hatthi* and *kunthu*) are equal (Viy. 101a; 314b). But it rests on the *apaccakkhāṇa*. It is not *virai* and *avirai*, but *paccakkhāṇa* "renunciation" (Ṭhāṇ. 44a, 112b) and *apaccakkhāṇa*, and acc. to Viy. 266b even the mixture of either, that was given a systematical description. So far as the *pacc.* is represented by the monastic vows and by the *aṇu-vvaya* it is called *mūlaguṇa-pacc.* (Viy. 295b) and *uttaraguṇa-pacc.* when represented by the *guṇa-* and *sikkhā-vaya*. Here, however, not indicating the content but the mode of performance, there follows a sequence of 10 forms (also Ṭhāṇ. 498a) showing the

1. Comp. K. 4, 1; Nis. 11, 72ff.
2. SBE 22, XXII ff.
3. For Sūtra 7, 6 see also SPAW 1929, 607.

pacc. to happen on account of something in the future or either in the past, to be enforced despite indisposition, etc. Its purity, acc. to Ṭhāṇ. 349a, demonstrates itself by faith, discipline, learning, conserving, and a harmonious character. In this connexion we may refer to the failure of a monk described by Ṭhāṇ. 246 a as the four *duha-sejjā* concerning heresy, insatiability, dissipation, and fastidiousness. Their opposites are the so-called *suha-sejjā*.

§173. We continue to deal with the "stoppage" (*saṃvara*) by considering its media in the sequence of groups established by Umāsvāti T. 9 in starting from the number of the sub-members. Many of these sub-members will be found in more than one group. Since the Canon knows but some of them, it is ignorant of their common aim as such. First we have the control (*gutti*) of the mind, the speech, and the body (Ṭhāṇ. 111 b; Samav. 8a). In each of these cases, acc. to Utt. 24, 19ff., it represents itself by refraining from *saṃrambha*, *samārambha*, and *ārambha*, by which the comm. (comp. also Sthān. on Ṭhāṇ. 403b) understand two stages of preparation and the performance of forbidden thinking, speaking and acting. The same relate the 1st and 2nd *gutti* to the four possibilities of "true, wrong, either and neither of the two" (and hence in each of them attentiveness is asked for), and the physical *gutti* to the omission of an action doing harm to other beings. Though all this was comprised by the *ārambha*, etc. already, Umāsvāti in commenting on T. 9, 4 is, on the whole, more concrete in interpreting the three *gupti*.

In Utt. 24 the *gutti* are treated along with the 5 *samii* (accordingly Samav. 13 b).[1] We might call them their sisters if the comments were right which by these 8 *pavayaṇa-māyāo* (so called in 24, 1) understand the "mothers of the sacred teaching."[2] This ought to read *p.-māīo*, *-māūo* or *-māyaro*. But actually it means "vessels (*mātrā*) of the teaching", since he

1. On the other hand the 5 *samii* together with the 5 vows add up to the *samāhi* (Ṭhāṇ. 473a) frequently quoted in monastic poetry, comp. Āyār., Sūy., Utt.

2. CHARPENTIER, Utt. p. 365 even has "mothers of the faith".

only who is solicitous of discipline and circumspection (*samii*) will take in its spiritual content. Pre-stages of the 5 *samii*—along with such, if not expressly mentioned, of the two first *gutti*—will be found in the interpretation of the 1st principal vow (Āyār. II 15 I), i.e. the circumspection (1) observed in walking (*iriyā*) and (4) the way of taking utensils in one's hand and of either setting or laying them down (*āyāṇa-bhaṇḍa-nikkhevaṇā*). Along with these two, the latter now going by the name extended to *āy.-bh.-matta-n.*[1] we have (Ṭhāṇ. 323a; Samav. 10a) the circumspection (2) observed in speaking (*bhāsā*), (3) in looking for alms (*esaṇā*), and (5) in relieving nature (*uccāra-pāsavaṇa-khela-singhāṇa-jalla-pāriṭṭhāvaṇiyā*). We are also referred to 8 *samii* to which the *maṇa-*, *vai-* and- *kāya-s.*, not *-gutti*, are added (Ṭhaṇ. 422b). In all cases we are concerned with the preservation of life. When walking in a street a monk must not look farther than one *juga* in order not to overlook something near him; his speech must be free from passions, from laughter, fear, loquacity, and slander; the alms must be given and received in the way allowed, and they must be in the condition they have to be (§ 154); all objects handled must be carefully inspected and wiped off; when relieving nature and throwing away something the monk is expected first to scrutinize the place chosen for that purpose for its remoteness (§ 148). All items concerning locomotion on land and on water are treated in detail, though not with regard to the *samii*, by Āyār. II 3, while Dasav. 7 refers to the mode of speech.

§174. From the domain predominantly devoted to questions of discipline Umāsvāti in dealing with what he calls *dharma* (T. 9, 6) again turns to that devoted to ethics. The *dharma*, i.e. the monastic morality, consists in forbearance (*kṣamā*), humility (*mārdava*), candour (*ārjava*), indifference towards the sweets of life (*śauca*), truthfulness, self-discipline, asceticism, abstention, voluntary poverty, and spiritual obedience. For the model to this sequence see Ṭhāṇ. 296b,

1. We should expect *bhaṇḍa-matt'āyāṇa-nikkhevaṇā*.

(in two halves) and 473b. While *śauca* and *ākiṃcanya* are missing they give *mutti* ("abandonment") and *lāghava* ("contentedness") instead of them, but Samav. 120b has *soya*, and along with Ṭhāṇ. 233b it refers to *ākiṃcaṇiyā*, resp. *akiṃcaṇayā* in related connexions. *uvasama*[1] (the representative of *khanti* or *khamā*), *maddava*, *ajjava*, and *saṃtosa* are, acc. to Dasav. 8, 37f., the counterparts to *koha*, *māṇa*, *māyā*, and *lobha*. In the *uttama bambha*, as Samav. calls it,[2] the sequence rendered by Umāsvāti culminates.[3] For asceticism (*tava*) comp. § 178, for *saṃjama*, § 177, and as to the whole see JACOBI's comments on the Sūtra. In the texts referred to abstention (*ciyāga*, also *cāya*) means the abandonment of sinful thoughts, acc. to others it stands for the communication of knowledge (i.e. the *dāṇa* of the propertyless), whereas acc. to passages as Dasav. 2, 2f. (*cāī* it is the abstention from concrete pleasures. Samav.. 35a describes the *bambha* as being 18fold by abstaining from an offence in thinking, speaking, and acting (3) with regard to worldly and heavenly pleasures (*orāliya* and *divva kāma-bhoga*) (2) in one's own doings, in those caused, and in those approved of (3). The theory of both the *kāma* and the *bhoga*[4] is reported by Viy. (309b), acc. to which the former along with others refer to sounds and forms, the latter to smells, tastes, and connexions by touching. Acc. to their different tendencies the souls behave partly as *kāmī*, partly as *bhogī*, and partly as *kāma-bhogī*, and the same applies to the beings according to the sensual organs they have. From these arrangements it follows that the idea of the *bambha* comprises far more than merely the abstention from sexual feeling,. This is shown by Ṭhāṇ. 444a referring to the 9 *bambhacera-gutti*, and the comment made on the word *brahmacarya* of the Sūtras answers to it.

1. K. 1, 35: *uvasama-sāraṃ sāmaṇṇaṃ* "the nature of monkhood is forbearance".

2. This accounts for *uttama* in T. 9, 6 with Umāsvāti and in the Dig. version.

3. This merely bears analogy to the *daśa-lakṣaṇaka dharma* Manu 6, 92 of which JACOBI reminds us. There is no interdependence.

4. In Ṭhāṇ. 263b *bhoga* appears along with *sokkha*. He who is unable to abstain form either kind of pleasure and looks for others of their sort is called a *pasappaga*. *kāma* and *bhoga*, on the other hand, are not included in the 10 *sokkha* Ṭhāṇ. 87a.

§175. To the tenfold *dharma* Umāsvāti in T. 9, 7 adds the twelve pessimistic reflections (*anuprekṣā*). They include the reflections on the transitoriness of things, the helplessness of man, the painful roaming about in the Samsāra, the loneliness of man, (5) on the difference in essence between the soul and both the body and all earthly things, on the inward impurity of the body, on the influence, the stoppage, and the annihilation (10), on the world, on the scarcety of enlightenment (*bodhi-durlabhatva*),[1] and on truth (*dharma-svākhyāta-tattva*). This sequence again, since we do not find it in the Canon, is only the work of the Sūtra author whose authorship, moreover, seems to betray itself by the insertion of the abstract expressions *āsrava*, *saṃvara*, and *nirjārā*. The four first *anuprekṣā* derive from Uvav. § 30 V', and according to the *dharmya* meditation (§ 180) they are the *aṇicca-*, *asaraṇa-*, *egatta-*, and *saṃsārâṇup-pehā*. If only for this reason it seems improbable that the relative statements made in the Mahānis.[2] should have exercised any influence on Umāsvāti, since here the Saṃsāra takes the fifth place behind *ann'anna*, the difference in essence (*anyatva*). But, after all, the Mahānis. generally speaks of *bhāvaṇā* instead of *aṇuppehā*; the "impurity" (*aśucitva*) is missing, and new is the *titthagarehiṃ tatta-cintā-bhāvaṇā*.

As early as in the Uvav. we equally come across abstractions drawn from the ideas conveyed to us by the monastic poetry with its pessimistic character. Some example by means of catchwords may serve to illustrate the *anuprekṣā*: *kus'agge jaha osa-bindue . . . evaṃ manuyāṇa jīvie* Utt. 10, 2; *kus'agga-jala-bindu-cancalaṃ jīviyaṃ* Uvav. § 23 (accordingly Dasav. 11, XXI); *nálaṃ te tava tāṇāe vā saraṇāe vā* Āyār. 6, 24f., comp. Sūy. II 1, 38, 41; *aṇavadagga dīha-m-addha cāuranta-saṃsāra-kaṃtāra* Utt. 29, 22 and elsewhere; for other comparisons see Bhattap. 86, 141;[3] *ego aham aṃsi, na me atthi koi na yâham avi kassai* Āyār. 37, 7, in Mahāpacc. 13 metrically shaped and

1. Thus with p. 195 of the Bhāṣya instead of *bodhi-durlabha* of the Sūtra.
2. The AUTHOR, Mahānis. p. 66.
3. Comp. v. KAMPTZ, Sterbefasten p. 23 f.

related to; *ekko uppajjae jīvo, ekko c'eva vivajjai, ekkassa hoi maraṇaṃ, ekko sijjhai nīrao*, etc. loc. cit. 14ff. The impurity of the body is drastically represented in Nāya 8.

The three last *anuprekṣā* are intimately connected with one another and range in a logical sequence once again blurred in the Mahānis., though here the real meaning of *loka* is elucidated by *loga-vitthara* representing the feeling of the immensity of the world full of wandering souls.[1] In addition to this sense of space we have the sense of time which, in the course of innumerable forms of existence, feels the possibility of hearing the teaching and of acquiring salvation through it to be extremely small. Utt. 3 is the first to deal with this idea; comp. also Dasav. 11, VIII; *dullabhe khalu bho gihīṇaṃ dhamme gihi-majjhe vasantāṇaṃ*. The 12th *anuprekṣā*, finally, refers to the contents of the teaching as it was preached. That it results from the thinking of the Titthagaras is, acc. to the Mahānis., equally an object of consideration.

§176. He who gives himself up to the reflections mentioned above arrests the influence of Karman. By this determination our *aṇuppehā* is distinguished from the one referred to in Utt. 29, 22 where its objects are differently demonstrated. Considering the context the latter inheres in the department of instruction or, more precisely, in that of studying (§ 150).[2] As another medium of the *saṃvara* the *anuprekṣā* are followed in T. 9, 2 by the resistance to the 22 troubles (*parīsaha*). The classical passage recording them is Utt. 2 acc. to which also Samav. 40b lists them. The temptations are: hunger and thirst, heat and cold, stinging insects (*daṃsa-masaga*)[3] and nakedness (*acela*);[4] resentment (*arai*) at the monastic duties, women; (compulsory) migratory life (*cariyā*), (compulsory) studying (*nisīhiyā*) and (compulsory poor) quarters for the night (*sejjā*); abusive language (*akkosa*) and ill-treatment (*vaha*); (compulsory) requests and rejection; illness, injuries caused

1. Acc. to Umāsvāti it concerns the complexity of the world.
2. UPADHYE Journal Or. Inst. Univ. Baroda 8, p. 6-9.
3. From Uvav. 87 it follows that *two* kinds of insects are meant.
4. This pair certainly goes back to an association of ideas, though Utt. 2, 12f. fails to express it.

by blades of grass (*taṇa-phāsa*) and dirt; (flattery by) manifestations of reverence. Differences exist among the three last *parīsaha*. Acc. to the comm. (20) *pannā* indicated the presumption of knowledge, but[1] the pertinent passages Utt. 2, 40f. console for the lack of knowledge (*annāṇa*) as being the inevitable result of corresponding former actions. This agrees with the following passages 42f. correctly relating to (21) *annāṇa*, (the resentment at) not understanding. (22) *daṃsaṇa* (thus also Samav). most probably indicates the (pride in) faith, though the passages 44f. describe the opposite, i.e. heresy. This corresponds with *adarśana* in Umāsvāti. JACOBI's manuscripts have also *sammatta* along with *daṃsaṇa*.[2] In the Samav.-Ṭīkā even the subjects are exchanged one for the other: we have as (20) *jnānam; kvacid ajnānam iti śruyate*,[3] (21) *darśana=samyag-darśana* and (22) *prajnā* "consideration". At any rate the naming of the three objects is conspicuously inaccurate and, hence, not in harmony with the preceding. The *par.* are equally dealt with by Sūy. I 3, 1 though unsystematically. Among the concrete temptations we have (loc. cit. 3, 1, 13) as a new item the *kesa-loya*, i.e. pulling out one's hair (§ 137). It also counts among the 22 *parīsahôvasagga* Uvav. § 116 and nearly consonant Viy. 99 b[4] which in their names and their sequence bear resemblance to ours. *uvasagga* are obstacles either put in a monk's way by godly persons, humans and animals or developing within and on himself (*āya-saṃceyaṇijja*, Ṭhāṇ. 280a, where detailed statements concerning the different kinds will be found).[5] Though not counted the words are associated also in

1. With good will stanza 40 may be interpreted as being a lamentation and 41 (or 41b) as the answer to it given by a conceited monk.

2. Thus Utt. ed. JAYANTAVIJAYA in the text, but *darśana* in the comm. of Kamalasaṃyama.

3. Of the same content in Viy. 390b (ibd. a brief characterization of all 22).

4. They start with *nagga-bhāva*.—The author of the Mahānisīha cannot be blamed for having incorporated the same phrase into his text as was done by the AUTHOR, Mahānis. p. 66.

5. In this connexion the actions and their motives seem to be confused. Obstacles, for instance, derive from scorn, hostility, fear, greediness, defence, they consist in bad company, dropping down, falling asleep or in the atrophic shrinkage of the members etc.

other respects, e.g. Āyār. I 38, 3=22=Sūy. I 16, 4. The sequence rendered by the Uvav. probably is secondary, though it is hard to see why the orderly sequence was abandoned.—Viy. 388f. and, accordingly, T. 9, 12-17 teach on what kinds of Karman the different 22 feelings of uneasiness depend and how many of them may occur with one individual simultaneously. By the way they think about ill-treatment they have to suffer the *chaumattha* and the Kevalin differ from each other (Ṭhāṇ. 306a). They both comprehend the necessity of their sufferings, but while in doing so the former wants and has to promote his own salvation, the latter wants to put an example.

§177. Umāsvāti has brought the media of *saṃvara* in the number of their members up to 22 and now opens a brief new sequence with the (right) conduct (*caritra*, T. 9, 18) taking the first place. He knows of five different kinds: 1. *sāmāiya* or either the temporary (*ittariya*) or lifelong (*āvakahiya*) pious conduct in general as before the ordination (comp. § 138); 2. *cheôvaṭṭhāvaṇiya*, the conduct after the first or the repeated ordination (comp. § 161) (*uvaṭṭhavaṇā*); 3. *parihāra-visuddhiya*, the conduct under the "exceptional position" dictated by atonement as *nivvisamāṇaga* and as *nivviṭṭhakāiya*) (§ 136); 4. *suhuma-saṃparāya* representing a conduct showing but very slight lapses[1] of either one morally changing for the worse (*samkilissamāṇa*) or one morally improving; 5. *ahakkhāya* representing the conduct which (both with the *chaumattha* and the Kevalin) comes up to the enunciated ideal. These Prakrit words originate from Viy. 909a; Ṭhāṇ. 322b; Uvav. § 30 II. though the two first passages do not relate them to *caritta* but to *saṁjama* (or *saṃjaya*) thus equating conduct with self-discipline.[2] By 4. the theory of the saṃjama is associated with the teaching of the *guṇa-sthāna* (§ 183). *saṃjama* and its opposite frequently mean the protection of or, resp., the

1. This probably is the actual meaning of the word rendered by *kasāya* by the commentators.

2. Comp. a.o. *saṃjama tti cāritram* Sthān. 440b. This *s.* presents itself in the discipline regarding the inward sense, the speech of the body, and the belongings of a monk Ṭhāṇ. 233b. For another, schematic division of the *s.* comp. Ṭhāṇ. 322b.

damage done to life. Comp. *chasu saṃjaya* Dasav. 3, 11; 7, 56·
(3) *asaṃijama* means hurting a being's feelings appertaining to it by virtue of its organs of sense (e.g. *beindiyā ṇaṃ bhante jīvā* (acc. pl. !) *samārabha(māṇe) ... jibbhāmayāo sokkhāo vavarovittā bhavai, jibbhāmaeṇaṃ dukkhenaṃ saṃjogittā bhavai* Ṭhāṇ. 284a; also 368b). In the same relation the *saṃjama* is five-, seven- and tenfold (Ṭhāṇ. 322b; 403b; 472b) in which case, however, also lifeless objects are being considered. Following the tenfold *saṃjama* we see that in the 17fold Samav. 32b caution in praxis comes into its own by *pehā, uvehā, avahaṭṭu* and *pamajjaṇā* (careful watching, examining, removing and wiping off).

§178. In dealing with asceticism which, acc. to T. 9, 19ff., follows the conduct we are no longer in the exclusive province of the *saṃvara*. For Umāsvāti teaches T. 9, 3 that asceticism does not only serve for "stoppage" but also for "annihilation" which, by the way, according to him, though with a certain inconsistency between 9, 2 and 9, 8, makes itself equally felt in the resistance to temptations. In conformity with this importance it has for the ultimate aim asceticism, (*tava*) within its division into external and internal forms presents itself in various shapes. The most detailed information is supplied by Viy. 921a=Uvav. § 30 which we follow on the condition that in the face of the characteristic mixture of ethical and concrete demands we shall state but the principal divisions of the latter, while for details we refer to our representation of the monastic life (§ 156). So then *external* asceticism first of all consists in dropping one's meals, in restricting oneself to but few objects and little food, in doing the round for alms which may be subjected to many different special regulations, and in abandoning spiced food. Frequently *tava* means merely fasting in this wider sense. Physical asceticism exercised by forced positions (§ 157) and by doing without fineries stands fifth. All these points are plainly material, whereas only the second, the restriction of quantity (*omoyariyā*, also Ṭhāṇ. 147a), equally means an ethical dictate to the monk to reduce anger, pride, fraud, greed, noise (*sadda*) and quarrel (*jhanjhā*), to be *appa-koha* etc. Thus moderation (*bhāv'om.*)

stands side by side with temperance (*davv'om.*),[1] in connexion with which we observe that in the first case *udara* (belly) as a component part of the word has lost its significance. External asceticism ends up in the monk's withdrawing from his surroundings (*paḍisaṃlīṇayā*, comp. Ṭhāṇ. 322b): by reaching the state of indifference (*rāga-dosa-niggaha*) towards all that the five senses offer, by the suppression and taming of the four passions, by the avoidance of displeasing and the promotion of pleasing activities (*joga*) of the inner sense, of speech and body, and, finally, once more plainly concrete by confining himself to the resting-place secluded from all worldly dealings and temptations. This last point is all that Umāsvāti in T. 9, 19 took over from Uvav. § 30 VI, from which we may conclude that he did not fully agree with coordinating the other *paḍisaṃlīṇayā* to external asceticism, and for that reason he suggested it in T. 9, 26 when dealing with internal asceticism. But the old classification rested on the material nature of body, speech, and all senses, while the reflection which conquers the passions depends on the inner sense acc. to T. 2, 25.

§179. *Internal* asceticism also knows of six media as does the external one (Ṭhāṇ. 364b). Here we have the subjection to confessions and atonement (§ 158; 161). Second follows good behaviour (*viṇaya*) towards knowledge, faith and conduct, furthermore in thinking, speaking and acting in which it makes no difference whether the object is of a spiritual kind or not, and in the way of proving oneself helpful, tactful (*desakāla-nnū*) and friendly.[2] Third ranges the readiness to spiritual service (§ 149) and fourth the study (§ 150). In T. 9, 20 follows fifth the abandonment (*vyutsarga*) of all outer and inner groundworks of existence in which the latter are represented by the body and the passions and the former by the twelvefold *upadhi*.[3] Umāsvāti does not go into details. In the Uvav. the

1. LEUMANN, Aup. s.v. *omoyariyā*.

2. In this connexion we must not overlook the statement made by Viy. 637 a acc. to which respectful treatment is not found in the hells, not among elemental beings and lower animals, whereas higher animals know of it, only that they are ignorant of offering a seat (!).

3. For the relation of the beings to the 3 *uvahi* (and parallel *pariggaha*) Karman, the body and the belongings see Viy. 749b.

corresponding follows only sixth behind the *jhāṇa* which for its being the larger subject will be treated later. The *viosagga* there referred to (though generally written *viussagga*)[1] disengages from all both material and immaterial (*davva-v.* and *bhāva-v.*), i.e. from the body, the surroundings (*gaṇa*), the belongings (*uvahi*) and food on the one hand and from the passions, the Saṃsāra and the Karman on the other.

§180. With Uvav. we turn back to meditation (*jhāṇa*, Ṭhāṇ. 188a; Samav. 9a; Āv. 14). It produces beneficial effects, and acc. to T. 9, 30 it even leads to liberation provided it is "pious" and "pure". For there are kinds of meditation not to be recommended. These *avajjhāṇa*[2] are invariably dealt with the other two; they are the impure forms of an attitude which in itself is beneficial as *annāṇa* is to *nāṇa*. The *aṭṭa jhāṇa*, the *gloomy* meditation, serves for the redress of discomforts and the preservation of the comforts of life. An exceptional case of the former is illness, of the latter enjoyment for which T. 9, 34 expressly specifies the wish for coming to possess certain ideal goods in the future existence. The name for it is *nidāna* (comp. also T. 7, 32). Along with *māyā* and *micchatta* the *niyāṇa* adds up to the sequence of the three "stings" or "thorns" (*salla*, § 168).[3] It is treated comprehensively in an explanation delivered by Mahāvīra, the Āyāiṭṭhāṇa, the 10th Dasā, and its external notes are lamentations, mourning, weeping, and wailing.[4] The *malignant* (*rodda*) meditation is out for damage, lies, robbery and the appropriation of material goods (*sārakkhaṇa*) and is perceptible by the strength (*ussanna-* or *osanna-*), the repetition, the variety, and the perpetuity of moral imperfections (*dosa*).[5] The *pious* (*dhamma*) meditation has four kinds or ranges (*paḍoyāra*) since it serves for penetrating (*vijaya*)[6] into the Jain

1. That yet and in spite of *vyutsarga* the correct word is *viosagga* was shown by LEUMANN Aup. see *vosirai*.

2. Comp. the *avajjhāṇayā* Ṭhāṇ. 147a.

3. For passages from later works see EDGERTON ABhI 8, 228-231. But it is out of the question to speak of a right to cultivate a *nidāna*. JACOBI Samarāiccakahā p. XIX, XXX has compiled the explanations of the word.

4 *vilavaṇayā* Uvav. 30 V, *paridevaṇayā* Ṭhāṇ. 188a.

5. "variety" is inserted here after the pāṭh. *nāṇāviha-dosa* indicated by Sthān. 190a. The orthodox text has for it *annāṇa-dosa*.

6. = *vicaya*, (*artha-*) *nirṇayana*.

commandment (*āṇā*), for the aberrations (*avāya*),[1] and for the outcome of actions (*vivāga*) and the consequent different shape (*saṃṭhāṇa*) of the beings.[2] It is characterised by taking delight (*rui*) in *āṇā*, *nisagga*, *uvaesa*, and *sutta*. *nisagga* is said to be the "natural condition" (*svabhāvo'nupadeśaḥ*) of some who are not in need of instruction, i.e. the *patteya-buddha* (§ 14). Instead of the latter two Ṭhāṇ 188a has *sutta* and *ogāḍha*. *ogāḍha* is said to be the "neighbour" (*sādhu-pratyāsannībhūta*) whom to see being instructed equally causes delight (*rui*). The starting-point (*ālambaṇa*) of the *dhamma jhāṇa* is the method of the instruction (§ 150); its mood (*aṇuppehā*) is determined by the reflections mentioned in § 175. In the same way and in the same place the *pure* (*sukka*) mediatation is being dealt with. Its characteristics are purity and renunciation in all external affairs and the absence of emotions and confusions; it refers to forbearance, abandonment (§ 174), candour and humility; its moods are governed by *avāya*, *asubha*, *aṇantavattiyā*, and *vipariṇāma*, i.e. by the thoughts directed to aberrations, evil things, the endless number of existences, and the perpetual transformation. By *asubha* the internal impurity of the body may be meant. Rather than by all these more or less colourless expressions we come to understand the nature of and the way how to practise the *sukka jhāṇa* more clearly by being given an account of its *paḍoyāra*. This kind of meditation is concerned with one individual object within the range of the *śruta-jnāna* meditated

1. JACOBI in T. 9, 37; from the empirical facts. In this he is guided by T. 1, 15 where we should rather read *avāya* instead of *apāya*.

2. Acc. to Abhay. we are concerned with the shape of the universe.—In Yogaśāstra 7-10 Hemacandra has some different division of the *dharma-dhyāna* (though it is not before 10, 7; 11, 1, that he says that it relates to the latter). The four subvarieties *piṇḍastha*, *padastha*, *rupastha*, and *rūpâtīta dh.-dhy.* advance from bodily objects of meditation to magic characters, to the image of the Arhat and, finally, to the bodiless *paramātman* (comp. BÜHLER, Hc. p. 84, partly after BHANDARKAR who follows Sakalakīrti's Tattvārthasāradīpikā, Report 1883-84, p. 110f.). In Yog. 11 Hc. then renders the *śukla-dhy.* with the division as offered in the Uvav., if only for the sake of completeness, see third next footnote. He wrote the Prakāśas 1-4 along with the following for practical use, and, what is more, probably in order to oblige his prince (comp. BÜHLER p. 36) he dealt with experiments in Pr. 5 and 6 which have nothing at all to do with the Jain doctrine, and in 7-10 with such to which he attached this relation only artificially. For the above definition of *rūpa-stha* makes it quite plain that the four subvarieties are non-Jain by origin.

upon in either some or only one of its conditions (*paryāya*), so that, accordingly, we have either the *puhatta-viyakka* (for the the object is taken "for itself") *sukka jh.* or the *egatta-viyakka sukka jhāṇa.*[1] Acc. to T. 9, 45 *viyakka* (*vitarka*)=*śruta*. In the first case there may be a transition (*vicāra*) leading from the meditation on one object over to that of another, in the second consciousness continues to concentrate on one, and, accordingly, *saviyāri* and *aviyāri* are added to the two *viyakka*. Here, moreover, the pure meditation is gradated into *suhuma-kiriya s. jh.* and *samucchinna-kiriya sukka jhāṇa*. In the first there is but very little activity left, in the latter none at all. *kiriyā* in this connexion means *joga*, the display of the inner sense, speech, and body (§ 84). These uppermost grades are exclusively proper to the Kevalin, and that when, with the exception of vegetative activity (e.g. of breathing), he has ceased to exercise *yoga* and when, in the *selesī*-stage (§ 186), he is devoid of this final remainder as well (Uvav. § 153; Paṇṇav. 436b). In other words, the time it lasts is most limited or, rather, next to nil. Since the Kevalin is beyond the danger of having a relapse the *jhāṇa* of either grade is called *appaḍivaī* and *aṇiyaṭṭī*[1] (the latter in T. 9, 41; *vyuparata-kriyā-nivṛtti*). It is characteristic of the post-canonical view taken by T. 9, 27f. that it introduces physical conditions for the faculty of meditation. Those only who possess a most excellent physique (*saṃhanana*, § 65) are fit for lasting it out, and even they will do so for the time of one *muhūrta* only. Indeed the two highest grades do not occur any longer since—after Jambu's Nirvāṇa—nobody ever again became a Kevalin.[3] Nor is this the view shared by Umāsvāti since he assigns the different kinds to monks of different moral maturity (T. 9, 35ff.). For *gloomy* and *malignant*

1. That *puhatta-* and *egatta-viyakka* are adj. to *sukka-jjhāṇa* is demonstrated by the two other forms *suhuma-* and *samucchinna-kiriya*.

2. The activity of the inner sense which in conformity with that of speech ceases *before* that of the body is of a material nature and must not be confused with the cognizant activity of the spirit.

3. Acc. to Hc. 11, 4 the complete *śukla-dhyāna* is not exercised at present since it asks for the best physique possible and for the knowledge of the Pūrvas.

is the meditation of him who either completely or partially fails to observe the vows (*avirata* and *deśa-virata*, the latter with ref. to laymen), and gloomy as well is the meditation of him who possibly proves negligent (*pramatta-saṃyata*, § 183). His counterpart, i.e. he who proves reliable (*apramatta*-s.), exercises the *pious* meditation. This kind, however, along with the two first grades of *pure* meditation is proper to him who suppresses the passions, as it is proper to those who succeeded in annihilating them (*upaśānta-kaṣāya* and *kṣīṇa-kaṣāya*).

§181. Umāsvāti in commenting on T. 10, 7 (p. 316 of the ed.) says that the monk who has come to be on the first two grades of the *śukla-dhyāna* possesses miraculous powers (*ṛddhi*) a number of which are quoted by the commentator. This, however, is but an attempt to incorporate the magic faculties (*iḍḍhi, laddhi, siddhi*) frequently mentioned in the Canon into the system, by the way, in a rather unfitting place, for he who has come to reach the "pure" grade of meditation may be supposed to be above those magic tricks[1] presently to be mentioned. For not only that they do not belong to this grade of meditation, they have nothing at all to do with the road leading to salvation. In their being referred to we have to see a concession made to the popular belief ascribing certain supernatural powers to the men exercising asceticism all over the country. Acc. to Uvav. § 24 (comp. Hc. Yog. 1, 8; Mahānis. p. 75) it is "some" monks not differentiated in detail to whom this is done. Their powers are inexhaustible (*koṭṭha-buddhi*), they develop the object independently out of its very first beginnings (*bīya-b.*) and then work it up' (*paḍa-b.*).[2] In studying they have the gift of combination (*payâṇusāri*),[3] and they seem to be capable of taking in the most different lectures at the same time (*saṃbhinna-soya*).[4] As to

1. Limitations of the *iddhi* are ref. to by Ṭhāṇ. 354b; they are given mainly by the fundamental laws of the world.

2. Collecting, as it were, the rain of knowledge (*nāṇa-vuṭṭhi*) in the cloth of intellect (*buddhi-paḍa*), Cuṇṇi on Sūy. nijj. 18; Abhayadeva on Uvav. 24.

3. Or the gift of never to forget what one has learned, *padānusmārin* (JACOBI, Sthav. p. 9; 2nd ed. p. XCV).

4. That it applies to hearing is shown by Mahānis. 1, 46 *saṃbhinna-'ui*.

cognition they occupy the fourth grade where the *ujju-mai* goes along with the *viula-m.* (§ 80). Other gifts impress the masses more strongly: these monks are capable of distributing curse and blessing, to touch them is considered as beneficial as are their excrements, they procure milk, honey, and butter, and they cause supplies never to run short.[1] The curse (*sāva*) does not figure prominently in the texts, and its rôle is taken rather by the magic flash of fire which may be hurled by some infuriated monk or god. An action of that kind is the *teya-nisagga*, and we read Viy. 678a how he who is struck is immediately burnt to ashes by the *teya* or the *teya-lessā*. Thān. 520b, however, also refers to other cases in which the fiery missile causes blisters (*phoḍa* and *pula*) and acts upon its object in a more indirect way. The *teya-lessā* accumulates (*saṃkhitta* Viy. 666b)[2] through asceticism and, accordingly, it also goes by the name of *tava-teya*.[3] Hurling is done by means of a *samugghāya* (Viy. 665b; 678b), and probably it is here that we have the model for the homonymous practices in the system (§ 89). It is worth remarking that Mahāvīra counters the hot missile of his opponent (*sā'usiṇā t.-l.*)[4] with a cool one of his own *sīyaliyā t.-l.*) (Viy. 666a) which is contrary to the nature of the subject.

Such monks, moreover, are capable of producing objects by magic, of changing into them (Viy. 757a), and of moving in the air without support. These latter faculties which obviously were particularly popular with common people are equally referred to by Viy. in which the spiritually advanced state of the monk is characterized by calling him *bhāviy'appā*.[5]

1. *akkhīṇa-mahāṇasiya* following *khīrāsava* etc. demonstrates how the latter expressions are expected to be understood. Neither have we the Karman technical meaning of *āsava* nor any relation to the sweetness of speech indicated by Umāsvāti in calling these faculties *vādika*.

2. Sthān. 149b on Ṭhāṇ. 147b where three motives for accumulation are referred to is incorrect in giving *laghūkṛta* as an explanation.

3. The instr. reads but *taveṇaṃ teeṇaṃ*.

4. Erroneously printed *sīôsiṇā*, but Vy. 668a has *svāṃ svakīyām uṣṇāṃ tejo-leśyām*.

5. A *bh.'a.* is *iḍḍhimaṃ* as are the Arhat and the secular heroes (Ṭhāṇ. 331b).

Such performances can also be enacted by a god; in the system of the *iḍḍhi*, acc. to Ṭhāṇ. 172a, it is the *viguvvaṇā*. Viy. 154a; 190a in referring to both the monk and the god insist on saying that it means simply an effect on the senses and nothing real whatever (*aṇagārassa bhāviy'appaṇo ayam eyārūve visayá-mette buie, no c'eva ṇaṃ saṃpattīe vikuvviṃsu vā vikuvvai vā vikuvvissanti vā.*[1] For performing such an effect material particles not proper to the performer have to be attracted, and only by applying them, *bāhirae poggale pariyāittā*, he will succeed in producing it (Viy. 189a ff.; 283a; 315a; 643a; 750b; Jīv. 374b; Ṭhāṇ. 104b) in which case the texts differentiate such *poggala* that adhere to the performer from such adhering to the speaker or else to some third place (*tattha-gaya, iha-g.*[2], *annattha-g.*). The performance is called *veuvviya-samugghāya*, and Viy. 153b; Jambudd. 268b; Jiṇac. 27 describe it in the way a god performs it (§ 89). We may assume that it is the *veuvviya-* or, perhaps, the *teya-s.* that may, though not must, be applied either totally or partially (!) in order that a god or a monk thanks to his bright *lessā* (§ 97) may perceive godly persons (*samohaeṇaṃ asamohaeṇaṃ* or *asamohayâsamohaeṇaṃ appāṇeṇaṃ jāṇai pāsai* Viy. 283b; Jīv. 141b). Conjurations by magic occur in abundance comprising the most different objects and persons (naturally not with souls of their own, Viy. 751b) in which connexion also women play a fairly important part (comp. Viy. 189a; 627a), and monks or gods walking in the air are equally discussed in detail. There is nothing to it but to believe that they are capable of lifting themselves over an obstacle as is the Vebhāra mounta in (Viy. 190a; 643b), and by dozens of examples we are shown (Viy. 190a f.; 626b) that a monk is able to float in the air in all positions possible. In doing so he either takes human sitting or bearing positions or imitates the ways animals behave. Thus a monk floating in the air may, for instance, do so with his head down like the bat (*vaggulī*). The theory of floating in the air discriminates (Viy. 793b) between *vijjā-cāraṇa* and *janghā-c.*

1. *visae tti gocaro vaikriya-karaṇa-śakteḥ... viṣaya eva v.-mātraṃ kriyā-śūnyam... saṃpattīe tti yatho'ktârtha-sampādanena* Vy. 155a.

2. *prajnāpakâpekṣayā iha-gatān (pudgalān)* Vy. 283b.

The latter have gone through a more severe praxis of asceticism and, hence, they are capable of performing more than others are. Umāsvāti's explanation (p. 316) seems to include the reverse by saying that the *janghā-c.* are able to walk on flames, smoke, rain, rays, spider-threads, etc. while the *viyadgati-c.* can do without these expedients. From this we might conclude that *vijjā* here contained the word *viyat*, though Viy. says that those concerned acquire *vijjāe uttaraguṇa-laddhiṃ khamanti* (?). For the spiritual value attached to these faculties it is significant that in cases, those who own them die without confessing. This indicates the deservedly small estimation of such tricks, and Mahāvīra accordingly voices it by telling as suggested to him, the story of the nun Paṇḍarajjā reported by v. KAMPTZ.[1] On the other hand and contrary to our feeling to exercise magic powers was not supposed *māyā*. Against this it is frequently stated that only an *amāī* is capable of exercising them (§ 62; 168). Uvav. § 24 the *cāraṇa* are followed by the *vijjāhara* (the successive word *āgāsaivāī* is probably an attribute) so that here the *vijj.* are counted among spiritual persons. In fact, however, as follows from Jambudd. 71b, they represent an individually differentiated class of people ruled by princes and said to have their permanent residence on the Veyaddha mountains (§ 124). These beings of good nature who in fairy-tale literature play an important part[2] walking in the air thanks to their nature, not by deserts as do the secular heroes along with the Arhats (Ṭhāṇ. 356b; comp. also 331b). Here, too, as in the case of the Bhavaṇavāsī, the spirits of the air[3] of the popular belief have been assigned their place in the system.

§182. The expressions *upaśama* and *kṣaya* applied in § 180 appear as early as in the teaching on the conditions (*bhāva*) for which Viy. 722a refers to Aṇuog. 113b ff.,[4] comp. Ṭhāṇ.

1. Sterbefasten, p. 32. But Vajra (§ 23) is praised for his magic tricks, particularly for his faculty of walking in the air (Āv. 766 ff.).

2. Comp. a.o. ALSDORF ZDMG 92, 464 ff.

3. JACOBI in Literaturbl. f.d. orient. Philol. 2, 48 tried to derive *vijjāhara* from *viharati* (*vijarhara*).

4. Taken from normal life, however, are the 4 *bhāva* compared by Ṭhāṇ. 234b with water of different turbidity and resulting in a corresponding post-existence in hell etc.

376b. Umāsvāti renders it in T. 2, 1 ff. We start 1st with the condition of substantiality (*pāriṇāmiya bhāva*) which takes the 5th place there. The soul—to quote from Aṇuog. but what specially refers to it—is destined or not to salvation (§ 101). The remaining *bhāva* caused to the soul are produced by Karman. 2nd, the realization (*udaya*) of the 8 Karman kinds in it transposes it into the *udaiya* condition which, accordingly, is the norm. 3rd, by self-control the *mohaṇijja* Karman adhering to the soul can be suppressed to a degree that it keeps peace (*uvasama*) without being realized. This condition is called *uvasamiya*. 4th, if the Karman is not only suppressed but has fallen victim to annihilation (*khaya*) we come to have the *khaiya* condition proper to the Kevalin. 5th, ranging by name between the two preceding we have the *khaôvasamiya* condition presenting itself when the 4 kinds of the *ghāi-kamma* (§ 87) do not realize *vipākataḥ*, but *pradeśataḥ* only. This differentiation does not follow from Aṇuog. itself, whereas from Hemacandra's comment it does. It rests on the view held by Viy. 65a that the *aṇubhāva*, i.e. the *vipāka*, of a Karman (T. 8, 22) need not be felt, while with the *paesa-kamma* this is always obligatory (§ 85). Since in the *uvasamiya bhāva* the Karman does not come to develop at all the *khaôvasamiya bh.* is inferior to it. Hence, logically, it must range after the *udaiya*. A 6th condition Umāsvāti passes over in silence: the *saṃṇivāiya*, representing several of the preceding *bhāva* occurring simultaneously. The combinations possible are scrupulously listed by Aṇuog. 122 a ff.

§183. The *upaśānta-* and the *kṣīṇa-kaṣāya* in particular will be found among the *guṇa-ṭṭhāṇa*, or, if we recur to the Canon, among the 14 *jīva-ṭṭhāṇa* Samav. 26b. They are homonymous with the *guṇa-ṭṭh.* The comm. does not take special notice of this, and yet it must have known the name *guṇa-ṭṭh.* for the logical and practical grades leading to liberation. He who stands on these "grades of soul" leading up to perfection is called, 1. *micchā-diṭṭhi*,[1] heretical, 2. *sāsāyaṇā-sammad-d.*,

1. Also written *micchad-diṭṭhi* frequently. A double d, however, is only justified with *sammad-d.* (*samyag-dṛṣṭi*).

in the temporary foretaste of true faith,[1] 3. *sammamicchā-d.*' neither heretical nor orthodox, but a mixture of either, 4. *aviraya-sammad-d.*, not observing the commandments, of right faith, 5. *virayaviraya*, partly following the road directed by the commandments (*deśa-virata*) with ref. to the layman, 6. *pamatta-saṃjaya*, controlled, but not without negligence, 7. *appamatta*-s., controlled and in being so reliable, 8. *niyaṭṭi-bāyara* and 9. *aṇiyaṭṭi-b.* charged with the passions in their normal strength and at any rate not in their subtlest forms, 10. *suhuma-saṃparāya uvasāmaga* or *s.-s. khavaga*, harbouring but the smallest possible measure of the passions, 11. *uvasanta-moha*, who has suppressed the *mohaṇijja-kamma*, 12. *khīṇa-m.*, who has annihilated it. Either bear the Sanskrit name of *upaśānta-* and, resp., *kṣīṇa-kaṣāya-vītarāga-chadmastha.* The 13. place is occupied by the *sajogī kevalī*, the Kevalin activating the inner sense and both body and speech, the 14. by the *ajogi k.* not activating them (§ 186) . This passage of the Samav. is the only one in the Canon containing the 14 grades, but we are missing any detailed comment on them. As to the *niyaṭṭi* and the *aṇiyaṭṭi* leading from the 8th up to the 9th grade such a comment would have contained some indication of the complicated procedures which in the later Karman theory we find being related with the *guṇa* grades. For v. GLASENAPP, Karman p. 83f., refers to it[2] in rendering details regarding three procedures (*karaṇa*) by means of which the soul prevents fresh *mohaṇijja* (§ 87) from developing. The third of them is called *aṇiyaṭṭi-karaṇa*, while the (second) procedure to be exercised by the (8.) *niyaṭṭi-bāyara-saṃparāya* is not called *niyaṭṭi-* but *apuvva-karaṇa*. Those mentioned are preceded by the *ahāpavitti-karaṇa*. Of these three procedures merely the *apuvva-k.* is referred to in the Canon, though but sporadically (Viy. 434b; Nāyādh. 152b;[3] Jambudd. 278b) and, as is the case with the *guṇa-ṭṭh.*, without going into details. Yet after

1. Comp. v. GLASENAPP, Karman p. 62.

2. Add Śīlānka Ācār. 270a. Samarāicc. p. 47 quotes the three procedures.

3. Here explained as 8. *guṇa-sthāna* by Abhayadeva.

all the *apuvva-k.* is called *kamma-raya-vikaraṇa-kara.* Moreover in Samav. 39b we find a note on the *mohaṇijja kamma* of the *niyaṭṭi-bāyara* which (along with respective notes on that of the *abhavasiddhiya* and the *bhavasiddhiya*—§ 101—Samav. 45b; 47b) points at the later theory in that—to conclude from the word *santa-kamma*—it knows the expression *sattā* for the potential existence of Karman missing in the Canon in other respects (§ 85) and at least three of corresponding computations of *kamm'aṃsa* (=*uttara-prakṛti*).

Sporadic as all these references may be, yet they indicate that the older texts contained what the Karman theorists are so careful in recording at great length. The source from which they drew their knowledge is said to have been the Diṭṭhivāya, the 12th Anga.

This equally applies to the teaching on the *seḍhi* or "ladders" which the soul ascends in either suppressing Karman or freeing itself from it. It is mentioned but once, i.e. by Uvav. § 153 referring to *guṇa-seḍhi,* and here again we are left in the dark as to its theoretical background.

Strongly mechanical as is the character of the Karman teaching represented above, this character now comes to tell in a still stronger way. By the three procedures it is intended to prevent the soul from developing, as it cogently must, fresh *mohaṇijja kamma* when old *m.k.* is realizing. Now, one of the processes in the course of the second procedure (*apuvva-k.*) is the *guṇa-seḍhi,* i.e. an annihilation of Karman particles. The purpose of this process is to bring about the condition called *sammatta.* But yet there is still some *mohaṇijja* left resting in the soul, and it is this Karman which the *uvasama-seḍhi* is intended to systematically prevent from materializing, while the *khavaga-seḍhi* is to annihilate successively all kinds of Karman whatever. The latter in doing so leads to the state of Kevalin. Now the *guṇa-ṭṭhāṇa* are divided among the *sammatta* and the two *seḍhi* as is indicated by the names of the last of the *g.-tth.* The *uvasama-s.* is ascended on the 4., 5., 6. and 7. grade to lead, if but for a short time, up to the 11. from which summit. No sooner than it was reached, the soul descends again.

For the 14 grades far from constituting a temporal sequence are but a sequence determined by actions since on them the soul moves either up or down according to how and what it acts. But it is precisely activity, i.e. life, that the theorists given to abstracting leave out of consideration in their representations. For details comp. v. GLASENAPP, though his view that here psychological mazes are still waiting for being explored will hardly turn out to be true, since it appears that here the Jains have cultivated psychology without soul.

§184. We started this chapter by regarding the similes characterizing the individual peculiarities of man on the grounds of practical experience. And so, before we turn to the crowning point where the road of salvation culminates and all individuality vanishes into nothing, we may conclude it by referring to an equal simile which with the same probability as the preceding ones we feel justified to ascribe to Mahāvīra's personal knowledge of the imperfections and virtues of human nature. We hear of distinctions being made between the "hollow" (*pulāga*),[1] the "spotted" (*bausa*), the "sinful" (*kusīla*), the "free" (*niyaṇṭha*), and the "absolved" (*siṇāya*). The text introducing these names is lost, but from the last of them it follows that it referred to the *snātaka* of the Brahman life. In the *siṇāya* we have the Kevalin. The *niyaṇṭha* is one grade below him, so that this word corresponding by derivation with the *nigganṭha*[2] does not signify the common monk but one of outstanding qualities by many of which he already equals the *siṇāya*. Contradictory to this the collective name for all five kinds is also *niyaṇṭha*[3] while the remaining three stay below it in quality. The *kusīla* is sinful either on account of obvious offences and passion or merely owing to the lowest grade (§ 87) of the latter according to which he is called *paḍisevaṇā-k.* and *kasāya-k.* Thus altogether we have six kinds[4] with which Viy. 890b ff. is concerned

1. Literally the "empty ear".
2. Comp. PISCHEL, Gr. § 333. But what we have before us is the prep. *ni*, not *nis*.
3. But *nigganṭha* acc. to Ṭhāṇ. 336a.
4. Mahānis. 3 classifies about 200 different kinds. Comp. the AUTHOR, Mahānis. p. 68.

by treating them from 37 different angles both concrete and metaphysical,[1] though T. 9, 49 considers but 7 of them. They include only few allowing us to understand by them the valuation of the lower grades. The *pulāga*, for instance, does not, as is the case with the *bausa* and others, rise to imitating the praxis of the Jina, called *jiṇa-kappa*, but he remains in the *thera-k.*; by his offences he afflicts both the *mūla-guṇa* and the *uttara-g.*, i.e. both the five vows[2] and the ten renunciations (§ 172), and his learning, if it goes beyond Puvva 9, 3, remains within the range of nine Puvvas. As against that the *bausa* leaves the vows unviolated, and he at least knows the text concerned with the 8 *pavayaṇa-māyā* (§ 173) (for us Utt. 24), whereas of the Puvvas he knows not more than ten. Among the most detailed we have the description regarding the differences in conduct (*caritta-pajjava*, Viy. 898b) on which the whole gradation certainly rests. Within their classes the "hollow", the "spotted", and the "sinful" are either superior, inferior, or equal to one another in all grades[3] imaginable, while without them in the orthodox sequence they are by ∞ times inferior to one another. It is only the two *kusīla* that behave towards the *pulāga* and the *bausa* as they do towards their own kind,[4] and the *niyaṇṭha* goes together with the *siṇāya*. The *saṃyama-sthāna* referred to in the Bhāṣya commenting on T. 9, 49 are not an immediate reflection of this *caritta-pajjava*.

§185. In turning to the *annihilation* (*nijjarā*) the way Umāsvāti treats it in T. 9, 47 we are reminded of the previously mentioned *guṇa-ṭṭhāṇa*, since for the better part the tenfold gradation of the annihilators as rendered by this text corresponds with them. This gradation shows at its beginning the (provisionally merely) true believer (*samyag-dṛṣṭi*), the layman (*śrāvaka*), the monk (doing no more than) keeping the vows (*virata*) and parting with the passions in their coarser forms

1. For the first of them dividing each into five see also Ṭhāṇ 336 a.

2. Strangely enough they are here called *āsava* (*pancaṇhaṃ āsavāṇaṃ paḍisevejjā* Viy. 893b).

3. This is expressed in a way that one may be inferior to the other by $\frac{1}{\infty}$ $\frac{1}{s}$ or $\frac{1}{x}$ (comp. § 21) or superior to him by ∞, or x times.

4. But the *paḍisevaṇā-k.* is ∞ times more than the *pulāga*.

(*ananta*-—scil. *anubandhi*, § 87—-*viyojaka*). The higher grades are characterized by the absence of the *mohaṇijja kamma* dividing into the one disturbing the faith and the other disturbing the conduct (§ 87). The monk annihilates the former (*darśana-moha-kṣapaka*), is about to suppress the latter (*upaśamaka*, comp. § 182), and has succeeded in doing so (*kṣīna-moha*). The highest grade is the *jina*. On each of these grades Karman is annihilated, i.e. on every next higher ∞ times more than on the preceding. However, as little as with the closely related *guṇa-ṭṭhāṇa* does this mean a cogently temporal succession of grades, but merely a kind of statistical statement which like them is not recorded by the Canon.

The medium for annihilation is asceticism. This is taught by T. 9, 2 as being its second purpose next to the one of effecting *saṃvara*. The annihilation of resting Karman by asceticism is, as it were, the artificial way opposite to the natural manifesting itself by sensing Karman, and which as well may be called consumption. For the latter comp. the discussions on the correlation of *nijjarā* and *veyaṇā*, § 86. It is closely connected with the statement that a monk by 4½ days, fasting will annihilate more Karman than a denizen of hell in millions of years (Viy. 704a). To a high degree, acc. to Ṭhāṇ. 170b, our annihilation is exercised by a monk by his urge to studying and to special castigation (*egalla-paḍimā*, § 139), by a layman by his urge to giving away his fortune and to devoting himself to lifelong monkhood, by either, however, (as confirmed by Samth. 108) by the desire for death fasting (§ 165). It is evident that only by performing the intention here indicated by the words *kayā ṇāṃ* . . *viharissāmi* etc. he who cherishes this desire will be successful in reaching his aim. The question to what extent the *nijjarā* shortens the chain of existences of a pious man after his death pertains to metaphysics. As long as it does not suffice to remove the Karman substance adhering to the soul it must continue on its course. Frequently (in Viy. 128b; 168b; 179b) and later Mahāvīra is questioned about the destinies awaiting a certain person after his death and he is able to supply most detailed information about the future up and down of their souls. But we find general statements being made as well. They depend on the point concerning the loyalty (*ārāhaṇā*) of the believer. Ṭhāṇ. 159a; Viy. 418 b in theoretically dealing with this loyalty gradate it within the range of cognition, faith and conduct into three grades for each, while Ṭhāṇ. 98a also renders it as *dhammiyā* along with *kevali-ārāhaṇā*. The first of these two is proven by knowledge and conduct, the second bears as its fruit the termination put to the chain of existences, the *anta-kiriyā* (§ 101), or either a godly existence by which it comes to be *kappa-vimāṇôvavattiyā*, an expression intending to say that it will lead to the state of Kevalin later. These different kinds and grades of loyalty now offer the base for a certain number of future births, i.e. upto 7 or 8 acc. to the Paiṇṇas;[1] beings with nothing but an otherworldly existence awaiting them are called *bisarīra* (Viy. 851b; Ṭhāṇ. 61b; 250b). The uppermost grade, however, destroys that base and leads up to salvation at the end of the present life, and it is in particular death-fasting that is said to be qualified for it. Acc. to what we have formerly learned from Ṭhāṇ. it carries with it a great annihilation and this, at least indirectly, accounts for Viy.'s repeatedly (189b; 231a; 375a; 497b; 794a) allowing the act of confession, especially the one before death, to flow from the *ārāhaṇā* or "loyalty". In the Paiṇṇas it is made quite clear[2] that the monk ending by fasting either enters into the highest possible heavenly region of Savvaṭṭhasiddha (§ 129) or arrives at the place reserved for the Siddhas. The latter postulates that the monk be in the possession of the *kevala*-cognition. In accordance with the rôle self-castigation plays in the system, even the biography of Mahāvīra (Āyar..II f.; Jiṇac. § 120) scarcely speaks of intellectual struggles and exertions but all the more of th enormous physical efforts directed to suppressing human nature, and, in the end, yielding both omniscience and omnivision as a reward for them. Ultimately the physical side comes to the front completely. the Paiṇṇas[3] along with the legends

1. Comp. v. KAMPTZ, Sterbefasten p. 39.
2. v. KAMPTZ loc. cit. p. 21 f.
3. Comp. the AUTHOR, Mahānis. p.2 9 f., 72.

from which they draw and the Mahānisīha make the fasting monk and the martyr come to obtain the *kevala* by virtue of their activities and sufferings, by which instead of immersing themselves in the sacred teaching as actually required, they content themselves with a minimum of formulae and separate words effecting the requisite annihilation by being brought to mind.

§186. The monk and the nun who have come to be free from the four obscuring, interfering and hindering kinds of Karman are in the possession of omnicognition, the *kevala-nāṇa*[1], and are *uppanna-nāṇa-daṃsaṇa-dhara . . . kevalī tīya-paccuppanna-m-aṇāgaya-viyāṇaga savvannū savva-darisī* (a.o. Viy. 114a; for greater details comp. Uvav. § 16). Only what can be felt, their individuality, their social standing, and their amount of life still adhere as Karman to their souls. As taught by metaphysics it assimilates the three first, so far as it is necessary, to the one mentioned last (*visamaṃ samaṃ karei*) and expels its surplus by an act of ejaculation called *kevali-samugghāya* and demonstrated in § 89 with ref. to Uvav. § 141 ff. While this was an entirely physical operation we now see the functions of the inner sense and of speech come in again. They exclusively move within the sphere of what is true and what is neither true nor wrong by which we have to understand instructions, orders, questions etc. (§ 74). In what Uvav. § 150 says about the physical activities left to such a one and said to consist in walking, standing, sitting, lying, passing beyond, lifting and handing something in different respects, the physical functions are completely neglected, as though in cases the condition of the *sajogī kevalī* asking for a description (Uvav. § 151; Ṭhāṇ. 49b; *guṇā-ṭṭhāṇa* 13, comp. § 183) did not include the entire teaching activity along with the master-life of a Kevalin like Mahāvīra displaying to the full (Ṭhāṇ. 306a) knowledge, vision, conduct, asceticism, and will. The activity of the senses (*āyāṇa*),

1. How we are to distinguish between an *ohi-nāṇa-kevalī*, a *maṇapajja-va-n.-k.* and a *kevala-n.-k.* (along with such as *jiṇa* and *arahā* of the same kind, Ṭhāṇ. 174a) Sthān. fails to explain.

however, has ceased (Viy. 223b=286a), since the Kevalin is not in need of it any longer.

Uvav. 30 V calls the *sukka-jhāṇa* on the last grades by the names of *suhuma-kiriya* and *samucchinna-k.* ('§ 180) in which connexion *kiriyā* means as much as *joga*. The attributive words *appaḍivāi*, resp. *aṇiyaṭṭi* exclude a relapse into the former activity. Hence this meditation—and this view is shared by tradition (Aup;. Sthān.)—must refer to a state of mind proper to the state of Kevalin. But the description offered by Uvav. § 141 ff. says nothing about meditation. Yet an indication of it may be found in Uvav. § 152 describing the manifestations of the inner sense and of both speech and body in the moment when they have been brought to a standstill as being diminutive and underbidding in size any measure feasible for other beings. The Kevalin is now *ajogī* for a small period of a few seconds and during it he annihilates the Karman of the last four kinds previously mentioned. This act puts an end to his earthly life and to his existence in the Saṃsāra. No more than (Uvav. § 155) a burnt seed is able to produce a sprout can a soul free from Karman experience a new incarnation. His entering into that stage is signified by the established expression of *selesiṃ paḍivajjai* (Uvav. § 153-155=Pannav. 607 f.; Viy. 252a; 725b; Dasav. 4, 23). Here the idea of one's reaching the top of a mountain makes itself felt,[1] particularly as in the Uvav. the *selesi* is linked up with the *guṇa-seḍhi*, i. e. the progessive scale of the virtues, though it does not go back *śilā* but to *śīla*[2] as indeed Prajn. 609b has it.

§187. After the last remainders of Karman have been annihilated the soul leaves (Uvav. § 153) its casing, i.e. the Karman body, and at the same time also the body of energy along with the physical body (§ 62); thanks to the buoyancy essentially proper to it (§ 92) it darts within 1 *samaya* in a straight line up to the place of the Siddhas above the region of

1. "Er gelangt zum Gipfel-Grad" the AUTHOR, RL 7, 28. The comm. (comp. Aup. s.v.) take *śaileśī* for the state of the *śaileśa* by which they understand the *unshakeable* Meru or him strengthened by asceticism.

2. The Digambaras indeed write *silesī* (Gomm. Jiv. 65). *selesī* is to *śileśa* as *sāmāyārī* is to *samācāra*.

Isīpabbhārā (§ 135). The younger texts like to speak of the *śiva ṭhāṇa*,[1] whereas in the older ones emphasis is placed not so much on the aim to be reached as on the process of reaching it, i.e. the *siddhi* or *mutti*, causing the word *nivvāṇa* not being frequently used, but comp. Utt. 23, 83.

The released soul[2] joins the Siddhas floating there in endless numbers 1-2 *joy.* below the boundary of the universe only up to where the fundamental fact of motion (§ 57) is capable of transporting it. All Siddhas (Uvav. § 168-189) touch it (*puṭṭhā log'ante*). This is brought about by the fact that they all interpenetrate each other (*annonna-samogāḍhā*) with all their units. They measure two thirds of the body (filled out completely by the soul, as we have seen) they had in the last moment of their earthly existence, a notion most certainly going back to observing the corpse having shrunk. The Siddhas are soul, soul pure and simple.[3] For the moment of transition as described above the Kevalin is attributed the "formally distinct" grasping (*nāṇa*) of the object as an individual one along with its momentary qualities (§ 82) (*sāgārôvautta*, Uvav. § 153). But he also has the "formally indistinct" way of grasping (*daṃsaṇa*) the object without its temporal attributes in a purely abstract and universal manner. Both, the *sāgāra nāṇa* as well as the *aṇāgāra daṃsaṇa*, are equally proper to the Siddha.[4] Pure cognition of that kind complies with the nature of the soul which is a spiritual function exclusively (§ 71). And it is this boundless realization of the nature of the soul alone and not some sensation or other for which, indeed, all preconditions whatever are wanting, that conveys what we may call eternal bliss.

1. Hence also the word *śivâvāpti* in Somaprabha, Śṛṅgāravairāgyataraṅgiṇī 33.

2. Its 31 virtues (*siddhâiguṇa*, Samav. 55b) rest on the absence of all Karman.

3. This is certainly meant by *jīva-ghaṇa* Uvav. § 154; 178=Pannav. 607b. The comm. however (and it is they whom the AUTHOR RL 7, 30, 2 followed) understand by it a compactness of soul units (§58).

4. The transl. rendered by the AUTHOR RL 7, 30 must, accordingly, be more exact.

GLOSSARY (§§)

aimuttaga-canda 67
airatta 48:5
aisesa 141
akaṇḍuyaga 157
akati-saṃcaya 94
akamma-bhūmi 117
akamhā-bhaya 88 n.
akaraṇayā 160
akāma-nijjarā 117
akicca-ṭṭhāṇa 158
akiriyā 16, 168
akiriyā-vāī 83
akevalin 81
akkosa 176
akkhara 74
akkhīṇa-mahāṇasiya 181 n.
agaṇi-kāya 99
agāra-dhamma 170
agurulahu 61
agga-mahisī 132, 166 n.
aggi 110 n.
aggeī 58
aghāi-kamma 87
anga-paviṭṭha 40
anga-bāhira 40, 44, 48:5, 50, 151
ang(ula) first occurrence 58
acakkhu-daṃsaṇa 82
acakṣur-darśana 15, 82
acarama 81
acitta 61, 105 n.
accāsaṇā 69
ajīva 57,61,76, 83
ajogī 81, 183, 186
ajjava 174
ajjā 49
ajjhattha 99
ajjhavasāṇa 96
ajjhāroha 106
ajjhovagamiya 86
ancala 35
anjali 163
aṭṭa 180
aṭṭha-jāya 137
aṭṭahama-bhatt(iy)a 156, 163
aṭṭhā-daṇḍa 170
aṇagāra 84, 89 n., 181
aṇagāra-sāmāiya 151
aṇagāriyā 137
aṇanga-paviṭṭha 40, 151
aṇaṭṭha(°ā)-daṇḍa 170
aṇaṇhaya 16
aṇ'atta 137
aṇattavaṃ 168 n.
aṇaddha 59 n.
aṇanta 57 n., 87
aṇanta-guṇa 21
aṇanta-vattiya 180
aṇantara 81
aṇantara-purakkhaḍa 128
aṇantara-siddha 21
aṇantar'āgaya 101
aṇantar'āhāra 96

aṇantâṇubandhi 87
aṇavakankha 99
aṇavaṭṭhappa 162
aṇavaṭṭhayā 161
aṇavadagga 175
aṇasaṇa 156
aṇāiya 60
aṇāgāra 82, 187
aṇābhoga-(niv)vattiya 96, 99
aṇicca 175
aṇiṭṭhubhaga 157
aṇiṭṭhaṃtha 21, 60
aṇidāya 86
aṇimisa 154 n.
aṇiyaṭṭi-bāyara 183
aṇiyaṭṭī 180, 186
aṇissiya 72
aṇīya, °yâhivai 132 n.
aṇu 68
aṇuoga 38, 53
aṇugama 53
aṇugghāima, °iya 51, 162
aṇugghāḍa 162
aṇujāṇai 171
aṇudisaṃ 140
aṇunnavaṇī bhāsā 74
aṇunnā 53, 141, 150
aṇuparihāriya 162
aṇupālittā 170 n.
aṇuppavāya 38
aṇuppehā 150, 175f., 180
aṇubhāga, °va 85, 87, 182
aṇu-vvaya 77, 163 n., 172
aṇusaṭṭhi 165
aṇevaṃbhūya 86
aṇonna-samogāḍha 187
aṇḍaya 64, 118 n.
aṇhaya 84, 167f.
atittha 81
atihi-saṃvibhāga 170
atīta 71
atta-māyā 96
attha-joṇi 13 n.
atthi n'atthi 38
atthikāya 57
atthiya 154 n.
atth'oggaha 72
adarśana 176
adinn'ādāṇa 16, 170f.
ad-uttaraṃ 121
adukkhī 88
addha-cakkavāla 21
addhā 57f.
addhâuya 93 n.
addhāṇa-gamaṇa 69
addho'vamiya 57
adhamma 57f., 76, 168
adharma 10
ananta-viyojaka 185
anavasthita 78
anākāra 82
anindriya 71
anukta 72
anuprekṣā 175
anta-kiriyā 101, 185
antara 12, 60, 68, 96

antara-dīva(ga) 116f.
antarāiya 87
antī 168
andhakāra 48:5
ann'anna 175
anna-m-anna 162
annautthiya 20, 149
annāṇa 70, 79, 168, 176, 180
annāṇiya 83
annāṇī 79
anno jīvo, annaṃ sarīraṃ 175
anyatva 175
apaesa 59 n.
apaccakkhāṇa 87, 100, 172
apajjatta 63, 101, 104
apajjattiya 74
apajjavasiya 60
apaḍhama 81
aparissāī 159
apavartana 90
apasattha 149
apāya 72, 180 n.
apuṭṭha-vāgaraṇa 54
apuvva-karaṇa 13, 183
apuhatta 55
appa 90
appa-kammatarāga 99
appa-koha 178
appaḍikuṭṭha 165
appaḍivāī 180, 186
appamatta 80
appamatta-saṃjaya 183
apramatta-saṃyata 180
aprāptakāritva 67
abandhaga 91
abahi-lesa 97 n.
abāhā 85, 90
abuddha 152
abbuya 64
abbhakkhāṇa 170 n.
abbhahiya 96
abbhuṭṭhāṇa 136
abbhuṭṭhittae 160
abbhovagamiya 86
abhava-siddhiya 101
abhigama 103 n.
abhigraha 156
abhijāti 97 n.
abhijāya 97 n.
abhinna 68
abhisega-silā 115
abhihaḍa 154
amajjha 59
amāī 62, 168, 181
amuha 159
ammā 64
aya-gola 104
arai(-rai) 167, 176
aravinda 74 n.
arahaṃ 14, 20 n., 25, 37 n.
arihanta 18 n.
aruṇa 119
artha-naya 76
aliya-vayaṇa 171
alukkhī 59, 88 n.
aloga 84 n., 103

alog'āgāsa 57
alpa-bahutva 21
avakkanta 108
avakkamiya 86
avaktavya 77
avagāhaṇā 57
avagraha 72
avacūr(ṇ)i 43
avaccijja 16
avajjhāṇa(yā) 180
avattavva 77
avatthu 76
avaddhaṃsa 167
avadhāna 78
avadhi 78, 80f.
avanda(ṇijja) 149 n.
avara-ṭṭhiya 137 n.
avaraṇha 150 n.
avahaṭṭu 177
avāuḍa 157
avāya 72, 180
avāya-daṃsī 159
aviukkantiyaṃ 94
aviosaviya-pāhuḍa 156
avigaraṇa 147
aviṇaya 168
aviṇīya 156
avibhāima 59 n.
avibhāga-paliccheya 85
avimuttayā 71
aviyārī 180
avirai 168, 172
avirata, °ya 180
avīci-davva 96
avvattaga-saṃciya 94
avvatta-daṃsaṇa 15
avvāvanna 64
avvocchitti 76f.
aśucitva 175
asaṃkhejja 57 n.
asaccāmosa 74
asajjhāiya 150
asaṃjama 177
asadda 60
asaṃdiddha 72
asannī 91, 167
asamāhi 51, 158
asamohaya 181
asaṇa 154
asaraṇa 175
as(s)āyā-veyaṇijja 89, 167
asāsaya 77
asunna-kāla 93
asubbha 60, 180
asura 105
asoccā 78
asti 77
ahakkhāya 177
ahacchanda 139
ahâu-nivvatti-kāla 57 n.
ahātacca 15
ahā-pariggahiya 142
ahā-bāyara 89
ahā-rāiṇiyāe 138
ahā-riyaṃ 110
ahā-landaṃ 147

ahā-lahusaga 160
ahā-saṃvibhāga 170
ahā-suhuma 89
ahiṃsā 28
ahigaraṇa 172
ahigaraṇiya 100
ahigaraṇī 70, 172
ahiyāsaṇā 69
ahe-loga 58, 107, 110 n.
aho 58

āicca 48:5
ā'iḍḍhi 96
āinna 46, 166
āu-kāya 59 n.
āuga-pāṇa 67
āuttaṃ 74
āuya-kamma 87, 89f., 95
āuya-bandha 90
āusaṃ(ta) 42, 137
āesa 79
ākaḍḍhai 86
ākiṃcaṇiyā 174
ākiṃcanya 174
āgama 41, 75, 160
āgarisa 90
āgāsa 57, 76
āgāsâivāī 181
āghoṭayati 89
ājīviya 167
ājnā-prāmāṇya 21 n.
āṇamai 66
āṇavaṇiya 99
āṇā 160, 180
āṇā-pāṇa 67
āṇupuvvī 87, 99
ādā 70 n.
ādāna 16 n.
ādāṇiya 16
ādi 59
āditya 125
ādejja 16
ādeśa 79
ādhākarma 154 n.
ānīta 155 n.
āpucchaṇā 136
ābṛhati 90
ābhaṭṭha 163 n.
ābhiog(iy)a 124, 132, 167
ābhiṇibohiya 73, 75, 79
ābhoga 71, 96
ābhoga-nivvatiya 96
āmisa 168
āya-kamma 96
āyambil(iy)a 156, 162
āyaya 21, 60
āyarakkha 132
āyariya 49:12, 139ff., 150, 162, 164
āyariya-uvajjhāya 141
āyariyatta 141
āyava 48:5, 87
āya-saṃceyaṇijja 176
āya-sarīra-khetta 96
āyā 38, 61, 70
āyāṇa 67, 173, 186
āyāvaṇā 157

āyāvettae 157
ārambha 163, 173
ārambhiya 100
ārā(d)haṇā 163, 170, 185, 189
ārāhiṇī-bhāsā 74
āriya 117
ārovaṇā 162
ārjava 174
ālambaṇa 180
āloettae 16, 158
āloyaṇā 159, 164
āvakahiya 156 n., 165, 177
āvatta 166, 168
āvaraṇa 86
āvaliyā 48:5, 57, 60
āvasaha 147
āvassaya 40, 77, 149, 164
āvassiyā 136, 151
āvāga-patta 86
āvāsa-pavvaya 121
āveḍhiya-pariveḍhiya 85
āśrava 30 n., 84
āsa-rayaṇa 101
āsaissāmo 74
āsava 84, 99, 167f., 181 n., 184 n.
āsāyaṇā 57, 149, 158
āsāliyā 63
āsura 167
āsrava 84, 86, 168, 175
āhākamma 154
āhāra 96, 156
āhāraka, °ga 62, 89
āhārāiṇiyāe 138
āhāriya 84
āhārei 60, 96 n.
āhohiya 18, 81
āhohī 81

ingāla-kariyā 105
ingiṇi-maraṇa 165
icchā-kāra 136
icchā-parimāṇa 170
iḍḍhi 48:5, 62, 80, 125, 133, 181
iḍḍhimaṃ 181
iḍḍhimanta 80 n.
ittariya 156
itthi-rayaṇa 101
itthī 166 n.
Inda-maha 150
inda 118 n., 131
indā 58
indiya 67, 72, 75
indiya-pāṇa 67 n.
imā Rayaṇappahā 112
iriyā 173
iriyāvahiya 84, 99
issariya 87
iha-gaya 90, 181
iha-bhaviya 90

īkṣaṇa 82
īriyā 99
īriyāvaha 84
īsā 132
īsāṇī 58
īsiṃ pabbhāra-gaya 157

īsiṃ-purevāya 110
īhā 72

ukkāliya 40, 151
ukkiṭṭha 137
ukkuḍaya 157
ukkoseṇaṃ 21, 58
uggama-dosa 153
ugghāima, °iya 51, 162
ugghāḍa 162 n.
uccāra 157, 173
ujju-mai 80, 181
ujju-sutta 76
ujjuy'āyaya 21, 95
ujjoya 87
uṭṭhāṇa 83, 125
uḍupaka 103 n.
uḍu-baddha 146
uḍḍha 58
uḍḍha-muinga 103
uḍḍha-loga 129
uttara-guṇa 170 n., 172, 184
uttara-pagaḍi 85
uttara-paṭṭa 145, 147
uttara-prakṛti 183
uttara-veuvviya 62
uttāṇaya 157
uttāṇa-sāī 157
udaiya 86, 182
uddaga-joṇiya 94
udagattā 94
udaga-rasa 123 n.
udaga-viyaḍa 154
udaya 84, 88, 91, 97, 182
udaya-saṃṭhii 48:5
udiṇṇa 86
udīrai 60, 160 n.
udīraṇā 86
udīriya 86
uddavaṇayā 66
uddāittā 66
uddiṭṭha-bhatta 163
uddisittae 141, 150
uddesaṇâyariya 150
uddesiya 154
udbha-bhojana 155 n.
upakaraṇa 67
upadeśa 189
upapāta, °da 92 n.
upayoga 71, 82
upavāsa 162 n.
upaśama 182
upaśamaka 185
upaśānta-kaṣāya 180, 183
upādhi 179
upāśraya 163
uppatti 168
uppattiya 73 n.
uppala 94, 106
uppāya 15 n., 38
uppāya-pavvaya 133
uppāyaṇa-dosa 153
ubbh'asaṇa 155 n.
ummāya 69
ura-parisappa 118
urāliya 62

uvautta 79
uvaesa 180
uvaoga 48:4, 57, 71, 82
uvaog'addhā 71
uvakula 48
uvakkama 90
uvaggaha 100, 145
uvaghāya 87
uvacaya 67, 72
uvaciṇai, °ṇāi 64, 84
uvaciya 86
uvajjhāya 139, 151, 161 n., 164
uvaṭṭhavaṇā, °ṭṭhā° 136, 138, 177
uvaṭṭhāvettae 138
uvabhoga 87, 170
uvarima 150
uvavajjai 94, 96
uvavāya 47, 63, 92
uvavāsa 163
uvasagga 176
uvasanta-moha 183
uvasama 174, 182
uvasama-seḍhi 183
uvasamiya 182
uvasaṃpayā 136
uvasāmaga 183
uvassaya 147
uvahāṇa 156
uvahi 179
uvāsaga-paḍimā 51, 163
uvās'antara 107
uvehā 177
uvaṭṭaṇā 85, 94
uvaṭṭei 85, 94
uvveha 113
usabha-vāhaṇa 131
usiṇa-joṇiya 94, 107 n.
ussappiṇī 13, 57, 61 n., 120
ussāsa 66

ūsassai 66
ūsāsa 161

ṛju-sūtra 76
ṛddhi 181

ega 175
ega-nāṇī 81
ega-rāiya 146, 163
egao-khaha 21
egao-vaṃka 21, 95
ega-ṭhāṇa 162 n.
eg'aṭṭhiya 106
egaṭṭhiya-paya 38 n.
egatta 175
egatta-viyakka 180
egalla-paḍimā 139, 185
egalla-vihārī 157
egâsaṇa 156, 162
eg'indiya 104
eyai 60
erāvaṇa-vāhaṇa 131
evaṃbhūta, °ya 76
eṣyati kāle 60
esaṇā 173
esaṇijja 153

esaṇiya 171

okacchiya 143
ogāḍha 58, 68, 180
ogāhaṇā 60, 65, 72
oggaha 72, 147, 153
oggaha(ṇa) 143
ogha-saṃjnā 71 n.
ojas 96 n.
omakoṭṭhayā 71
omaceliya 143
omaratta 48:5 (p. 103)
oma-rāiṇiya 138
omoyariyā 156, 178
oya 21, 60, 122
oyaṭṭaṇā 85, 90
oyaṭṭei 85
oyaṇa 77
oy'āhāra 96
orāliya 62, 174
ovamma 75
ovīlaga 159
osaṇṇa 71, 180
osanna 71, 139
osappiṇī 12, 57, 61 n., 120
osa-binduya 175
osahi 106
oha 71, 145
ohāṇa 71
ohāvai 139
ohi 73, 78, 80, 98
ohi-nāṇa 46:7, 186 n.

kai 28
kakkasa 167f.
kankhā-mohaṇijja 88
kankhiya 88
kaccha 132
kancaṇaga-pavvaya 115
kancuya 143
kaḍa 86
kaḍa-jumma 21 n.
kaṇag'āvalī 156
kaṇḍa 115 n.
kaṇṇa-kalaṃ 126 n.
kaṇha 97
kaṇha-rāī 60, 134
kati-kaṭṭhaṃ 127 n.
kati-saṃciya 94
kathā(naka) 189
kantāra-bhatta 154
kanthaga 166
kanda 106
kandappiya 167
kappa 129, 131, 136
kappa-ṭṭhii 136, 142
kappa-ṭṭhiya 136, 162
kappa-vimāṇôvavattiya 185
kappâīya 131
kappāga 162
kappôvaga 131
kamaḍhaga 144
kambala 143
kamma 38, 83f., 87ff.
kamm'aṃsa 183
kammaga 62, 84

kamma-ṭṭhiīya 84
kamma-niyāṇa 84
kamma-pagaḍi 85, 87, 100
kamma-bhūmaga 117
kamma-bhūmi 117
kammā-vāī 83
kammiya 73 n.
kammôvaga 84
kaya-vvaya-kamma 163
karaṇa 84, 86, 183
karaṇôvāya 96
karisa 64
karman 78
kalakala 126
kalambuya-puppha 67
kalala 64
kalā-savanna 21 n.
kali-oya 21
kalusa 88
kalpa-traya 143
kallāṇa(ga) 34, 162 n.
kavala 155
kavittha 125
kavvaḍaya 21
kasāya 84, 87, 167f., 184
kasāya-samugghāya 89
kasāy'āyā 70
kāiya 100
kāu(ya) 97, 108 n.
kāussagga 161
kāgiṇī 13
kāma 174
kāma-bhogī 174
kāya-kilesa 157
kāya-ṭṭhii 69, 93
kāya-bhavattha 64
kāya-tigicchā 69
kāyasā 171
kāruṇya 172
kāla 57, 77
kāliya 40, 151
kiikamma 148f.
kiṃṇara 79 n.
kiḍḍā 69
kiṇha-pakkha 125
kinnara 79 n.
kibbisiya 134, 167
kimi-rāga 168
kiriya-ṭṭhāṇa 99
kiriyā 86, 99
kiriyā-vāī 51
kivvisiya 134
kīya-gaḍa 154
kīrtideva 30
kīliyā 65
kīva 137
kuṇḍa 124 n.
kunthu 78, 172
kumāra 14
kumāra-bhicca 69
kumbha 30 n.
kummāsa 77
kula 23, 25, 48, 87, 139, 141, 148
kulaka 189
kulagara 13
kulôvakula 48:5 (p. 102)

kuvala 31
kus'agga 175
kusīla 52, 139, 184
kūḍa 114f.
kūḍa-pāsa 100 n.
kevala 13, 18, 81f., 185
kevala-daṃsaṇa 15
kevali-pannatta 101
kevali-samugghāya 47, 89, 186
kesa 69
kesa-loya 176
kesariyā 144
kouya-karaṇa 167
koṭṭiṇī 25 n.
koṭṭha-buddhi 181
koḍākoḍi, koḍi° 103 n., 126, 128
koḍha 65
korava 166
kosa 125
koha 168 n., 174
kriyā 100
kleśa 97 n.
kṣamā 174
kṣaya 182
kṣīṇa-kaṣāya 180, 182
kṣīṇa-moha 185

khaiya 86
khaôvasamiya 78
khaṇḍa 58, 78 n., 113
khattiya-kumāra 17
khanti 174
khandha 59, 76
khandha-karaṇī 143
khamaṇa 162 n.
khamā 174
khamā-samaṇa 29 n.
khamāvei 159
khaya 86
khara 166
kharakaṇṭaya 163
khalunka 166
khavaga-seḍhi 183
khahayara 118
kh'āi 101 n., 127 n.
khāima 154
khāmei 151, 159
khāra-tanta 69
khitta see khetta
khippa 72
khīṇa-moha 183
khīr'āsava 181 n.
khu khu 21
khujja 65
khujja-karaṇī 143
khuḍḍa, khuḍḍāga 21
khubbhai 60
khura 137
khurappa 67, 108 n.
khura-muṇḍaga 163
khetta 77
khetta-sama 112
khett'āriya 117
khela 173
khomiya 143

gai-ppavāya 48
gai-raiya 128
gaccha 30, 34f., 52, 139
gacchāgacchiṃ 139
gaṇa 22, 25, 30, 34, 139, 148, 179
gaṇa-saṃgahaṇa 140
gaṇahara 22, 139f.
gaṇâvaccheiya 139f.
gaṇâvaccheiyatta 140
gaṇi-piḍaga 37, 45:4
gaṇi-saṃpayā 51, 140
gaṇin 140
gaṇiya 57
gaṇī 140
gabbha 63f.
gabbha-ghara 76
garahai 160 n.
garahaṇa 162 n.
garbha 63
gaha 126
gahaṇa 57, 72
gahaṇ'esaṇā 153
gāuya 65
gāo 74
gāṇaṃgaṇiya 139
gāma 146
gāmâṇugāmaṃ 146
gāratthiṇī 163
gāratthiya 149, 163
giddha-paṭṭha 165
giṃhā 106 n., 146
gilāṇa 148
gihī 163
gīy'attha 52, 151
guṇa 59, 76f.
guṇa-ṭṭhāṇa 183ff.
guṇarayaṇa-saṃvacchara 156
guṇa-veramaṇa 163 n.
guṇa-vvaya 170, 172
guṇa-seḍhi 183, 186
guṇa-sthāna 91, 177, 183
gutti 54, 173
gupti 173
gummāgummiṃ 139
guru 162
guviya 107 n.
guvviṇī 137
geṇhai 60, 68
gocchaga 144
go-tittha 121
godohiya 157
gopāla 74 n.
gomuttiyā 168 n.
goya 90 n.
goya-kamma 87, 168 n.
gorjī 36
gola 104
gola-vaṭṭa-samugga 25

ghaṭṭai 60
ghaṇa 21, 60, 64
ghaya 156
ghara-samudāṇa 153
ghāi-kamma 87, 182
ghās'esaṇā 153
ghuṇa 153 n.

cauttha-bhatt(iy)a 34, 156
cauddasa-puvvī 38
caurāsī 189
cakka 58
cakkavaṭṭī 13, 115, 133
cakkavāla 21
caṇḍa 132
caṇḍāla 134 n.
canda 48
canda-gora 14
canda-paḍimā 156
candaga-vijjhā 50
candra 30
candraka-vedhyaka 50
camma 143, 145
camma-kosaga 143, 145
camma-(pali)ccheyaṇaga 143
camma-rayaṇa 13
cayai 92ff.
cayaṇa 92
cayaṇôvavāya 48:5 (p. 103)
caraga-parivvāyaga 167
carama 81
carita 189
caritta 87, 89, 177
caritta-pajjava 184
caritra 189
carima 21, 89 n.
cariya 189
cariyā 176
calai 60
calaṇiyā 143
cāī 137, 174
cāujjāma 16
cāummāsiya 159
cāulôdaṇa 163
cāuvaṇṇa 137 n.
cāya 174
cāra 48
cāra-ṭṭhiīya 128
cāraga 13 n.
cāritra 177
ciṇai, ciṇāi 64, 84
cita 71
citta-samāhi 51
cintā-suviṇa 15
ciya 86
ciyāga 174
cilimili 143
cīvara 143
cīvāsī 31
cūrṇi 43
cūliyā 31, 38, 52
ceiya 18, 154
ceiya-rukkha 18
ceiy'ālaya 31
cela 143
cela-cilimiṇiyā, °liyā 143, 145
caitya-vāsa, -vāsin 31
cola-paṭṭā 143

chaumattha 15, 81f., 176
chakka-samajjiya 94
chaṭṭha-bhattiya 156
chadmastha 81

chandaṇā 136
chavi 133 n.
chavi-chheya 13 n.
chāumatthiya 89
chāyā 97
chinna 127
chihāli-dhāraga 163
cheôvaṭṭhāvaṇiya 177
cheya 40, 136, 161
cheya-ggantha 40
chevaṭṭha 65

jai 120 n., 137
jakkha 112 n.
jakkh'āiṭṭha 69
jakkh'āvesa 69
jakkh'ālitta 150
jagaī 121 n.
jagad-guru 28
jangolī 69
janghā-cāraṇa 181
jamā 58
jaya (jagat) 91
jarā 69 n.
jarāuya 64
jala-bindu 175
jalayara 118
jalla 173
java-majjha 156 (p. 275)
jahanneṇaṃ 21, 58
jāi 87
jāgara 152
jāgariyatta 152
jāṇai pāsai 66, 78f., 82
jāṇaṃ 163
jāma 69
jāyaṇā bhāsā 74
jāyā 132
jāla-kaḍaga 121 n.
jāvajjīvāe 171
jiṇa 14
jiṇa-kapp(iy)a 26, 143, 184
jiṇa-ghara 25
jiṇa-paḍimā 25
jiṇa-magga 26
jina 185
jibbhiyā 114
jimha 120 n.
jīda 137 n.
jīmūta 120 n.
jīya 160
jīva 10, 57, 84f., 88, 91, 94, 121
jīva-ghaṇa 187
jīva-ṭṭhāṇa 183
jīva-phuḍa 62
jīvā 113
jīv'āyā 70
juga 173
jumma 21, 60
jain'ābhāsa 30 n.
joisa 48, 126
joisiya 125
joga 48, 84f., 96, 167f., 178, 180, 186
jog'āyā 70
joṇi 63
joṇi-voccheya 63 n.

joyaṇa first occurrence 62
jnāna 176

jhanjhā 178
jhallarī 103
jhāṇa 152, 180
jhūsaṇā 170

ṭīkā 43
ṭolā 32

ṭhavaṇa 144
ṭhavaṇa-kula 153
ṭhavaṇā 77
ṭhāṇa 45:3, 147, 157
ṭhāṇâiya 157
ṭhāvaṇā-guru 159
ṭhii 69, 85, 98
ṭhiya 68
ṭhiya-lessa 98 n.

taṇa 106
taṇa-phāsa 176
tatta-cintā 175
tattva 169
tattha-gaya 181
tappa 103
tap-paḍhamayā 142 n.
tabbhava-maraṇa 165
tamā 58
tamu-k(k)āya 60, 134 n.
tava 16, 87, 174, 178
tavassī 148
tasa 66, 84 n., 118
taha-kkāra 136
tahā-rūva 137 n.
tā 48:5, 127 n.
tāṇa 175
tāyattīsa 132
tār'agga 48
tāra-ggaha 126
tārā-gaṇa 125
tāvasa 79, 167
tigicchiya 69
tittha 12, 81, 121
titthagara 12, 14ff., 81
tinnāṇôvagaya 18
ti bemi 42
tirikkha-joṇiya 64, 104
tiriya-bhitti 18
tiriya-loga 113
tirīṭa 143
tivihaṃ tiviheṇaṃ 171
tunga 30 n.
tuḍiyā 132
tuṇḍiyā 144
tumba 132
teu 97
teoya 21 (n., p. 42)
teya-nisagga 62, 181
teyaga 62, 89
tericchiya 167
trasa 66
trasa-nāḍī 95

thambhai 168

thaya 50
thalayara 118
thāvara 84 n., 118
thibuga 105
thīṇ'addhi 87
thūbha 25, 79 n.
thūlaga 170
thera 23 n., 26, 136, 138, 140f., 148, 158, 162
thera-kappa 26, 144, 184
thera-kappiya 143
thera-bhūmi 141
theraga 31

daṃsa-masaga 176
daṃsaṇa 82, 87, 169, 176, 187
daṃsaṇa-sāvaya 163
daṃsaṇ'āvaraṇa 87
daḍharahā 132
daṇḍaga 145
daṇḍa-nīi 13
daṇḍa-samāyāṇa 99
daṇḍ'āyaiya 157
datta 30 n.
datti 156
dabbha-saṃthāra 147
darisaṇ'āvaraṇa 87
darśana 176
darśana-moha-kṣapaka 185
daviya 57 n.
daviy'āyā 70
davva 57, 61, 66, 68, 76f.
davv'indiya 67, 71
daśapūrvadhārin 38
dasā(o) 46:7, 69
dasāra-maṇḍala 13
dahi 156
dāna 174
dāra 55, 168f.
dāvaddava 46
dāvara 21
dāvei 154
dāhiṇ'āvatta 166
dikkhā 138
dikkhettae 138
dig-ambara 26
digiṃchā 176
diṭṭhasāhammavaṃ 75
diṭṭhi 169
diṭṭhiya 99
divasiya 159
divva 174
disā 58, 140
disākumārī 110
disā-pokkhiya 79
disāhatthi-kūḍa 115
disi-dāha 150
disi-vvaya 170
dīkṣā 30, 138
dīpikā 43
dīva 122
dīva-samuddāiṃ 113 n.
dīviccaga (°ya) 46, 110
dīha 21 n., 90 (āuya), 114
duāikkha 16 (p. 31)
duḥkha 172

dukkaḍa 159
dukkāla 26
dukkhī 88
duddhara 72
dubbhi 60, 67 n.
dummaṇa 167 n.
durabhi 67 n.
duvihaṃ tiviheṇaṃ 171
duha-sejjā 172
duhao-khaha 21
duhao-vaṃka 21, 95
dūijjai 146
dūra 127
dūsamā etc. 13, 120
deula 25
deva 30 n., 105, 112 n., 125, 132 n.
deva-kibbis(iy)a, °kivvi° 134, 167
deva-nikāya 134 n.
devayā-paḍimā 164
devâhideva 14
devinda 50
deśanā 189
deśa-virata 180
desa 58f., 61, 76, 84, 96
desa-kāla-nnu 179
desa-viraya 163
desâvagāsiya 163, 170
doccaṃ pi 89 n., 95 n.
dosa 99, 153, 158, 167f., 180
dosiṇā 48:5
dohada 49:8, 64
dravyârthika 76
dvīpa 110 n.

dhaṇiya 84
dhaṇu first occurrence 65
dhaṇu-paṭṭha 113
dhamma 16, 57, 76, 168, 175
dhamma (dharmya) 180
dhamma-kahā 46, 150
dhamma-jāgariyā 152
dhamm'antevāsī 16 n.
dhammâṇuoga-cintā 150
dhamm'āyariya 141
dhammiya 185
dharma 174f., 180n.
dharma-lābha 30
dharma-vṛddhi 30
dharma-śālā 163
dharma-svākhyāta-tattva 175
dharmya 175
dhāraṇā 72
dhārettae (gaṇaṃ) 140
dhik-kāra 13
dhīra-purisa 48
dhuva 72, 125
dhuva-Rāhu 48:5
dhyāna 181

nakkhatta-vijaya 48:5
nakṣatra 48:5
nagara 146
nagar'āvāsa 124
nagga-bhāva 176 n.
nandā 69
namo arihantāṇaṃ etc. 161 n.

namo tthu ṇaṃ 101
naya 53, 75ff.
naraga 108 n.
nava-ṇīya 156
naha 69
nāga 30 n., 105, 112 n.
nāgakumāra-vāsa 170
nāgadanta 25
nāṇa 16, 38, 53, 75f., 80, 88, 186f.
nāṇ'āyā 70
nāṇ'āvaraṇijja 87
nāṇī 79
nāma 77, 166
nāma-kamma 87, 89
nām'āuḍiya 76
nāya 46, 150
nāya-vihi 154, 163
nārāya 65
nālī 95, 108 n.
nioya 104
nikāiya, nikāei 85
nikkhamai 126
nikkheva 53, 77
nikkhevaṇā 173
nigaṇṭha 27 n.
nigoda, °ya 93, 101, 104
niggantha 45:2, 51, 137, 184
niggantha pavayaṇa, pā° 37
nigganthī 51, 97 n., 137
nigganthī-pavvāviyaga 137 n.
niggoha 65
nicchūḍha 89
nijjarā 86, 175 (nirjarā), 185
nijjarei 60
nijjavaga 159
nijjāi 69
nijjiṇṇa 88
nijjūhei 139
niṇhava 18 n.
nitiya 139, 154
nidā 86 n.
nidāna 180
nidāya 86
niddā 87
niddā-niddā 87 (p. 180)
niddha 59
nidhatta 85
ninditttae 160
nippheḍaṇa ,°ṇā 140
nimantaṇā 136
nimitta 15 n.
nimitt'ājīvaga 167
niyaṃsaṇiya 143
niyaṭṭi-bāyara 183
niyaṇṭha 17 n., 137, 154f., 184
niyamā 91, 100
niyāṇa 51 n., 168, 180
niyāṇa-kāraṇa 13
niyāṇa-bhūmi 13
niyāṇa-maraṇa 165
niratiśaya 81
nirantara 96
niray'āvāsa 108
niruvakkama 90
nivṛtti 67
nilleva 93

nivvattaṇā 67, 72, 96
nivvattayā 72
nivvattiya 96
nivvāṇa 16, 187
nivvigai 164
nivviṭṭha-kāiya 136, 177
nivvisamāṇa(ga) 136, 177
nivvīiya 156, 162
nivveḍhei 126
nivveyaṇī 150
niṣikta 90
nisagga 180
nisarai 68
nisīhiyā 51, 136, 147, 151, 157, 176
nisega 85
nisejjā 145
niseha 51
nissāsa 66
nihatta, °ttei 85, 90
nihi 13
nīti 13 n.
nīl'uppala 14
nīsasai 66
nīsāe 18
nisīhiyā 136
negama 76
necchaiya 76
netā 48
neraiya 77, 109
neraī 58
nesajjiya 157
nesatthiya 99
naigama 76 n.
no-indiya 72, 75
no-kasāya 87
no-jīva 10

paiṭṭhiya 84
paunjai 78 n.
pauma 116
pauma-gora 14
paesa 57ff., 76, 85, 92
paesa-kamma 182
paesiya 59, 77
paoga 48, 82 n., 99
paogasā 60
paosa 150
paosiya 100
pakuvvaga 159
pakkha 48:5
pakkhiya 159
pakkhī 74
pakkhev'āhāra 96
paccakkha 75
paccakkhāṇa 16, 38, 87, 163 n., 170 n., 172
pacchakkhāṇ'āvaraṇa 87
paccāyāi 66
paccīsī 189
paccūsa 150
pacchā-kaḍa 164
pacchāga 143
pacchitta 161
pacchitta-sutta 52
paccho'vavannaga 98 n.
pajjatta 63, 101, 104

pajjatti 63
pajjattiya 74
pajjava 60
pajjava-jāya-lessa 98 n.
pajjunna 120 n.
pajjosavaṇā 146
pajjosavaṇā-pancamī 24 n.
panca-namokkāra 161 n.
panca-mangala 52
panca-mahavvaiya 16
panca-muṭṭhiya 137
panca-rāiya 146
pancendiya 105
paṭṭa 145
paṭṭa-dhara 34
paṭṭ'āvalī 34, 189
paṭṭhavaṇā, °vei 160
paḍa-buddhi 181
paḍaṇa 150
paḍala 144
paḍāgā 62
paḍikkamai, °maṇa 159, 161
paḍiggaha(ga) 142, 144
paḍijāgarettae 170
paḍiṇiyattai 95
paḍipucchaṇā 150
paḍibaddha 106
paḍimā 156f., 161, 163f.
paḍiyāṇiyā 143
paḍilehai 148
paḍivatti 47:3, 48:5
paḍivāī 78
paḍivāsudeva 13
paḍisaṃlīṇayā 178
paḍisaṃveei 86
paḍisattu 13
paḍisevai, °ṇā 184
paḍihāriya 147
paḍoyāra 180
paḍhama 21, 81
paḍhama-pāusa 146
paḍhama-samaôvavannaga 96
paḍhamâṇijoga 38 n.
paṇihāṇa 84 n.
paṇḍiya-maraṇa 165
paṇḍura 110
patad-graha 144 n.
pa-telasa 18 n.
patta 94
pattiyāmi 169
patteya-buddha 14, 81, 180
patteya-sarīra 106
pattôvā-rukkha 166 n.
patthaga 76
patthaḍa 108 n.
patthāvāya 110
padastha 180 n.
panta 156
pannavaṇā 77
pannavaṇī bhāsā 74
pannā 69, 176
pabbhārā 69
pamajjai, °ṇā 148
pamatta 133
pamatta-saṃjaya 62, 183
pamāṇa 76

pamāya 88, 168
pamha 97
paya 148, 150 n.
payara 60
payalā 87
payalāei 87 n.
payalā-payalā 87
payāṇa 15
payâṇusārī 181
para 148
para-bhaviya 90
paramātman 90
para-m-ahohiya 81
para-veyāvacca-kamma-paḍimā 156 n.
paramâṇupoggala 58 n., 59
paraṃpara 81
paraṃpara-siddha 21
paraṃpar'āgaya 101
par'āghāya 87
parikamma 21 n., 38
pariggaha 71, 142, 171, 179 n.
pariggahiya 100
pariṭṭhāvaṇiyā 173
pariṇamai 60
pariṇāma 10, 60f., 67
pariṇāmai 96 n., 98
pariṇāmayā 96
pariṇivvuya 22
paridevaṇayā 180 n.
paribhāsa 13 n.
paribhoga 170
paribhog'esaṇā 153
parimaṇḍala 21, 60, 65
parimāṇa-kaḍa 163
pariyaṭṭaṇā 150
pariyāiṇayā 96
pariyāittā 181
pariyāei 89
pariyāya 138
pariyāya-thera 138
pariyāraṇayā 96
pariyāvannaga 104
parisā 132
parisāḍei 89
parispanda 84
parisphuṭa 82
parihāra 161f.
parihāra-kappa-ṭṭhiya 162
parihāra-ṭṭhāṇa 167
parihāra-visuddhiya 177
parihāriya 162, 164
parīṣaha, °saha 176
parokkha 75
parokṣa 75
paryāya 180
paryāyârthika 76
paryuṣaṇā 189
pala 64
paliovama 57
paliyanka 103
pallava 35
pavaga 96
pavattiṇī 140, 158
pavattī 140, 164
pavancā 69
pavayaṇa-māyā 173, 184

pavāya 38
pavāya-kuṇḍa 114
pavāya-daha 114
pavāla 106
paviṭṭha 67
pavisai 126
pavesaṇa(ga) 93
pavva 125
pavva-Rāhu 48:5 (p. 103)
pavvajjā 137
pavvā 132
paśyattā 82
pasattha 98 n.
pasappaga 174 n.
pasū 74
pāusa 106 n.
pāôvagamaṇa 165
pāṭhântara 43
pāḍivaya 150
pāḍihāriya 147
pāḍucciya 99
pāḍha 38 n.
pāṇa 66, 70, 92, 104, 154
pāṇamai 66
pāṇâivāya 99f., 170 f.
pāṇ'āu 38
pāṇi-vaha 171
pāṇu 66
pāya 142, 144
pāyacchitta 160f.
pāya-puṃchaṇa 142, 145
pāya-lehaṇiyā 145
pāyāla 121
pāranciga, °ya 161f.
pāriṇāmika, °ya 101, 182
pāriyāvaṇiya 100
pārihāriya 162, 164
pārei 156
pāva 84, 169
pāvayaṇa 37
pāva-suya-pasanga 15 n., 69
pāsaṇayā 82
pāsaṇḍika 27 n.
Pāsâvaccijja 16
pāsavaṇa 159, 173
pāsillaga 157
pāhuḍa 38, 48:5, 156
pāhuḍa-pāhuḍa 48:5
piiya 64
piccaṃ 74 n.
piccha 30
piṇḍa 154
piṇḍavāya 153, 155
piṇḍastha 180 n.
piṇḍ'esaṇā 154
piṇḍiyā 64
pittiya 69
piyangu 14, 110
pihula 21
pīḍha 147
pīdhâṇīya 132
pukkhala-saṃvaṭṭaga 120
puggala 59 n.
pucchaṇī bhāsā 74
puṭṭha 58f., 67f., 86, 99, 187
puṭṭhiya 99

puḍhavi-kāiya 104
puḍhavī 107 n.
puṇṇa 169
putta 16 n., 64
pudgala 84, 96 n.
purekkhaḍa 71
purao kaḍa, kaṭṭu 90, 140
purāṇa 189
purima ṭhāṇa 96
purim'aḍḍha 156, 161
purimaṇḍala 162 n.
purisa(-jāya) 166
purisakkāra-parakkama 83
puris'ādāṇīya 16
purohiya 13
pula 181
pulāga 184
pulāga-bhatta 155
puvva 37f.
puvvaṇha 150
puvva-sejjāyarī 18 n.
puvvôvavannaga 98 n.
puhutta 55
puhutta-viyakka 180
pūjya-vyākhyā 66 n.
pūrṇimā 33
pūrva 37
pūrva-pakṣa 38
pūrvânuyoga 38
pṛthaktva 67 n.
pṛthutva 67 n.
pejja 99, 167f.
peyāla 170
pesī 64
pess'ārambha 163
pehā 177
poggala 57, 58f., 69, 84, 88, 94, 96, 125, 181
poggala-pariyaṭṭa 57, 61
poggalī 67
poyaga 64, 84
porāṇa 72
porisi-cchāyā 48, 127 n.
porisī, °rusī 18, 48, 148, 150f., 155
posaha-sālā 170
pohatta 67
prakaraṇa 29, 189
prakīrṇaka 134 n.
pracaya 67
prajnā 176
pratara 21 n.
pratipatati 78
pratimā 32
pratyakṣa 75
pradeśa 85
prabandha 189
prabodhita 28
pramatta-saṃyata 180
pramoda 172
praśasti 34 n., 189
praśnôttara 189
prastaṭa 108 n.
prāṇa 67n.
prekṣaṇa 82

phaḍḍa 139

phaḍḍāphaḍḍiṃ 139
phandai 60
phala 86
phalaga 147
phāsuya 153
phuḍa 105
phumphuy'aggi 66
phusamāṇa 60 n.
phoḍa 181

bausa 184
baddha 86
baddha-spṛṣṭa 67
baddhellaga 48, 71
bandha 84f., 87, 91
bandhai 91
bandhaga 91
bandhaṇa 84
bandhī 84
bambha 118n., 174
bambhacera-gutti 174
bambhayārī 163
bambhī livi 117
bala 83, 87
baladeva 13, 117
bala-pāṇa 67 n.
balā 69
bali 30
bahalatā 67 n.
bahiddhā-dāṇa 16
bahil-lesa 97 n.
bahu 72
bahu-kaṇṭaga 154
bahu-bīyaga 105
bahu-y-aṭṭhiya 154
bahu-sama 113 n.
bahuviha 72
bāyara 59 n., 60, 68, 104f.
bāla-maraṇa 165
bālā 69
bālâvatthā 137
bāhalla 67
bāhā 113
bāhiraya 96, 181
bāhulya 67 n.
bimba 32, 64
bisarīra 185
bīya-buddhi 181
buddha 20 n., 81, 152
buddh'anta 125
buddhi 73
bodhi-durlabha 175
bola 126
brahmacarya 174

bhagavaī 48, 56
bhagavaṃ 18
bhaijjai 100
bhaṇḍa 173 n.
bhaṇḍaga 142
bhatta 120 n., 157, s. aṭṭhama, cauttha
bhatta-paccakkhāṇa 165
bhatta-paccakkhāya(ga) 165 n.
bhattasālā 25 n.
bhadanta 43
bhadra 30 n.

bhante 17
bhayaṇāe 91
bhava-ṭṭhii 69, 93
bhavaṇa 111
bhavattha 81
bhava-dhāraṇijja 62
bhava-paccaiya 78
bhava-siddhiya 101, 183
bhav'āuya 93 n.
bhāga 48
bhāva 75, 77f., 80, 182
bhāvaṇā, °na 45, 46:10, 167, 171, 175, 189
bhāv'indiya 67, 71
bhāviy'appā 89 n., 181
bhāṣya 43
bhāsā 68, 70, 74, 163, 172
bhāsâriya 117
bhikkhā 156 n.
bhikkhāga 153 n.
bhikkhāyariyā 153
bhikkhu 137
bhikkhuṇī 137
bhikkhu-paḍimā 51, 74, 157
bhinna 68
bhilanga-sūva 163
bhuya-parisappa 118
bhūi-kamma 167
bhūmi 107
bhūya 70, 112 n.
bhūya-vijjā 69
bhūṣaṇa 30
bheya 60, 88
bheya-ghāya 126
bhoga 87, 174
bhogī 174
bhomejja-nagara 112

ma-kkāra 13
mai 73
mai-annāṇa 73
maṃsa 154
maṃsa-cakkhu 30 n.
mangala 161 n.
maccha 154
majjhaṇha 150 n.
majjh'antiya 127
majjhima 19
maḍ'āī 154 n.
maṇa 61, 70, 173
maṇa-bhakkhī 96
maṇa-pajjava 73, 80, 186 n.
maṇasā 171
maṇussa-khetta 80
maṇussī-gabbha 64
maṇo-gaya 80
maṇḍala 48:5, 126, 139 n.
maṇḍala-bandha 13 n.
maṇḍaliya 15
maṇḍaliya-pavvaya 123
maṇḍali-rāya 14
mati 73
matta 173
mattaga 144
maddava 174
manaḥ-paryāya 80

manu 13
mandā-vāya 110
mammuhi 69
maya 168
maruyā devā 134 n.
masūra 77
maha 150
maha-ggaha 126
mahattariyā 110
maha-ddaha 114
maha-vvaya 171
mahā-kammatarāga 99
mahā-nagara-dāha 66
mahā-niraya 108
mahā-purisa 56
mahā-vāya 110
mahiḍḍhiyatarāga 69
mahoraga 63
māi-ṭṭhāṇa 158, 168
māiya 64
māī 62, 158, 168
māu(ya) 64
māu-oya 64
māuya-paya 38 n.
māṇa 168 n., 174
māṇusa 133 n.
mādhyasthya 172
māyā 168, 174, 180f.
māyā-mosa 167
māyā-vattiya 100 n.
māraṇ'antiya 89, 95 n.
mārdava 174
māsa 157
māsiya 157
māhaṇa 45:2, 137
māhātmya 189
micchatta 87, 168, 180
micchā me dukkaḍaṃ 159
micchā-kāra 136
micchā-daṃsaṇa 100
micchā-diṭṭhi 79, 168f.
mitta-dosa 99
mithyātva 87
miyā 74
milakkhu 117
missa 93
mīsā 60
mukkellaga 48
mukkha-vastrikā 145
mucchā 168
muṇḍa 137
muṇḍāvettae 137
mutti 174, 187
muddh'anta 125
mummuhī 69
musā-vāya 170f.
muha-ṇantaga 145
muha-pottiya 145
muha-vaṇa 114
muhutta 48, 62 et passim, 127
mūla 40, 106, 127, 161f.
mūla-khidi 162
mūla-guṇa 170 n., 172
mūla-naya 76
mūla-bhāṣya 29 n.
mūla-bhūmi 162

mṛṇmukhī 69 n.
mṛpāṭikā 65
meccha 117
meṇḍha-visāṇa 166
mehuṇa 171
mokṣa 101
mosa 74
moha 51
mohaṇijja 87, 169, 182f.
mohaṇīya 78

yakṣa, yakṣiṇī 14
yati 36
yoga 84ff., 167 n.
yoga-paṭṭaka 145

rajoharaṇa 145 n.
rajju 21 n., 103
ratta 106 n.
raya 84 n.
raya-ugghāya 150
rayaṇa 62
rayaṇ'āvalī 156
rayaṇi 65
raya-ttāṇa 144
rayaharaṇa 142, 145
rasa 64
rasa-pariccāga 156
rasaya 63 n.
rasāyaṇa 69
rahassa 21 n.
rāiṇīya 138
rāiya 159
rāī-bhatta 171
rāī-bhoyaṇa 155, 171
rāga 30 n.
rāga-dosa-niggaha 178
rādi 138 n.
rāma-kesavā 13
rāya-kahā 154 n.
rāya-piṇḍa 154
rāya-vuggaha 150
rāsī 10, 21 n.
riyai 110
rui 169, 180
rukkha 79 n., 106
rucaka 58 n.
rūkṣa 59
rūpastha 180
rūpâtīta 180
rūvi 61, 78
roemi 169
rodda 180

lagaṇḍa-sāī 157
langa 30 n.
laṭṭhi(yā) 145
laddhi 71f., 74, 181
labdhi 62
lahu 162
lāghava 174
lābha 87
linga 81, 88 n.
livi 117 n.
liṣyate 97 n.
lukkha 59

lukkhī 59, 89 n.
lūya-siraga 137
lūha 156
lesa 97
lesā-paḍighāya 127
lesā'bhitāva 127
les(s)ā 48:5, 97ff., 181
lo'ujjoya 133
loka 71 n., 175
loga 58, 76, 84 n., 103
loga-ṭṭhii 84, 121
log'anta see loy'anta
log'andhayāra 133
loga-pāla 110
loga-matthaga 103
log'āgāsa 57
logâṇubhāva 121
lobha 168 n., 174
lom'āhāra 30, 96
loya (loca) 137
loy'anta 107, 187
loya-sannā 71

vaira-majjha 156
vairôsabha 65
vaissa 19 n.
vaôvaṭṭhāvaṇa 140
vaṃśā 113 n.
vaṃsa 113 n.
vaṃsī-patta 64
vakkanti 63, 92
vakkamai 94, 106 n.
vakkhāra-pavvāya 115
vaggaṇā 61, 97
vaggulī 181
vajja-pāṇi 131 n.
vajja-risabha 65
vajja-saṃṭhiya 61, 68
vanjaṇa 72, 74
vaṭṭa 21, 114
vaṇa 115
vaṇa-khaṇḍa 116
vaṇa-dav'aggi 66
vaṇa-saṇḍa 121
vaṇassaikāiya(tta) 94, 104, 106 n.
vaṇṇa-vihīṇa 33
vattavva 77
vattha 142
vaddhai, vaddhāvei 17
vaya (vayas) 69
vaya (vrata) 171
vara-vaira 103
vargaṇā 62
varṣā 113 n.
valaya 107
valaya-maraṇa 165
vali 30
vavarovittā 177
vavahāra 21 n., 51, 76, 160
vas'aṭṭa-maraṇa 165
vasati-nivāsa 31
vasahi 76
vaha 176
vāiya 69, 137
vāukāya, °yāya 66, 105
vāgaraṇī 46:10, 74

vācaka 25
vācanā'ntara 43
vāmaṇa 65
vām ('āvatta) 166
vāyaga-vaṃsa 48
vāyaṇā 150
vāyaṇâyariya 150
vāyavva 58
vāruṇī 58
vāvahāriya 76
vāsa-ghara 25 n.
vāsā 106 n.
vāsāvāsā 146
vāsudeva 13, 117
vāsyā 113 n.
vāha 50
viigicchiya 88
viukkamai 94
viuṭṭettae 160
viula-mai 80, 181
viuvvaṇayā 96
viussagga 161
viossagga 179
vikalpa 77
vikahā 154 n.
vikuvvai 62, 181
vikṛti 156
vikovaṇayā 69
vikkhamba 113
vikkhevaṇī 150
vigaī-paḍibaddha 156
vigal'indiya 67
viguvvaṇā 181
viggaha 95
viggaha-gai 95
vicaya 180
vicāra 180
vijaya 115, 180
vijjā 11, 38, 50
vijjā-cāraṇa 181
vijjāhara 124, 181
vijju 110 n.
vijjukumārī 110 n.
vijnapti 34 n., 189
viṇaya 149, 179
vitarka 180
vidaṇḍaga 145
vidisā 58
vidhi-caitya-gṛha 31
vinnāṇa 16
vipariṇāma 180
vippariyāsa 84
vibhanga-nāṇa 79
vimalā 58
vimāṇa 48:5, 125, 127
vimohai 133
viyakka 180
viyaḍa 63
viyad-gati 181
viyaya-pakkhī 63
virai 172
virata 185
virayâviraya 183
virāhiṇī bhāsā 74
vilaṭṭhi 145
vilavaṇayā 180

vivaraṇa 43
vivāga 180
vivāga-patta 86
vivega 161
viśreṇī 95
visamaṃ samaṃ karei 186
visaṃbhoiya 139
visaya 67, 79, 181
visujjhai 98 n.
visuddha (tarāga) 76
viseḍhi 95
visohettae 160
vihāya-gai 87
vīi-pantha 153 n.
vīivayai 125, 133
vīci-davva 96
vīra 30 n.
vīr'āsaṇiya 157
vīriya 83, 165 n.
vīsasā 58, 60, 88
vīsumbhai 165 n.
vukkamai see viukkamai
vṛtti 43
veijjai 67 n.
veiyā 116, 121 n.
veuvviya 62, 89, 181
veei 67 n., 86f.
vekacchiyā 143
veṇaiya 73 n., 83
vemāya-niddhayā 59
vemāyā 66
veya 87, 91
veyai 60
veyaṇā 86f., 89, 99
veyaṇijja 87f., 91, 167
veyaraṇī 99
veyāvaccā, °vaḍhiyā 148
verajja-viruddha 154 n.
veramaṇa 16, 163 n., 171
velā 110
vehāṇasa-maraṇa 165
vocchitti 76f.
vodāṇa 16
vosirai 180 n.
vyavahāra 76
vyutkrānti 63
vyutsarga 180 n.

śakaṭôddhi 58 n.
śakti 59
śabda (-naya) 76
śalākā-puruṣa 13
śikṣā-pada 170
śivâvāpti 187
śauca 174
śyāma 112
śrāvaka-pratiṣṭhā 33
śruta-devatā 14, 33
śreṇī 21
śveta-paṭa 26
śvetâmbara 26

saingāla 153
sao 96
saṃyama-sthāna 184
saṃrambha 173

saṃlehaṇā 165, 170
saṃvacchariya 159
saṃvara 169, 173, 175, 177, 185
saṃvarai 160 n.
saṃvasittae 139
saṃvāsa 133 n.
saṃvuḍa 15, 84
saṃvṛt(t)a 63
saṃveganī 150
saṃvegī 36
saṃsaṭṭha 154
saṃsatta 139
saṃsāra 175
saṃhanana 65
sakaṣāya 81
sakahā 25
sakkhi 43
saṃkama 85
saṃkāmai 85
sankiya 88
saṃkiliṭṭha 98 n.
saṃkilissamāṇa 177
saṃkha 76
saṃkhaḍi 154
saṃkhā-dattiya 156
saṃkhitta 181
saṃkhejja 21, 39 n., 57 n.
saṃgaha 76
saṃgahiya 84
saṃgha 30, 137, 148
saṃghaṭṭana 30
sacitt'āhāra 163
sacca 38, 74
saccāmosa 74
sajjhāya 150
saṃghayaṇa 65
saṃghāṭaka 144
saṃghāḍī 143, 157
sajogī 81, 98, 183, 186
saṃciya 86, 94
saṃjama 16, 174, 177
saṃjaya 80, 177
saṃjalaṇa 87
saṃjogittā 177
saṃjoyaṇā 153
saḍḍha 163
saṃṭhāṇa 21, 60, 65, 67, 74, 180
saṃṭhii 48:5
saṃṭhiya 79
saṇapphaga 63
saṃṇivāiya 182
saṃṇivāya 48
satta 70
satta-sattamiyā 156
sattarī 189
sattā 85, 183
sa-dāra-saṃtosa 170
sadda 60, 178
saddahai 169
saddahaṇ(ay)ā 162 n., 169
sadhūma 153
santa 96
santa-kamma 85, 183
saṃtai-bhāva 71
santara 96
s'antarā 162

santar'uttara 143
saṃtosa 174
saṃtharai 155
saṃthāraga 147
sannā 71
sannī 71, 91
sapajjavasiya 60
sapaḍikkamaṇa 16
saparyāya 82
sapta-bhangī 77
sappi 156
sabalā 51, 158
sabbhāva-payattha 169
sabhā 131
sabhāva 101
sama-cauraṃsa 65
sama-śreṇī 95
samaiya 96
samaṇa 17, 137
samaṇa nigganṭha 137
samaṇa bhagavaṃ 18
samaṇa-bhikku 45:2
samaṇa-bhūya 163
samaṇ'āuso 48, 137
samaṇī 137
samaṇujāṇai 171
samaṇôvāsaga, °siyā 163 n.
samatta-painna 18
samabhirūḍha 76
samaya 57, 59 n., 187
samayaṃ 60 n.
samā 12, 120
samāiṇṇa 109 n.
samācāra 136
samādhi-maraṇa 26
samābhaṭṭha 163 n.
samārambha 173
samāhi 156, 173 n.
samāhi-pāṇa 165
samii 54, 146, 173
samiya 132 n.
samukkasaṇā 141
samugghāya 86, 89, 95, 181
samucchinna-kiriya 180 n., 186
samudāṇ(iy)a 99, 153
samudda 122
samuddisittae 150
samosaraṇa 18
samohaṇai 89, 95 n.
samohaya 181
saṃpai 76
saṃpatti 181
saṃparāiya 84, 99
saṃbukka 166
saṃbhinna-sui 181 n.
saṃbhinna-soya 181
saṃbhunjittae 139
saṃbhoiya 139
saṃbhoga 25, 139, 159
sammai 118 n.
sammaṃ-bhāviya 159, 164
sammatta 87, 162 n., 169, 176, 183
sammad-daṃsaṇa 15
sammad-diṭṭhi 169
sammā-micchatta 87
sammā-micchā-diṭṭhi 169, 183

sammucchai 127
sammucchaṇā 63
sammucchima 63 n.
sammoha 167
samyag-dṛṣṭi 185
saya 45:5
sayaṃ 86, 96
sayaṃbuddha 81
sayaya 189
saraṇa 175
sarīra(ya) 62, 64f., 89 n.
salāī 69
salinga 81
salila-kuṇḍa 114
salla 158, 168, 180
sallahattā 69
sallehaṇā 165, 170
savaṇa 16
savaṇayā 101
savattī 163
saviyārī 180 (p. 315)
savva 59, 84, 96
savvaobhadda-paḍimā 156
savva-kāma-guṇiyaṃ 156
savva-tthova 21
savvannu 186
saśrī 125
sasī 48:5
sāima 154
sāiya 60, 65
sā'usiṇa 181
sākāra 82
sāgara 30 n.
sāgarovama 45:4, 57, 120
sāgāra 82, 187
sāgāriya 147, 154, 163f.
sāci 65
sāḍa 143
sāṇa-vaṇīmaga 153 n.
sādi 65
sādhu 36
sāmaṇṇa 174 n.
sāmantôvaṇivaiya 99
sāmāiya 53, 70, 163, 170, 177
sāmāṇiya 132
sāmāyārī 136, 187 n.
sāmudāṇa 153
sāmuddaga 46, 110
sāmprata 76
sāyaṇī 69
sāyā-veyaṇijja 167
sārakkhaṇa 180
sāriya 147, 163
sārūviya 159
sālā 106
sāva 181
sāvaga 163
sāvaṇī 69
sāviyā 163
sāsāyaṇa-sammad-daṃsaṇa 183
sāhaṇaṇā 60
sāhatthiya 99
sāhā 23, 26, 139
sāhāraṇa-sarīra 106
sāhu 137
sāhuṇī 137

siṃha 30 n.
sikkhā-vaya 170
sikkhāvei 138
singhāṇa 173
siḍhila 84
siṇāya 184
siṇeha-kāya 59
siṇeha-bhāva 120
sitâmbara 26
siddha 81, 96 n., 101, 187
siddhānta 41
siddhâiguṇa 187 n.
siddh'āyayaṇa 25
siddhi 16, 181, 187, 199
sippa 118 n.
simbhiya 69
siya, siyā 77, 91, 100
siva ṭhāṇa 187
sissa 150
sissiṇī 150
sihā 121
sīôsiṇa 63, 181
sīyaliya 181
sīla-vvaya 163 n., 170 n.
sīlesī 186 n.
sīha-nāya 126
sīha-nikkīliya 156
sīhabbhava 14
suṃsumāra 63
suadhijjhiya 16 n.
sukka 97, 180
sukka-jhāṇa 186
sukka-pakkha 125
sujjhāiya 16 n.
sutta 38, 43, 45:2, 141, 180
sutta-jāgara 15
suttatta 152
sutta-porisī 151
sudakkhu-jāgara 152
supaiṭṭhaga 103
subbhi 60, 67 n.
subha 60
sumaṇa 167 n.
suya 53, 87, 160
suya-ṇāṇa 73ff.
surabhi 67 n.
surā 77
suvaṇṇakumāra-vāsa 170
susamā 13, 48:6, 120
suha 86
suha-vimoyaṇatarāga 69
suha-veyaṇatarāga 69
suha-sejjā 172
suhuma 60, 101, 104, 118 n.
suhuma-kiriya 180 n., 186
sūijjai 45:2 n.
sūcī 45:2
sūri 34
sejjā 147, 157, 176
sejjā-saṃthāraga 147
sejjāyara 147
sejjâsaṇiya 147
seḍhi 21, 60, 95, 124, 183
seṇāvai 13
sena 30 n.
sêya 60

seya-kāla 60
selesī 180, 186
sesavaṃ 75
seha 148
seha-nikkhamaṇa 140
seha-nipphedaṇa, °ṇā 140
sehāvei 138
sokkha 174 n., 177
somaṇ'antiya 159
somā 58
soya 65
saukṣmya 60 n.
stava, stuti, stotra 189
styāna-(g)ṛddhi 87 n.
strī-mukti 30
sthānaka 32
sthāvara 66
sthiti-bhojana 155 n.
sthaulya 60 n.
snātaka 184
snigdha 59
spṛṣṭa 67
syāt 77
syād-vāda 77
svapna-darśana 15

ha-kkāra 13
hatthi 172
hatthi-rayaṇa 101
hariya 106
hāsa 87 n.
hiyâṇukampaga (°kampanta) 132 n.
heṭṭhilla 150
hemanta 146

Index of Proper Names (§§)

Aihoḷe 27
Aimutta 46 (8), 137 n.
Akalanka 26 n., 29f.
Akbar 28
Aggibhūi 20
Angacūliyā 19 n., 26, 31, 56
Anga-Magadha 24
Angavijjā 56
Angai 49 (10)
Accuya 15
Ajātasattu 18, 23
Ajitadeva 35 n.
Ajja-Candaṇā 20
Ajja Sāma 48
Ajjuṇaga 46 (8)
Ancal(iy)a-Gaccha 35
Aṃju 46 (8: 10)
Aṇuogadārā 53
Aṇuttarovavāiyadasāo 46 (9)
Aṇojjā 17
Anurādhapura 27 n.
Antagaḍadasāo 46 (1:8)
Andhaka-Vṛṣṇi 49
Abhaya 49 (8)
Amoghavarṣa 29
Ambaḍa 47 (1)
Ariṭṭhaṇemi 46 (1: 2, 8: 1), 49 (12)
Arhadbali 30
Alakkha 46 (8: 6)
Avarakankā 46 (1: 6)
Avāḍa-Cilāya 13
Aśoka 23f., 28
Ahmedabad 32

Āurapaccakkhāṇa 50 (4)
Āgamika 33
Ājīvika, °ya 18, 46 (7: 7), 97 n.
Āncalika 35
Āṇanda 46 (7: 1), 163
Ātmabhāvanā 50
Ānanda 22
Āyāra 45
Āyāradasāo 51
Ārādhanā 29 n.
Ārāhaṇā 50 (6)
Ārāhaṇāpāḍāga 50
Ārya Rakṣita 23
Āryarakṣita 35
Āvassayanijjutti 55
Āsaḍa 52

Indabhūi see Goyama I
Indra 150
Indranandin 30 n., 137
Isibhāsiyāiṃ 56

Īsara 52

Ujjayinī 24, 26
Ujjuvāliyā 18
Ujjhiya 46 (11)
Uttarajjhāyā 54

Udayagiri 27
Udāī 94
Udāyana 18 n., 46 (8)
Udāyin 23
Uddyotana 28, 34 n.
Upakeśa-Gaccha 34
Umāsvāti 29, 103
Umbaradatta 46 (11)
Uvangacūliyā 83
Uvavāiya 47
Uvāsagadasāo 46 (7)
Usabha 15f., 25
Usabhadatta 17
Usuyāra 54

Ṛṣabha 15

Ekkāi 46 (11)

Os, Osvāl 34
Ohanijjutti 55

Aupapātika Sūtra 47
Auṣṭrika 34

Kaṃsa 16
Kakutstha 13 n.
Kakkī 28
Kaṭuka 33
Kaṇha Vāsudeva 13, 46 (6: 16), 46 (8)
Kadamba 27
Kaniṣka 23, 25
Kappa 51
Kappavaḍiṃsiyāo 49 (9)
Kammavivāgadasāo 46 (11)
Kalinga 24
Kalpasūtra 1f., 51
Kalkin 28
Kalyāṇa (town) 30, 33 n.
Kavila 13
Kahāuṃ 27
Kāmakesa 46 (7)
Kārkala 13 n.
Kālaka 24, 104 n., 146 n.
Kāśyapa 17
Kāṣṭhā-saṃgha 30
Kissa Saṃkicca 18
Kuṇāla 23
Kuṇālā 24
Kuṇḍakoliya 46 (7)
Kuṇḍagrāma, °pura 17
Kutscha 103 n.
Kundakunda 29f.
Kumārapāla 28, 33
Kumārasena 30
Kumārila 29
Kuvalappabha 52
Kuvalayamālākathā 28
Kūṇiya 18, 23, 47, 49 (8)
Kṛṣṇa 13
Keśin 34
Kesī 47 (2)
Kailāsa 15
Konka, Venka, Kuṭaka 15
Konkan 74 n.
Koṭika-Gaccha 34

Koṭivarṣa 24, 26
Koḍinna 17 n.
Koṇḍakunda 29 n.
Kosambī 18
Kauṇḍinya 17
Kauśāmbī 24
Kauśika 17

Khaṇḍagiri 24
Khandaga 156
Kharatara-Gaccha 34, 36
Khāravela 24, 30

Ganga 27f.
Gangadatta 46 (8)
Gaṇivijjā 50 (8)
Gandhahastin 45
Gaya-Sukumāla 46 (8)
Gardabhilla 24
Girnār 15
Gujarat 28, 31, 33
Guṇaratna 30
Gupta 28
Guptigupta 26
Gottāsa 46
Godāsa 26
Gopucchika 30
Gopya-saṃgha 30
Gommaṭa 13
Goyama Indabhūi 20ff., 45 (5)
Gosāla Maṃkhaliputta 18, 26 n.
Gautama Buddha see Buddha

Causaraṇa 50
Canda 49 (10)
Candāṇana 25
Candāvejjhaya 50
Candra-Gaccha 34
Candragupta 23, 26
Candragupti 26
Candra Sūri 49 (8)
Campā 15, 18, 47 (1), 49 (8)
Cāṇakya 23, 26
Cāmuṇḍa Rāya 13 n.
Cāmuṇḍā 34
Cāmuṇḍika 34
Cālukya 28
Citta 47 (2), 54
Cilāya 46
Culaṇīpiyā 46 (7)
Cullasayaga 46 (7)
Ceḍaga 18, 48 (8)
Cellaṇā 18, 49 (8), 51

Channiya 46

Jagaccandra 34
Jamāli 17
Jambuddīvapannatti 48 (6)
Jambū 22
Jambhaga 15
Jambhiyagāma 18
Jayantī 101
Javaṇa 117
Jasoyā 17
Jātaka 14 n.

Jāli 46 (9)
Jiṇacariya 51
Jiṇadatta 46, 120
Jiṇapāliya 46
Jiṇarakkhiya 46
Jinacandra 26 n.
Jinadatta 31, 34
Jinadāsa 29, 51
Jinabhadra 29, 52
Jinavallabha 31
Jinahaṃsa 45
Jineśvara 31, 34
Jiyasattu 46
Jīyakappa 52
Jīvābhigama 47 (3)
Jaisalmer 27
Jnātṛ 17

Ṭhāṇa 45 (3)

Ḍhuṇḍhiyā 32, 36

Tandulaveyāliya 50
Tapā-Gaccha 34ff.
Taptī 27
Tamluk 24
Tāmraliptī 24
Titthogālī 50
Tibet 119
Timisaguhā 60
Tisalā 17
Tissa 27 n.
Teyaliputta 46
Toramāṇa, °rāya 28

Thāṇīya 23 n.
Thāvaccāputta 46
Therāvalī 51

Dakkhiṇa-Mahurā 30
Daḍhapainna 47 (1)
Dasaveyāliya 54
Dasão, Dasāsuyakkhandha 51
Dāsīkharbaṭa 25 n., 26
Diṭṭhivāya 23, 38, 48, 55f., 76 n., 91, 150 n., 183
Dīgha-Nikāya 16, 18, 97 n.
Dīvasāgarapannatti 47 (3)
Dujjohaṇa 46
Dūsagaṇi 53
Dṛṣṭipāta, °vāda 38
Delhi 28
Devakī 17
Devagupta 28
Devadatta 76
Devadattā 46
Devanandin 30, 84
Devarddhi 29, 38, 51
Devasena 26 n.
Devānandā 17
Devindatthaya 50
Devendra 14 n., 164
Dovaī 46
Dramila 24
Dvāravatī 16

Dhanna 46 (6 and 9)
Dhammantari 46 (11)
Dhammarui 46
Dharmakīrti 29
Dharmaghoṣa 164
Dharmasāgara 32ff.
Dharmasena 38
Dhāriṇī 47 (2)
Dhruvasena 51

Nanda 23, 26, 46
Nanda Vaccha 18
Nandiṇīpiya 46 (7)
Nanditaṭa 30
Nandivaddhaṇa 18, 46 (11)
Nandiseṇa 46 (11), 52
Nandī 53
Nami 16
Nayavijaya 36
Narasiṃha 35
Nava Tatva 1 n.
Nāila 52, 120
Nāgārjuṇīya 43
Nāgapurīya-Gaccha 35
Nāgasirī 46 (6: 16)
Nāgpur 35
Nāṇaka-Gaccha 35
Nāndyāvarta 14, 25
Nāya 17
Nāyādhammakahāo 46 (6)
Nālandā 18
Nigoyachattīsī 104 n.
Niṇṇaya 46 (11)
Nirayāvaliyāo 49 (8)
Nisaḍha 49 (12)
Nisīha 51
Nītisāra 30
Negamesi see Hari N.
Nepāl 23
Nemi 25 n.
Noṇamangala 27

Pauma 49 (9)
Paumaṇābha 49 (6: 16)
Paumāvaī 46 (8), 49 (9)
Paesī 47 (2)
Pakkhiya-Sutta 55, 159
Pajjanna 132
Pajjosavaṇākappa 51, 136
Pancakappa 52
Paṇḍarajjā 181
Paṇhāvāgaraṇāiṃ 46 (10)
Patanjali 10, 172
Padmadeva 35
Padmanandin 30
Padmāvatīcaritra 1 n.
Pannavaṇā 48 (4)
Pallaviya 35
Paseṇai 47 (2)
Pāṭaliputra 23, 37f., 76
Pāḍalipura 26
Pāṇḍava 46 (6:16)
Pātrakesari 29
Pārasa 117
Pārasnāth 15
Pārśva 3, 15, 34

Pārśvacandra 35
Pāvapurī 19
Pāvā 15, 19
Pāśacandra (-Gaccha) 35
Pāsa 16, 26, 34, 46 (6), 47 (2), 49 (10)
Pāsâvaccijja 136
Piṇḍanijjuti 55
Piyadaṃsaṇā 17
Puḍhavisirī 46 (11)
Puṇḍarīya 46 (6: 19)
Puṇḍravardhana 24, 26
Punnāṭa 26
Pupphacūlā(o) 46 (6), 49 (11)
Pupphiyāo 49 (10)
Puṣkara 30 n.
Puṣpadanta 30
Pūjyapāda 30
Pūraṇa Kassapa 26 n.
Poggala 79
Poṭṭila,°lā 46 (6)
Porisīmaṇḍala 48
Paurṇamīyaka 33
Pratikramaṇa Sūtra, etc. 55
Prabhava 22
Pralamba Sūri 51
Praśnottararatnamālā 29 n.
Prasenajit 47 (2)
Prītivarmika 23 n.

Phaggusirī 120

Bambha 23 n., 48
Baladeva 17, 49 (12)
Basukuṇḍ 17
Bahassaidatta 46 (11)
Bahuputtiyā 49 (10)
Bāṇgaṛh 24
Bāravaī 46 (8), 49 (12)
Bālaśiraḥśekhara 51
Bāvis Ṭole Panth 32
Bāhubali 13 n.
Bindusāra 23
Bimbisāra 18
Bihar 26
Bīja 33
Buddha 19, 22
Buddhaghosa 18
Buddhisāgara 50
Bṛhatkathākośa 26
Bṛhad-Gaccha 34
Benares 36
Besāṛh 17
Boḍiya Sivabhūi 26, 55

Bhagavaī 45 (5)
Bhattaparinnā 50
Bhadrabāhu 23, 26, 37, 43
Bhadrabāhukathā 26
Bharaha 13, 48 (6), 60, 119
Bharahacakkicariya 48 (6)
Bhāgavata-Purāṇa 15
Bhānucandra 28
Bhāraha (Mahābhārata) 77
Bhāvavijaya 14 n.
Bhīkanjī 32
Bhuvanatunga 50

Bhūtabali 30
Bhūyā 49 (11), 139 n.
Bhūyāṇanda 94
Bhoja 28

Makāi 46 (8)
Makkhali Gosāla see Gosāla
Maṇḍalappavesa 48 (5)
Maṇḍiyaputta 22
Mathurā 23, 25, 27, 30, 39 n.
Madurā 30
Manu 13, 174 n.
Mandara 15
Manmatha 13 n.
Maraṇavibhatti 50
Maraṇavisohi 50
Maraṇasamāhi 50
Marwar 32
Malakka 119
Maladhārin 148 n.
Malayagiri 43, 51
Mallaki 19
Malli 15, 30
Mallī 46 (6)
Mahabbala 49 (9)
Mahāgiri 23, 38
Mahānisīha 52
Mahāpaccakkhāṇa 50
Mahābhārata 77
Mahāvaṃsa 27 n.
Mahāvideha 13, 16, 119
Mahāvīra 14, 16ff., 25, 30, 45ff., 48 (5), 49 (8 and 10), 51, 117 n., 139, 152, 181, 184f.
Mahāsaga 46 (7)
Mahāsumiṇabhāvaṇā 15
Mahesaradatta 46 (11)
Māthura-saṃgha 30
Māyandī 46 (6)
Migāvaī 18 n.
Miyāputta 46 (11)
Mihirakula, °gula 28
Munja 28
Muttra 25
Mūla-saṃgha 30
Medhamālā 52
Meha 46 (6)
Moggarapāṇi 46 (8)
Maisūr 13 n., 26 n.

Yaśā 34 n.
Yaśodeva 55, 159
Yaśodharman 28 n.
Yaśobhadra 23
Yaśovijaya 34 n.
Yāpanīya 30
Yenūr 13 n.
Yogadṛṣṭisamuccaya 29 n.
Yogabindu 29 n.
Yoga-Sūtra 172

Rakkhiya 23 n.
Rajjā 52
Rajputana 29 n., 32
Ratnanandin 26
Rayaṇadīva 46 (6)

Rājāvalīkathe 26 n.
Rāḍh, Rāṛh 18
Rāmāyaṇa 77
Rāyagiha 18, 49 (8)
Rāyapaseṇaijja 47 (2)
Rāṣṭrakūṭa 28f.
Rāhu 48 (5), 125
Ṛṣabha 15
Revaī 49 (12)
Romaga 117
Rohagutta 23 n.
Rohiṇī 17, 46 (6)

Lakkhaṇadevī 52
Lava 32
Lāḍha 18, 24 n.
Licchavi 19
Lunka, Lonka, Launka 32
Lumpāka 32f., 35

Vaira 52
Vaggacūliyā, Vanga° 31, 56
Vajjabhūmi 18
Vajra 23, 38
Vajranandin 30
Vaṭa-Gaccha 34
Vaṭṭakera 29f.
Vaṇhidasāo 49 (12)
Vaddhamāṇa see Mahāvīra
Vanavāsi-Gaccha 34
Varadatta 49 (12)
Vardhamāna see Mahāvīra
Vala(bhī) 26 n., 39
Vavahāra 51
Vāubhūi 20
Vāṇārasī 49 (10)
Vāsudeva see Kaṇha
Vikrama 24, 28
Vikramacarita 24 n.
Vijaya 46 (11)
Vijayacandra 35
Vijayadeva 36
Vijaya-śākhā 36
Vijayasiṃha 36
Vijayasena 28
Viṇīyā 13, 119
Viṇhu 48 (5)
Viṇhusirī 120
Videha-dinna 17
Vidyānanda 29
Vidhipakṣa-Gaccha 35
Viyāhacūliyā, Vivāha° 26, 31, 56
Viyāhapannatti, Vivāha° 45 (5)
Vivāgasuya 46 (11)
Viṣṇu-Purāṇa 15
Vīra see Mahāvīra
Vīrangaja 120 n.
Vīracandra 30 n.
Vīratthaya 50
Vīraśaiva 29
Vīrācārya 55
Vīs Ṭole Panth 32
Vṛṣṇi 49 (12)
Veṇūr 13 n.
Vebhāra 181
Veyaḍḍha 119

Veṣadhara 32
Vesamaṇa 15
Vesāliya 17
Vesālī 18, 49 (8)
Vehalla 49 (8)
Vaiśālī 17
Vaiṣṇava 29

Śankheśvara-Gaccha 35
Śayyambhava 22
Śāntarakṣita 29
Śānti 26 n.
Śānticandra 48 (6)
Śīlānka (Śīlācārya) 29, 31, 43
Śubhācandra 81
Śaiva 29
Śravaṇa Beḷgoḷa 13 n., 26, 29
Śrāddhadinakṛtya 164

Saṃlehaṇāsuya 50
Saka 24
Sakka 15, 131f.
Saga 117
Sagaḍa 46 (11)
Saṃkheviyadasāo 56
Saṃghadāsa 29, 51
Saccasirī 120
Saḍḍhajīyakappa 164
Saḍḍhadiṇakicca 164
Saḍḍhapaḍikkamaṇa-Sutta 164
addālaputta 46 (7)
aṃthāra 50
amantabhadra 29

Samavāya 45 (4)
Samuha 46 (11)
Samprati 23f.
Sambhūtavijaya 23
Saṃbhūya 54
Sammeta, °ya 15f.
Sayānīya 18 n.
Saramaṇḍala 21
Sarvadeva 35
Sāgaradatta 46
Sādhu-Paurṇamīyaka 33
Sāmaññaphala-Sutta 16, 18
Sārdha-Paurṇamīyaka 33
Sālihīpiyā 46 (7)
Sāvatthī 18, 49 (10)
Siddhattha 49 (12)
Siddhasena 29, 47 (2), 52, 78, 82
Siddhasena Divākara 24, 29
Sirikalasa 30
Sirī 46 (11), 49 (11)
Siva 79
Sivabhūi 26
Sīhasena 46 (11)
Suṃsumā 46
Sukāla 49 (8)
Sukumāliyā 46
Sujjhasirī 52
Sudaṃsaṇa 46 (8)
Sudatta 46 (11)
Sudharman 22
Subāhu 46 (11)
Subuddhi 46 (p. 91)
Subbhabhūmi 18

Subhaddā 49 (10), 139 n.
Sumai 52
Sumangalavilāsinī 97 n.
Sumati 15
Suya 46 (6)
Suyahīlaṇuppatti 56
Surādeva 46 (7)
Suṣaḍhacaritra 52
Susthita 26
Suhamma 22, 53
Suhavivāga 46 (11)
Suhastin 23ff.
Suhma 18
Sūyagaḍa 45 (2)
Sūrapannatti 48 (5)
Sūriyābha 47 (2)
Sejjaṃbhava 22
Seṇiya 18, 51
Selaga 46 (6)
Sevaḍa 26 n.
Soma 23 n.
Somā 49 (10)
Somila 49 (10)
Soriyadatta 46 (11)
Skanda 150
Skandila 39 n.
Sthānakvāsī 32
Sthūnā 24
Sthūlabhadra 23, 26, 38

Hatthipāla 19
Hari Negamesi 15, 17, 64, 132
Hariesa 54
Harigupta 28
Haribhadra 23 n., 27, 29, 31, 137 n.
Harṣakula 45 (2)
Halsi 27
Hāthīgumphā 24
Hīravijaya 28
Hūṇa 28, 117
Hemacandra 23, 28
Hoysaḷa 28

Subject Index (§§)

accommodation 147
actions 99
activity of the body 57, 66
act of dejection 148
addressing Mahāvīra 17
addressing monks 137
adultery 170
aggregates (khandha) 59
agnostics 83
ājnānika 77
alms-bowl 144
alms round 153
amount of life see quantity of life
anatomy 65
animals (pets) 147
animals and monachism 55, 101
animals, classification of 63, 104, 118
animals expressing themselves 74
animals, respectful treatment of 179 n.
animate crown jewels 101
animate dust 145, 153
animate elements 105
anekāntavāda 77
Angas 37, 40f., 45ff.
annihilation (of karman) 185
Apabhraṃśa 6
apology 38, 45 (2)
Ardhamāgadhī 6, 20, 117 n.
ārdhapālika, °phālaka 26
arithmetics 21
arson 181
articulated evidences 73f.
āryā (primitive form) 42, 45
āryā (common form) 42
Aryans 117
asceticism 156, 178f., 185
astronomy (Jain) 21, 48 (5f.), 125
atoms (poggala) 58f., 61
atomism of time 57 n.
atonement (pāyacchitta) 161
Aulūkya-philosophy 10
Aupacchandasaka 42
attraction of matter 62, 84, 96
aversion to images 33

barbarians (milakkhu) 117
beggars compared with fishes 153 n.
beggars compared with worms 153 n.
behaviour of monks 149
bhāsa (bhāṣya) 43
bhūta 150
binding of karman 84
black fields 134
bodies, kinds of 62
body, shape, size 65
bones, beings without 65
bowing down 149f.
Brahman 13, 14, 17, 29, 49
breath(ing) 61, 66, 67 n., 79, 105, 132, 145, 172, 184
Buddha see Buddhists
Buddhists 1, 3, 20 n., 37, 47, 83, 165,

172

calculation(s) 21
calendar 140, 150
cannibalism 49 (8)
canon, redaction of 29, 39
canon, survey 41
canon, of the Digambaras see Digambara canon
categories (ṭhāṇa) 45(3)
category texts 42
causes of diseases 69
cauterization (khara-tantra) 69
celestial bodies 128
centre of the world 107 n., 134
change of stages (pavesaṇa) 93
Chedagrantha 35
Cheyaggantha, Cheyasutta 40f., 51ff.
chronicles (paṭṭâvalī) 34
chronology 122
classes of beings 67
clothing of monks and nuns 26, 143
clothing question 26
clouds 62, 105, 120, 121
coagulation (sammucchaṇā) 63
cognition (nāṇa) 72, 75, 78ff.
colours of gods 110
colours of humans 18
colours of matters 57, 61
colours of the Jinas 14
colours of the soul 97
commandments 16
commentaries 43
community (saṃgha) 137, 139
comparisons 20, 57f., 66f., 84, 92, 96, 103, 135, 153 n., 181, 186
conception 64
conception of Mahāvīra 57
conclusion, logical 75
conditions (pajjava), of atoms 60
confession 33, 35, 50 (āura°), 137, 149
confession formula (paḍikkamaṇa) 151(4)
confusing karman (mohaṇijja-kamma) 69, 78, 87
consumption of karman 90
cosmography see astronomy
council 23, 37, 39
countless (uncountable) 21
craving, pregnancy 64
creation of beings 63f., 118
cremation of corpse 48(6), 165
cross position of embryo causing death 64
crown jewels 7, 101
crown jewels (14 rayaṇa) 13, 101
cult 25
cult of images 32
cuṇṇi (cūrṇi) 43
curse (and blessing), 62, 89, 181

daily routine 148
darkness 60, 125, 133f.
darkness, aggregate of matter 134
darkness, taking food after (rāī-bhoyaṇa) 171

dasā-texts 42
death 69, 90
death, cause of 90
death, hour of 98
death in the house 150
death year of Mahāvīra 19
density of matter 58, 61
deportments 10 (kappa), 136, 149
development (pajjati) of beings 63
dialogue-texts 42
dice playing 21
Digambara 26, 30 etc.
Digambara canon 29 n., 39, 40
digestion by Kevalin 30, 62
dimension(al order) 60
direct cognition (paccakkha-nāṇa) 75
diseases 69
dissenters see heretics
dogs, set on Mahāvīra 18
dohada 49, 64
dreams 15, 26
duplication of celestial bodies 128
duration of life 69
dust, animate 145, 153

earth souls 105
earthquake 107 n., 110 n.
eastward orientation 137
eating at night (rāī-bhoyaṇa) 171
ebb and flow 121
eclipses 125, 150
egg-born (aṇḍaya) beings 64
ejaculation 186
elements 105
elixirology 69
emblems of the Titthagaras 14
embryo 64f.
embryo-life 64
embryology 50 (Tandulaveyāliya)
embryonal state of Mahāvīra 17, 18, 30
energy, latent 62
entities, fundamental 57
epic lectures 77

face-cloth (muha-pattī) 145
famine in Ujjayanī 26
fasting to death (sallekhaṇā) 26 (Candragupta), 28, 137, 165, 185
fear, object of 87 (p. 181), 87 n., 109
female deities, goddesses 66, 132
fertility, human 64
festive days 34 n., 150
fiery body (teyaga-sarīra) 62
figures, liking for 21
filth 148 n.
fineness and coarseness 60
fire, flame souls 105
fire walk 181
fish (eaten by monks) 154
food 154, 164
food taking after darkness 171
fortune-telling 69 n. (p. 151)
former life, later effects of 137
founders of civilisation (kulagara) 13
four passions 21
function of speech 74

fundamental facts, entities 57

gender, grammatical 74
generation (gabbha-vakkanti) 63
geometry 21, 60
germinative faculty of plants 63 n.
germinative life 67
giver and alms 154f.
gloomy meditation 180
god and monk 46 (7), 47(2), 49(10 and 12), 133
gods, manifestation of 133
gods of the lower world 110
god visits the earth 133
goddesses see female deities
gotra 48 (Sūrapannatti), 126
gourd as alms-bowl 144
group leaders (gaṇa-hara) 22, 139
guest, monk as a 147
guilt 158, 168
Gujarātī 6
gynaecology 64

hair, non-growth of 69
hair, tearing out, etc. 137
hand-broom 30, 145
hell-beings 21, 65, 71, 109, 185
hells 45(2), 108f.
hemaphrodites 65
heretics, heresy 26, 77, 83, 149
heroes 45(4)
Hinduism 11
historical details 49(8)
honey 156, 181
horoscope 140
horse making khu khu sound 21
hot spring, explanation for 21
human anatomy 65
human appearance of a world (loka-puruṣa) 103
human body, structure, shape, size 65

I (āyā) 70
idol worship 32
illness due to gloomy meditation 180
imagination, process of 73
imperial crown treasures 13, 101
indirect cognition (parokkha-nāṇa) 75
Indo-China 119
infinity 21, 78
influence (aṇhaya) 84
inscriptions 23, 27
insignificant appearance as consequence of intensive activity 91
instincts (ābhoga) 71
instruction 150
intake of matter (āhāra) 96
interpenetration (of units) 58
inward sense (māṇa) 61, 63, 70, 169

jagatī 42
Jain church 23
Jaina-Māhārāṣṭrī 6
Jaina-Śaurasenī 6
Jina statues 24ff., 32, 163, 180n.

Kāṇādas 10
karman 84, 167, 186
karman, annihilation of 185
karman, kinds of 85, 87, 91
karman body 95
kevala-cognition 22, 81f., 186
kevalin 58, 71, 81f., 84

laity 46(7), 137, 163f., 170
latent energy 62 (p. 139)
laughing, causes for 87 n.
leaving (changing) the gaṇa 139
left and right 65
light as matter 60
lines, seven possible kinds of 21 (p. 40)
list of peoples 117
logic, Digambara 77
lower world 107ff.
lower world gods 110
loyalty 185 (p. 326)

madness (ummāya) 69
magic 181
magic characters 180 (p. 314 n. 2)
magic flash of fire 181
magic power 62
Mahāvīra's year of death 19
manifestation (uvavāya) 63
manifestation of gods 63
mantras 101 (namo tthu ṇaṃ)
manuscripts 1, 2, 4, 150
Marāṭhī 6
martyr 185 (p. 327)
mass of all that is (atthikāya) 57
material quality of sense organs 60, 67
matter, units of 58
maximum and minimum 21
meals, changing, leaving out, restricting 156
meat (eaten by monks) 154, 156
medicine 69
meditation 152, 180f., 186
menstrual blood 64
merit 169
metaphysics 185
metres 42
minor vows 46(7),
Mīmāṃsā 29
miscarriage 64
Mohammedans 29
monastic mode of life 136, 138, 164
monk's age (pariyāya) 138, 162
monk's alms-round 153
moving (capability of) 66
moving in the air 181 (p. 317)
muha-pattī (face cloth) 145
Mūlasutta 41
Muṇḍaka-Upaniṣad 137 n.
music, condemned in sanctuaries 31
mythology 14f., 48, 131

nadir 58
nails, non-growth of 69
Nāga-stones 139 n.
nakedness 26, 30
nakṣatra 48, 125, 126

names of Mahāvīra 17, 51
names of peoples 117
Nandyāvarta 25
napkin (muha-pattī) 145
narrations of similes (naya) 150
natural phenomena 21, 107 n., 110 n., 132, 150
necessary formulae (āvassaya) 151, 164
New Testament references 20 n., 46
Nijjutti 29 n., 43
nobles see princes
non-Aryan 117
non-world (a-loga) 21, 103, 107
northern lights (disi-dāha) 150
novices 137f.
numbers 21, 39 n., 45 (3;4), 57f., 62, 67, 99, 103, 168ff. etc.
nuns 20, 30, 143 etc.
nuns and monks 137

offence against live matter 170
omens 15, 50 (in Gaṇivijjā)
omniscience 22, 87, 186
one to three-eyed beings 67 n.
orientation towards the east 137
originator (vīsasā), lack of 58
outfit (139), 142f.

paediatrics (kumāra-bhicca) 69
Paiṇṇa 40, 50
palpability 57, 61
paradise state 112, 117
passions 21, 84, 87, 168
Patteya (Pratyeka)buddha 14, 56
peaceful condition of karma 182
peoples, list of 117
persecution of Jains by Muslims 29
pessimistic reflections (anuprekṣā) 175
pessimistic monastic poetry 175
pets see animals
physical culture 148
physicians 69
physiology 63
pi (π) 21
places occupied by gods 130ff.
places of worship 79
planets 48(5)
plant beings 94, 104
plants 106
pole (square cube) 58
popular belief 18, 69, 112, 181
possession (jakkhâvesa) 69
Prākrit 6, 29, 43
pre- and post-existence 93
pregnancy whim 64
princes and nobles 18, 28f., 147 n., 150, 154
procedures, three (karaṇa) 183
procreation 71
propaedeutic texts 53
property of the monk 142, 171
psychotherapy (bhūya-vijjā) 69
published series (grantha-mālā) 2ff.
punishment 13, 109, 158
Pūrva, Puvva 23, 38, 56, 62

quantity of life 87, 90, 186

radiation of magic power 62
rain 94, 120, 132 (divine)
rainy season 106, 146
reflections (anupreksā) 175
reflexes 86
reforms 31f., 35f.
regional gods 133
reincarnation (uvavāya) 92, 95
relative number (alpa-bahutva) 21
relativity of statements 77
relics (Jiṇa-sakahā) 25
renunciation (paccakkhāṇa) 172
respect, lack of for superiors (āsāyaṇā) 149
resting place (sejjā) 147
right and left position of embryo 65
right conduct (caritta) 136, 177
righteousness 169
routine, daily 148
Ṛṣis in Isibhāsiyāiṃ 56

saffron dress of the Saṃvegis 36
sāl tree 18, 94
salutation with dharma-lābha etc. 30, 149
salvation capability 101
salvation finder 14
salvation preacher 14
Sāṃkhya 10
Sanskrit 6, 29, 43
schism 17, 26, 30, 29, 38
scripts, 18 kinds of 117
seasons 106, 146
seeing 82
seniority, monk's 40, 138, 161f.
senses 67, 71
sermons 26, 55, 46, 150, 166
seven lines 21
seven or eight future births 185
seven religions 21
sex 64, 66
sexuality 48(1), 66, 133
shadow as matter 60
shaving 137
sick, prohibited becoming monks (nuns) (pavvajjā) 137
siddhas 47(3), 159, 187
siddhas, their abode 135
similes 20, 166
sitophobia 69
sixteenfold passions 87
size of gods 110
śloka 42, 73
smell 57, 61
sorcery 40, 181
soul colours 57, 97
soul, grades of (jīva-ṭṭhāṇa) 183
soul, original concept of 10
soul shafts (nālī) 95
soul, size of 10, 58
sound as matter 60, 67f.
source texts 102, 136
southern half, its size 111, 130
space 57
speech 61, 63, 68,74

sperm 64
spirits, etc. 112
spiritual function (uvaoga) 71, 82
staff 145
stages of life (dasā) 50, 69 (Tandulaveyāliya)
Sthānakavāsī 4, 32
still birth 64
stoppage of karman influence 169
study hours 40, 150f.
stūpa 25
substance (davva) 57, 61
suicide 165
sun and moon 48(5), 125ff.
Suparṇa 110, 139 n.
superiors 140f., 148
sūtras (Umāsvāti's) 29
Śvetāmbara 26
symbols of the Titthagaras 14
symptoms of decline in religion 26, 31, 33, 120
syādvāda 29 n., 77
synod see council
systems, Mahāvīra's borrowing from other 10

taking the vows (uvaṭṭhāvaṇā, dikkhā) 138
Tamil 29
tastes, kinds of 57, 61
toxicology (jangolī) 69
temples 25, 163
temptations 54, 176
ten stages of life (dasā) 69
terrestrial warmth 127
therapeutics 69
time, measurement of 57
time, unit of (addhā-samaya) 57
time, wheel of 12, 120
three-eyed 67 (p. 146 n. 3)
Titthagara 15, 126, 133
tonsure see shaving
transformation body 62
transposition body 62
travelling monks, nuns 27, 146
tree planting 49 (10)
trees 18 (p. 36, Sāl tree), 106, 113
triṣṭubh 42
true and wrong (sacca, mosa) 74

units of time and matter 57f.
universal history 48
untouchable gods 134 n.
untruthfulness (musā-vāya) 170
upper world 129
urine drinking 156
uterus 63f.
uterus, form of 64
Uvangas 40, 47

Vagga-texts 42
Vaiśeṣika 10
vaiśya 26
vaitālīya 42
Veḍha 13 n., 42, 46 (10), 47, 51, 69 n.
Veḍha-texts 42

vegetarianism 154
vibration of soul units (parispanda) 84
(p. 174)
vows 46, 138, 165, 170

walking on fire 181
wandering monks, nuns 27, 146
warmth as matter 60
washing the body 49(11)
water, animate 105
water, boiled 154
will 83
wind, animate and inanimate 105 n.
wind-beings 62
windbody (vāuyāya) 66
wind, theory of 110
wish, for ideal goods in the future existence (nidāna) 180
world-centre 107 n.
world-emperors 13
world history 48(6)
world laws (loga-ṭṭhiī) 84, 121
world periods 120
world profile 104, 134

yakṣa 11, 69

zenith 58
zoology see animals

ADDITIONS

p. 13, 16	Even in a quite recent and very useful book V. A. *Sangave*: Jaina Community, a social survey, Bombay 1959—no German book is recorded in the large Jainist bibliography.
p. 22, footnote 1	The etymology of Gommaṭa (i.e. Cāmuṇḍarāya)=Manmatha is refuted by *Upadhye* in Anekānta, Vol. 4 (1942). See also *the same* in Ind. Hist. Qu. 16 (1940).
p. 50, 8	It is equally possible that Śvetāmbara art faithfully continued in representing the Jina as a naked man, while his Śvet. followers long since wore clothes generally.
p. 50, 18	As to *sevaḍa* comp. *Zachariae* in Kleine Schriften, p. 43 and Festschrift Winternitz, p. 176.
p. 50, footnote 7	In the original German edition Devasena's Darśanasāra ed. Nāthūrām Premī, Bo. s. 1974, was registered on p. 212 (not translated). The text was published critically by *Upadhye* ABHORI 15 (1934), p. 198 ff.
p. 56, 13	Uddyotana's Kuvalayamālā was published by SJS Vol. 49 (1959).
p. 61 ff.	The spiritual genealogy in the Śākhās and Gacchas of both the Sena- and Balātkāra-Gaṇas and the Kāṣṭhā-Saṃgha is given by V. P. *Johrapurkar* in his book Bhaṭṭāraka Saṃpradāya, Sholapur 1958. According to him, the Digambara Bhaṭṭārakas from the 13th Century were highly representative religious rulers all over India and enjoyed near to princely authority.
p. 66, 14	Not acknowledged are the Oha- and Piṇḍanijjutti, Mahānisīha, Jīya- and Pancakappa, and the Paiṇṇas.

p. 79, 26 Āvnijj. 777 (399[b]) has *cheasuttāṇi*.

p. 109, 28 ff. For 3 mss. of the Titthogālī see *Kapadia*, Descr. Cat. XVII, 1, p. 356 ff. 1233 or 1251 Gāhās. The Ārāhaṇāpaḍāgā, 990 G., was composed by Vīrabhadra in S. 1078, see ib., p. 328 f., and thus cannot be called a canonical Paiṇṇa. Nor can, as it would seem, the Titthogālī.

p. 112, 33 *Comm.* : Bhāsa, Visesaṇisīhacuṇṇi by Jinadāsa *mahattara*. *Ed.* : see Vavahāra.—Ed. by Amar Muni and Kaṇhailāl "Kamal". Vol. 1-4. Agra 1957-60. This ed. was preceded by a cyclo-styled type-script one prepared Vijayaprema Sūri, Bo. V. S. 1995. The recent ed. on its title-pages bears the name of Visāha Gaṇi *mahattara* as the *praṇetṛ* of the Nis. This name was taken from 3 concluding Gāhās (though before the colophon). In them the text is evidently said to have been copied for the Gaṇin (*tassa lihiyaṃ=tasya paṭhanārthaṃ likhitam*). The titles of *gaṇi* and *mahattara* betray a comparatively late epoch.

p. 172, footnote 4 To be added two monumental editions, viz. that one due to Hiralal *Jaiṇ* of the Ṣaṭkhaṇḍāgama of Puṣpadanta and Bhūtabali with the Comm. of Dhavalā of Vīrasena, 16 Vols., Amraoti 1940-58; and the Mahādhavalasiddhāntaśāstra, Mahābandha, ed. by S. C. *Diwakar* and Phoolchand *Sastri*, Jnānapīṭha Mūrtidevī J. Gr. M., Prākṛta-Grantha, in progress (9 Vols.), Ban. 1947 ff.

p. 180, 22 The *mohaṇijja kamma* is the only subject of Guṇadhara's (a Dig. author) Kasāyapāhuḍa with Yativṛṣabha's Cūrṇi and Vīrasena's Jayadhavalaṭīkā, ed. by Phūlcand and Kailāśacand, Vols. 1-7 ff., Caurāsī Mathurā 1944-58. ff.

p. 196, 3 ff About the *lesā* see *Upadhye* in Proc. Trans. All India Or. Cgr. VII, p. 391-398 and Jain Gazette 31, p. 14.

p. 271 footnote 3 A scholarly discussion of *phāsuya* by Mme C. Caillat, JAs. 1960, p. 42-64.

p. 273, 1 its object must be deprived of life (......) by somebody else. An example is given by Mahāvīra (Viy. 686 b). The passage is of extreme interest with regard to what follows on p. 273. Comp. the *author* ZDMG 104, p. 262.

p. 298, 26 The *Author* in a footnote Worte p. 43 has called the attention upon the words *ujjhiuṃ bāle* Sū. 2, 2, 6 f (307 a) where the *aṇaṭṭha-daṇḍa* or futile doing is specified. We here in a rather furtive manner find the irrational conception—"except children"—that Karmic consequences are in force not earlier than after puberty has been reached. *Jacobi* in his translation follows Śīlānka's wrong interpretation *sad-vivekam ujjhitvā ātmānaṃ vā parityajya bālavat*. The Cuṇṇi is silent.

p. 307, 2 Definition and survey of *anuprekṣā* by *Upadhye* in the introduction to his critical ed. of Svāmī-Kumāra's Kārttikeyānuprekṣā, RGŚM 2, Agas (near Anand) 1960.